Canadian Environmental
Policy and Politics

Third Edition

Canadian Environmental Policy and Politics

Prospects for Leadership and Innovation

Edited by

Debora L. VanNijnatten
Robert Boardman

OXFORD
UNIVERSITY PRESS

OXFORD
UNIVERSITY PRESS

70 Wynford Drive, Don Mills, Ontario M3C 1J9
www.oupcanada.com

Oxford University Press is a department of the University of Oxford. It furthers the University's
objective of excellence in research, scholarship, and education by publishing worldwide in

Oxford   New York

Auckland   Cape Town   Dar es Salaam   Hong Kong   Karachi   Kuala Lumpur   Madrid
Melbourne   Mexico City   Nairobi   New Delhi   Shanghai   Taipei   Toronto

With offices in

Argentina   Austria   Brazil   Chile   Czech Republic   France   Greece   Guatemala
Hungary   Italy   Japan   Poland   Portugal   Singapore   South Korea
Switzerland   Thailand   Turkey   Ukraine   Vietnam

Oxford is a trade mark of Oxford University Press in the UK and in certain other countries
Published in Canada by Oxford University Press
Copyright © Oxford University Press Canada 2009
The moral rights of the author have been asserted
Database right Oxford University Press (maker)
First Published 2009

Library and Archives Canada Cataloguing in Publication

Canadian environmental policy and politics : prospects for leadership and innovation / edited by
Debora L. VanNijnatten and Robert Boardman. – 3rd. ed.

Previously published under title: Canadian environmental policy.

Includes bibliographical references and index.

ISBN 978-0-19-542905-3

1. Environmental policy—Canada.   2. Environmental protection—Canada.
3. Environmental policy—Canada—Case studies.
I. Boardman, Robert   II. VanNijnatten, Debora, 1967–

GE190.C3 C35 2009   333.70971   C2009-901087-9

Cover image: Jeff Foott / Getty Images

Oxford University Press is committed to our environment. The text pages of this book are printed on
Forest Stewardship Council certified paper, harvested from a responsibly managed forest,
which contains 100% post-consumer waste.

Preserving our environment

Oxford University Press chose to print the pages of this
book on recycled paper and saved these resources[1]:

energy	water	greenhouse gases	solid waste
27 million BTUs	53,535 L	1,553 kg	826 kg

39 trees were saved for our forests

Printed by **Webcom Inc.**
on Legacy Offset 100% post-consumer waste.

[1]Estimates were made using the Environmental Defense Paper Calculator.

FSC

Mixed Sources
Product group from well-managed
forests, controlled sources and
recycled wood or fiber

Cert no. SW-COC-002358
www.fsc.org
© 1996 Forest Stewardship Council

Printed and bound in Canada
1 2 3 4 -- 12 11 10 09

Contents

For ShanLin Yuan

and

For Christine

Contributors

Robert Boardman recently retired from Dalhousie University, where he was McCulloch Professor of Political Science.

Stephen Bocking is Professor and Chair, Environmental and Resource Studies Program, Trent University.

Steven Brown is Associate Professor of Political Science, Wilfrid Laurier University, and Director of the Laurier Institute for the Study of Public Opinion and Policy.

Stewart Elgie is Associate Professor of Law and Co-Director, Environment Research Institute, University of Ottawa.

Michael Howlett is Burnaby Mountain Chair in the Department of Political Science, Simon Fraser University.

Carolyn Johns is Associate Professor, Politics and Public Administration, Ryerson University.

Bruce Lourie is President of the Ivey Foundation, and a member of the Board of the Ontario Trillium Foundation.

Douglas Macdonald is Senior Lecturer, Centre for the Environment, University of Toronto.

Mary Louise McAllister is Associate Professor of Environment and Resource Studies, University of Waterloo.

James Meadowcroft is Canada Research Chair in Governance for Sustainable Development, and Professor in the School of Public Policy and Administration and the Department of Political Science, Carleton University.

Robert Paehlke is Emeritus Professor of Environmental Studies, Trent University.

Sarah Pralle is Associate Professor of Political Science in the Maxwell School, Syracuse University.

Jeremy Rayner is Professor and Head, Department of Political Science, University of Regina.

Ian H. Rowlands is Professor of Environment and Resource Studies, and Associate Dean, Research, Faculty of Environment, University of Waterloo.

Mark Sproule-Jones is Emeritus Copps Professor of Political Science, McMaster University.

Chris Tollefson is Professor of Law, University of Victoria.

Glen Toner is Professor of Public Policy and Director of the Research Unit in Innovation, Science and Environment, School of Public Policy and Administration, Carleton University.

Marcia Valiante is Professor of Law, University of Windsor.

Debora L. VanNijnatten is Associate Professor of Political Science and Director of the Masters' in International Public Policy (MIPP) Program, Wilfrid Laurier University.

Graham White is Professor of Political Science, University of Toronto Mississauga.

Mark Winfield is Assistant Professor of Environmental Studies and Coordinator, Joint Bachelor of Laws/Master of Environmental Studies Program, York University.

Introduction

Debora L. VanNijnatten and Robert Boardman

In terms of government-directed efforts aimed at improving environmental quality, there has arguably been some progress since the first edition of *Canadian Environmental Policy* was published in 1992. Emissions of nitrogen oxides, volatile organic compounds, and particulates from industry and electricity generation continue to decrease as air pollutant requirements kick in. Certain plant and animal species that are at risk due to pollution or resource harvesting have been brought under the protection of federal or provincial legislation, and recovery strategies are being put in place. Species protection has also been enhanced by the recent expansion of the national and provincial parks and protected areas network. In addition, a larger share of both residential and industrial solid waste is diverted through recycling, composting, and deposit-return systems. Moreover, there are greater efforts by provincial agencies to ensure healthy drinking water supplies across the country, largely through increased attention to non-point source pollution such as agricultural run-off. The routine operations of many business and government organizations are also greener as a result of environmental audits on waste systems and attention to energy use.

Despite these grounds for optimism, however, it must be said that Canada's overall environmental policy record has been rather disappointing. It would be difficult to argue, for example, that Canadian governments have, in recent years, been truly ambitious in terms of setting environmental policy goals. While there have been some laudable steps, the Canadian environmental policy regime has not tended to be 'stringent' in the sense of imposing rigorous targets to change the behaviour of industry, societal actors, and governments themselves in an effort to achieve high levels of environmental quality. The rhetoric of sustainable development has been employed at all levels of government, but the real implications for Canadian society and the economy of the 'sustainable' part of the equation have not influenced the overall objectives of government policy to the degree necessary. Certainly, Canada is not alone here; all developed nations are struggling with the operationalization of sustainable development in the context of advanced capitalism. However, Canada (at the time of writing) is the only OECD country lacking a national sustainable development strategy that might provide an umbrella for setting the kinds of goals needed to bring about the transformative changes undoubtedly required. Environmental policy leadership has been a relatively scarce commodity in Canada.

And if the goals of our environmental policy regime have not been particularly ambitious or stringent, neither have we been innovative with respect to means. The two are, of course, linked; timid goals do little to encourage innovations in policy instrumentation. There is ample evidence to show that Canadian federal and provincial governments have generally been reluctant to *require* behavioural change on the part of industry and societal actors, such that the environment is protected or enhanced. And this is despite court decisions that have consistently expanded the scope of all governments to address environmental concerns, as Marcia Valiante points out in Chapter 3. While regulation is a mainstay of the federal and provincial environmental policy regimes, the Canadian practice has been to build considerable discretion into legislation in order to allow policy-makers to respond to more immediate political and economic incentives. Even more telling is the fact that both the federal and some provincial governments have over the past decade opted to raise barriers to employing regulation in the name of competitiveness and under the guise of 'reducing the red tape' that businesses face.[1]

And, neither have governments in Canada moved enthusiastically to try policy instruments that might be regarded as more 'business-friendly', such as the creation of markets for pollution through tradeable permit systems. Yet other policy instruments that create action in ways different than regulation—including ecological fiscal reform ('tax-shifting') and informational regulation—are also thin on the ground in Canada. Indeed, in this respect, there has been remarkably little progress since we wrote the Introduction to the second edition of *Canadian Environmental Policy* in 2002 and noted that the rush to 'voluntarism' had peaked, that criticisms of its effectiveness were gaining ground,[2] and that alternative policy instruments were under discussion.[3] Governments have been reluctant to regulate but they have also—perhaps until very recently—been reluctant to try anything new. Thus, innovation in terms of how we go about achieving our environmental policy goals has also not generally been a feature of the Canadian environmental policy regime.

Aims of the Book

This volume takes as its point of departure the relative lack of both environmental policy leadership in terms of policy goals and the lack of innovation in policy instrument choice in Canada. Our authors explore the various reasons for these tendencies as well as their consequences, which are becoming ever more visible in the natural environment around us. They also discuss the prospects for change and the constraints that face those who wish to inject more leadership into the regime. At the same time, some chapters point to promising developments, such as co-management boards in the Northwest Territories, innovations associated with Sustainable Forest Management and eco-infrastructure, local bans on cosmetic pesticides, and various strategies to promote renewable electricity. These experiments indicate the potential for a different kind of environmental policy future, even if initial efforts have not always been quite as successful or consistent as advocates had hoped.

It is important to further clarify what this third edition of *Canadian Environmental Policy* is and is not about. Two important aspects of environmental debates are not the focus of the book, though some of the chapters touch on these. First, the authors are not engaged in policy advocacy, in the sense of assessing government actions on the environment and using these analyses to propose and defend specific courses of action. However, there is no neat and uncrossable line here. Anyone discussing the environment will likely have their own preferences about what governments should and should not be doing, and the contributors to this volume are no exception.

Second, the focus is firmly on governments and their public policy-making activities. At the broadest level, we are concerned with governments' environmental policy goals, their policy instrument choices, the outcomes in terms of environmental quality, and the possible interactions among these. Policy goals refer to the stated or expected ends of the course of action to which a government is committed, as when Canada's federal government agreed to achieve a six per cent reduction in greenhouse gases below 1990 levels by 2012 under the terms of the Kyoto Protocol. Policy instruments refer to the actual means or devices that governments have at their disposal to achieve policy goals. Regulation, subsidies, taxation, and voluntarism are all examples of policy instruments. Continuing with our Canadian climate policy example, a key question has been: What is the appropriate mix of policy instruments—encouraging voluntary industry action to reduce emissions (as has been the case for much of the past decade), imposing emissions cuts through regulation, or instituting some sort of taxation on emissions—which will enable Canada to achieve its Kyoto goal? Environmental policy outcomes refer to measures of environmental quality, such as levels of pollutants in ambient air, water, soil, or plant and animal life. Although one cannot assume a direct relationship given the complex reality of environmental policy and politics, the most recent results of Canada's Greenhouse Gas Inventory showing that emissions increased 22 per cent between 1990 and 2006[4]—the biggest percentage increase among G8 countries over the same time period—indicates, at the very least, that the right mix of policy instruments to achieve Canada's climate policy goals has not yet been found.

Some of our readers might worry that this focus on governments leaves individuals or environmental organizations outside government out of the picture. We are not denying that individuals can and do contribute to environmental problem-solving through the decisions they make about water use, organic produce, transportation, voting, the consumption of less heavily packaged goods, household energy use, and conservation, among others. Further, environmental groups have critical roles in relation to environmental education (in its broadest sense), on-the-ground activities such as land management for biodiversity conservation, and policy analysis and advocacy. Some of these topics enter the discussions in this book, for example in the ways that environmental groups exert influence on the policy choices that governments make; Stewart Elgie's examination of the role of environmental groups in Chapter 14 in pushing for species at risk legislation is a case in point. For the most part, however, our mandate is to discuss and evaluate the environment-related policy actions of Canada's federal, provincial, territorial, aboriginal, and municipal governments.

It is certainly the case that public debates on environmental policy reveal different framings of the roles and optimal activities of governments. Some assessments ignore or downplay them. Some environmentalists feel that real, sustainable contributions to solving environmental problems should be geared to individuals or to local communities. Others take the conviction further and suspect that governments are part of the problem, that they are large and powerful entities too concerned with protecting the interests of large and powerful corporations, and woefully inadequate to the task of bringing creativity and long-term thinking to the critical tasks associated with protecting the environment. While the authors in this book have varying views of the roles, capacities, and appropriate actions of governments, a common starting-point is the belief that environmentally good actions by governments are possible, and that they form an integral part of the overall task of achieving higher levels of environmental quality. Indeed, much thinking on environmental policy in Canada has traditionally sprung from a broad philosophical outlook that defends a view of governments as participants in the tasks of solving society's problems. Canadians are disturbed when they see governments evading these responsibilities. This response has deep roots in Canadian political culture; it is not specific to any particular political party.

That said, different kinds of preferences and values underlie evaluations of government performance. One question underlying many of the studies in this book is how 'effective' environmental policies are. The answer depends, of course, on the criteria used. Should we, for example, base a judgment on a government's own statements or assumptions about its expectations and goals? How do we factor in the viewpoints of critics, who may have different expectations and advocate different goals? Costs, in terms of expenditures in human and material resources, and opinions about the repercussions of effects in the economy (and jobs!), are a big part of this picture from the perspective of government policy-makers. Assessments of costs have been a significant feature of debates on Canadian policy options on climate change, and notions of fairness are unavoidably a part of environmental policy-making, as government actions have consequences in terms of shifting the distribution of costs and benefits in society. It is fair to say that the authors in this volume are interested primarily in whether these choices appear to be aimed at (and seem likely to result in) higher levels of environmental quality.

In terms of the substantive focus of this volume on 'environmental policy', there is no simple way of encapsulating environmental problems in such a way that the full range of issues, and government actions on these issues, is included. The environmental agenda is huge and all-encompassing. Early problems were related to the conservation or protection of particular sites, as in the creation of national parks in the early twentieth century. Then, governments at various levels began to deal with problems such as waste management and sewage treatment in cities. Pollution problems—including air quality in cities and water quality in lakes and rivers with important fisheries—became in many ways the defining characteristic of environmental policy for much of the past half-century. The concept of 'pollution' has in the past two decades expanded to include the effects in Canada of global climate change through the by-production of carbon and other compounds, and the influence these have on the chemistry of the atmosphere. A further set of problems relates to sustainable development. These encompass the issues just noted, but also tend to emphasize the importance of activities involving the use of renewable natural resources, such as forests, and significant aspects of others whose physical supply is fixed, such as minerals and fossil fuels. We have tried to include a representative range of case studies, whether through entire chapters devoted to a policy sector or via case studies used to illustrate insights in the contextual chapters.

Finally, an important task in terms of understanding Canadian environmental policy is examining the governance structures which underlie policy choices. Issues connected with 'governance'—which we can define broadly as the activity of making authoritative public choices[5]—are critical, as the optimal ways of making decisions on environmental policy are far from self-evident. Sustainable development arguments rest on participatory and collaborative notions about how environment and resource policy decisions should be made, and it is certainly the case that environmental policy-making in Canada has become more inclusive in various ways. Glen Toner and James Meadowcroft argue in Chapter 6 that Canada was initially an acknowledged innovator with respect to societal participation and multi-stakeholder dialogues on policy issues. Indeed, many of the chapters here refer to participatory decision-making processes in such areas as forest management, local government decision-making, pesticide policy reform, endangered species legislation, water pollution policy, and climate policy.

Yet, the picture is more complex and more deeply-rooted than merely government consultation with new actors in the environmental policy-making process. In an era where traditional state authority is 'bleeding' upward to supra-state, downward to sub-state, and outward to non-state actors, decision-making power, control, and legitimacy directed at public ends increasingly straddles the boundaries of the formal political system and non-state sectors and structures. As Peters and Pierre suggest, 'political power and institutional capacity is less and less derived from formal constitutional powers accorded to the state and more from a capacity to wield and coordinate resources from public and private actors.'[6] Michael Howlett, Jeremy Rayner, and Chris Tollefson refer to the phenomenon of 'governance shift' whereby institutional arrangements 'move from relatively formal, top-down coordination rules towards more informal and ambiguous arrangements subject to continuous negotiation' in Chapter 13. Thus, conventional political institutions are increasingly supplemented, in some cases supplanted by, other 'sites' of governance. A fitting example is the complex of institutions and processes put in place to respond to court-imposed obligations to consult and accommodate the interests of Aboriginal peoples. According to Graham White (Chapter 9), there are 'myriad governance provisions . . . designed to include Aboriginal people and their perspectives in public policy decisions relating to wildlife management and environmental regulation.'

Stephen Bocking provides some indication of the significance of governance arrangements in Chapter 5 when he notes that, '[g]overnance requires attention to not just the substance of policy, but the procedural mechanisms required for networks of actors to be guided towards sustainability.' Locating and scrutinizing these sites of governance helps to unravel the question of *why* it is that we end up with rather timid policy goals and little experimentation with alternative policy instruments. For example, Douglas Macdonald argues in Chapter 11 that the governance regime for climate change policy in Canada, resting as it does on weak intergovernmental consensus-building processes, is one reason for our inability to achieve national policy goals in this area. Carolyn Johns and Mark Sproule-Jones (Chapter 15) argue that governance arrangements in the water policy arena are characterized by 'state managerialism' and are inappropriate to addressing the tasks associated with the Next Generation policy agenda, which require more thorough-going change to the existing set of stakeholder interactions.

The Impetus for Action

Even if Canada's environmental policy record has been less than inspiring to date, interesting developments seem just around the corner. One might argue that we have reached a 'strategic inflection point'[7] in terms of our environmental policy regime, whereby conditions have changed materially, the rules of the game are different, and the current trajectory is becoming difficult to sustain. As compared with the context facing the editors and contributors of the first edition of *Canadian Environmental Policy* (in 1991) and the second edition (in 2002), the pressures for environmental action seem broader, more varied, emanating from many different sources, and perhaps harder to ignore. The critical question, then, is whether governments in Canada recognize and can adapt to factors of major significance auguring for greater leadership and more effort aimed at innovation.

The first of these factors is that the environmental problems confronting Canadians and their governments have multiplied and magnified. Canada has not generally done a good job of maintaining uniform databases with environmental information; State of the Environment reporting was unfortunately discontinued under the Chrétien Liberals in 1996, leaving a serious knowledge gap. Instead, for the period 1997–2003, there are reports on particular ecosystems (e.g., Great Lakes, Boreal Shield) or pollution issues (e.g., forest health and municipal wastewater effluent), but no data across media that can be compared year-by-year. These individual reports are worrying, however, and they build to similar conclusions. For example, the report on the Boreal Shield, Canada's largest ecozone, laid out the multiple stresses—such as clear-cutting, mining, and climate change—that will change this landscape dramatically over the coming decades.[8] Another focusing on water use by the agricultural sector noted that '[d]rought is a significant threat to the water supply in the Prairies and Ontario.'[9] A look around the websites of environmental advocacy groups shows a wide range of thorough analysis, and highlights the deepening environmental hazards associated with climate change, Alberta's oil sands, urban sprawl, nanomaterials, endocrine-disrupting substances, and incineration of toxic wastes, to name but a few. And, of course, our greenhouse gas emissions, and thus our contribution to global climate change, have increased considerably.

Perhaps not surprisingly then, Canada's environmental policies have attracted a surprising amount of often trenchant criticism—both domestically and internationally. For students of environmental policy in Canada, even a quick look through annual reports of Canada's Commissioner for the Environment and Sustainable Development highlights the multiple and cross-cutting failures of the federal government. The most visible failure, of course, is our inability to meet our Kyoto target. The 2006 Commissioner's report offered a scathing critique of the federal approach to climate change; it found 'inadequate leadership, planning, and performance' and an approach 'lacking foresight and direction', creating 'confusion and uncertainty'.[10] The 2005 report, surveying a range of issues including oceans management, national parks management, drinking water safety, and biodiversity, concluded that: 'A recurring theme throughout this year's Report is that the federal government suffers from a chronic inability to see its own initiatives to completion; it starts out but rarely, if ever, reaches the finish line.'[11] More recently, in his 2007 annual report, the Commissioner focused on the weaknesses in departmental sustainable development strategies which 'have not achieved their intended purpose', have been 'a major disappointment' and are 'not taken seriously' by senior managers. Even when, as in the Conservatives' Clean Air and Climate Change Act, the federal government has proposed to undertake initiatives in key environmental policy areas, critics have pointed to a lack of fresh thinking on urgent problems.

This chorus has been joined by voices from outside the country. It is probably fair to say that external criticisms generally have little influence on environmental policy inside Canada. However, they do sometimes reinforce domestic critiques, especially when, as recently, they appear to arise out of a sense that Canada has taken deliberate steps to shed its former image as an international role model of environmental attentiveness and leadership. Towards the end of the first decade of the twenty-first century, international references to Canada's reputation on environmental policy are dominated by concerns about oil sands developments and the retreat from Kyoto. In late 2006, Prime Minister Stephen Harper abruptly cancelled a summit meeting with the European Union after EU officials made it clear that Kyoto would be on the agenda. Sustained criticisms of Canada's record on climate change also surfaced at the UN climate change conference held in Nairobi in 2006, in Bali in late 2007, and more recently in Poland. Canada is also open to international censure for its investments in biofuels and the contribution these investments are making to the world food crisis. These and other criticisms met Prime Minister Harper when he spoke in May 2008 at the international meeting in Bonn of the parties to the Convention on Biological Diversity.

It is also the case that the public is increasingly aware of both the environmental challenge before us and also our failures in meeting this challenge. In July 2007, the environment and global warming were seen in a TNS Canadian Facts poll as the issue they were most concerned about among 'all the issues facing the world today',[12] 91 per cent of respondents agreed that global warming was the most serious issue facing Canadians, and 70 per cent felt that federal and provincial governments are not doing enough in this regard. A 4 September 2007 Environmental Monitor poll found that 70 per cent of respondents considered pollution laws inadequate, and that their top environmental concern was global warming.[13] In a poll conducted by McAllister Opinion Research from 29 April to 9 May 2008, over 70 per cent of respondents considered British Columbia's recent introduction of a carbon tax 'a positive step'.[14] The most recent polls certainly indicate competition for the attention of Canadians among the many issues confronting them, particularly the economic downturn. Yet they also show that the healthy majority of Canadians continue to be 'definitely, if not extremely, concerned about climate change' and that they want the federal government to maintain equal priority on both the economy and the environment rather than focus primarily on economic security.[15]

The causes of higher levels of public concern for the environment are many and varied. The change of government in Ottawa in 2006 no doubt helped to concentrate public attention on environmental issues. After assuming the reins of power with a decidedly offhand attitude toward environmental policy, and cutting climate change programs in the early months of its mandate, the Harper Conservatives have paid considerably more attention to this 'file' since late 2006. In addition, one cannot discount the impact on Canadians of the 'Bush factor' and the political consequences of an aggressively anti-environmental US President facing off against a very vocal pro-environment opposition personified by the Nobel Prize-winning former Vice President, Al Gore.

An additional reason for higher levels of public concern is likely that media coverage of environmental issues has increased substantially and has also been more critical. There is a circular process at work here. Media coverage responds to a sense on the part of editors and reporters that Canadians are interested in these issues, and reports then reinforce concerns. Coverage of Alberta's oil sands development has been especially intense. A media audit tracking the tone and depth of coverage of Canada's oil sands found that 80 per cent of articles on the topic between January 2007 and May 2008 reported a 'high negative sentiment' toward the oil sands, while topics specifically related to climate change reached 70 per cent.[16] Arctic warming trends and the impact on polar bears—long a symbol of Canada—have also figured prominently in coverage. The announcement that a giant ice shelf, 3,000 to 4,500 years old, had broken free from the coast of Ellesmere Island in the Canadian Arctic, creating an enormous, 66 km² ice island and leaving a trail of icy blocks in its wake, generated headlines all over the world. The media was also very active on the bisphenol A issue in 2008, highlighting potential risks from water bottles and baby food containers. Indeed, the widening range of links between environmental degradation and human health concerns—cancers, fertility, respiratory illnesses—can have a powerful impact on the public consciousness.

Many other issues continue to be highlighted by the news media. Some of these are local or provincial in character yet have impacted environmental policy debates across the country. They include reports of mining companies dumping toxic tailings into Canadian lakes, and the lax federal regulations that have facilitated this; the waste incineration practices encouraged in Ontario, despite the environmental costs; the controversy surrounding the proposed landfill site at Danford Lake, north of Gatineau; and continuing problems of mercury contamination, for example in northern Québec. All of these combine to create an impression of mounting environmental problems.

There is considerable debate about the extent to which this increase in public alarm represents a 'third wave' of environmental concern, how long the 'wave' is likely to last, and whether Canadians are actually willing to make real sacrifices for the environment (e.g., higher energy prices), particularly as the economic downturn deepens. Certainly, the evidence provided in Robert Paehlke's chapter might lead one to expect that public concern will not endure in tough economic times and, indeed, the polls referred to above indicate that these questions are open to interpretation. Yet, it is also clear that the present climate of public opinion—influenced in part by the ascent of an activist and environmentally-inclined Democrat to the White House—affords Canadian governments considerable leeway *right now* in terms of seizing the reins of environmental policy leadership, particularly as regards climate change. One might also argue, as does Paehlke, that this third wave is indeed distinctive in terms of its emphasis on climate change, a problem whose far-reaching impacts are beginning to be noticed and cannot be solved without taking the sustainability challenge much more seriously.

Moreover, partisan politics may prod government action as well, although this dynamic seems rather ambiguous from the vantage point of the post-2008 election landscape. The increase in concern about the environment appeared to be more politically salient in the run-up to the election;

the Green Party of Canada (GPC) had attracted increasing levels of support in recent provincial and federal elections and, as of the spring of 2008, the GPC was drawing between 8–12 per cent of voter support, according to various public opinion polls.[17] The election of Elizabeth May, long-time environmental activist and former Executive Director of the Sierra Club, on the first ballot at the Green Party's leadership convention, also seemed to indicate a new era for the GPC. However, the inability of Liberal Leader Stéphane Dion to again any traction for his 'Green Shift' (ecological fiscal reform) platform—indeed the Liberals' share of the vote *decreased*—does not bode well for green partisan politics. A further difficulty is that the Liberals, NDP, and GPC appear to be in direct competition for green votes, which has proven beneficial for the Conservatives, who have taken a decidedly more moderate approach to environmental policy.

Further, there has been a gradual reconfiguration of stakeholder interests and strategies. There can be no doubt that the private sector is still a major constraint on enhanced regulatory initiatives, with a preference for the kind of voluntarism that led to initiatives such as the Responsible Care program in the chemicals sector or self-regulation, as with the Forest Stewardship Certification. The Canadian Council of Chief Executives continues to argue that many companies and sectors have already put in place 'beyond regulation' performance systems on the environment, and they urge the wider adoption of these kinds of best practices as an alternative to regulation.[18] However, the alignment of business interests is becoming more complex. As Stewart Elgie points out in Chapter 14, private sector interests are not always cohesive vis-à-vis government action on environmental issues, and they may choose to work with environmental groups in advocating certain environmental policy stances. Moreover, the presence of a relatively new and burgeoning environmental industry sets up a different kind of industry interest, one that welcomes new government mandates requiring such things as environmental retrofits, new technologies, and audits. The Ontario government cites over 2,400 companies in that province alone in the environment goods and services sector.[19]

For their part, environmental nongovernmental organizations have begun to adopt strategies that have already served their American counterparts well, building coalitions of organizations and networks in order to launch national, and more powerful, campaigns. Both Sarah Pralle's chapter on the spread of local bans on cosmetic pesticides and Stewart Elgie's chapter on the species at risk campaign illustrate this well. In addition, various chapters, for example by Pralle, Elgie, and Douglas Macdonald, also point to the ways in which environmental groups attempt to 'divide the opposition' by forming alliances with various affected industries.

All of this is occurring on a backdrop of significant international forces impelling the environment, and especially climate change, onto the global agenda. The 4th Assessment Report of the United Nations' Intergovernmental Panel on Climate Change, released in 2007,[20] provided detailed and authoritative scientific evidence of the anthropogenic forces that are driving the twenty-first century changes in the world's climate. While the Kyoto agreement has failed, there is active international debate and diplomacy on the options for a new deal for the period after 2012. Despite sustained US opposition, issues such as climate change and biodiversity have in the last few years become regular features of the G8 meetings.

Closer to home, and perhaps more importantly, climate change took top billing in the US presidential election campaign, with both the Republican and Democratic nominees pledging to set a greenhouse gas emissions cap for the nation as a whole. The favoured approach to implementing this cap seems to be an emissions trading regime, which is expected to build on efforts already underway at the subnational level—including the Western Climate Initiative and the Regional Greenhouse Gas Initiative—to establish cross-jurisdictional cap-and-trade regimes. As a number of provinces are in active negotiations to join these subnational regimes, this is also serving to push Canadian climate change policy forward. The victory of Barack Obama and the move of more activist Democrats into key committee posts in Congress signals that a legislated cap on greenhouse gas emissions, new vehicle emissions standards, and a cap-and-trade regime will emerge sooner rather than later.

The Task Before Us

Given the magnitude of the policy challenge before us, created in part by the inertia that critics have detected in prevailing approaches, along with the various factors pushing for action, this suggests that considerably more forceful action by governments, and a deeper exploration of alternatives, is needed. But, in what direction should we be heading? What would actually constitute environmental policy leadership and innovation? Collectively, the authors and editors of this volume make the case that governments need to set more ambitious short- and long-term goals, and employ a wider range of policy instruments to achieve these goals. As Mark Winfield expresses this task in Chapter 4: '[a] more ambitious and integrative approach to both the establishment of environment policy goals and their implementation will be needed.' Ian Rowlands (Chapter 12) elaborates on the need for integration 'across policy approaches and across issue areas'. It has also become increasingly clear that we need to pay much closer attention to what we are actually achieving in terms of environmental outcomes.

But, what should the reference points be? How might we think about a different kind of environmental policy future? From a comparative perspective, one broad characteristic of Canadian environmental policy which stands out relative to that of other countries is our primarily 'First Generation' orientation. First Generation policies, the foundation of environmental policy regimes established in the 1970s, are those which focus on specific kinds of pollution for which sources can readily be identified, generally large point sources such as smokestacks or automobile emissions. First Generation policies target these 'end-of-pipe' emissions to a specific media (e.g., air or water) through the specification of technology standards and processes. This is a front-end approach, concerned primarily with designing compliance systems. It is also one which sees the primary relationship as that between the government regulator and the polluter, and policy-making as a function of negotiations between the two. There can be no doubt that first-generation policy, as perhaps best exemplified in traditional 'command-and-control' regulatory regimes, produced substantial improvements with respect to many types of pollution, and it has proven particularly helpful in dealing with industry laggards. At the same time, it is also clear that the First Generation thinking which underlies such regimes is too narrow in itself to address the environmental problems generated by increasingly complex, diverse, and interdependent societies, such as the challenge of moving away from a carbon-based economy.

By contrast, in the US and many European countries there are signs of a shift to 'Next Generation' thinking, which refers to a collection of ideas about environmental policy and policy-making that together promote a reorientation of approach along two interrelated lines.[21] First, in terms of goal-setting, Next Generation policies take a more holistic, 'place-based' approach concerned with the health of entire ecosystems. Mary Louise McAllister (Chapter 8) describes an ecosystem perspective as one which focuses on natural planning units, takes an interdisciplinary approach, includes cross-scale considerations and incorporates a sustainability ethic. The focus is no longer on specific point source emissions to specific media, but on preventing pollution in the first place, on maintaining healthy systems. Second, Next Generation policies are concerned with putting in place results-based implementation regimes in line with this ultimate goal. Advocates of Next Generation policy argue that we should employ the full range of instruments—regulation,[22] economic instruments, tax incentives, informational regulation—in whatever combination will deliver the necessary improvements in environmental quality. Policy-making of the Next Generation variety is also of necessity more collaborative and participatory, given the broad range of knowledge and expertise required of such an approach; this certainly implies the kind of governance shift described above.

Although Next Generation terminology may be used at the level of policy rhetoric in Canada, in most cases it does not seem to have permeated down to the level of actual policy to any serious extent. Of course, there are myriad forces that constrain Canadian governments from moving in this direction, from being environmental policy entrepreneurs or innovators; shifting gears towards policy responses of the Next Generation is certainly not a straightforward task. For one thing, a common theme underlying the chapters in this volume in the lack of federal leadership, a habit that will be difficult for the current government to break, particularly given its ideological predispositions. Successive Liberal governments, first under Chrétien, then Martin, appear to have viewed their role as environmental policy facilitators, and directed their efforts to putting in place conditions for others—the provinces, industry, civil society groups, and citizens—to take action gradually. Mandating firm, shorter-term policy goals, and using all possible federal levers to attain these goals, has not been in the playbook. The climate change policy case is, of course, the foremost example of this.

This reluctance to don the mantle of environmental policy leadership has been even more evident in the case of the Harper Conservatives. That said, in late 2006 the government read the political winds and announced a flurry of new initiatives in various areas in early 2007. For example, the Conservatives have undertaken to 'report regularly on the results achieved in addressing the top environmental concerns of Canadians', including air and water, nature, and climate change.[23] At the time of writing, the federal government was also working with the National Round Table on Environment and Economy to implement its recommended sustainable development indicators for the country. Further, the Conservatives supported a bill sponsored by Liberal Member of Parliament John Godfrey, the *Federal Sustainable Development Act*, which, as James Meadowcroft and Glen Toner explain in Chapter 6, attempts to address some of the failings of the current federal approach to implementing sustainable development across government. And, while criticisms of the Conservatives' climate policy, *Turning the Corner*, are thick on the ground, it must be acknowledged that a regulatory framework for achieving emissions reductions in particular industry sectors—though on an intensity basis rather than a hard cap—is being put in place for the first time.

Actually, though, the most vigorous activity over the past decade with respect to Canadian environmental policy has not taken place at the federal level—it has been at the subnational level. Subnational governments—provincial, local, and territorial—have become more significant, in various ways, to the environmental policy enterprise. While we noted the growing importance of provincial environmental policy activities in the second edition of *Canadian Environmental Policy*, this trend has become even more pronounced. Our authors point to a new assertiveness on the part of provinces in areas such as climate policy, renewable energy, Great Lakes watershed management, sustainable forest management, mercury pollution reduction, and pesticides reduction. This is not to say that provinces have been successful environmental policy leaders or innovators, but merely that they have provided more leadership and undertaken more innovation than the federal government. And, Mary Louise McAllister nudges us in Chapter 8 to broaden our perspective to take into analytical account the growing variety of initiatives being undertaken by municipal governments. An interesting aspect about local, and in some cases provincial, initiatives is that they seem to constitute a new phenomenon of 'innovation without jurisdiction'. In other words, while in some cases lower level governments do not possess actual constitutional or legal jurisdiction for the subject matter of environmental policy, they have nevertheless found ways of taking environmental policy action using whatever policy levers are close at hand. In the case of the territories, as Graham White points out in Chapter 9, new governance provisions under comprehensive land claims have fundamentally changed the rules of the game with respect to environment and resource management in the North, both broadening the field of players and also pushing the previously dominant federal government to the margins of policy discourse.

While action at the subnational level may be laudable, and in many cases necessary, there are legitimate concerns about the impact of our highly decentralized federal system on the achievement of sustainable development in Canada. Our authors make it clear that the patchwork of provincial environmental policies, noted in the second edition of *Canadian Environmental Policy*, continues to be in evidence. The result is different mixes of policy instruments in different jurisdictions. For example, as Douglas Macdonald notes at the beginning of Chapter 11, we have no coherent national climate change policy; instead, we have a plethora of plans, federal and provincial, which differ markedly from each other with regard to both the goals chosen, and also the policy instruments which will be used to achieve these goals. Michael Howlett, Jeremy Rayner, and Chris Tollefson document in detail the wide range of activities that provinces have taken in the name of 'sustainable forest management' (Chapter 13), and Ian Rowlands describes the different provisions being put in place in individual provinces to achieve very different goals for increasing the supply of renewable electricity in Chapter 12. One might hypothesize that bottom-up harmonization of environmental policy is possible—and chapters by Sarah Pralle (Chapter 17) and Debora VanNijnatten (Chapter 7) muse on this possibility—but it is not clear how and whether 'the integrated and comprehensive approach' advocated here as a necessary part of our environmental strategy can be achieved with this extent of difference. Arguments about federal states as laboratories of innovation aside, Canadian federalism exhibits particular 'pathologies,' in the words of Glen Toner and James Meadowcroft (Chapter 6), which make environmental policy activism and integration difficult.

Another constraint on environmental policy leadership and innovation is, rather bluntly stated, bureaucratic politics and inertia. The battle of wills between Environment Canada and Natural Resources Canada, particularly with respect to climate change policy, is well documented.[24] NRCan has amended its core statute to include sustainable development and is currently into its 4th Sustainable Development Strategy.[25] However, the department is widely seen as harbouring a bias toward fostering resource development, which makes it an unlikely partner for ambitious climate change policy. Indeed, the department has acted as a brake on the establishment of firm emissions reduction mandates applied to industry or even, as Stephen Bocking points out in Chapter 5, on the pursuit of environmentally friendly science and technology choices. NRCan is also seen to have exhibited a bias on behalf of the mining industry in discussions of mercury pollution reduction, according to Bruce Lourie (Chapter 16). Yet other departments have shown themselves to be less than helpful in moving the country toward sustainable development: Toner and Meadowcroft note the reluctance of officials in Finance Canada even to experiment with ecological fiscal reform; Mark Winfield (Chapter 4) observes that officials in Fisheries and Oceans Canada have been reluctant to enforce regulations that protect fish and waterways; and Stewart Elgie (Chapter 14) discusses the opposition of Environment Canada officials (!) to a mandatory protection regime for species at risk.[26]

Furthermore, although we appear to be on the verge of a shift in policy instrument choice, with much more serious consideration of market- and tax-based instruments and how they might fit into a broader sustainability framework, it is not clear that Canadian governments are prepared for this shift, or are devoting the necessary resources to undertaking this shift. Policy capacity is clearly lacking. This theme reverberates throughout the volume. Mark Winfield notes that combining various policy instruments into an integrated regime requires 'much greater policy development capacity on the part of government agencies advancing such approaches' (Chapter 4) but Toner and Meadowcroft lament a lack of sustainable development capacity among both senior management and staff in the federal bureaucracy. Carolyn Johns and Mark Sproule-Jones point to declining environmental policy capacity in Chapter 15 as one reason for the currently excessively narrow view of water policy goals and instrument choice. Stephen Bocking (Chapter 5) expresses concern about the deep cuts to science and technology which impact our current ability to produce effective environmental policy. And, Robert Boardman notes that our ability to meet global environmental challenges alongside the international community requires 'greatly improved capacities for governance, and vastly expanded knowledge bases' (Chapter 10); he indicates that we are ill-prepared in this respect.

Moreover, the continental dimension of Canada's policies on the environment has grown and become further institutionalized as a result of changes on the North American scene. While we have been debating the impacts of greater trade integration with the United States and Mexico on our environmental policy maneuverability for some time, we have not yet come to terms with the implications of greater *political and policy integration* with our southern neighbours, a trend which may or may not be related to trade. As we keep our eyes trained on a more sustainable future, we will have to bear in mind that governments at various levels in Canada—but particularly the provinces—see their environmental policy context in a different way than they did a decade ago. The impetus for action on environmental problems and the policy choices that have been made, particularly at the subnational level, may very well reflect the traditions of the United States, not Canada. This new reality will have to be incorporated into the national environmental regime.

Chapter Overview

The chapters in this third edition of *Canadian Environmental Policy* have been guided by a set of questions: Is there evidence of environmental policy leadership and innovation? What are the major obstacles? Where do we see promising developments that might serve as a starting point for new approaches?

The book is divided into four sections. In the first section, 'Canadians and their Environment', we begin by looking at public support for environmental policy leadership and innovation. In his birds-eye view of environmentalism in Canada in Chapter 1, Robert Paehlke traces the prospects of the environmental movement through three distinct 'waves' during which public concern about environmental degradation was high: through the 1970s; from the late 1980s into the early 1990s; and over the past five years or so. Paehlke argues that the Canadian environmental movement has had its greatest successes during these three waves of strong environmental concern among the general public and extensive attention from the media. During each of these periods, the movement has played a critical role in questioning the existing political and economic order and pressuring governments to act, though their philosophical orientation and programming has changed significantly across the three periods. However, he also explains that the ability of the movement to press for environmental leadership is constrained by economic conditions and, relatedly, trends in public opinion, as well as by the difficulty of maintaining a presence both inside and outside the economic and political systems. The continuing challenge of the environmental movement, then, is to achieve policy initiatives—whether regulations, tax shifts, or a system of incentives for businesses and consumers—in such a way that improvements will continue when public attention has turned for a time to other issues, as threatens to be the case now.

Steven Brown, in his Chapter 2 analysis of voter support for the Green Party of Canada, explores the prospects for Green parties on the federal and provincial political scenes, and their potential to frame the terms of political debate in the direction of environmental policy leadership. Brown employs newly released public opinion data from Ipsos Reid to paint a profile of the GPC's support base, which appears to be composed of somewhat younger self-employed professionals concerned about the environment, but is not otherwise markedly distinctive either demographically or politically from that of the Liberals and NDP. In other words, Green party voters do not reside on the fringes of the Canadian electorate. While this bodes well for the party's saleability across the Canadian electorate, Brown's analysis also reveals a significant weakness in Green party support; it is relatively fluid. Fully three-fifths of the GPC's voter support was new in the 2006 federal election, and a significant portion of these were ex-Liberals. This raises the possibility that these voters may simply migrate back to the Grits, particularly if they adopt an appropriately green mantle. In any case, rising voter support for Green Parties has altered the dynamics of partisan politics in observable ways.

In the second section, 'Making Environmental Law and Policy', four chapters survey the legal, institutional, and policy frameworks currently in place in order to assess opportunities for environmental policy leadership and innovation. Marcia Valiante, in Chapter 3, begins by arguing that, with respect to the Supreme Court's pronouncements, 'the cumulative message is that the Court is sympathetic to environmental protection, is open to innovative claims, and will not be an impediment to government action at all levels.' Federal powers in particular have been interpreted generously. Valiante shows that courts have supported environmental leadership by endorsing environmental values, legitimizing ambitious policy choices, giving environmental groups more scope to raise environmental arguments before the courts, and encouraging governments and project proponents to take environmental costs into account. While noting that the Court's actual substantive impact on environmental policy is minimal since most decisions simply uphold legislative or executive policy choices, Valiante makes the case that litigation is a gradual, cumulative strategy that can 'support and legitimize policy innovation'.

In Chapter 4, Mark Winfield provides something of a primer on environmental policy instruments and instrument choice in Canada. As Winfield notes, 'the choices that governments make about policy instruments have a large influence on whether stated policy goals are actually achieved.' He shows that there has been a marked lack of innovation in environmental policy instrumentation in Canada relative to the US and European countries; governments here have relied primarily on regulation accompanied by subsidies to help industries make the transition to cleaner technologies. There have been very few attempts to use instruments involving the creation of markets, the application of taxes and charges or the use of public information. Winfield links this tendency to a range of policy and political factors that act as obstacles to innovation—including federal–provincial relations, public opinion and nongovernmental actors—but also to the relatively limited range of goals that governments have pursued in their environmental policy initiatives. Winfield argues that Canadian governments must 'combine different instruments into comprehensive systems or "regimes" capable of achieving the kinds of deeper changes in economic and social behaviour, ... that are widely seen to be necessary to advance . . . environmental sustainability'.

In Chapter 5, Stephen Bocking addresses the role of science in environmental governance and in the pursuit of environmental policy leadership more specifically. Bocking explains that science performs essential functions in environmental governance: in identifying problems, contributing to policy formulation, guiding the management of resources, and providing a basis for adjudicating conflicts regarding the environment. The major challenge for governments in the pursuit of environmental policy leadership is to ensure that scientifically sound, relevant, credible, and politically legitimate knowledge is available to support these functions. Bocking indicates that governments are not currently meeting this challenge, as they have failed to bring science into the service of environmental governance in different ways—via basic research, regulatory science, advocacy science, and innovation science. As he argues: '[o]nly by applying a variety of models can science respond effectively to diverse requirements for environmental knowledge.' Bocking proposes a new model of science —'modest science'—which 'contributes distinctive knowledge, but is cognizant of the value of other forms of knowledge, and is also mindful of democratic imperatives as well as the boundaries between science and policy'.

Glen Toner and James Meadowcroft, in Chapter 6, examine the sustainable development policies, institutions, and practices put in place by the federal government. Toner and Meadowcroft set the tone for their analysis by noting that, in the 1990s, Canada was considered an innovator and leader in terms of the institutional change process required by sustainable development, yet '[f]ew would say this is the case today.' Their chapter provides an examination of various sustainable development mechanisms, including strategic environmental assessment, the Commissioner for Environment and Sustainable Development, departmental sustainable development strategies, and the National Roundtable on Environment and Economy. They conclude that these do not, by any means, add up to a government-wide strategy for change. The authors detail those characteristics of our political system which act as serious barriers to the kind of transformative change required by sustainable development, including federal–provincial relations, executive dominance, partisan politics, bureaucratic inertia, and erratic public support. In the end, however, Toner and Meadowcroft conclude that this is a story of the failure to lead, both operationally in terms of putting in place national priorities and appropriate policies, improving coordination across government and carefully monitoring what has been accomplished, but also politically—it is a failure of 'political spirit'.

The third section of the volume, 'Environmental Governance at Multiple Levels', examines the potential and opportunities for environmental policy leadership and innovation at the subnational, local, territorial/aboriginal, trilateral, and international scales. In Chapter 7, Debora VanNijnatten explores the mechanisms by which North American ideas and actors influence Canadian environmental policy at multiple governance levels—bilateral, trilateral, and cross-border regional—and asks whether these influences have acted to constrain or encourage environmental policy innovation in Canada. She argues that the most significant interaction in recent years has been at the cross-border regional level, although there have also been noteworthy initiatives at the trilateral level. In many cases, these North American dynamics, far from being a constraining influence, have instead helped to create opportunities for environmental policy action and innovation in Canada. At the same time, however, the cross-border regional dynamic has served to reinforce the differences in environmental policy approach which already exist among provinces, and between the provinces and federal government. This divergence complicates even further the perennial problem of building a more integrated and ambitious environmental policy regime in Canada.

In Chapter 8, Mary Louise McAllister presents us with something of a paradox. Although one would not expect municipal governments in Canada to be environmental policy leaders or innovators, given their jurisdictional constraints and dependence on property taxes, there might be some grounds for rethinking this assumption. McAllister traces the movement of cities from a focus on being providers of efficient services and economic development, to zoning for the purposes of creating the 'city beautiful', to the emergence of 'city healthy' and sustainability campaigns. She argues that socio-ecological systems perspectives have been influencing the manner in which local planning and practitioners carry out their work, as evidenced in the work of the Royal Commission on the Future of the Toronto Waterfront, in the role that cities have come to play in biosphere reserves, and in the new emphasis on 'green infrastructure'. While significant constraints on local governments remain, there are some promising developments in urban areas that are at the nexus of large concentrations of population and economic activity.

Graham White, in Chapter 9, takes us to Canada's far North to consider environmental governance in a very different setting. White assesses actions taken by the new environmental regulatory 'co-management' boards created under the comprehensive land claims agreements in the territorial North, specifically the Mackenzie Valley Environmental Impact Review Board (MVEIRB) and Mackenzie Valley Land and Water Board (MVLWB). These boards, through majority Aboriginal membership, are intended to put in place 'stringent processes for environmental regulation for resource extraction and infrastructure processes'; this is critical given the economic, cultural and spiritual significance of the land to Aboriginal people. After surveying MVLWB and MVEIRB processes and membership, as well as specific decisions taken, White argues that, overall, 'their record, both in maintaining a high-quality regime of environmental impact assessment and of imposition of mitigation measures, and in assuring that the concerns and the approaches of local Aboriginal people are taken into account, is one of solid accomplishment.' In fact, White argues, here we have a good example of the holistic, place-based approach advocated by Next Generation enthusiasts.

Robert Boardman rounds out this section with an analysis of international environmental governance in Chapter 10. He argues that international and domestic environmental policies can be mutually supportive in the pursuit of environmental leadership. Canadian officials have at various times used international mechanisms to promote environmental objectives, such as Arctic contamination, the survival of polar bears, and chemical pollution. Looking 'downward', international agreements and the institutions they spawn create 'networks of obligations' which can encourage action in Canada; for example, Canada's participation in the Convention on Biological Diversity was a critical push toward federal legislation on endangered species. Moreover, Boardman discusses the way in which 'ideas and instruments seep through borders', as the policy approaches of forerunner countries such as Germany and the Scandinavian countries diffuse via bodies such as the OECD to 'laggards' such as Canada. Indeed, comparisons between Canada and other countries have become handy tools for critics of domestic policy. Boardman cautions that this complex mix of influences supporting environmental policy leadership may be weakening as 'a systemic timidity' overtakes Ottawa's approach to many international issues.

The final section of the book investigates the record of environmental policy leadership and innovation in seven different areas: climate change, renewable electricity, forest management, endangered species, water pollution, mercury pollution, and pesticides use. Douglas Macdonald, in Chapter 11, begins with climate change policy, which he himself describes as the 'hard case' of Canadian environmental policy, 'requiring commitment, leadership and policy innovation far beyond anything seen to date'. Macdonald's conclusions? We have seen very little commitment, leadership, or innovation; instead, 'we have no coherent policy, we have given up on Kyoto and emissions continue to rise.' Macdonald unravels the story of two decades of policy failure, arguing that four factors have been particularly significant to this story: the large regional variations in the cost of emission reductions and thus in provincial interests; the presence of a 'highly motivated veto state' (the province of Alberta); the absence of motivated leader (particularly the federal government); and the inadequacy of intergovernmental mechanisms for national environmental policy integration. Macdonald indicates that Canadians have not come to terms with the magnitude of the policy challenge, which requires direct engagement with the problem and process of burden-sharing, with politics in Alberta and with the potential US influence.

In a complementary Chapter 12, Ian Rowlands examines Canadian provincial policies to promote the increased use of renewable resources in electricity supply systems. He shows that strategies to promote increased use of renewable resources have, to varying degrees, relied upon government targets/obligations, competitive procurement, market mechanisms, and consumer initiatives. Rowlands argues that the most innovative thinking about the development of renewable electricity policy is informed by broader ideas regarding 'integration'—across policy approaches, using a variety of regulatory, taxation, and market instruments; and across issue areas, recognizing the horizontal connections between electricity policy and broader objectives related to sustainability and issues like climate change. According to this metric, Canadian provinces have made tentative steps in this direction—with Ontario playing a prominent role here—but Rowlands concludes that more innovation is required.

Next, in Chapter 13, Michael Howlett, Jeremy Rayner, and Chris Tollefson examine the degree to which the 'old' forest governance has been replaced by a 'new' forest governance operating under the ambitious sustainable forest management (SFM) paradigm. In a policy-making context which saw the incorporation of significant new actors in the forest policy community, the SFM paradigm, a central goal of which is biodiversity conservation, has been transmitted to Canada through various iterations of the National Forest Strategy (NFS) as well as the certification movement. Accompanying this evolution is experimentation with new forest policy instruments, as traditional prescriptive regulation and direct subsidies have come to be accompanied by new experiments involving performance standards, incentives, codes of conduct, certificates, and procedural instruments, including intensive local and regional planning efforts and consultative and participatory policy-making efforts. However, the authors argue that the move toward the SFM-inspired forest governance has been uneven, and many key features of the traditional regulation and subsidy approach to forest policy (for example, such as centralized control over such important elements of forest production as allowable cuts and land tenure by hierarchical government departments and specialized forest agencies) are deeply entrenched and have proven highly resistant to change.

In Chapter 14, Stewart Elgie leads us through the decade-long campaign by a coalition of environmental groups in Canada to get a national law to protect endangered species on the books. Employing an analytical framework which highlights the impact of institutions, actors, and ideas on policy development, Elgie shows us how federalism and executive dominance acted as obstacles to the incorporation of ambitious policy proposals put forward by environmental groups, with the aid of the scientific community, into a Species At Risk Act (SARA). He also notes the influence of cross-national learning, whereby the US experience with endangered species legislation was used by all actors to push their particular agendas. Through concerted entrepreneurial efforts, the environmental coalition was eventually successful not only in getting legislation, but also in increasing the stringency of key provisions. As Elgie explains, one of the most interesting aspects of the SARA story was that, in many ways, the timing for a federal environmental law reform initiative was bad; nevertheless, the unique combination of events and drivers in this case resulted in environmental policy leadership.

We then move into the realm of pollution control, with Chapter 15 on water policy by Carolyn Johns and Mark Sproule-Jones. The authors review water pollution policy efforts in Canada through reference both to the broader policy context and to policy responses in two specific cases in the Great Lakes: contamination of Randle's Reef in Hamilton Harbour and the Walkerton drinking water crisis. The authors argue that although Canada has come some way since its 'First Generation' policy efforts, progress toward 'Next Generation' water pollution policies in the past decade has been slow and variable. To a great extent, the lack of progress can be attributed to the resilience of traditional water allocation regimes which favour economic water users in a resource management context characterized by state managerialism. This, in turn, has impacted Canada's ability to move forward in key areas, such as the integration of water quantity and quality; the incorporation of climate, air, and land use in cross-medium approaches; and linking natural and social systems at the watershed scale in an effort to achieve 'integrated water resource management.'

In Chapter 16, Bruce Lourie examines the challenges that Canada faces with respect to the regulation of toxic substances, using the case study of mercury reduction policy. Lourie begins his examination by observing that, 'if mercury use and exposure cannot be managed under Canada's toxic pollution policy framework, it becomes hard to imagine whether any toxic substance can be adequately controlled.' However, Lourie provides little reason for optimism. He argues that the Canadian federal government, and particularly Natural Resources Canada, through the continued support for and promotion of inaccurate and misleading research, has deliberately sought to create scientific uncertainty in order to influence the regulatory agenda. Lourie sets out two factors that may explain this surprising stance: the fact that NRCan is a 'client-focused' agency, with these clients being primarily the extractive industries; and the prevalence of industry funding of regulatory science. Indeed, Lourie notes that corporate agendas have influenced science–policy debates in other areas, including lead, asbestos, and greenhouse gases; there is, according to Lourie, fundamental flaws in Canada's procurement, oversight, and use of science in environmental policy-making.

Finally, Chapter 17 by Sarah Pralle ends the volume on a rather optimistic note. Canadian pesticide politics, she explains, has 'bucked' the rather dismal trends identified in various chapters in this volume, including the dominance of neo-liberal, de-regulatory agendas, budget-cutting, and a federal withdrawal from the environmental policy scene. Instead, the pesticides case shows environmental policy leadership from above, in the form of new regulations under a revised Pest Control Products Act, and from below, in the form of municipalities across the country banning the non-essential use of cosmetic pesticides. Pralle provides a number of insights into potential sources and strategies for environmental policy leadership with respect to how the dynamics of competition among different levels of government in Canada can facilitate action, how officials within government can act as policy entrepreneurs, how environmental groups worked together to facilitate action, and how the American influence can be a force for upward harmonization of policy.

Notes

1. M. Winfield, 'Environmental Governance in Canada: From Regulatory Renaissance to Smart Regulation'. Keynote address given at the annual Journal of Environmental Law and Practice Conference, Saskatchewan, June 2006. Published in *Journal of Environmental Law and Practice (JELP)* 17: 69–83.

2. See, for example, various chapters in Robert B. Gibson, *Voluntary Initiatives: The New Politics of Corporate Greening* (Peterborough: Broadview Press, 1999) and Kathryn Harrison, 'Voluntarism and Regulatory Governance', in E.A. Parson, ed., *Governing the Environment: Persistent Challenges, Uncertain Innovations* (Toronto: University of Toronto Press, 2001), 207–46.

3. Debora L. VanNijnatten and Robert Boardman, eds, *Canadian Environmental Policy: Context and Cases* (Don Mills: Oxford University Press, 2002), xii–xiii.

4. Environment Canada, 'Canada's 2006 Greenhouse Gas Inventory'. Available at http://www.ec.gc.ca/pdb/GHG/inventory_report/2006/som-sum_eng.cfm (accessed 1 February 2009).

5. Lamont C. Hempel, *Environmental Governance: The Global Challenge* (Washington, DC: Island Press, 1996), 10.

6. G. Peters and J. Pierre, 'Development in International Relations: Towards Multi-level Governance', *Policy and Politics* 29, 2 (2001): 132.

7. The term 'strategic inflection point' was coined by Andy Grove of Intel to describe the period of massive change that affects an organization's situation and competitive position. It is the point at which an organization either takes a decision to change its corporate strategy to pursue a different direction and risk immediate decline.

8. Environment Canada, 'Ecological Assessment of the Boreal Shield Ecozone'. Minister of Public Works and Government Services Canada, 2000. Available at http://www.ec.gc.ca/soer-ree/English/SOER/CRAengfin.cfm#light (accessed 20 June 2008).

9. Agriculture and Agri-Food Canada, 'The Health of our Water: Toward sustainable agriculture in Canada'. Minister of Public Works and Government Services Canada. Available at http://www.agr.gc.ca/nlwis-snite/index_e.cfm?s1=pub&s2=hw_se&page=1 (accessed 20 June 2008).

10. Office of the Auditor General of Canada, '2006 September Report of the Commissioner of the Environment and Sustainable Development'. Available at http://www.oag-bvg.gc.ca/internet/English/aud_ch_cesd_200609_0_e_14982.html (accessed 20 June 2008).

11. Office of the Auditor General of Canada, '2005 September Report of the Commissioner of the Environment and Sustainable Development'. Available at http://www.oag-bvg.gc.ca/internet/English/aud_ch_cesd_200509_0_e_14947.html (accessed 19 June 2008).

12. TNS Canadian Facts, 'Environment and Global Warming Top Issues, Canadians Say'. Media Release, 25 July 2007. Available at http://www.tns-cf.com/news/07.07.25-green-power.pdf (accessed 20 June 2008).

13. McAllister Opinion Research, 'Poll: Increasing Majority Call Canada's Pollution Laws Inadeqate'. Media Release 4 September 2007. Available at http://www.globescan.com/news_archives/em07_pr/em07.pdf (accessed 20 June 2008).

14. The Pembina Institute for Appropriate Development, 'Strong National Support for British Columbia's Carbon Tax: Survey'. Media Release, 26 May 2008. Available at http://www.pembina.org/media-release/1641 (accessed 20 June 2008).

15. Environics Research Group, 'No longer business as usual: Is the environment dead as a public issue now that we are in a recession?'. Available at: http://erg.environics.net/media_room/default.asp?aID=692 (accessed 1 February 2009).

16. Fleischman Hillard International Communications, 'Media Audit: Analysis'. Available at http://www.oilsandsfuture.com/media-audit.php (accessed 20 June 2008).

17. http://www.nodice.ca/elections/canada/polls.php.

18. http://www.ceocouncil.ca/en/creating/env_lead.php.

19. Ontario's Environment Industry: Protecting the Future (2006). Available at http://www.ene.gov.on.ca/cons/5754e.pdf.

20. The Synthesis Report is available at http://www.ipcc.ch/ipccreports/ar4-syr.htm.

21. See, for example, M.R. Chertow and D.C. Esty, *Thinking Ecologically: The Next Generation of Environmental Policy* (New Haven, CT: Yale University Press, 1997); D.F. Kettl, ed., *Environmental Governance: A Report on the Next Generation of Environmental Policy* (Washington, DC: Brookings Institution Press, 2002); N. Gunningham, 'Reconfiguring Environmental Regulation: Next Generation Policy Instruments'. The International Development Research Centre. Available at http://www.idrc.ca/en/ev-110171-201-1-DO_TOPIC.html (accessed 17 July 2008).

22. Some advocates are concerned with making regulation more 'flexible', i.e., setting a general goal or performance standards and letting each employer decide how to meet it, although this is a matter of considerable debate in the literature.

23. Environment Canada, 'Tracking Key Environmental Issues'. Available at http://www.ec.gc.ca/TKEI/toc/toc_e.cfm (accessed 20 June 2008). The data contained in the first report is quite dated, however, and does not give one a sense of the most recent trends.

24. See, for example: Debora L. VanNijnatten and Douglas·Macdonald, 'The Clash of Energy and Climate Change Policies: How Ottawa Blends', in G. Bruce Doern, ed., *How Ottawa Spends 2003–2004* (Don Mills: Oxford University Press, 2003).

25. http://www.nrcan-rncan.gc.ca/sd-dd/strat/strat_eng.html.

26. There is an interesting discussion of the roles of four key agencies on sustainable development (Environment Canada, Industry Canada, NRCan, and Transport Canada) in Francois Bregha, 'Missing the Opportunity: A Decade of Sustainable Development', in Glen Toner ed., *Innovation, Science, and Environment: Canadian Policies and Performance 2008–2009* (Kingston and Montreal: McGill-Queens University Press, 2008), 30–52.

Canadians and their Environment

1

The Environmental Movement in Canada

Robert Paehlke

With the advantage of hindsight, most analysts date the origins of the North American environmental movement to the 1962 publication of Rachel Carson's *Silent Spring*. Prior to that, the conservation movement, with its principal focus on the protection of habitat and wilderness, functioned back into the nineteenth century.[1] Compared to the conservation movement, the environmental movement had a broader, three-dimensional focus on pollution, the protection of biodiversity, and what would come to be called 'sustainability'. This broader movement had much greater political appeal because it emphasized things that concerned more people—the air that we breathe and the water that we drink—essentially urban-oriented issues, as well as issues like resource availability and price that have a direct effect on economic well-being.

In Canada, the environmental movement did not take hold in the public imagination until later in the 1960s and the early 1970s when organizations like Pollution Probe at the University of Toronto (1969), the Ecology Action Centre in Halifax (1971), and the Society Promoting Environmental Conservation in Vancouver (1969) were established. Comparable groups sprang up all across the country in most cities of any size and many of these groups, including these three, are still active today. Also dating to this era, which might be called the first wave of environmentalism, were Environment Canada (then called the Department of the Environment), *Alternatives Magazine* (now published at the University of Waterloo), and the Faculty of Environmental Studies at York University.

This array of organizations supplemented and helped to alter the focus of existing conservation organizations that previously had centred almost exclusively on the protection of nature and wildlife habitat (and especially on the establishment of provincial and federal parks). The environmental movement focused on the places where most Canadians, by this time, were living: in cities. It stressed the excesses of the consumer-oriented society that had arisen in the decades following the end of the Second World War, principally the concern that resources including minerals, fish, forests, and energy, clean air, and water, would soon be a thing of the past. Consumption, it was widely argued, was so excessive and inefficient that resources either would be depleted or would produce intolerable environmental damage when extracted and processed. A classic statement of this view was the best-selling book *Limits to Growth*.[2]

To fully appreciate the comparatively radical character of the environmental movement of the 1960s and 1970s, we should first briefly look at the prior conservation movement. Some of the policy prescriptions that seemed impractical at the time have turned out to be quite prescient and might have helped to diminish some of today's leading environmental concerns.

The Origins of Environmentalism:
Early Conservation in Canada

Early conservation efforts in Canada were both real and important, but they did not have the early beginnings or wide support that similar efforts sometimes had in Europe or the United States. Conservation began with the development of scientific forestry in France and Germany in the seventeenth and eighteenth centuries and was transferred to North America by German forestry educators. Bernard Fernow, for example, founded the Schools of Forestry at Cornell University and the University of Toronto. Generally though, conservation efforts began much sooner in the United States than in Canada. As Monte Hummel put it, 'Americans were generally ahead of Canadians in concern for the conservation of resources. The concern probably resulted from the more extensive settlement in the US, which demonstrated the harm that civilization could do. In Canada a pioneer mentality of "unlimited" forests, lakes and wildlife persisted longer.'[3]

In 1847 Vermont Congressman George Perkins Marsh made his noted speech to the Agricultural Society of Rutland County, Vermont, in which he called out deforestation as the destruction of nature; in 1864 Marsh published his masterpiece *Man and Nature*. In 1851 Henry David Thoreau spoke to the Concord (Massachusetts) Lyceum and famously asserted that, '[i]n wilderness is the preservation of the world.' In 1854 he published *Walden; or, Life in the Woods*. These two books are perhaps the greatest works of conservation and both received wide attention, as did the nature paintings of both John James Audubon and the Hudson River School, including Asher B. Durand and Albert Bierstadt. The conservation movement was about the appreciation of nature and the wise, and scientific, use of resources, but it also questioned basic values and advocated the *preservation* of nature.

Audubon did more than paint nature; he declared that, 'the greedy mills told the sad tale, that in a century the noble forests . . . should exist not more.'[4] By the 1870s John Muir was establishing a national reputation as a writer who promoted the preservation of nature. In the 1880s he led the campaign to establish Yosemite National Park and in 1892 he founded the Sierra Club. Muir and some of the others had a mass following for conservation that was lacking at the time in Canada.

Nonetheless, Banff National Park—Canada's first national park—was established in 1885, only 13 years after Yellowstone National Park. Unlike Yellowstone National Park, Banff was founded primarily to promote tourism and the Canadian National Railroad, rather than to promote conservation; strong conservation language only entered the Parks Act in 1930. There were, however, notable Canadian conservation initiatives prior to this latter date. The first Canadian bird sanctuary was created in Saskatchewan in 1887 and in 1907–9 the federal government purchased 700 of the remaining bison (once 60 million strong) and placed them in national parks.[5] These conservation efforts were important but, in effect, very modest initiatives.

In 1909 Canada signed its first international environmental protection treaty, the Canada–US Boundary Waters Treaty that established the International Joint Commission. In 1916 the Migratory Bird Convention was co-signed with the United States. In 1909 Canada also established the Commission on Conservation, an independent agency devoted to forest conservation, water development, and a variety of conservation initiatives. The Commission strove to entrench a scientific conservation ethos in Ottawa, but succumbed to opposing political forces in 1921. During the 1930s and the war years that followed there was little, if any, opposition to development of any kind, though the war years did produce considerable interest in more careful resource use and recycling.

Environmentalism in Canada: The First Wave

Social critics in the 1950s looked at post-war prosperity and the changing shape of North American society and its economy, and began raising fundamental doubts. American conservationists like Fairfield Osborne, Harrison Brown, and Samuel Ordway, Jr questioned the efficacy of the emerging consumer-oriented society in a tone well beyond that of most early conservationists, save perhaps Thoreau and a few others.

These 1950s writings did not, however, dampen the post-war boom mentality. The tail-finned automobiles of the day kept getting larger and longer, and even more weighted down with chrome throughout the 1950s and 1960s. It was not until the scientifically-rooted assertions of Rachel Carson that the environmental era took hold. When these were amplified by the findings of the computer modelling in *Limits to Growth*, the arguments of those crying in the wilderness in the 1950s began to take hold.

Concern with pollution and resources was suddenly everywhere. It was as if the unintended costs of economic prosperity had been spray painted in Dayglo colours where previously they were swathed in camouflage. Environmentalism reached the broader public in ways that conservation had not, and alarm replaced passing concern. Governments, especially in North America this time, felt compelled to at least appear to be taking action to protect the environment. Throughout the 1970s legislative initiatives were frequent.

In 1969, the National Environmental Policy Act (NEPA) was passed in the United States and the term 'environmental assessment' entered our vocabulary (though the Canadian initiatives in this regard were slower in coming). Canadians and Americans alike were soon aware that their detergents were polluting the Great Lakes, as were a wide array of industries, especially in such locations as Sarnia, Hamilton, Cleveland, and Buffalo. Not long after the formation of the federal Department of the Environment in Canada, the rising concerns about resources were accelerated by the 1973 OPEC oil price increase. These price increases, and those that followed in 1979, brought the message of resource limits into everyday lives, especially of energy-profligate North Americans.

Environmentalism, it turned out, was different from conservation in several important respects. The new focus was on urban concerns, the possible limits that might arise given the way our economy functioned and how we lived our lives—all of which struck a popular chord. The newer environmental activists were still concerned with protecting nature and wilderness, but their first concern was with protecting human health and well-being. For a time, protecting nature seemed passé compared to what was painted as a fundamental crisis of industrial society itself and a direct threat to human survival. What environmentalists were saying was irretrievably political, since fixing the problem called for more ambitious action than protecting islands of nature and scenic beauty, as important as that might still be.

It was not long before Canadian environmental organizations and environmental scientists were challenging the pulp and paper industry over mercury and dioxins, and the Science Council of Canada was producing the groundbreaking study *Canada as a Conserver Society*.[6] This report, written by the noted metallurgist Ursula Franklin, called for a rethinking of the industrial economy in a way that got us 'more (economy) for less (resource use)'. This paralleled the view of Barry Commoner who argued that the root of our environmental problems was more poor technological choices than too large a human population or too much affluence.[7] It appeared in the same year as the first articulation of the 'soft path' ideas of Amory Lovins.[8] Lovins visited Canada many times and earned considerable influence here through the detailed analytic work of David Brooks and others active within the Canadian environmental movement.[9]

These works all struck a counterweight to two competing arguments: one, that there was no alternative but to proceed with major new conventional and environmentally risky energy developments to prevent economic collapse; or, two, that we needed to walk away from industrial society and learn to live with zero economic growth and zero population growth. This latter option—the anti-technological, often anti-urban, dimension of early environmentalism—is sometimes forgotten but was quite commonplace within the environmental movement of the early 1970s. This perspective stands in sharp contrast to today's very widely asserted argument that North America's best hope economically is the pursuit of green technologies, green jobs, and a green economy.[10]

In the short term, especially after the 1973 OPEC oil price increases, the pursuit of energy efficiency and, to a lesser extent, energy alternatives came to be widely accepted within government circles. The Department of Energy, Mines, and Resources (the predecessor to Natural Resources Canada) established an Office of Energy Conservation in 1974, headed by David Brooks (though in 1977, discouraged by insufficient action, Brooks left to head an Ottawa office for Energy Probe). The 1973 energy price increase and the pleadings of environmentalists were sufficient to cause the government to create an office, but not enough to cause government or industry to take decisive long-term action.

The environmental movement in effect advocated energy policy innovations that would have reduced Canada's greenhouse gas emissions more than a decade before climate change became a concern. In addition, even at this early date the North American automobile industry was seen by some analysts to be on a weak economic footing compared to high-quality foreign producers in the face of rising energy prices.[11] Environmentalist policy instincts were frequently ahead of their time and anticipated both environmental and economic problems that we have yet to resolve even 30 years later.

That said, after OPEC again raised oil prices in 1979, Canada entered a period that might be called the First Energy Crisis. Ironically perhaps, the largest gains in energy efficiency (and reduced use) were made as the first wave of environmental activism waned in the face of subsequent recessionary conditions in the early 1980s. Indeed, we might put forward the hypothesis that environmental concerns get pushed to the back burner in the public eye and in government whenever the economy weakens. These circumstances, as experienced in the early 1980s, meant that the things environmentalists most fervently desired would not come to pass.

Energy prices drove North Americans and Europeans (who were ahead of the game to begin with because their energy prices had always been considerably higher) to reduce energy use in a dramatic fashion between 1980 and 1985. People switched rapidly to smaller cars, took public transit, and insulated their houses; the economy slowed. Even when the recession eased, energy demand continued to decline until 1985, when oil prices fell dramatically in response to falling demand. This, in turn, allowed the North American auto industry to return, by the 1990s, to fuel inefficient vehicles on which profit margins are higher—and SUVs were born (and heavily marketed). This three-factor dynamic—rising environmental concern, rising energy prices, and the economic cycle—is important because it has since repeated itself and threatens to do so again now. When the economy falters, as in the early 1980s and the early 1990s, waves of pro-environmental opinion that can drive policy innovation tend to wane. Media and public attention turns to economic issues: job losses, inflation, and governmental deficits and debt.

Energy prices, in and of themselves, can produce environmental improvement through improvements in energy efficiency—heavier use of transit, the purchase of more fuel efficient appliances and vehicles, and so forth—even in the absence of surges in pro-environmental opinion or stronger environmental policy initiatives. At the same time, the fear of future energy shortages can simultaneously put pressure on governments to approve environmentally doubtful energy supply options, such as tar sands development in Canada and offshore or Alaska wilderness drilling in the United States. In early 1980s, for example, a declining economy rip-sawed by stagflation captured Canadians' attention and pushed forward into a waning of the first wave of the environmental movement and the election in the United States of Ronald Reagan, a President notably hostile to action on any and every environmental concern. Yet, despite government indifference there, high oil prices accelerated energy efficiency improvements and spurred offshore oil initiatives in, for example, the North Sea off of Norway and the North Slope of Alaska.

The Second Wave of Environmental Activism in Canada

Thus, by the mid-1980s, the North American economy had returned to more normal growth rates and improving energy efficiency, spurred by high oil prices, led to falling demand and an abrupt decline in oil prices. Strikingly, no sooner had prosperity returned and energy prices declined than widespread environmental concern again appeared in polling data. By January 1987 Canadians would again select the environment as the leading answer to open-ended polling regarding their concerns—above jobs, health care, or inflation.[12] This restored priority to the environment followed a number of events and revelations including the Exxon Valdez oil spill off of Alaska, extensive reports regarding the hole in the ozone layer, and acid rain impacts. Some of the strengthening concern regarding the environment was also public reaction to the long-standing open hostility to environmental protection exhibited by noted political figures, especially Ronald Reagan.[13]

This second wave of environmental activism was different from the first in several important ways. First, it was less apocalyptic in its mood and tone, and its rejection of industrial society holus bolus was more infrequent. Second wave environmental activists were more pragmatic and more willing to work with governments and businesses and in return, governments and business were more willing to work with environmental activists. In Canada, this cooperation was manifest in such things as business–government–environmentalist Round Tables,[14] green products,[15] and voluntary compliance initiatives.[16] Some of these second wave initiatives were more successful than others, and some were seen as cooptation.[17] Regardless, the environmental movement of the late 1980s could be characterized as having moved from protest and confrontation to cooperation and professionalism. Some within the movement welcomed this change while others were more wary.

This shift over the nearly 20 years from the peak of the first wave to the second is hardly surprising. Some of the movement's leaders during the second wave were the same people powering the first wave, but they were older, with families and mortgages to pay. Others were graduates of then-newer university programs in environmental studies. More than that, business and government leaders could no longer imagine that the environmental movement was a fad, likely to soon fade as the issue attention cycle (in Downs' noted term) waned.[18]

The second wave was also different in terms of issues. More often, the newer set of issues was international in character, rather than local or national. The premiere second wave issue in Canada was acid deposition, referred to most often at the time as acid rain. Other issues with an international character included ozone depletion, which led to an international treaty known as the Montreal Protocol; the depletion of tropical rainforests (a visit to which, for a time, came to be almost a *sine qua non* of being a rock star); and the then just-emerging concern with the possibility of climate change.

The campaign against acid rain must be counted as a singular success not only for the movement that lobbied the Canadian government, but also for the Canadian tail which—for once—wagged the American dog. More than half of the acid falling on Canadian lakes originated in the United States, particularly from Midwest coal-fired power plants in states like Ohio and Illinois. There are lessons to be learned from the campaign that led to a treaty signed in 1991 by President George H.W. Bush and Prime Minister Brian Mulroney. The first reason for the campaign's success lay in the place that the endangered lakes of Ontario and Québec, as well as salmon streams in Nova Scotia, hold in Canadian hearts, especially those of established families from Toronto and Montreal. The Canadian Coalition on Acid Rain (CCAR) used this leverage very effectively. Second, Canada acted first to significantly reduce its contribution to the problem from a number of influential industries including nickel smelting and Ontario Hydro. The United States could not, as it might in other cases, respond by telling Canada to clean up its own act. Third, and perhaps most important, Canadian environmental organizations lobbied directly in the United States, and joined with US states that were themselves adversely affected by acid depositions from both the US Midwest and Ontario.

The second wave of environmental activism was less successful in getting effective action on the protection of tropical rainforests or on climate change. In the former case, the nations where the damage was taking place had few economic options and were thus less responsive to pressure from the international environmental movement. Indeed, at one point, the Ambassador from Brazil suggested that instead of halting cutting in his nation, the United States should replant Manhattan. In the case of climate change the issue was new, the evidence was less compelling than it has become since, and the changes necessary to reverse long-term climate effects were especially central to the global economy and thus politically unpalatable. In 1988, Toronto hosted one of the early international climate change conferences with federal government involvement, but the level of action sought at the time from governments was modest, since few anticipated how quickly the changes were to become fully visible.

Some environmentalists and scientists, however, understood the challenges involved in reducing greenhouse gas emissions. Virtually all aspects of the global economy run on fossil fuels and there is no inexpensive way to remove carbon dioxide from the waste stream, especially from the waste stream of moving vehicles. At the time, and for more than a decade to follow, low oil prices were to prevail. Vehicles that achieved reasonable fuel economy again all but disappeared from North American highways and driveways in favour of vans and SUVs. The premier issue of the third wave of environmental activism (and the second crash of the North American auto industry) was in the process of creation in auto showrooms, even as the second environmental wave was still active.

Somehow, in the absence of high energy prices and imminent threats of energy shortage, the connections were not made by consumers or by governments, let alone the North American auto industry of the 1990s. Big cars and big houses were very popular and suburban sprawl around Canada's major cities continued apace. The auto and oil lobbies blocked strong action on fuel efficiency. In Ontario, the government of Mike Harris even slashed insulation standards for new houses in an attempt to improve industry profits. As early preparations for the Kyoto climate change conference were underway in 1996, the Chrétien government and the Klein government in Alberta provided heavy new incentives for investments in oil sands extraction, even though it was known that oil from that source involved three times the carbon dioxide emissions per barrel than conventional oil.[19] Political and business pressures were addressed with one hat on and environmental matters with another, with government figures talking all the while about the need to integrate environment and economy.

That notion of environment–economy integration was at the heart of the second wave of environmentalism and for many in both business and government it was a sincere view of what changes were necessary. For others, however, it may have been, and may still be, the case that what is important is that environmentalists avoid ignoring economic factors. Political leaders at the same time are expected to forget the environment when significant economic issues—investment and jobs—are on the table. That is precisely what happened in the 1990s, although this response was harder to maintain as energy prices headed sharply upwards following the US invasion of Iraq and as evidence mounted regarding the impacts of climate change.

The second wave of environmentalism, as the first, also faded in the face of economic difficulties, this time in the early and mid-1990s. This period was also characterized by a widespread and intense sense that government budget deficits had been too high for too long. Accordingly, there was wide support for cutbacks to public spending, as long as it did not affect key programs like health care. Under several provincial governments, environment and natural resources ministries bore more than a proportional share of those cuts. This was especially true in provinces with Progressive Conservative governments. The Harris government in Ontario (1995–2000), for example, cut the budget of the provincial Ministry of Environment and Energy by 37 per cent between 1994–95 and 1996–97 and the Ministry of Natural Resources budget was reduced by 22 per cent during the same period.[20]

At the federal level, much of Canada's internationally vaunted 1990 Green Plan also fell by the wayside in the face of federal budget-cutting (even in its first two years); its provisions were allowed to sunset after six years. Many Green Plan promises went unfulfilled, including the reduction targets on greenhouse gas emissions and the passage of regulations for priority toxic substances.[21] This time a combination of economic hard times, waning public and media attention to the environment, and *low* energy prices led to lost ground environmentally throughout the 1990s. Program reductions, declining enforcement, and rising energy consumption and greenhouse gas emissions were common during this period all across Canada.

Thus, the environmental movement was able to urge public concern to higher levels in the late 1980s and to get action on several key issues, most notably acid rain. Yet, before the ink was even dry on the Green Plan, the budget for the implementation of a broad array of agenda items was falling away. Within a few years momentum had disappeared altogether. Even when prosperity returned by the late 1990s, environmental opinion and effective governmental environmental action were slow to rebound, in part because the world had, in the meantime, changed.

For one thing, global economic integration had proceeded apace. The North American economy was fully integrated and it became difficult for Canada to take environmental actions that were out of line with US environmental actions, and US environmental actions had slowed during the waning years of the Clinton administration and then all but disappeared with the election of George W. Bush in 2000. More than that, Canadian manufacturing was under increasing pressure from producers in Mexico, China, and other countries with far less stringent, or less stringently enforced, environmental regulations than those in Canada, the United States, or Europe. In the meantime, the leadership on new environmental actions was clearly passing from North America to Europe.

Through the second wave and since, both environmental problems and the solutions to those problems were often based at the global scale—except, as we will see shortly, for some solutions that self-consciously sought to return aspects of production to the local scale. Canadian environmental organizations, throughout the 1980s and to the present, have been actively involved in environmental treaty initiatives including acid precipitation, climate change, upper atmosphere ozone depletion, persistent organic pollutants (POPs), hazardous waste exports, deforestation, and biodiversity protection. In recent years, as a third wave of environmental activism seems to be emerging, the focus has turned even more intensely to the global level.

The Third Wave: Focus on Climate Change

By 2002, it had become politically difficult for the Chrétien government to delay any longer on ratification of the Kyoto Protocol to which it had agreed four years earlier. It recommended ratification despite the fact that both the Progressive Conservatives and the Canadian Alliance stood firmly against proceeding and despite the fact that delay in acting had put Canada's emissions massively over the Kyoto targets. The Canadian public, however, had increasingly come to the view that climate change was a genuine threat and that Canada had an obligation to act. Indeed, today's third wave of environmental concern has emphasized a single issue to a much greater extent than the previous two waves had done. Indeed, climate change is much more dominant in the third wave than acid rain ever was in the second.

While the emphasis of most Canadian environmental organizations has been on climate change for five or more years now, the solutions to this problem involve economic, technological, and lifestyle changes so broad that they subsume the concerns of many earlier environmental movement campaigns. Effective climate change action includes increased energy efficiency, changes in the design of buildings and transportation systems, increased use of alternative (renewable) energy sources, increased recycling (less wasted material means reduced energy use), forest restoration and protection, and improved agriculture and land use generally. Indeed climate change action plans such as those produced by the National Round Table on Economy and Environment (NRTEE) look very much like a comprehensive plan for enhanced environmental sustainability.[22]

As well, the third wave has seen a renewed emphasis on food quality and the environmental production of food. Organic food production has always been an important concern of environmental activists, but concern with all aspects of food production, including the relationship between climate change and the food system, has now spread into the wider society.[23] In this spirit, the emphasis in recent years has been on the concept of 'food miles', that is, how far does the food Canadians consume travel from the farm to table? The less the distance travelled, the less energy is expended, the fewer preservatives must be added, the fresher the food, and the greater the likelihood that consumers of food will know the producers of the food. Leadership on this issue has come from noted chefs and farm organizations like the National Farmers' Union.[24] Thus, rather than environmental organizations being pitted against the 'food industry' or 'industrial agriculture', it is food producers themselves that are providing environmental leadership.

This issue meshes very well with questions surrounding global economic integration as a means of resisting environmental regulations and it was given a considerable boost in 2007 by public concern regarding food, including pet food, imported from China. As well, the issue meshes nicely with concerns over climate change; the further food travels, the more greenhouse gases are emitted in the transportation process. With regard to both food and climate change, the environmental movement has become even more deeply involved with the core technologies and organization of the contemporary global economy.

This involvement happens at both the local level and on a large corporate scale. Small farmers' markets feature local and organic produce, but the giant, multi-billion dollar North America-wide food retailer Whole Foods has arisen as well. The Danish wind turbine producer, Vestas, is also now operating on a global scale and wind energy production has attracted billionaire Texas oil investor T. Boone Pickens. Other major corporations that participate actively in, and profit significantly from, green product production and sales include Home Depot, General Electric, and Toyota. This result of the environmental movement is a long way from the protest movement of the early 1970s.

Thus, the third wave is distinctive from the first two waves in terms of issues, but it is also very different in terms of the relationships between the environmental movement and both the economy and political and electoral processes. An additional reason for that difference is the recent rise in the political viability of the Green Party of Canada. Some green activists and supporters of environmental policy initiatives now have the option of more direct involvement in the electoral process rather than seeking to influence the government of the day, whatever its political character. It should be noted as well that many environmental movement activists continue to support other political parties, especially the New Democratic Party or the Liberals.

Canada's Green Party was late in emerging when compared to Europe, Australia, or New Zealand, but it has gained considerably greater support than has the Green Party in the United States. Both of these differences can be explained in terms of electoral and constitutional systems and to a lesser extent political culture. Many European nations use some variation of proportional representation and virtually all have parliamentary systems. These factors avoid discouraging the development of new parties and are often associated with multi-party systems. Canada, like the United States and Great Britain, has single member constituencies which make it harder for new parties to proliferate because getting a small proportion of the vote rarely results in gaining any seats and the resulting opportunity for party-building.

Canada, however, does provide public funding for campaigns and it does so with a relatively low electoral result (four per cent of the national vote). This has proved to be a boon for the Green Party. By contrast, the United States does nothing to encourage smaller parties and the presidential system means that any vote for a small party can produce a political outcome that those casting the vote find to be very negative. Thus, in the year 2000, a small number of votes for Ralph Nader (a Green candidate) resulted in George W. Bush defeating Al Gore (one of the leading environmentalists in North America) in Florida and thereby nationally. Green party votes in the United States, especially at the national level, have not been very significant since that event. In contrast, the Green Party vote in Canada has grown in recent years, as Steven Brown notes in Chapter 2 of this volume.

Thus, the federal Green party was successful enough to receive public funding based on electoral success and selected a very experienced leader in Elizabeth May, the past head of the Sierra Club of Canada. Thereafter, some polls in early 2008 showed the party to have support of up to 10 per cent of voters, but in the October election despite improving its vote the party was again unable to win a seat as the Conservatives again attained minority government status.

Even though the Green Party was unable to win seats, its presence in the electoral process attracted votes from other parties and may well have caused others to give greater prominence to environmental policy in order to garner the support of those that might otherwise vote Green. Arguably, that is partly why the federal Liberals came out in support of a carbon tax, a move widely seen as politically high-risk. Green Party presence may also explain why environmental policy gained prominence in the leader's debates for the first time.

However, it should also be noted that the Liberal's advocacy of a carbon tax arguably was badly timed (initially announced in the face of rapidly rising gas prices) and ineptly explained and defended by Stephane Dion. The Conservatives launched attack ads against both Dion and the tax and the Liberal Party lost ground to the Conservatives, the NDP, and the Greens.

Finally, there is another characteristic of the third wave that had become visible in the 1990s and since has solidified as the third wave emerged. Global leadership in environmental policy and politics has shifted geographically from North America to Europe. The conservation movement had some roots in German scientific forestry, but it took hold most strongly in North America and it was in North America that the first National Parks were established. Further, during both the first and second waves of environmentalism environmental policies such as environmental impact assessment and 1970s anti-pollution legislation were pioneered in North America. Health concerns led to bans on exposure to second-hand tobacco smoke and other important steps here as well.

However, as the emphasis of the environmental movement has turned to energy policy, sustainability, and climate change, global leadership has been centred in Europe much more than in Canada and the United States, both of which have consistently lagged in terms of public policy and economic adaptation. Municipal, state, and provincial governments have made an effort here, but North America's national governments have been stunningly ineffective while Europe's have made commitments, set goals, and either acted to achieve reductions or at least have avoided the sharp increases in greenhouse gas emissions that have been the norm in Canada and the United States.

Conclusion:
From Protest to Participation to Party Politics

When compared to its early days in the late 1960s it can be seen that today's Canadian environmental movement has adapted a great deal. What began as a protest movement with leaflets being given out on street corners, governments and businesses being picketed, and smokestacks being scaled so that banners could be unfurled is now actively participating in the halls of power—both corporate and political—on a daily basis. Some environmentalists may find this new respectability discomfiting, but most are happy to have some influence and are willing most of the time to compromise. Most environmentalists also welcome new, more environmentally friendly automobiles, sustainability-certified wood products, and organic produce at a farmers' market or at their local supermarket.

Older supporters of environmental organizations can remember when organic produce was only available in a few countercultural outlets and when recycling could only be engaged in at often distant depots staffed by volunteers from environmental organizations. Now corporate leaders speak of positioning themselves in terms of green products and every automobile company is trying to catch up with Toyota in the hybrid market. Even the shift in the value of the Euro relative to the US dollar as an international currency is connected to the extent to which Europe has gotten ahead of North America in creating an energy efficient (and thereby sustainable) society and economy. These changes indicate that environmentalism is a very long way from being a protest movement: it has been integrated into the Canadian economy, society, and polity.

This shift came, essentially in three stages: protest (in the late 1960s and early 1970s), participation (late 1980s and early 1990s), and integration (post-2003). The rise of the Green Party embodies that integration in the political process and the involvement of some (but by no means all) businesses and even business schools in the creation, production, and marketing of green products shows the extent to which greenness now has a central role in our economy. At the same time, the environmental movement must be cautious about becoming too comfortable with its new status. Co-optation and a reversal are still real possibilities.

Other parties can selectively absorb parts of the green party platform in diluted form and reduce the Green vote accordingly. That is obviously both good and bad for environmental policy progress. Corporations can produce products that are only marginally less problematic for the environment, an action which makes more and more people comfortable with making small changes (driving a hybrid car, but still living in a distant suburb and driving long distances every day and using the money they save on gas on a winter holiday in the Caribbean). Continuous education and a measure of the genuineness of product and lifestyle changes are essential. The movement is also, as we have seen, always vulnerable to losing influence in the face of economic hard times. A successful environmental movement must have a presence both inside and outside the economic and political systems. Changes need to be carried through within these systems; however, to maintain a critical perspective about change at least some of the movement must always be sufficiently autonomous to critically judge what further changes might be necessary.

Support for environmental protection clearly moves in broad cycles. The Canadian environmental movement has had its greatest successes during waves of strong environmental concern among the general public and extensive attention from the media. The current economic downturn may, of course, pose new challenges regarding environmental policy, but also perhaps some opportunities because the Obama administration has pledged to use a greener energy policy as one means of helping to revitalize the US economy. To maximize success the Canadian environmental movement must advance policy initiatives—be it regulations, tax shifts, or a system of incentives to businesses and consumers—that suit the times and that will allow improvements to continue if and when public attention turns to other issues.

Questions for Review

1. How important historically has been the influence of the American environmental movement on developments in Canada?
2. Which issues, cases, and campaigns have had the greatest impact on the rise of the environmental movement?
3. Why have environmental issues since the 1980s become among the most important concerns of Canadians?
4. To what extent and in what ways have environmental groups encouraged policy activism and innovation in Canada?

Notes

1. For a much longer discussion see Robert Paehlke, *Environmentalism and the Future of Progressive Politics* (New Haven: Yale University Press, 1989).
2. Donella H. Meadows, et al., *The Limits to Growth* (New York: Universe Books, 1972).
3. Monte Hummel, 'Environmental and Conservation Movements'. Available at http://www.thecanadianencyclopedia.com (accessed 1 July 2008), 3 pages.

4. Cited in Roderick Nash, *Wilderness and the American Mind* (New Haven: Yale University Press, 1967), 97.

5. Hummel, 2.

6. Science Council of Canada, *Canada as a Conserver Society* (Ottawa: Science Council of Canada, 1976).

7. Barry Commoner, *The Closing Circle: Man, Nature and Technology* (New York: Bantam Books, 1972).

8. The initial articulation of the soft energy path came in Amory Lovins 1976 article 'Energy Strategy: The Road Not Taken?', published in *Foreign Affairs*, also published as Chapter 2 in his *Soft Energy Paths* (New York: Ballinger, 1977), 25–60.

9. In Canada there was a province by province soft energy path analysis competed by Brooks, Ralph Torrie, Susan Holtz (of the Ecology Action Centre) and others published in *Alternatives* starting with the Summer/Fall, 1979 issue. Brooks later published *Zero Energy Growth for Canada* (Toronto: McClelland and Stewart, 1981).

10. See for example the Green Party of Canada's platform *Vision Green* (available from http://www.greenparty.ca) or a variety of policy documents at http://www.barackobama.com.

11. See, for example, Emma Rothschild, *Paradise Lost: The Decline of the Auto-industrial Age* (New York: Vintage, 1974).

12. See poll results published in *Toronto Globe & Mail* (21 January 1987), A1.

13. Membership in US environmental organizations rose significantly through the early 1980s despite focus at that time on stagflation and other economic concerns. Those who remained focused on the environment were more likely to see their concern through into activism out of fear that Reagan would make things much worse. This activism spread into Canada and increased as the economy stabilized in the mid-1980s.

14. Michael Howlett, 'The Round Table Experience: Representation and Legitimacy in Canadian Environmental Policy Making', *Queen's Quarterly* 97 (1990): 580–601.

15. Patrick Carson and Julia Moulden, *Green Gold: Business Talking to Business about the Environmental Revolution* (New York: Harper Business, 1991).

16. Robert B. Gibson, ed., *Voluntary Initiatives and the New Politics of Corporate Greening* (Peterborough: Broadview Press, 1999).

17. Toby M. Smith, *The Myth of Green Marketing: Tending Goats at the Edge of the Apocalypse* (Toronto: University of Toronto Press, 1998).

18. See Anthony Downs, 'Up and Down with Ecology: The "Issue-Attention Cycle"', *The Public Interest* 28 (Summer 1972): 38–50.

19. For a more extensive discussion on this point see Robert Paehlke, *Some Like It Cold* (Toronto: Between the Lines, 2008).

20. See Robert Paehlke, 'Canada', in Helmut Weidner and Martin Jänicke, eds., *Capacity Building in National Environmental Policy* (Berlin: Springer-Verlag, 2002), 123–146.

21. G.B. Doern and T. Conway, *The Greening of Canada* (Toronto: University of Toronto Pres, 1994).

22. National Round Table on Environment and Economy, *Advice on a Long-Term Strategy on Energy and Climate Change in Canada* (Ottawa: NRTEE, June 2006).

23. See the discussion of the public response to pesticides as early as the 1920s in Robert Paehlke, *Environmentalism and the Future of Progressive Politics* (New Haven: Yale University Press, 1989).

24. The activation of chefs regarding green agricultural practices has been led by Alice Waters of Berkeley, California, founder of Chez Panaisse, which is sometimes ranked as the best restaurant in the United States. Waters is credited with the creation of California cuisine emphasizing fresh local, organic ingredients. In this same spirit is Michael Stadlander, a noted Ontario chef and of the superb downtown Vancouver restaurant Rain City Grill.

2

The Green Vote in Canada

Steven D. Brown

For decades, environmentalists in Canada have lamented the absence of public pressure on governments to focus serious attention on the country's environmental problems. Political observers have traditionally regarded the environment as an 'armchair issue'—one that attracts the public's attention when more material concerns seem to be in check, but one that rarely moves people to act on their concerns. Governments can manage such issues effectively with lip service rather than ambitious and innovative policy development. As the first decade of the new millennium draws to a close, are there signs that this situation is changing? Consider the following:

- In the 2004 Canadian federal election, the Green Party of Canada fielded candidates in every constituency and attracted support from about 4.3 per cent of those casting a vote, an increase of more than 500 per cent over the support it received just four years earlier (.81 per cent). In the subsequent January 2006 federal election, the Greens held on to this vote share (4.5 per cent), and increased it again to 6.8 per cent in the October 2008 election.
- In 2005, the BC Green Party polled 9.2 per cent in that province's election.
- In November 2006 'the environment' overtook 'health care' as the most important problem facing the country, and remained the number one concern for the next 18 months. As the decade closes, it remains among the top three concerns for Canadians.
- In October 2007, the Green Party of Ontario attracted the support of 8.2 per cent of Ontario voters, a three-fold increase over its base four years earlier.

Perhaps the most significant aspect of these developments is that they are not just attitudinal political expressions—there is a *behavioural* dimension to them as well. It is one thing when environmental issues manage to out-duel more materialist concerns for priority on the public's agenda. It is quite another when significant minorities of that public decide to empower Green Parties with their votes. On the surface, at least, the stakes associated with continued government inaction are now higher and riskier.

However, policy responses by potential governing parties will depend on the character of the political pressures they perceive, and these will be shaped, at least in part, by the composition of the 'attentive public' in this policy domain, that is, those prepared to base their vote on this issue.[1]

Who, then, are these 'significant minorities' for whom environmental concerns constitute an apparent basis for partisan support? Do they have a distinctive socio-demographic and political profile? What kinds of environmental policy responses are they seeking?

This chapter addresses these questions through analysis of a survey conducted following the federal election of 23 January 2006. The survey was administered to a sample of about 35,000 members of an Ipsos Reid Canadian panel who were invited to complete it online after casting their ballot on election day. While this is not a probability sample of the Canadian electorate, it is broadly representative of that electorate and has been reweighted with known parameters to make it even more so.[2] The survey is ideal for present purposes because it furnishes Green Party and 'environmental' voters in sufficient numbers to permit a finer-grained analysis of their social, demographic, and political character.

Canadian Green Parties in Context

Canadian Green parties present themselves as local representatives of a global environmental movement. Although originating in Europe in the1970s, the movement now has party organizations in most electoral jurisdictions in the developed world, as well as many in the developing world. While the public tends to identify Green parties with environmental causes, most Green parties—in Canada and elsewhere—subscribe to a common set of principles; since 2001 the *Charter of the Global Greens* has also included a commitment to social justice, participatory democracy, nonviolence, sustainability, and respect for diversity.[3] This set of principles is said to describe the substance of a 'new politics' dimension.

The Green Party of Canada (GPC) was founded in 1983 and has fielded at least a partial slate of candidates in every subsequent election. Beginning in 2004 and in every federal election since, the party has nominated a full slate of candidates.[4] As a consequence it has achieved a degree of financial stability by easily surpassing the two per cent threshold of support necessary to receive a per-voter subsidy through Canadian party financing legislation. Green parties have also formed at the provincial level in all Canadian provinces except New Brunswick. British Columbia and Ontario have the strongest organizations and support bases, but the Alberta and Quebec parties have also shown increased strength—in the four to five per cent range—in recent provincial elections.

As political actors, Greens have enjoyed modest electoral success globally. They have participated in many—mostly European—coalition governments (e.g., Finland, Germany, Belgium, France, Italy, Sweden, and Ireland), have elected representatives to numerous other legislatures (e.g., Australia, New Zealand, Estonia, Latvia, European Parliament, Switzerland, and the US states of California and Maine), and have had success at the local government level in many countries. In Canada, Green parties have not yet elected any representatives to national or provincial legislatures. However, Table 2.1 compares the recent electoral support record for Canadian Green parties with that of other countries where the Greens *do* have legislative representation. The table suggests that what distinguishes the Canadian record from these more successful experiences is not the level of support received from voters, but the electoral system in which parties must compete. Simply put, Canadians' support for the Green alternative is not atypical of support that Greens receive elsewhere in the developed world; indeed, Ontario and British Columbia are among the jurisdictions with the strongest Green showing in recent elections. What distinguishes Canada from the rest of these countries is its first-past-the-post electoral system; all of the other countries in the table have adopted some variant of proportional representation which rewards parties with seats proportionate to their electoral strength.

Table 2.1 Electoral Support for Green Parties in Canada and Selected Countries

Country	Legislature	Year	Green Support (%)
Quebec	**National Assembly**	**2008**	**2.00**
Switzerland	National Council	2007	3.60[a]
Canada	**H. of Commons**	**2006**	**4.50**
Alberta	**Legislative Assembly**	**2008**	**4.58**
Ireland	Dail	2007	4.69
Sweden	Legislative Assembly	2006	5.24
New Zealand	H. of Representatives	2008	5.30
Czech Republic	Chamber of Deputies	2006	6.30
Canada	**H. of Commons**	**2008**	**6.80**
Netherlands	Lower House of Dutch Parl.	2006	7.00
Estonia	National Legislature	2007	7.00
EU	European Parliament	2004	7.30
Germany	Federal Parliament	2005	8.10
Ontario	**Legislative Assembly**	**2007**	**8.20**
France	European Elections	2004	8.43
Finland	Parliament	2007	8.50
British Columbia	**Legislative Assembly**	**2005**	**9.20**
Belgium	Senate	2007	9.44[b]
Australia	Senate	2007	10.0[c]
Austria	National Council	2008	10.40

a) Includes the votes for both the Green Liberal party of Switzerland and the Green Party of Switzerland.
b) Includes the votes of both the Ecolo and the Groen parties
c) 'First choice' only in the proportional representation system.

While Green parties in Canada, without representation, can have no direct impact on the legislative agenda, their growing presence on the political scene can nevertheless affect that agenda in at least two significant ways: first, by forcing other parties whose support bases are at risk to adjust their platforms accordingly; and second, by framing the debate regarding appropriate policy directions. Understanding the Green's electoral base, then, is important to understanding the party's potential policy impact.

Profiling the Green Voter in Canada

Motivation

Perhaps the most basic question to ask about Green voters is why they have chosen to support this particular party. Certainly, the party presents itself as a champion of environmental causes, but it also endorses the central tenets of 'new politics' with an emphasis on social justice issues, pacifism, and de-centralized democracy; moreover its platform advances a position on virtually every issue on the political agenda.[5] There is also the possibility that some Green voters are simply expressing their disappointment or disenchantment with mainstream parties. Unlike electoral systems with pro-portional representation, the Canadian single-member constituency system provides relatively few political options for 'protest' voting. To what extent, then, is the Green vote a negative vote rather than a positive one, or a vote cast for idiosyncratic reasons?

Two questions from the 2006 election-day survey address these issues at least in part. First, the survey panelists were asked directly which of a series of issue concerns was most important in shaping their vote.[6] Second, they were asked whether they liked *any* of the parties running in the election.[7] Green voters' responses to these questions suggest that environmental concerns are clearly central to the party's electoral support base, but such concerns by themselves are not adequate to describe the cohort's motivation.

Table 2.2 summarizes the most frequent responses to the 'issue-linked-to-vote' question for each of five party cohorts. On the one hand, the Green party cohort, in comparison to the other parties, comes closest to approximating a single-issue support base. Almost half of the Green voters cite 'pro-tecting the environment' as the reason for their vote, with no other issue cited by more than a small fraction of the cohort. However, it is also the case that just over half of the Green voter cohort *did not cite the environment* as the reason for their vote; they cited a broad selection of other concerns. There is also hint of a 'new politics' and 'protest' motivation in the cohort's responses when asked about their feelings regarding the parties running in this election (data not shown). While only about 12 per cent of the total sample 'strongly agreed' that they didn't like any of the parties competing in the election, the percentage of Green voters expressing this level of alienation was 34 per cent (with

Table 2.2 The Five Most Frequently-cited Issues 'Mattering Most' to Vote, by Partisan Cohort

Liberal Voters (N=9200)	Conservative Voters (N=12876)	NDP Voters (N=7434)	Bloc Voters (N=4261)	Green Voters (N=1868)
Managing the economy (27%)	Cleaning up corruption (32%)	Social programs like childcare, pensions (25%)	Cleaning up corruption (31%)	Protecting the environment (48%)
Fixing our healthcare system (16%)	Reducing taxes (12%)	Fixing our healthcare system (23%)	Fixing our healthcare system (16%)	Cleaning up corruption (12%)
Keeping Canada together (15%)	Managing the economy (11%)	Cleaning up corruption (11%)	Managing the economy (13%)	Fixing our health-care system (9%)
Moral issues like abortion and same sex marriage (14%)	Moral issues like abortion and same sex marriage (11%)	Moral issues like abortion and same sex marriage (10%)	Social programs like childcare, pensions (11%)	Managing the economy (6%)
Social programs like childcare, pensions (12%)	Criminal justice and public safety issues (10%)	Managing the economy (7%)	Protecting the environment (8%)	Moral issues like abortion and same sex marriage (6%)

another 35 per cent merely 'agreeing'). Such a response, coupled with the fact that 'cleaning up corruption' was the second most frequently cited reason for voting Green, suggests that the Green Party's appeal is not adequately captured with its environmental stance, but may well also include an element of 'old politics' rejection.

One additional aspect of these 'issue-linked-to-vote' responses is not apparent from the table but is worth noting here. The Green party tends to be the party of choice among those reportedly basing their vote on environmental concerns. While only about five per cent of all voters cited 'protecting the environment' as the reason for their vote, just less than half of them (47 per cent) voted Green in 2006. This has significance because it suggests that the party is viewed widely as the appropriate option for those seriously concerned about the environment. And given that proportions in recent polls citing the environment as Canada's 'most pressing issue' have more than doubled since these data were collected, it helps to explain why Green support levels have also continued to grow through 2008.

Partisan Origins

Since the GPC electoral share has grown from less than one per cent in 2000 to about 4.5 per cent in 2006, it is obvious that most of the party's support base has either migrated from other partisan camps or has newly entered the electorate. Appreciating the partisan origins of GPC supporters is useful because it provides clues to the developing ideological character of the party, and it identifies the mainstream parties most threatened by the party's growth. In the 2006 election-day poll, only two questions were asked that pertained to past partisan behaviour: one asked whether 2006 was the first federal election in which the respondent had voted; and the other question asked about the respondent's vote in the 2004 election.

Figure 2.1 displays the composition of the Green vote in terms of the voter's reported behavior in the previous 2004 election. Since GPC electoral gains were mostly between 2000 and 2004 with little change between 2004 and 2006, Figure 2.1 portrays only the *recent* partisan origins of the Green support base. As a consequence, it is not surprising that the largest component of the 2006 cohort— at 40 per cent—is the Green vote from 2004. What is surprising, however, is that this 'stable' component is as small as it is. Retention rates for the other parties between the 2004 and 2006 elections ranged from 60 per cent for the Liberals to 89 per cent for the Conservatives. Given that the GPC's aggregate support level changed only slightly (an increase of 0.2 per cent) between these elections, the finding that about three-fifths of the party's vote in 2006 was new suggests enormous fluidity in the party's support base. Apart from the 'core' Green component, former Liberal supporters, at 23 per cent, comprise the largest partisan grouping in the 2006 cohort; defectors from the other three parties are also found in the cohort, but their representation is modest by comparison. Consistent with experiences elsewhere, the Greens did well with new voters and especially with 're-entering' voters—those who sat out the 2004 election. In this sample, the GPC attracted seven per cent of the new vote and over eight per cent of the re-entering cohort in 2006 (data not shown).

The finding that 60 per cent of the Green vote is new but that aggregate support for the party has remained largely unchanged begs the question: where did about 60 per cent of the 2004 Green vote go in 2006? Our answer to this question must be tentative because the 2004 recall question did not specifically identify the Green party alternative; instead, the survey grouped Greens with other minor parties in that election. However, given the nature of minor party support in 2004 and using reported behaviour in 2006, some tentative inferences about the destinations of these 'lapsed'

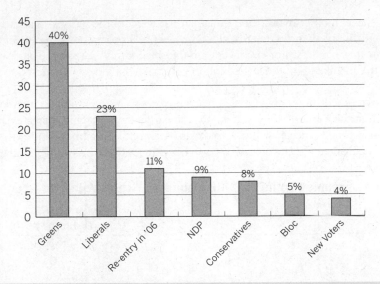

Figure 2.1 Partisan Origins of the 2006 Green Party Vote

Greens are possible. They suggest that the partisan character of the party's support base has changed substantially between the two elections. In 2004, the Greens attracted much more balanced support from former Liberals, Conservatives, and New Democrats (data not shown). In 2006, the party lost about as many voters as it gained, but the exchange was decidedly asymmetric in partisan terms: there was a large net gain of former Liberals and sizeable net losses in the neighbourhood of 12 per cent to each of the Conservative and New Democratic parties.

Demographic Profile

A substantial body of literature has accumulated in the past two decades seeking to explain the rise of ecological movements and green politics in terms of socio-cultural developments in post-industrial societies.[8] Much of this literature shares a common focus on the distinctive socio-demographic profile of those found to be associated with such movements. Indeed, the profile has been sufficiently distinctive and sufficiently ubiquitous to be labelled by many scholars the 'new class' or the 'new middle class'. Members of the 'new class' tend to be younger, highly educated, and frequently working in professional or social service occupations. While the profile seems to apply well to ecological social movements, there are many national variations when applied to Green party members and voters in different countries. In Germany, for example, the Green party attracts support from the 'new class'—albeit an aging 'new class'—but also disproportionately from students and urban dwellers.[9] In Britain and Australia, Greens draw support heavily from public sector employees.[10] In France and Belgium, on the other hand, Green party supporters tend to be somewhat older than their German counterparts, are not especially highly educated, are more occupationally diverse, and come from more rural communities.[11]

A survey of Canadian Green Party *members* by Cara Camcastle in 2005 revealed that the 'new middle class' thesis does apply in some respects to the Canadian case.[12] GPC members are better educated than those in other mainstream Canadian parties, and the party also attracts more members from young cohorts than do other parties. However, the occupational profile of GPC members is anomalous in that public sector employees are the *smallest* rather than the largest occupational cohort within the membership; the largest cohort comprises members who describe themselves as 'self-employed'.

Table 2.3 provides a demographic profile of Green *voters* from the 2006 election-day survey. The table indicates that there are certainly elements in the party's demographic character that are consistent with the 'new politics' thesis, with Camcastle's portrait of GPC members, and with findings from other countries. Canadian Green voters *do* tend to be younger than the voting population generally,

Table 2.3 Demographic Profile of 2006 Canadian Green Voters (percentage)

		Green Voters (N=1868)	All Voters (N=
Age	Under 35	35	27
	35–54 years	44	42
	Over 55	21	31
Education	HS or less	16	21
	Some U or College	49	51
	U degree +	35	28
Gender	% Female	51	51
Family Income	Under $40K	32	31
	$40–79K	36	41
	$80–119K	21	19
	Over $120K	11	9
Labour Force Role	Employee	55	53
	Self-employed	13	11
	Unemployed	6	4
	Retired	9	18
	Student	12	8
	Homemaker	5	7
Occupation in Labour Force	Executive/Managerial	12	14
	Professional	31	28
	Clerical/Sales	19	22
	Technical/Skilled	13	12
	Unskilled	8	8
	Other	18	18
Community Size	Major City (1 million +)	26	27
	Medium City (100–999K)	33	32
	Small City, Town or Rural	41	41

and they are especially under-represented among voters 55 years or older. GPC voters also tend to be better educated than most voters, with 35 per cent (versus 28 per cent) claiming at least one university degree. The party's support base is *not* distinctive in terms of its gender mix, its urban–rural composition or, for the most part, its average household income, but these findings, too, are not inconsistent with most experiences elsewhere.

In much of the 'new class' literature, occupation is a key marker variable. This is because it is thought to reflect differential exposure to critical perspectives and differential levels of autonomy from market forces—both of which figure prominently in explanations of the rise of new social movements.[13] While the election-day survey did not gather sufficient information about voters' occupations to address these issues directly, it does provide some pertinent information about the occupational profile of Green voters. Table 2.3 presents this information from two perspectives. The first describes the voter's role in or out of the labour force, and the second profiles the general nature of the voter's employment responsibilities. From these distributions, it can be seen that, as expected, the Green party does relatively well with students and with those in professional occupations, and less so with those in mainstream market-sensitive occupations (executives, and those in managerial, sales, and clerical roles). The party also does quite poorly with retired individuals. While the data do not permit us to distinguish public from private sector employees, they do allow us to distinguish those who are employees from those who are self-employed. It can be seen here that the pattern identified by Camcastle for GPC *members* is only faintly in evidence for GPC *voters*— the self-employed are represented here in about the proportion we would expect in the population, and do not constitute a dominant component of the Green support base.

While this analysis reveals some mildly distinctive features of the Green vote, it does not describe a party demographic on the margins of the Canadian electorate. Indeed, the overall impression one gets from Table 2.3 is of a party that, in most respects, mirrors the demography of the country.

Political Orientations

From her survey of Green Party membership in Canada, Camcastle concluded that the GPC was an 'ecological centre party'.[14] By this, she meant that the membership's policy priorities and strategies placed them decidedly to the ecological or post-materialist end of the 'new politics' dimension, but at the *centre* of the conventional left–right dimension. She noted that the GPC membership, as a group, exhibit elements of 'new politics' thinking in placing priority on protection of the environment and development of educational opportunities, in supporting the decentralization of political and economic processes, and in expressing more acceptance of alternative lifestyles. However, she also noted that the party membership was much more ambivalent about the role of government in society—a central criterion for distinguishing 'left' from 'right' in Canadian politics. The GPC members were certainly skeptical of big business, but, as a group, they were also reticent about government ownership in the Canadian economy, expressed concern about waste in the government's delivery of social services, and preferred indirect (rather than direct) government involvement through use of the taxation system to encourage sustainability and to redistribute wealth more equitably. As Camcastle observed, this centrist positioning of the membership makes the Canadian party quite distinctive within the global community of Greens, where, almost invariably, ecological and left positions are found to be related.[15]

Does this pattern of political orientation also describe the cohort of Canadian Green *voters*? The 2006 election-day survey does not deal directly with political ideology.[16] However, it does ask about the voter's policy views in a number of different ways and the Greens' responses to such questions, relative to those of other party supporters, yield some useful clues about political orientation. We approached the analysis in three ways.

The first of these approaches draws on responses to the 'issue-linked-to-vote' question introduced above,[17] and addresses the relative salience of post-materialist concerns within the Green party camp. The standard measure of post-materialism, first developed by Ronald Ingelhart in the 1970s, provides respondents with a list of four societal goals, two of which are held to be materialist in nature and two post-materialism in nature.[18] Respondents are asked to select the two that are most important to them. A post-materialist index score is then computed by subtracting the number of materialist goals selected by the respondent from the number of post-materialist goals selected. The 'issue-linked-to-vote' question in the 2006 election-day survey provides a basis for developing a similar index score, but one that applies to the aggregate level of party cohort. That is, a party's post-materialism score can be calculated by subtracting the proportion of its voters which selected a 'materialist' issue in rationalizing their vote from the proportion that selected a 'post-materialist' issue. Although the survey offered panelists 13 issue options from which to choose, not all of them easily classify as either materialist or post-materialist. However, an argument can be made that the following four issues fall generally on the materialist side of the divide: (1) reducing taxes, (2) criminal justice and public safety issues, (3) managing the economy, and (4) employment/jobs. Similarly the following four issues would seem to be more post-materialist in nature: (1) protecting the environment, (2) managing moral issues like same sex marriage and abortion, (3) social programs like childcare, pensions, and (4) fixing our healthcare system. Using these as the basis for scoring the party cohorts, Table 2.4 summarizes the results. The rankings of the party support bases are not surprising: the Green party cohort tilts most strongly in the post-materialist direction, thanks largely to its pre-occupation with the environment issue. However the NDP is not far behind, with its dual focus on health care and social programs. On balance, the Bloc is more post-materialist in its concerns, but considerably more divided than the other two parties. As befits supporters of 'big tent' parties, the Liberals and Conservatives are fairly evenly balanced between the two orientations, with the Liberals tilting slightly in the post-materialist direction, and the Conservatives tilting modestly in the materialist direction.

Table 2.4 Materialist versus Post-Materialist Orientations of the Five Canadian Party Cohorts

	Proportion Selecting Post-Materialist Issues (%)	Proportion Selecting Materialist Issues (%)	Post-Materialist Index Score[1]
Green Party	68.2	15.9	+52.3
NDP	63.6	18.9	+44.7
Bloc Quebecois	40.9	23.6	+17.3
Liberal	42.9	38.2	+4.7
Conservative	24.4	34.6	−10.2

[1] The post-materialist index score is the numeric difference between the proportion in each party which cited a 'post-materialist' reason for their vote and the proportion citing a 'materialist' reason.

A second glimpse of the Green party's political orientation can be caught in their responses to three questions addressing economic and social dimensions in Canada's political space. The first of these deals with *the role of government in society*, and asks which of the following two statements comes closer to the respondent's view: 'Government should do more to solve problems' or 'Government is doing too many things that should be left to businesses and individuals.' Two other questions ask about their positions on the *social issues of abortion and gay marriage*.[19] For these three issues, Figure 2.2 compares the support level for each of the five party cohorts against a common benchmark—the electorate's overall aggregate level of support for the position. Hence, the height/depth of the bar relative to the x-axis in the graph indicates how atypical the party cohort in question is on that issue.

From the graph, it can be seen that Conservative party voters are significantly at odds with the other mainstream party cohorts on all three issues. While about 58 per cent of the electorate as a whole thought the government should be doing more to solve problems, Conservative voter support for this suggestion was 38 per cent—or 20 points below the aggregate level. Similarly, 49 per cent of the electorate supported the legalization of gay marriage, and 40 per cent supported legalizing abortion in all cases, but the Conservatives' support for these proposals was well below both levels—24 per cent less for gay marriage and 13 per cent less for abortion. On the other side of the divide, the Liberal and NDP supporters tend to cluster together across all three issues; Bloc supporters resemble them for two of the issues, but are considerably more supportive of abortion 'in all cases'.

What of the Green Party cohort on these issues? Interestingly, the Greens closely resemble the NDP and Liberal voter groups for the two social issues (i.e., legalizing gay marriage, and support for abortion in all cases), but they are quite distinctive in their response regarding the role of government. On that issue, Greens tend to fall neatly between the Conservatives and the other three parties, at approximately the overall aggregate level of support.

While the issues here clearly do not adequately cover either the 'new politics' or 'left–right' dimensions, the Green response patterns are suggestive. First, they suggest that the views of Green party

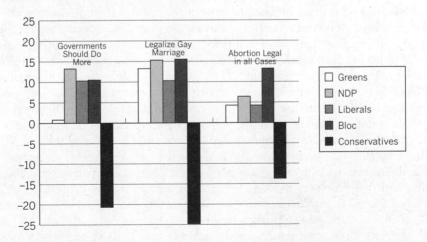

Figure 2.2 Issue Positions of Partisan Cohorts Above or Below Total Sample's Support Level

voters are generally consistent with what Camcastle found for Green party *members*. Both are generally supportive of left libertarian social issues but both seem open to non-governmental or market strategies to achieve policy objectives. Second, these findings indicate no evidence that the views of Green supporters are 'radical' in any respects. On social issues, they are virtually indistinguishable from Liberal or NDP supporters, and on the role of government, they seem, as a group, to tread a middle path.

The survey provides a third means of locating Green voters in Canadian partisan issue space. Survey panelists were not asked their positions on a full menu of political agenda items, but they did answer a battery of questions identifying which of the mainstream parties and party leaders would best handle an extensive list of eighteen possible government objectives.[20] Because the survey did not offer a 'Green' party alternative in this battery, the Green voters' were being asked essentially to assess which parties they saw as most proximal to them.

Table 2.5 makes two comparisons based on these responses, and both use the NDP response pattern as a benchmark or 'control group'. Panel #1 of the table—the first two columns—reports the relative frequencies with which Green and NDP voters cite the NDP as best for each job. That is, it addresses the question: to what degree do Green party supporters see the NDP as the mainstream party closest to their policy preferences? Panel #2 of the table—the second two columns—focuses on NDP and Green preferences when choosing between the Liberal and Conservative options. It is generally conceded that the NDP sees itself as closer to the Liberals than to the Conservatives on most policy dimensions; if so, its supporters should tend to choose the Liberal option when, for some reason, they find their own party or leader wanting on a particular policy dimension. Comparing Green and NDP patterns in this situation allows us to see the degree to which Green supporters also share that perception.

Not surprisingly, perhaps, Panel #1 reveals that NDP supporters, as a group, prefer their party over the others for handling *every* policy objective—in many cases, by overwhelming proportions. Indeed, NDP voters opt for their party an average of 71 per cent of the time over these 18 policy objectives. It can be seen that the Green response pattern resembles this to a great extent, but it is a paler imitation. To be sure, Green supporters make the NDP option their modal response for handling 11 of the 18 objectives; as well, the NDP is a strong consensus (72 per cent) choice for handling the Greens' #1 priority (the environment); it is the modal choice for being closest to respondent's *values* and for understanding respondent's *needs*; and it is the modal choice for handling four of the Green party's five priority issues (from Table 2.1). However, it is also true that the Green consensus for the NDP option is far from overwhelming for most objectives, averaging a mere 43 per cent over the 18 objectives. So it is fair to say that the NDP is seen as the closest party by the typical Green voter, but there is still considerable variation within the Green cohort on this question.

Panel #2 of Table 2.5 compares the choices made by NDP and Green supporters when they selected either the Liberal or Conservative options. The percentages in these columns are based only on those NDP and Green voters who chose the Liberal or the Conservative party as best able to handle an objective, and the percentage specified here reflects arbitrarily how frequently they chose the Liberal party in this two-party competition. Do the Green and NDP supporters share the same left-to-right linear view of the Canadian partisan dimension?

The table suggests that NDP supporters certainly tend to have such a linear view. When choosing between these old line parties, NDP voters stray from the Liberal option only for objectives which tend to have low NDP priority (reducing taxes, fixing the US relationship and fighting crime) or objectives which have tripped up the Liberals in recent years (running a scandal-free government,

Table 2.5 Comparing NDP and Green Voters in Their Choice of (1) NDP as Best Able to Handle Problems, and (2) Liberals Rather than Conservatives as Best Able to Handle Problems (percentage)

	Panel #1 NDP is best able . . .		Panel #2 Liberals rather than Conservatives . . .	
	NDP Voters (N=7434)	Green Voters (N=1869)	NDP Voters (N= **)	Green Voters (N=**)
Reducing taxes	43*	23	37	37
Managing compassionate & cost-effective social programs	82*	50*	72	68
Managing the economy	48*	23	71	61
Providing government that is closest to your values	85*	49*	67	60
Representing your province in Ottawa	70*	34	60	52
Keeping Canada together	56*	29	78	67
Managing moral issues like same sex marriage and abortion	68*	41*	73	70
Fixing our relationship with the US	43*	22	36	32
Understanding the needs of young people	88*	66*	47	34
Running a scandal-free and ethical government	89*	64*	24	29
Protecting the environment	89*	72*	57	59
Keeping their promises	88*	59*	43	37
Understanding the needs of people like you	89*	55*	65	55
Representing Canada in world affairs	46*	22	76	66
Fixing our health care system	82*	54*	59	50
Making our communities safe from crime	60*	33	38	34
Presenting a positive vision of the future	79*	46*	67	57
Providing the best overall government	78*	40*	72	57
Average over all objectives	71	43	58	51

(*) Indicates that this is the modal response by that voter cohort. (**) N in cells varies according to how many NDP and Green voters chose either the Liberal or Conservatives as best able to handle the problem in question. For the NDP, N varies between 751 and 4198. For the Green party, N varies between 443 and 1388.

and delivering on promises). Green voters as a group look very much like the NDP cohort when they select between these major parties. That is, they tend to choose the Liberal party for most objectives, and they opt for the Conservatives in exactly the same few policy areas. Even so, there is a modest difference between the cohorts in that the Greens quite consistently exhibit a weaker tilt to the Liberals. In 13 of the 18 policy areas, the Green cohort, relative to the NDP cohort, is more evenly divided between the Liberal and the Conservative options. This difference is nicely captured in each cohort's average level of support for the Liberal option (versus the Conservative option) across the policy domains—58 per cent for the NDP cohort compared to 51 per cent for the Greens.

Implications and Conclusions

The Green Party's recent emergence as a political force in Canadian politics raises questions about its possible impact on environmental policy in this country. Certainly, the party's impact will be adversely affected by the electoral system it confronts in Canada; as well, its effectiveness will depend on the acumen of its leadership and on the vulnerabilities of other parties in the system. Moreover, the options and strategies it adopts will also be constrained by the character of its electoral support. What does this chapter's analysis of that character suggest for the GPC as a political actor? Several observations seem warranted.

First, Green voters have a variety of motives for choosing the party, but concern for the environment is clearly the dominant one, mentioned by almost half of its supporters. This makes it likely that the environment will remain the signature issue for the party for the foreseeable future and that, as a consequence, environmental issues will have an ongoing champion in the partisan political arena. By itself this represents a change, but a development with special significance in light of the 2008 global economic meltdown and the resulting shift in agenda for the mainstream parties to economic recovery.

Second, and perhaps more importantly, the Green party is the party of choice for voters who are pre-eminently concerned with the environment—almost half of such voters opted for the party in 2006. Since we know that environmental concerns have continued to grow since these data were collected in January 2006, the availability of the Green option is likely to pressure other parties to give environmental policy a higher priority in order to forestall defections.

It would seem that the mainstream parties are not equally vulnerable to this threat of defection. While we can't trace the partisan origins of current Green voters with certainty, it appears that the largest identifiable group is comprised of ex-Liberals, and that the party cohort as a whole occupies the same issue space as New Democrats. On social issues the two cohorts—New Democrats and Greens—are virtually indistinguishable. When comparing their policy priorities, the Greens are modestly more post-material, but the NDP voters resemble them far more than they do any other party. As well, Greens as a group tend to prefer the NDP approach to those of the major parties in most policy domains, and, like NDP supporters, they tend to see the Liberals as the next closest option. Given this pattern, it appears that the 2008 minority Conservative government of Stephen Harper is less vulnerable to Green defections from its support base and therefore less likely to feel pressure, at least from domestic forces, to adapt its policy program accordingly.

Third, the Green vote in Canada seems not to be a voice for radical change or transformational politics. Apart from seeing the environment as the country's primary policy priority and apart from supporting a party that has little current chance of gaining parliamentary representation, Green voters are not on the margins of Canadian politics. At least for the topics covered in this survey, their views closely resemble the mainstream of Canadian society. While they *do* resemble Green voters elsewhere in that they tend to be younger, better-educated and drawn disproportionately from professional and student occupations, it would be an exaggeration to describe the party as distinctively 'new class' in its demographic composition. These characteristics are modest tendencies only.

As well, the Green–NDP affinity noted above has limits. Simply stated, the Greens are more diverse in their political views, and hence, as a group, they appear to straddle the traditional left–right political spectrum more broadly than the NDP. For example, the Greens are significantly more open to the Conservative approach in the areas of health care, managing the economy, social programs, vision, and representing 'my' values. But nowhere is this straddling more in evidence than in the cohort's views regarding the role of government in solving problems. Indeed, the Greens' mix of leftist views on social issues and centrist positions on how to solve political problems is arguably the cohort's most distinctive feature.

None of this is particularly surprising, given the party's membership profile, and especially given the party's centrist platform on economic issues. However, it is significant for at least two reasons. First, it suggests that the party leadership is not out of step with its voting base and can work with either a Liberal or a Conservative government without alienating that voting base. Second, it suggests that this electoral constituency will probably not be the source of pressure on the party to adopt the more ambitious, entrepreneurial and innovative policies that environmental activists have advocated and hoped for.

A major caveat should accompany all of these observations. While the patterns noted above are undeniable, they may also be transitory because the Green party support base may not yet have congealed. Upwards of three-fifths of the 2004 Green cohort did not return in 2006, but the party attracted about the same number of new supporters as they lost. The fact that gains and losses were not randomly distributed across the other parties—the losses in 2006 were mainly to the New Democrats and Conservatives, and the gains were largely from defecting Liberals—suggests that the nature of the party's core support can change with the fortunes of the mainstream parties. Indeed, there is a good possibility that at least some of its supporters are voters who are disaffected with their 'normal' party, and regard the Green party as a convenient, but likely temporary, place to park their vote.

Questions for Review

1. To what extent is voter support for the Green Party secure or fragile?
2. How significant is Canada's electoral system (first-past-the-post) in restricting the prospects of the Greens?
3. Which social groups are most likely to generate Green voters?
4. Do you think the Greens would gain and retain more voter support by (a) advocating more radical changes towards a sustainable society, or (b) taking the path towards a mainstream centrist party? Which strategy is more likely to put pressure on the governing party to be more activist with regard to environmental policy?

Notes

1. See David J. Elkins, *Manipulation and Consent: How Voters and Leaders Manage Complexity* (Vancouver: UBC Press, 1993).
2. The data were collected by the Public Affairs Division of Ipsos Reid using their Canadian online panel. This was an 'opt-in' sample; all panel members are invited to participate once they have cast their ballot, and the resulting sample of respondents is then reweighted to reflect the electorate. Because this is not a probability sample, it is difficult to establish conclusively that it is representative of the electorate in attitudinal and behavioural terms, but the fact that it has yielded reliable estimates of other known parameters should enhance confidence that it is doing so in this analysis as well. In the analysis 1,869 respondents, or 5.2 per cent of the total sample, indicated that they had voted for the Canadian Green Party in the 2006 election. Since the party support level in the election was actually 4.5 per cent, it should be noted that the sample used in this paper modestly over-represents Green party support for this election. The author is indebted to Ipsos Reid which has generously made the data available for this re-analysis. However the company bears no responsibility for interpretations found here.
3. Retrieved 14 May 2008 from http://www.globalgreens.info/globalcharter.php.

4. In fact, the GPC nominated candidates in all but one constituency in the 2008 federal election. Through an agreement with the Liberal Party of Canada, the GPC declined to nominate a candidate in the constituency of Liberal leader Stephane Dion—Saint Laurent-Cartierville—on the condition that the Liberals would not nominate a candidate in Green Party leader Elizabeth May's constituency—Central Nova.

5. See the Canadian Green Party website at http://www.greenparty.ca (retrieved 14 May 2008).

6. Question wording was: 'Which one of the following issues mattered most in deciding which party's candidate you voted for today: fixing our health care system, cleaning up corruption, managing the economy, protecting the environment, reducing taxes, social program like childcare, pensions, moral issues like abortion and same sex marriage, employment/jobs, keeping Canada together/National unity, fixing our relationship with the US, criminal justice and public safety issues, immigration policies, preserving the Atlantic Accord?'

7. Respondents were asked how much they agreed or disagreed with the following statement: 'I don't really like any of the parties that we have to choose among in this election.'

8. For an overview of this literature, see Robyn Eckersley, 'Green Politics and the New Class: Selfishness or Virtue', *Political Studies* 37 (1989): 205–23.

9. See Detlef Jahn, 'The Rise and the Decline of New Politics and the Greens in Sweden and Germany', *European Journal of Political Research* 24 (1993): 177–94.

10. See W. Rudig, L.G. Bennie, and M.N. Franklin, *Green Party Members: A Profile* (Glasgow: Delta Publications, 1991) and Ariadne Vromen, 'Who are the Australian Greens? Surveying the Membership', *Proceedings of the Australian Sociological Association Conference* (Tasmania: TASA, University of Tasmania, 2006).

11. Ferdinand Muller-Rommel, 'The Greens in Western Europe: Similar but Different', *International Political Science Review* 6 (1985): 483–98.

12. Cara Camcastle, 'The Green Party of Canada in Political Space and the New Middle Class Thesis', *Environmental Politics* 16, 4 (2007): 625–42.

13. See Eckersley, 'Green Politics and the New Class', 218–19.

14. Camcastle, 'The Green Party of Canada', 636.

15. See, for example, J. Meadowcroft, 'Green Political Perspectives at the Dawn of the Twenty-first Century', in M. Freeden, ed., *Reassessing Political Ideologies* (London: Routledge, 2001), 175–92.

16. The survey did attempt to tap the voter's general political orientation with the following question: 'On most political issues do you consider yourself to be a liberal, a moderate, or a conservative?' However, the public tends to confuse 'liberal' and 'conservative' labels with the Canadian mainstream parties of the same names; as a consequence, it is not very useful for comparing modal self-descriptions across different party groupings.

17. See note 6 above.

18. See Ronald Ingelhart, *The Silent Revolution: Changing Values and Political Styles Among Western Publics* (Princeton, NJ: Princeton University Press, 1977).

19. The 'abortion' question was phrased as follows: 'Which is the closest to your position. Abortion should be . . .legal in all cases, legal in most cases, illegal in most cases, illegal in all cases, or don't know?' The gay marriage question was phrased as follows: 'Which comes closest to your views about gay and lesbian couples, do you think . . .they should be allowed to legally marry, they should be allowed to legally form civil unions, but not marry, there should be no legal recognition of their relationships, or don't know?'

20. The wording of the question was: 'Which party and leader [Paul Martin and the Liberals, Stephen Harper and the Conservatives, Jack Layton and the NDP, or (in Quebec only) Gilles Duceppe and the Bloc Quebecois] would do the best job of dealing with each of the following if they win today's election—reducing taxes; managing our social programs in a way that is both compassionate and cost-effective; managing the economy; representing your province in Ottawa; keeping Canada together; managing moral issues like same sex marriage and abortion; fixing our relationship with the US; understanding the needs of young people; running a scandal-free and ethical government; protecting the environment; keeping their promises; understanding the needs of people like you; representing Canada in world affairs; fixing our health care system; making our communities safe from crime; presenting a positive vision of the future; providing the best overall government?'

PART

II

Making Environmental Law and Policy

3

The Courts and Environmental Policy Leadership

Marcia Valiante[1]

Canadian courts have regular opportunities to decide a wide range of environmental matters. Cases before them raise questions involving interpretations of the Constitution or legislation, reviews of administrative decisions, original suits for damages, or prosecution and sentencing of regulatory offences. This chapter considers the influence of litigation on the direction of Canadian environmental policy. Of particular concern, in keeping with the theme of the volume, is if and to what extent courts use these opportunities to contribute to environmental policy leadership. By necessity, this review will be selective; prosecutions and sentencing in regulatory offences will not be addressed in this discussion.

Courts have traditionally been considered conservative and elitist defenders of privilege, not crucibles of innovation. Yet, particularly since the advent of the Charter of Rights, more individuals and public interest groups turn to litigation to advance their agendas than was true in the past in Canada.[2] Although the Charter has as of yet been mostly irrelevant for the development of substantive environmental policy, other reforms, such as relaxed standing and intervention rules and the adoption of class action legislation and environmental bills of rights, have made it easier to get an issue before the courts. In addition, high profile decisions legitimizing environmental values encourage both environmental groups and individuals to use the courts to advance environmental policy particularly when their arguments are ignored in other political fora. Specialized environmental law groups such as the Canadian Environmental Law Association, Ecojustice, and Environmental Defence facilitate this approach.

Many lawyers necessarily have an abiding faith in litigation as a powerful instrument to effect social change and advance a progressive agenda. In an era of 'rights', public interest groups often share the belief that courts can make public institutions more responsive to their interests.[3] Yet the evidence supporting that faith is mixed.[4] Furthermore, whether it is even proper for unelected judges in a democracy governed by the principle of parliamentary supremacy to attempt to steer policy choices and force social change is hotly debated.[5] This chapter does not engage that ideological debate but accepts that courts have a defined role in our constitutional system that is generally carried out in a balanced and restrained manner. The focus here is more modest: to review significant environmental decisions for evidence of a link between them and environmental policy leadership.

The Context: Principles, Attitudes, Approach

Much attention has been paid to the Supreme Court of Canada's pronouncements supporting environmental protection.[6] Repeatedly, over two decades, the Court has highlighted environmental protection as 'one of the major challenges of our time',[7] a 'fundamental value in Canadian society', and a 'public purpose of superordinate importance'.[8] Further, the Court has accepted that 'our common future, that of every Canadian community, depends on a healthy environment.'[9] It has also endorsed key principles that support environmental protection, including the precautionary principle, the 'polluter pays' principle, intergenerational equity, sustainability, and public trust.[10] Beyond success in individual cases, the cumulative message is that the Court is sympathetic to environmental protection, is open to innovative claims, and will not be an impediment to government action at all levels.

However, this record of endorsement has had little impact on environmental policy. Most of the decisions upheld legislative or executive policy choices, did not dictate them, and subsequent cases have not yet yielded substantive policy shifts.[11] One hopes that this record will amount to more than judicial cheerleading. Certainly, hopes are high that it signifies moral leadership that will 'lead to a future with a much greater degree of environmental integrity' and 'will yield positive cumulative effects much greater than any single decision-maker could ever envisage'.[12]

In order to better understand the Court's approach in environmental cases, it is important to situate environmental cases within larger trends in the Court's jurisprudence. Such trends include adoption of a broad and purposive approach to statutory interpretation, increased reliance on international law in interpreting domestic law, restraint in federalism cases, and increased deference to the decisions of local governments. Some of these trends are discussed below.

To bring an action before the courts usually requires a person with a legal interest that has been affected, such as physical harm or damage to property. In constitutional and administrative law cases, however, the Supreme Court has developed special standing rules, allowing those not directly affected by legislation or a decision to challenge it.[13] The decision to allow standing is discretionary, and so it has an element of unpredictability. The Court's approach in most cases, however, has been to allow established environmental groups raising serious challenges to legislation or administrative decisions to do so.[14]

Another way to participate in litigation is to ask to intervene in a case brought by others. The purpose of intervention is 'to assist the court in ensuring justice is done and . . . important policy considerations are brought to the attention of the court'.[15] Interveners are particularly important in cases that could potentially affect an array of interests beyond those of the immediate parties. Although interveners cannot raise new causes of action, their submissions must be useful and different from those of other parties. The number and diversity of public interest groups intervening in the courts has increased significantly, particularly in Charter cases, and the Supreme Court rarely denies an application for intervener status.[16] While some judges have commented that the Court is burdened by too many interveners,[17] public interest interveners are routinely accepted in environmental cases that reach the Supreme Court. Studies indicate that they have a positive influence on decisions.[18]

A final threshold issue is the need to ensure that the case raises a legal and not a political issue. This is the issue of 'justiciability'. In a recent Federal Court case brought by Friends of the Earth for the purpose of getting the court to force the government to comply with the Kyoto Protocol Implementation Act, which had been passed by Parliament without government support, the outcome turned on this issue. The court held that the duties imposed under the act were not justiciable and thus could not be enforced by the court.[19]

Types of Legal Actions

Environmental matters come before the courts in many different forms, and each form raises different issues. The following sections explore some recent decisions in a few types of cases that have the potential to influence policy development: constitutional and Charter litigation, judicial review of administrative action, and civil actions.

Constitutional and Charter Litigation

Few division of powers decisions affecting the environment have reached the Supreme Court of Canada in recent years. It has long been settled that the environment is a matter of shared jurisdiction between federal and provincial governments, and since the early 1980s the Court has consistently upheld all challenged legislation, giving expanded scope to all governments to address environmental concerns. This approach is not limited to environmental cases; 'a consistent posture of judicial restraint—or generous interpretations of the scope of both provincial and federal jurisdiction—has been the defining feature of the Court's recent federalism jurisprudence.'[20] Over the last two decades, the Court has been reluctant to strike down either federal or provincial laws on federalism grounds. Instead, it has generously interpreted legislative powers of both orders of government, but federal powers in particular. The best example of a generous interpretation of federal law in an environmental case is the decision in *Hydro-Québec*, where the toxic substances provisions of the *Canadian Environmental Protection Act* were upheld as a matter of criminal law. In so doing, the Court expanded the traditional meaning of criminal law to save what was effectively a regulatory scheme. By accepting broad legislative policy scope in both orders of government, the Court has opened up space for policy innovation, but pushed federalism disputes and coordination problems onto the executive to resolve.

The *Spraytech* case illustrates this expansive view of governmental powers over the environment. Motivated by residents' health concerns, the municipality of Hudson, Québec adopted a by-law to ban the cosmetic use of pesticides on public and private property, relying on the power to act for the 'general welfare' of town residents found in Québec's municipal legislation. The by-law was challenged by commercial pesticide applicators and the Supreme Court upheld it on two grounds. First, the by-law was authorized by the general welfare power, continuing the Court's increasingly deferential approach toward broad municipal powers.[21] Second, the Court narrowed the test for determining when municipal by-laws conflict with federal and provincial laws; this effectively expanded the range of municipal authority.[22] Justice L'Heureux-Dubé noted, invoking international legal principles,[23] that the by-law was consistent with the precautionary principle.

Spraytech is one decision where the Court played a key role in supporting ambitious environmental policy and greater municipal jurisdiction over the environment. By its generous interpretation of municipal authority, the decision effectively allowed all three levels of government to regulate the use of pesticides. Emboldened by the decision, approximately 140 municipalities across Canada adopted similar by-laws, and many began to address other environmental issues. In 2004, Québec adopted a province-wide ban on the cosmetic use of pesticides, and Ontario passed legislation in 2008 to do likewise. It should be noted, however, that Ontario's legislation does not allow for more restrictive municipal by-laws, and thus pulls back from the possibilities set up by the Court's ruling.

There have been very few cases under the Charter of Rights related to the environment. However, a recent case illustrates how the goal of environmental protection can justify infringement of a fundamental freedom. The case[24] involved a challenge to Montreal's noise by-law by a night club that was prosecuted for using an outside loudspeaker to amplify music and provide commentary from the show inside as a way of attracting customers. The issues before the Court were whether the wording of the by-law was so vague as to be *ultra vires* and whether it violated the club's right to freedom of expression.

The by-law's restriction on 'noise' was ambiguous; however, the majority of the Court took a broad, contextual approach to statutory interpretation in upholding the by-law. It looked to the history of municipal control of 'nuisances', which always included the ability to control excessive noise, and relied on the 1995 *CP* case, an unsuccessful challenge of Ontario's *Environmental Protection Act*.[25] Overly vague laws violate Section 7 of the Charter—which guarantees 'life, liberty and security of the person and the right not to be deprived thereof except in accordance with the principles of fundamental justice'—but general language in environmental statutes is allowed because 'the subject matter does not lend itself well to precise language' and flexibility is needed for governments to be able to respond to unforeseen forms of pollution. The Court held that the Charter should not be used to hinder ambitious and flexible environmental legislation. This means that governments can enact generally-worded statutory prohibitions against pollution and leave the details to be worked out from time to time by administrators. This approach insulates governments from this type of Charter challenge by regulated industries but also prevents challenges from the public when governments fail to adopt ambitious regulations and policies.

The Court found that the noise by-law restricted freedom of expression. However, the by-law was upheld because its objective was pressing and substantial, its terms were rationally connected to achieving that objective, and the beneficial effects of restricting noise pollution outweighed the prejudicial effects on the protected right. In dealing with important social issues, elected officials are entitled to a measure of latitude. They must show only that they have tailored the restrictions to the exigencies of the problem in a reasonable way, and 'this is particularly so on environmental issues, where views and interests conflict and precision is elusive.' Thus, despite the location of the night club in the commercial area of a large city, residents do not have to 'be subjected to abuses of the enjoyment of their environment. . .'. As the judge said, 'the citizens of a city, even a city the size of Montreal, are entitled to a healthy environment.'

Constitutional decisions on Aboriginal rights may also influence the development of environmental policy. In particular, courts have referred to conservation as a compelling objective that can trump even constitutionally-protected Aboriginal rights.[26] These decisions often deal with the impacts of natural resource development on constitutionally-protected use rights or titles to land. Of particular interest to environmental policy is the line of cases that has established a 'duty to consult and accommodate' Aboriginal interests when decisions are made that could adversely affect them.

The duty to consult was first adopted in the context of justifying infringement of established Aboriginal rights.[27] More recently, the Court expanded the need for consultation and accommodation to include situations where government decisions or government-authorized actions might affect nascent rights. In the *Haida Nation* case,[28] the Court held that even though the Haida's claim to their traditional lands had not been proved, the province had a legal duty to consult with and, if appropriate, accommodate Haida concerns over timber harvesting when it made administrative decisions respecting tree farm licences. This duty is 'grounded in the honour of the Crown', which binds the Crown in all dealings with Aboriginal peoples and facilitates reconciliation between Aboriginal interests and Crown sovereignty. The duty is triggered whenever the government has 'knowledge of a credible but unproven claim' and contemplates conduct that might adversely affect that claim.[29] It has also been held to apply when treaty rights might be affected.[30] Once the duty is triggered, 'precisely what is required of the government may vary with the strength of the claim and the circumstances.' However, there must always be a meaningful process of consultation and good faith efforts on both sides. The stronger the claim, or the more significant the potential infringement, the more will be required of governments.

In a companion case to *Haida Nation*, the Court considered how these principles work in the context of an environmental assessment process.[31] Instead of a complete failure to consult, in this instance there was active involvement. The Taku River Tlingit First Nation (TRTFN) opposed construction of a road through their traditional lands as part of a proposed mine re-opening. TRTFN participated in a 3.5-year environmental assessment (EA) process but did not agree with the result; they challenged the process and the outcome. The Court held that BC was under an obligation to consult, but that the EA process fulfilled the province's obligation. TRTFN was a full participant, sitting on the project committee, sharing information, and expressing its views. The Province 'was not under a duty to reach agreement with the TRTFN, and its failure to do so did not breach the obligations of good faith that it owed them'.

The obligation to consult and accommodate Aboriginal interests directly affects the process by which resource and environmental decisions are made across Canada. Beyond the process, incorporating Aboriginal values via the need for accommodation may directly influence substantive policy direction with respect to the location, nature, and pace of future natural resource developments. However, judicial recognition of the duty to consult and accommodate does not guarantee that influence. Impediments to fruitful participation include lack of funds and capacity in many communities, emphasis on technical knowledge, lack of trust, and difficulty in participation in project implementation.[32]

Judicial Review of Administrative Action

Probably the most active area of environmental litigation is judicial review of government actions. Most environmental regulatory decisions are made by administrators acting under statutory authority. They design regulations and guidelines, interpret the meaning of statutory terms, apply these interpretations to facts, and exercise discretion in reaching decisions in individual cases, often balancing competing interests. Under some statutes, decisions can be appealed to specialized tribunals where all issues are open to reconsideration. Usually, courts do not become involved except in a limited way through an appeal on a 'question of law', or through judicial review. Judicial review is a mechanism for ensuring the accountability of administrative decision-makers through the courts, but on limited grounds. Judicial review influences the outcome in the particular case but can also influence policy through a definitive judicial interpretation of the statute or opinion on agency practices.[33]

The Supreme Court has struggled to clearly articulate the reach of this supervisory power. One particularly difficult issue is what degree of deference to give to administrators' decisions. In a March 2008 decision, the Court simplified its approach.[34] Certain types of decisions, including constitutional interpretations, questions of law outside a decision-maker's area of expertise, and true questions of jurisdiction, must be 'correct'. This means that a court will give them no deference and will substitute its view of what the right decision should have been. All other decisions will attract deference and can only be struck down if they are 'unreasonable'. This approach is intended to respect Parliament's choice to put certain decisions—including determinations of questions of fact, discretion, or policy—in the hands of expert or specialized administrators. The need to weigh multiple factors and interests means that several outcomes could be correct, so the courts will only 'inquire into the qualities that make a decision reasonable . . . the existence of justification, transparency and intelligibility and whether the decision falls within a range of possible, acceptable outcomes which are defensible in respect of the facts and the law'.

It is not yet clear whether the Court's revised approach will mean much change for judicial review of environmental decisions. Questions of statutory interpretation were usually reviewed on a correctness standard, and discretionary decisions on a reasonableness standard.[35] *Dunsmuir* suggests that even some statutory interpretation questions might now be given deference. Because most environmental legislation delegates broad discretion to administrators with little or no statutory guidance, it has always been difficult to successfully attack the resulting substantive decisions. Courts will generally only interfere with decisions that exceed explicit or implicit jurisdictional limits, decisions that cannot be justified on the evidence, or decisions in which fair procedures are not followed.[36] There are, however, some environmental statutes with mandatory duties or detailed criteria bounding discretion that provide greater opportunities for court supervision. One example is the *Species At Risk Act*, which mandates development of recovery strategies addressing certain criteria by specified deadlines.[37]

The *Canadian Environmental Assessment Act* attracts a great deal of judicial review. Environmental groups routinely challenge decisions made under the CEAA in the Federal Court. Most controversial projects find their way there, likely in part because the CEAA has no appeal provision and so judicial review is the only route of challenge. There are some mandatory provisions in the CEAA and most aspects of the process have been the subject of judicial review applications. Despite this, there have been few, and relatively limited, successes.

Two issues in particular have led to a lot of cases: defining the scope of a project, and evaluating the scope and completeness of the assessment carried out on a project. The scope of a project refers to what related undertakings must be evaluated. Numerous cases have challenged decisions to define projects in ways that split closely-related undertakings into separate projects, thus minimizing their individual impacts and making approval easier. The Act confers the power to scope a project on the 'responsible authority' and the Federal Court consistently defers to its choice.[38] The Supreme Court has refused to hear any of these cases.

The second issue refers to the mandatory factors that 'shall be considered' in every assessment. The Federal Court treats failure to consider a factor at all or failure to give a rationale for a conclusion as 'unreasonable'. However, where there is some evidence that the responsible authority considered the factors, even if that consideration is limited, courts have generally deferred to the responsible authority. The meaning of some factors, such as 'cumulative effects', which is a term not defined in the Act, has been left to the complete discretion of the responsible authority.

Environmental groups have tried unsuccessfully to use judicial review of CEAA decisions as a lever to constrain oil sands development. The *True North* case challenged the federal 'responsible authority's' decision to scope the project to include only those aspects of the oil sands development that required federal authorization under the Fisheries Act.[39] This avoided an in-depth comprehensive study of the entire project and downplayed the significance of potential adverse effects, thus facilitating federal approval. The Federal Court of Appeal held that this decision was a correct interpretation of the CEAA and was not unreasonable in light of Alberta's assessment of the project as a whole. This case marks a more restrictive view of the scoping power than in previous cases, but the Supreme Court refused to hear an appeal. In the Kearl Oil Sands case,[40] a joint federal–provincial review panel concluded that the massive development would not have 'significant adverse environmental effects' if mitigation measures and recommendations about regulatory standards were adopted. On judicial review, the trial judge agreed with the argument that the panel had not given any justification for its conclusion that the mine's contribution to greenhouse gas emissions would be insignificant. On the basis of the court decision, the federal government cancelled the authorization; this cancellation was upheld on an application to the court brought by the proponent. However, the review panel was quickly reconstituted, wrote a rationale confirming its initial conclusion, and submitted it to the federal government within a month. The government accepted the rationale and issued its final opinion that the authorization could be re-issued because it was satisfied that the 'project' would not cause significant adverse effects. Thus, as a result of the litigation, the project was not stopped or modified, only delayed for a few months. The environmental groups behind the judicial review gave up on pursuing the matter in the courts and intend to concentrate their efforts on different strategies to affect oil sands development.[41]

This record points to the limits of both judicial review and the CEAA. Important environmental decisions are essentially unreviewable as a consequence of discretionary and vague statutory language and a deferential stance by the courts. As a result, innovation depends on the choices made by the responsible authorities, but they may either have little environmental expertise or be motivated by competing political concerns.[42] Assessments are done project by project, with little opportunity to go behind a project and force an evaluation of the environmental impacts of the policy choice to support a resource development path. Judicial review provides little hope of getting courts to take a hard look at those policy choices. Even when courts have had the opportunity to review interpretations of the CEAA on a correctness standard, they have stayed close to the literal meaning of the Act, without using the broad principles in the Preamble and purpose sections, and have even accepted a narrowing of the process. They are reluctant to weigh in on the question of balancing development against environmental protection.[43]

A successful judicial review application may delay a project as more work is done, but is unlikely to stop a major development with high economic stakes, such as oil sands exploitation. Even so, there is value in pursuing these cases. Some projects have been shelved or re-designed as a result of CEAA litigation. Court scrutiny helps ensure that minimum statutory requirements are met, that pressure is kept on proponents and responsible authorities to be alert to relevant substantive factors in order to justify their actions as reasonable, that controversial projects are publicized, and that project direction, mitigation, and follow-up are influenced positively. The threat of litigation provides an incentive to proponents to do a better job from the outset. However, other strategies can also be influential. Active participation in panel reviews and efforts outside the courtroom also result in significant positive influence.[44]

Civil Actions

Civil litigation can have both a public dimension and policy implications.[45] This is most obvious in a successful claim for compensation for a government action that caused environmental harm. While a private defendant must pay damages for environmental harm, the economic burden of pollution shifts onto the polluter and off of individuals. The more such cases are recognized by the courts, the more entrenched the shift becomes. Governments may respond with policies that enhance regulatory obligations, but might also act to limit liability. Finally, civil actions provide an opportunity for individuals to police polluters and establish, through an impartial arbiter, appropriate standards of conduct for industry independent of government regulatory action or inaction.

Environmental cases come regularly, if not often, before the courts. To bring an action, one must frame it within a recognized 'cause of action'. For environmental harm, most cases are argued on the basis of the common law torts of nuisance, negligence, strict liability, and their parallels in the Québec Civil Code. There are many examples of successful claims, but the obstacles to success are many.[46] This section looks at a few issues considered in important, recent cases. These are class actions, environmental damages, and novel claims.

Class Actions

Class actions are a procedural device to allow all those affected by pollution or other harm to join their claims together into a single legal action against the polluter and/or regulator. Although group claims have always been allowed, class actions are needed for complex litigation that has a common cause and multiple individual effects. They serve three goals: (1) reducing duplication in proving claims, thereby reducing the costs of litigation; (2) overcoming some of the disincentives to individual action and thus advancing access to justice; and (3) modifying polluters' behaviour by ensuring they are more likely to pay the full costs of their harmful activities. Chief Justice McLachlan has said that pollution cases are especially well suited to class proceedings.[47]

In Canada, Québec led the way by adopting class action legislation in 1978, followed by several other provinces in the 1990s. Other than in Québec, and generally without reference to that experience, courts in the common law jurisdictions have struggled with application of the legislation in the context of environmental litigation.

A class proceeding must first be certified by the court. This pre-trial procedure becomes the primary battle ground because, if certification is denied, there is often little likelihood that individual claims will be brought against the defendant. On the other hand, if a claim is certified, settlement often results, and few cases go to trial.[48] A few cases have been certified which related to single incidents of pollution. For example, in Ontario, cases arising out of a fire at a plastics recycling facility, a sulphur dioxide release from Inco in Sudbury, and sewer back-ups resulting from a severe rainstorm have all been certified. More controversial have been cases involving nuisances or long-term exposure to contaminants leading to allegations of adverse health effects—the toxic tort cases.

The first decision from the Supreme Court on certification in an environmental claim came in 2001 as part of a series of certification decisions under the class proceedings rules in three provinces. Certification was sought in a nuisance action on behalf of 30,000 residents living in the vicinity of Metropolitan Toronto's landfill who were exposed to toxic gases, odours, litter, noise, and vibration. In the words of the Chief Justice, 'it is essential that courts not take an overly restrictive approach to the legislation, but rather interpret the Act in a way that gives full effect to the benefits foreseen by the drafters.'[49] On two of the statutory criteria, the court did give a generous interpretation.

While this generous attitude does give cause for hope that future cases will be certified, the Court refused to certify this case because it determined that a class proceeding was not the preferable procedure. In part this was because the pollution was not distributed evenly across the affected area or over time, therefore, individual issues predominated over the common ones. As one critic observed, requiring that common issues must predominate over individual ones 'suggests that private nuisance claims will rarely be certified'.[50] However, more recently, the Supreme Court confirmed that 'neighbourhood annoyance' claims under the Québec Civil Code were similar to common law nuisances, in that they did not require proof of fault, and could be brought as class actions.[51] The Court determined that the defendant cement plant was liable for damages even though it met all regulatory requirements and upheld a method of assessing damages that varied by location, in direct contrast to its approach in *Hollick*. This approach is more sensitive to the nature of environmental nuisance claims and the difficulty of assessing nuisance-type damages, and has breathed new life into the potential for class actions to advance such claims.

Health claims have proved more challenging. In 2005, the Ontario Court of Appeal certified a case regarding long-term exposure to toxic pollution as a class proceeding.[52] The potential class members seek damages due to historic nickel emissions from the Inco refinery in Port Colborne. The claimants originally alleged serious physical and emotional health effects, damage to property, and economic loss resulting from emissions over a 66-year period. However, when the claim was not certified and they were ordered to pay $200,000 in costs to Inco, they substantially revised their claim in hopes of having it certified. On appeal, the claim was simplified to one of negative impact on property values resulting from the release of an Environment Ministry report that found higher than expected nickel levels in soil samples in the neighbourhood near the refinery. The Court hinted that it would have followed *Hollick*, and not certified the original claim on the grounds that the individual issues overwhelmed the common ones, but it was satisfied that this impediment was overcome by dropping the claims for harm to health and going forward with the claim for diminished property value alone. Inco tried to appeal the certification to the Supreme Court, but was refused. Similarly, in 2007, citing *Hollick* and *Pearson*, the Alberta Court of Appeal upheld the certification of a case involving trichloroethylene emanating from property owned by Canadian Pacific Railway and migrating into groundwater, contaminating a large number of nearby homes.[53] Although concerned that the solvent 'posed a significant health risk to people, the Respondents pursued a class proceeding only on the ground that the Appellant is liable to them for the resulting damage to their property and corresponding reduction in property values and loss of rental income.' The health claims are being brought individually. By contrast, the Nova Scotia courts accepted the Sydney Tar Ponds case (discussed below under 'Novel Claims') as a class proceeding.

Class proceedings were adopted by legislatures to allow for remedies in cases that might not otherwise be brought to court, with the purpose of ensuring that polluters pay for the harm they cause and modify their behaviour. Overall, interpretation of that legislation has been generous but the success to date in environmental actions has been disappointing. Courts seem much more comfortable certifying the type of case that involves a single, discrete incident than cases of ongoing or historic pollution and the multiple complex effects that result.

Environmental Damages

The damages that are payable when environmental harm is proven can have an important influence on polluters' and governments' behaviour. Despite a trend to restrict damages in civil cases,[54] some recent decisions have gone in a different direction. In one, a landowner whose soil was contaminated by gasoline from a neighbouring service station received damages in an amount equal to the cost of remediating the site to a pristine condition. This level of clean-up was not required by the Environment Ministry's standard and it meant that defendant had to pay $250,000 more than the cost to remediate to the government standard for commercial lands. The court ruled that, alternatively, if the lower government standard was applied, then the landowner would be entitled to additional compensation for 'stigma' damage.[55]

In 2004, the Supreme Court ruled on the issue of compensation for environmental harm.[56] The case involved a claim by BC for damages caused by a fire to a leased forest on provincial Crown land. The company was found to be negligent but the province shared responsibility due to its inadequate fire-fighting efforts.

BC sought to recover its expenses for fire-fighting and the restoration of the burned areas, its loss of stumpage revenue from harvestable trees destroyed in the fire, and its loss of trees that could not be harvested for environmental reasons. For example, some trees were located on steep slopes and could not be harvested because of the risk of erosion, while others were in riparian buffers established to protect water quality, fish habitat, and other environmental values. The Court held that BC was entitled to compensation only for its expenses in fighting the fire and restoring the land. However, the case is important because the Court recognized public environmental rights enforceable by action of the Crown and adopted 'a principled approach to the assessment of environmental compensation common law'.[57]

A key question was the basis of the province's entitlement to damages for environmental loss. The Crown argued that entitlement flows not just from its status as a land owner, but also from its status as 'the representative of the people of British Columbia, for whom the Crown seeks to maintain an unspoiled environment'. All of the judges of the Supreme Court agreed that the Crown does have this inherent common law jurisdiction, known as *parens patriae*, to protect against interference with the public's rights. Those rights include rights in the environment and in common resources such as navigable waters, fish, beaches, air, and the sea. Historically, public rights were protected via 'public nuisance' actions brought by the Attorney General. Importantly, both the majority and the dissent confirmed that damages are an appropriate remedy in public nuisance cases, so that henceforth the Crown will not be limited to seeking an injunction. The Court went on to suggest that the traditional common law approach might even be appropriately expanded to embrace a 'public trust' as that concept has developed in the United States, even hinting that the Crown might owe fiduciary obligations to the public, opening it up to suits if it fails to protect the environment.

Alas, the majority concluded that it could not consider those issues in this case. Because BC had not raised those points earlier, it would be unfair to the defendant to rule on them. On this point, the dissent disagreed and was willing to expand the claim, accusing Justice Binnie, writing for the majority, of arguing against a narrow judicial construction and then adopting 'just such a narrow judicial construction by limiting the Crown's entitlement in this particular case to entitlement' as a landowner.[58] Nevertheless, how far the court is willing to go in developing the law will have to wait for another case. The door has been opened and the Court has indicated its willingness to engage the issues.

Another key element of the case was the approach to calculating damages. There was extensive discussion on the method used to calculate the value of harvestable trees in light of BC's stumpage system. On this point the majority and dissent disagreed about whether BC was entitled to recover damages in this case. The Court held that the calculation method should recognize and compensate for a range of losses, including the environmental services that the trees provide now and as a bequest to future generations, the passive use or 'existence value' of the forest, and the intrinsic value of natural heritage beyond its value to humans. These conclusions are important developments in the Canadian law of environmental damages. Even though such valuations will be difficult, 'ensuring that environmental costs are counted in the marketplace is a fundamental and necessary step towards building a sustainable society. . . . The law, through the determination of liability obligations, can play an important role in ensuring that environmental costs are factored in to business and market decisions.'[59]

Novel Claims

One way in which the courts can uniquely contribute to environmental policy innovation is by being open to arguments to adopt new categories of actions or to expand existing categories to take account of novel situations. The Supreme Court has repeatedly proclaimed the fundamental nature of environmental values to Canadian society and given encouragement about the positive reception that might await potential litigants. Yet, no 'environmental' cause of action has been judicially recognized, and the few statutory causes of action that exist are very narrowly drawn, and so are seldom, if ever, invoked. This forces potential plaintiffs to fit their claims into traditional categories, such as nuisance. Each of the existing categories has highly formalized criteria for success, standing rules, and so on. Some recent cases illustrate the openness of Canadian courts to novel claims.

Plaintiffs in a case involving toxic contamination from the Sydney Tar Ponds attempted to frame their claim around the concept of fiduciary duty, among other causes of action. Plaintiffs argued that the company and the governments of Canada and Nova Scotia owed fiduciary duties toward the local community arising out of ownership and operation of the steel plant and coking ovens. They contended that they were unaware of the risks and were particularly vulnerable to the decisions made about operation of the facilities that resulted in extensive pollutant discharges. They also argued that the governments owed them a fiduciary duty arising out of their regulatory functions, so that by failing to disclose the risks, and in fact actively misleading the community about risks, and by making operational decisions that exposed them to greater risk, defendants were in breach of this duty. They took their arguments from encouraging Supreme Court decisions.

Beginning with the *Guerin* case,[60] the Supreme Court characterized the obligations of the Crown toward Aboriginal peoples in dealings with land held by the Crown on their behalf as fiduciary ones. A fiduciary relationship is one where the fiduciary is held to very strict standards of conduct, including the requirement that he or she act so as to serve only the best interests of the beneficiary.[61] Justice Dickson in *Guerin* stated that the categories of fiduciary relationships are not closed, leaving open the possibility that the relationship between the Crown and Canadian citizens with respect to public resources or the environment could be conceived of as fiduciary, with a corresponding cause of action for breach of that duty. Justice Binnie hinted at this in *Canfor* but did not pursue it.

The Supreme Court has also alluded to potential obligations of private corporations toward the communities in which they operate. Traditional corporate obligations are fiduciary, requiring directors to act 'in the best interests of the corporation', often viewed as a duty to maximize share value above all else. In a 2004 decision, the Court tempered this view by interpreting the phrase 'best interests of the corporation' to mean something more than the 'best interests of shareholders', including other interests that could be considered by directors in managing a corporation: 'We accept as an accurate statement of law that in determining whether they are acting with a view to the best interests of the corporation, it may be legitimate, given all the circumstances of a given case, for the board of directors to consider, *inter alia*, the interests of shareholders, employees, suppliers, creditors, consumers, governments and the environment.'[62]

The tar ponds defendants brought motions to strike the claim as failing to disclose a cause of action. Even recognizing that 'the law is evolving with respect to fiduciary duties', the judge rejected out of hand that a fiduciary duty on the part of the governments arose out of a statutory or regulatory action, and that conclusion was not appealed. The judge did accept as 'arguable' that a duty might arise out of the 'private' function of operating the facilities, so that issue was allowed to go to trial against all of the defendants.[63] On appeal, the fiduciary claim was allowed to proceed to trial against the two governments but the claim against the corporation was struck out[64] because plaintiffs had not alleged any facts about the corporation's actions that gave rise to a reasonable expectation that it would act for the benefit of the community:

Not only were they strangers, Ispat was obliged to act in the best interests of others, its shareholders. . . . I do not see this obligation as being compatible with it being obliged to act in the best interests of the [plaintiffs]. To suggest on the facts alleged that Ispat owed a fiduciary duty to the [plaintiffs] to act in their best interests as opposed to in the interests of its shareholders would represent a fundamental change in the law of Canada, and one I am not prepared to countenance here.

On the other hand, facts were alleged that might give rise to a fiduciary duty between the governments and residents. Whether these facts can be established at trial remains to be seen. Even though the fiduciary argument was categorically rejected in the regulatory relationship, its acceptance in the 'private' relationship is a step toward raising the bar for government accountability.

Litigants also attempt to push the boundaries of recognized causes of action by asking the courts to expand their reach to new situations. Courts have said that the accepted classes of nuisance or negligence are not closed, so they are open to argument. A recent successful example relates to 'regulatory negligence', that is, negligence on the part of government in carrying out its policies.

The Berendsen case involved the rebuilding of a road in the 1960s by the Ontario Transportation Ministry. Asphalt and other roadbed wastes were removed and by arrangement with the landowner, were buried on a dairy farm, beside a watercourse. Years later when new owners, who were unaware of the waste, took over the farm they argued that they and their livestock were harmed from soil and well water contamination from the wastes. The Environment Ministry got involved, but did not agree that the well was contaminated so no remediation was done. The family sold what land they could and sued the Ontario government.

The province initially sought to strike out the claim because it was brought outside the six-month limitation period that applies to government acts.[65] The Supreme Court distinguished between 'public' duties and powers and 'private' ones undertaken by governments.[66] In this case, there was a public duty to repair highways but no duty to dispose of used asphalt in any particular way. When the Ministry chose to bury it on private land, that decision gave rise to a duty of care toward the individual landowner, though not toward the public generally. This finding allowed the family to pursue its claim.

At trial,[67] the judge adopted a generous reading of the law of regulatory negligence, holding that the Transportation Ministry had a duty to take reasonable care in deciding where and how to deposit road waste. The Ministry ought to have known, even in the 1960s before standards or setbacks were developed, that the material contained toxic substances and depositing such a large amount of waste near a residence and water could cause harm. Further, the judge held that the Environment Ministry's failure to require remediation 25 years later was negligent.

The law recognizes a duty of care only in relation to governments' operational, not policy, decisions. In this case, the court characterized all of the province's actions as operational decisions. The court rejected the Environment Ministry's reliance on its drinking water objectives as the standard for determining when water is contaminated and criticized the process for setting those objectives. If upheld on appeal, this ruling will mark a major shift—established standards will no longer be the brightline test of contamination and the adequacy of investigations and enforcement decisions will be more easily reviewable. Ministry operations will have to change or the agency will risk increased liability.

An example of an unsuccessful novel claim is the case of *Hoffman v. Monsanto*.[68] Here, organic farmers in Saskatchewan sought certification of a class action to recover damages from the manufacturer and distributor of genetically-modified canola resulting from commercial introduction. Plaintiffs alleged that because canola is open-pollinating, it inevitably spreads beyond the fields where it is planted; when it 'contaminates' a field of organic canola that crop cannot be marketed as organic, entailing economic loss and extra expense. The Saskatchewan Court of Appeal held that there was no negligence because of insufficient 'proximity' between Monsanto and the farmers to establish a duty of care toward them. There were also 'sound policy reasons' to negate a duty, that is, federal government approval of the unconfined release of the genetically-modified crop. The court struck out the nuisance argument because plaintiffs were suing the manufacturer, not the user: 'The implications of holding a manufacturer, or even inventor, liable in nuisance for damage caused by the use of its product or invention by another would be very sweeping indeed.' Similarly, there was no basis for trespass by the defendants because they did not directly interfere with plaintiffs' lands. These findings mean not only that a class action could not be certified, but that individual claims would also likely fail.

Some judges are more open to novel claims than others. It is generally difficult to get new claims recognized, particularly when they challenge long-standing legal doctrines. However, it seems easier to push forward incrementally at the boundaries of existing causes of action, as in *Berendsen*. Such decisions can lead to higher standards of care, resulting in behavioural and policy changes as polluters and regulators adapt.

Conclusions

Courts have a mixed record in leading environmental policy development. It is a complex question and difficult to tease out the impact of judicial decisions from other factors. While the record appears to lend support to the claim that judicial decisions do not themselves *cause* ambitious action, courts can play a crucial supporting role. Repeated statements by the Supreme Court endorsing environmental values and consistent support for progressive legislative choices reinforce shifting social attitudes in favour of environmental protection and help 'prepare the soil' and 'seed thoughts and knowledge and concern' for social change.[69] Some high profile decisions, such as *Spraytech* and *Haida Nation*, quickly cascaded into specific policy changes. Some, such as *Canfor*, had no immediate impact, but interpreted the law in ways that invite future litigants to raise innovative arguments. Others, such as judicial reviews of CEAA decisions, appear to contribute little to policy but do play an important role in ensuring that existing legislative mandates are taken seriously.

Policy-making by courts within our governmental system is controversial. Criticism of 'activist' judges making policy in Charter cases underscores the concern with their democratic legitimacy that also applies outside the Charter context. Yet judicial decision-making necessarily involves interpretive choices and those choices are value-laden. In this sense, courts do make policy. The trend has been toward increasing judicial acceptance of environmental values; however, there are no guarantees that judicial choices will consistently support progressive environmental protection policies.

One needs to be realistic about what litigation can accomplish. Each form of action is limiting in its own way and litigation by design changes the law incrementally. The process is slow and expensive and relies on committed litigants to challenge environmentally inappropriate decisions and raise innovative ideas that push judges toward more innovative decisions. The outcome is unpredictable. Defendants demand close scrutiny of the claims against them, and judges must justify their decisions with reference to legislative text, precedents, and legal principles. Leadership must also come from judges with knowledge and courage. Judicial attitudes can be conservative, especially in private law cases, and this can impede environmental activism. Judges resist substantive review of administrative decisions and defer to legislative intent and executive policy choices. Judicial review can prevent abuses of power, but is not designed to allow court-directed policy-making. Private actions with public dimensions are a growing area of litigation but, even here, 'policy' choices are left to the government.

Nevertheless, the law does evolve. While individual court victories may seem minor, the cumulative effects can be positive for environmental protection. Even backlash from a victory or a series of defeats can raise the public profile of issues and eventually influence policy development. Open standing and intervention rules allow more environmental interests an opportunity to raise broad contextual arguments before the courts. Deference insulates ambitious administrative decisions from challenge by regulated industries unhappy with that innovation.

Litigation is not a substitute for the 'long and hard task' of politics. Perhaps the best way to view the potential of litigation is as a strategy that supports and legitimizes policy leadership by legislatures and governments. But, without political action to lobby for stronger legislation, active participation to demand more ambitious administrative decisions, and education directed at cultural change, litigation alone is insufficient to achieve deep change:

It is a complex process, but politics are about collective action, and litigation is part of the process of determining the legitimate contours of collective action—but not the determinative factor. That responsibility lies with all of us.[70]

Questions for Review

1. Which principles and practices relevant to Canadian environmental policy have been articulated by the Supreme Court? Which cases have been most significant and why?
2. What is the environmental policy significance of the Court's judgments in aboriginal rights cases?
3. What has been the Court's view of the duties of companies and governments towards local communities and their environments?
4. To what extent has recourse to the courts aided environmental groups in achieving their environmental policy objectives?

Notes

1. The author would like to thank Joanna Wice and Tony Smits for their research assistance, funded by the Law Foundation of Ontario.
2. W.A. Bogart, *Good Government? Good Citizens?: Courts, Politics and Markets in a Changing Canada* (Vancouver: UBC Press, 2005), c. 2 generally.
3. Gregory Hein refers to them as 'judicial democrats': G. Hein, 'Interest Group Litigation and Canadian Democracy,' in P. Howe and P.H. Russell, eds, *Judicial Power and Canadian Democracy* (Montreal and Kingston: McGill-Queen's University Press, 2001).
4. See, W.A. Bogart, *Courts and Country: The Limits of Litigation and the Social and Political Life of Canada* (Toronto: Oxford University Press, 1994); G. Rosenberg, *The Hollow Hope—Can Courts Bring About Social Change?* (Chicago: University of Chicago Press, 1991). Bogart asserts that both sceptics and adherents find it impossible to prove or disprove that litigation alone causes significant social change.
5. A good summary of the competing arguments is provided in A.W. MacKay, 'In Defence of the Courts: A Balanced Judicial Role in Canada's Constitutional Democracy (2006–07)', *National Journal of Constitutional Law*, 21: 183–244. A cross-section of opinion on the middle ground, the so-called 'dialogue' theory, is found in Vol. 45 of the *Osgoode Hall L.J.*
6. See, for example, D.R. Boyd, *Unnatural Law: Rethinking Canadian Environmental Law and Policy* (Vancouver: UBC Press, 2003), 221–3.
7. *Friends of the Oldman River v. Canada (Minister of Transport)*, [1992] 1 SCR 3, at 16.
8. *R v. Hydro-Québec*, [1997] 3 SCR 213.
9. *114957 Canada Ltée (Spraytech, Société d'arrosage) v. Hudson (Town)*, [2001] 2 SCR 241, para. 1.
10. A detailed discussion is found in J.V. DeMarco, 'The Supreme Court of Canada's Recognition of Fundamental Environmental Values: What Could Be Next in Canadian Environmental Law?' *JELP* 17 (2007): 159–204, and J.V. DeMarco, 'Law for Future Generations: The Theory of Intergenerational Equity in Canadian Environmental Law' *JELP* 15 (2005): 1.
11. For example, a study of cases in which the litigants attempted to get courts to find that the precautionary principle is a mandatory rule of statutory interpretation (following the Supreme Court's endorsement of the principle) concluded that courts were extremely reluctant to give the principle normative content in the absence of legislative adoption: C. Kazaz, 'The Precautionary Principle Six Years After Spraytech, What Does it Mean?' in S. Berger, and D. Saxe, eds, *Environmental Law: The Year in Review 2007* (Aurora, ON: Canada Law Book, 2008), 141–150.
12. DeMarco, 'The Supreme Court's Recognition of Fundamental Environmental Values,' supra note x at page 204.

13. *Minister of Justice of Canada v. Borowski*, [1981] 2 SCR 575; *Finlay v. Canada (Minister of Finance)*, [1986] 2 SCR 154. The test requires a serious issue to be tried, a direct or genuine interest in the matter, and no other reasonable or effective manner to get the issue to court.

14. C. Tollefson, 'Advancing an Agenda? A Reflection on Recent Developments in Canadian Public Interest Environmental Litigation', *UNB Law Journal* 51 (2002): 175–195, at 183–5.

15. M. Campbell, 'Re-inventing Intervention in the Public Interest: Breaking Down Barriers to Access', *JELP* 15 (2005): 187–218.

16. MacKay, 'In Defence of Courts', *supra*, note x at 211.

17. J. Koshan, 'Dialogue or Conversation? The Impact of Public Interest Interveners on Judicial Decision-Making'. Available at http://www.ciaj-icaj.ca/english/publications/2003/koshan.pdf.

18. Campbell, 'Re-inventing Intervention,' supra, note x, and J.V. DeMarco, 'Assessing the Impact of Public Interest Interventions on the Environmental Law Jurisprudence of the Supreme Court of Canada: A Quantitative and Qualitative Analysis', *SCLR* (2d) 30 (2005): 299–332.

19. *Friends of the Earth v. Canada (Governor in Council and Minister of the Environment)*, 2008 FC 1183.

20. B. Ryder, 'The End of Umpire? Federalism and Judicial Restraint', *SCLR* (2d) 34 (2006): 345–77, at 345.

21. The shift toward greater deference to municipal decision-making began with the dissent of J. McLachlan in *Shell Canada Products Ltd. v. Vancouver*, [1994] 1 SCR 231, then was adopted by a unanimous court in *Nanaimo v. Rascal Trucking Ltd.*, [2000] 1 SCR 342, and continued in subsequent cases.

22. The Court adopted the 'impossibility of dual compliance test' that applies to conflicts between federal and provincial laws. In *Rothmans, Benson & Hedges v. Saskatchewan*, [2005] 1 SCR 188, the Court added the notion that a provincial enactment should not frustrate the purpose of a federal one, whether by making it impossible to comply with both, or by some other means. Also, this test applies only where the legislation does not provide for a different test: *Peacock v. Norfolk (County)*, (2006), 81 O.R. (3d) 530 (C.A.), leave to SCC refused.

23. The Court here continued the trend it started in *Baker v. Canada*, [1999] 2 SCR 817, of using international law principles endorsed by Canada to assist them in interpreting statutes or in assessing exercises of discretion. Scholars have noted that the Court often collapses all manner of international rules into merely persuasive authority even though some norms of international law are binding on them: J. Brunnée and S.J. Toope, 'A Hesitant Embrace: The Application of International Law by Canadian Courts', *CYBIL* 40 (2002): 3–60. If the Court had held that the precautionary principle was a rule of customary international law, it would have been binding in domestic law: *R. v. Hape*, [2007] 2 SCR 292.

24. *Montreal (City) v. 2952-1366 Quebec Inc.*, [2005] 3 SCR 141.

25. *Canadian Pacific Ltd. v. Ontario*, [1995] 2 SCR 1031.

26. *R. v. Sparrow*, [1990] 1 SCR 1075, *R. v. Gladstone*, [1996] 2 SCR 723.

27. *Sparrow*, note x. This was confirmed in later cases and expanded in the landmark *Delgamuukw* decision, [1997] 3 SCR 1010, which outlined in more detail the appropriate content of the duty.

28. *Haida Nation v. British Columbia (Minister of Forests)*, [2004] 3 SCR 511.

29. Such conduct may include the design of a process to evaluate a proposed development: *Dene Tha' First Nation v. Canada (Minister of Environment)*, (2008), 35 CELR (3d) 1 (F.C.A.).

30. *Mikisew Cree First Nation v. Canada (Minister of Canadian Heritage*, [2005] 3 SCR 388.

31. *Taku River Tlingit First Nation v. British Columbia (Project Assessment Director)*, [2004] 3 SCR 550.

32. P. Cassidy and C. Findlay, 'The Confluence of Environmental and Aboriginal Law,' in S. Berger and D. Saxe, *Environmental Law: The Year in Review 2007* (Aurora, ON: Canada Law Book, 2008), 15–42. There is concern also that BC is avoiding its obligations through deregulation in its forest practices regime: J. Clogg, 'Environmental Deregulation and the Crown's Constitutional Obligations to First Nations', in Berger and Saxe, 57–71.

33. However, Sossin notes that 'prevailing wisdom holds that judicial review is not an effective remedy of changing bureaucratic action, and that its utility, if any, lies in focusing public attention on particularly oppressive or discriminatory decision-making settings.' L. Sossin, 'The Rule of Policy: *Baker* and the Impact of Judicial Review on Administrative Discretion', in D. Dyzenhaus, ed., *The Unity of Public Law* (Oxford and Portland: Hart Publishing, 2004), 87–112.

34. *Dunsmuir v. New Brunswick*, 2008 SCC 9.

35. Although some were reviewed on a 'patently unreasonable' standard: e.g., *CPAWS v. Canada*, (2003), 1 CELR (3d) 20 (F.C.A.).

36. D.J. Mullan, 'The Role of the Judiciary in the Review of Administrative Policy Decisions: Issues of Legality'. Available at http://www.ciaj-icaj.ca/english/publications/1999/mullan.pdf.

37. S.C. 2002, c. 29. Environmental groups have brought judicial review applications for repeated failures to identify critical habitat in recovery strategies, including for the Nooksack Dace, Piping Plover, Killer Whale, and Sage Grouse. These applications have pushed the government to comply with the statutory requirements. Initiation of an application also influenced the Cabinet to list a species of salmon as endangered: *Rounthwaite v. Canada (Minister of Environment)*, (2007), 31 CELR (3d) 313 (F.C.)

38. The leading case is *Friends of the West Country Assn. v. Canada*, [2000] 2 FC 263 (C.A.). Construction of two bridges con-nected by a road was necessitated by proposed logging development. The responsible authority's decision to define each bridge as a separate project and not include the access road or logging development was upheld under s. 15. The court rejected the 'independent utility' test from US jurisprudence as a check on that choice. However, the RA was required under s. 16 to assess cumulative effects and in doing so did at least have to consider factors beyond the narrow scoped project.

39. *Prairie Acid Rain Coalition v. Canada (Minister of Fisheries and Oceans)*, (2006), 21 CELR (3d) 175 (Fed. C.A.). The coalition argued that the federal government should assess the project as a whole and evaluate its effects on all matters within federal jurisdiction. The destruction of Fort Creek was a consequence of the oil sands development, not a separate project in itself.

40. *Pembina Institute for Appropriate Development v. Canada*, (2008), 35 CELR (3d) 254 (F.C.).

41. Ecojustice, Media Release: Federal Environmental Review System for Tar Sands is Broken', 17 June 2008. Available at http://www.ecojustice.ca/media-centre/press-releases/federal-environmental-review-system.

42. A. Green, 'Discretion, Judicial Review, and the *Canadian Environmental Assessment Act*', *Queen's LJ* (2001–02): 785–807.

43. *Bow Valley Naturalists Society v. Canada*, (2001), 37 CELR (NS) 1 (F.C.A.).

44. S. Rutherford and K. Campbell, 'Time Well Spent? A Survey of Public participation in Federal Environmental Assessment Panels', *JELP* 15 (2005): 71–83.

45. L.N. Klar, 'Judicial Activism in Private Law', *CBR* 80 (2001): 215–240.

46. Tollefson, 'Advancing an Agenda?', supra, note x, discusses obstacles related to standing, costs and interim injunctions. A good overview of environmental actions is J. Benidickson, *Essentials of Canadian Law: Environmental Law*, 2nd ed. (Toronto: Irwin Law, 2002), c. 5.

47. *Western Canadian Shopping Centres Inc. v. Dutton*, [2001] 2 SCR 534.

48. There is a growing trend for defendants to push cases to trial: E.K. Gillespie and K.L. Dawson, '2007 Environmental Class Action Case Law Round-up', in Ontario Bar Association, *2008 OBA Institute of Continuing Legal Education, Environmental Law: Staying Aloft Amid a Flurry of New Developments*, 4 February 2008.

49. *Hollick v. Metropolitan Toronto*, [2001] 3 SCR 158.

50. H. McCleod-Kilmurray, '*Hollick* and Environmental Class Actions: Putting the Substance into Class Action Procedure', *Ottawa Law Review* 34 (2002–03): 263–306.

51. *St. Lawrence Cement Inc. v. Barrette*, 2008 SCC 64.

52. *Pearson v. Inco*, (2005), 20 CELR (3d) 258 (Ont. C.A.).

53. *Windsor v. Canadian Pacific Railway*, (2007), 32 CELR (3d) 194 (Alta C.A.).

54. B. Weintraub, 'Review of Significant Environmental Litigation in 2007: Continuing Trend to Restrict Damages and Liability in Civil Cases?' in *OBA Institute* 2008.

55. *Tridan Developments Ltd. v. Shell Canada Products Ltd.*, (2002), 57 O.R. (3d) 503.

56. *British Columbia v. Canadian Forest Products Ltd.*, [2004] 2 SCR 74.

57. Canfor, para. 8.

58. Canfor, para. 158, per J. LeBel.

59. S.A.G. Elgie and A.M. Lintner, 'The Supreme Court's *Canfor* Decision: Losing the Battle but Winning the War for Environmental Damages', *UBC Law Review* 38 (2005): 223–261, at 259–60. See also discussion in J.V. DeMarco, M. Valiante, and M.A. Bowden, 'Opening the Door for Common Law Environmental Protection in Canada: The Decision in *British Columbia v. Canadian Forest Products, Ltd.*', *JELP* 15 (2005): 233–55.

60. [1984] 2 SCR 335.

61. A fiduciary duty is recognized in the context of a relationship where one person can unilaterally exercise power to affect another's interests and that person is peculiarly vulnerable or dependent on the other. This is traditionally a matter of private law, but can also be recognized in public law: E. Fox-Decent, 'The Fiduciary Nature of State Legal Authority', *Queen's LJ* 31 (2005–6): 259.

62. *Peoples Department Stores Inc. (Trustee of) v. Wise*, [2004] 3 SCR 461 at para. 42.

63. *MacQueen v. Ispat Sidbec Inc.*, (2006), 24 CELR (3d) 286 (N.S. Supreme Ct.).

64. *MacQueen v. Ispat Sidbec Inc.*, (2007), 27 CELR (3d) 174 (N.S. C.A.).

65. *Public Authorities Protection Act*, R.S.O. 1990, c. P.38, s. 7.

66. *Berendsen v. Ontario*, (2001), 42 CELR (NS) 1 (SCC).

67. *Berendsen v. Ontario*, 2008 Ont. C.J. The decision is being appealed.

68. *Hoffman v. Monsanto Canada Inc.*, (2007), 28 CELR (3d) 165 (Sask. C.A.).

69. U. Franklin, *The Real World of Technology* (Montreal: CBC Enterprises, 1990), 120–1.

70. G. Torres, 'Some observations on the role of social change on the courts', *Drake Law Review* 54 (2007): 895–908, at 902.

4

Policy Instruments in Canadian Environmental Policy

Mark Winfield

Policy instruments can be broadly defined as the tools employed by governments to change the behaviour of individuals, communities, and organizations in ways needed to achieve desired policy outcomes, such as reductions in emissions of greenhouse gases or the production and use of toxic substances. As such, the employment of policy instruments represents a crucial stage in the policy cycle.[1] Policy instruments are the means by which governments move from the identification of problems and the changes in behaviour needed to address them, to the actual implementation of policy responses. They are the means through which governments attempt to translate policy into reality. As a result, the choices governments make about policy instruments have a large influence on whether stated policy goals are actually achieved. Part of the explanation for Canada's failure to meet its commitment under the Kyoto Protocol to reduce its greenhouse gas (GHG) emissions by six per cent relative to a 1990 baseline by 2008–2012, with emissions rising by 27 per cent instead,[2] may lie with poor choices of policy instrument made by a succession of federal governments in pursuit of the Kyoto target.

This chapter examines different types of policy instruments available to Canadian governments for achieving environmental policy goals. These include approaches intended to directly change behaviour, such as law and regulation; the application of taxes, charges, and subsidies to activities that governments wish to discourage or encourage; the dissemination of information about pollutant emissions and other environmental impacts of human activity; the creation of markets for ecological services like the absorption of air pollution; encouraging voluntary action by companies, communities, and individuals to reduce the environmental impact of their activities; and public information and education campaigns intended to motivate action at the individual, household, or classroom level. The role of less direct approaches to achieving environmental policy goals, such as procedural instruments like environmental impact assessment processes, is considered as well.

The chapter explores the ways in which governments approach decision-making about what tools might be best suited to dealing with a particular environmental policy problem, including such factors as the potential effectiveness, efficiency, and fairness of different options and their political and policy acceptability. Finally the chapter examines the Canadian experience with the use of different policy instruments in environmental policy.

One of the most striking aspects of Canadian practice, noted even by international observers, has been a lack of innovation in environmental policy implementation by Canadian governments. In comparison to other developed countries, Canadian governments have tended to rely on a very limited range of tools when pursuing environmental policy goals, principally regulation and subsidy. Similarly, compared to jurisdictions in the United States and the European Union, Canadian governments have rarely combined different instruments into comprehensive systems or 'regimes' capable of achieving the kinds of deeper changes in economic and social behaviour, such as major economy-wide reductions in emissions of greenhouse gases, that are widely seen to be necessary to advance the environmental sustainability of industrialized societies like Canada's.[3] The chapter explores some of the reasons for these outcomes, including the political, policy, and institutional barriers to such approaches in Canada. It also examines the question of the ambitiousness of the environmental policy goals that Canadian governments have set for themselves and the seriousness with which these goals have been pursued.

Types of Policy Instruments

Regulatory Instruments

Regulatory instruments have been the traditional tool of choice in Canadian environmental policy, particularly for the prevention and control of pollution. Regulatory tools rely on the establishment of legal obligations based in legislation that prohibit certain types of behaviour or that require the explicit permission of the government to engage in specified activities. Where such permission is given it typically may be subject to whatever conditions the government may choose to impose, such as the installation of equipment to limit emissions of pollutants. In effect, the state acts as a trustee of environmental resources, controlling access to them and making decisions about who should be allowed to use the environment for what purposes.

This regulatory model is strongly reflected in Canadian environmental legislation, particularly at the provincial level. Provincial environmental protection statutes typically prohibit engaging in activities that will result in pollution,[4] unless approvals have been obtained from the provincial environment ministry, and the activity is carried out in accordance with the terms and conditions of those approvals.[5] In addition, regulations may be adopted under environmental legislation that set specific rules in relation to particular activities. Regulations might be employed to prohibit the use or release into the environment of certain toxic substances or limit emissions of particular pollutants from specific industrial facilities or sectors.

Under environmental legislation, penalties are usually attached for engaging in prohibited activities without appropriate approvals, or carrying out activities that violate rules and conditions imposed by government. These penalties typically take the form of fines or imprisonment on conviction for an offence. Fines for environmental offences grew significantly in Canada from the mid-1980s onwards. Maximum fines under the initial round of environmental legislation adopted in Canada the early 1970s, were in the range of $5,000–$10,000 per offence. In practice, the actual fines imposed for environmental offences were typically far below even these modest maximums, with the result that violators simply regarded the penalties they received as the 'cost of doing business'. Major offences under the federal Canadian Environmental Protection Act, enacted in its current form in 1999, for example, can now be subject to penalties of up to one million dollars and up to five years imprisonment.[6] In practice, the application of maximum fines remains rare.

More broadly, the vigour with which Canadian governments have been willing to actually enforce environmental laws has been a longstanding issue in Canadian environmental policy.[7] Federal and provincial enforcement efforts peaked in the mid-late 1980s during the second wave of modern public concern for the environment in Canada, and fell off markedly in the 1990s as the public salience of the issue declined.[8]

Economic Instruments

Regulatory approaches, when they have been applied vigorously, have been highly effective in Canada in reducing pollution from industrial sources. The implementation of regulations by the governments of Ontario and Québec in the mid-1980s to control emissions of the pollutants that caused acid rain resulted in reductions in emissions of sulphur dioxide from the targeted sources, largely base metal smelting and coal-fired electricity generation facilities, by more than 50 per cent relative to a 1980 baseline by the mid-1990s. The emission reduction goals of the federal–provincial Eastern Canada Acid Rain Control program were achieved as a result.[9] Similarly, regulations have been used to successfully phase out the manufacturing and import of highly toxic or otherwise problematic substances, like polychlorinated biphenyls (PCBs) or substances that deplete the ozone layer.

Despite these successes, regulatory tools have been subject to criticism since the 1970s for being inefficient, inconsistently applied, and likely less effective in stimulating the kinds of deeper systemic changes in economic activities (such as dramatically reducing the use of fossil fuels) that seem likely to be necessary to ensure the sustainability of the global biosphere. As a result, economic policy instruments have been widely proposed as a complement or even alternative to regulatory strategies for achieving environmental policy goals.[10]

Economic instruments can take a number of different forms. Taxes or charges can be imposed on activities that governments wish to discourage or phase out. Such charges have the effect of raising the costs of these activities relative to alternative paths. Carbon taxes, which are based on the carbon content of fuels and, by implication, the amounts of GHGs likely to be generated through their use, for example, have been widely proposed as a means of achieving economy-wide reductions in the use of fossil fuels, like coal and oil, to combat global climate change. Sweden has been among the most prominent users of environmental taxes, imposing substantial taxes on the carbon and sulphur content of fossil fuels in the early 1990s.[11]

Governments can also pursue strategies of providing subsidies to encourage behaviour or the development of technologies that are seen to be more environmentally sustainable. The federal government, for example, has introduced a subsidy for the production of energy from renewable sources, such as wind power.[12] The government of Ontario, for its part, offers a fixed price above the usual market price for electricity generated from renewable sources.[13] Federal and provincial subsidies were central in the near universal installation of sewage treatment systems by Ontario municipalities in the Great Lakes Basin, a development that has been fundamental to the recovery of the water quality in the lakes over the past four decades.[14] Subsidies can also be employed as complements to regulatory initiatives to assist affected business in dealing with the capital costs of installing new pollution prevention or control technologies. Federal regulations on water pollution from the pulp and paper sector, first introduced in the 1970s, were accompanied by substantial subsidies for the 'modernization' of pulp and paper mills.[15]

Integrated strategies of environmental taxation, subsidization, and broader tax reform are sometimes referred to as ecological fiscal reform (EFR).[16] Under EFR strategies, the funds raised through environmental taxes and charges are recycled into subsidies for more environmentally sustainable behaviour or technologies, and even into broader reductions in employment and income taxes. The revenue from Sweden's carbon and sulphur taxes, for example, has been used to reduce personal income taxes.[17] Such strategies are generally seen to enhance the political acceptability of environmental taxes by ensuring no increase in the overall tax burden on households and businesses.

Rather than governments trying to prescribe the behaviour of individuals and companies through regulation, economic instruments rely on the responses of these actors to price signals in the marketplace in order to achieve policy goals. A potential weakness with the use of environmental taxes and charges is that it can be difficult to predict the precise level of taxation needed to prompt sufficient changes in activity to obtain the desired policy outcome.

A second form of economic instrument involves the creation of markets for certain types of activities, like the emission of pollutants or the harvesting of natural resources. The underlying theory is that by creating a limited number of permits to engage in a targeted activity, and then allowing market participants to decide whether to purchase the number of permits required to continue their existing activities (like emitting greenhouse gases) or to change their behaviour to reduce the number of permits they need, the resulting markets will establish economic values for the permitted activities. Companies will then make the most economically rational decisions, from their perspectives, about what strategy to pursue. Economists argue that these types of trading systems are more economically efficient than traditional regulatory models.[18]

Actual experience with emission trading systems is limited. A trading system for sulphur dioxide was established under amendments to the US federal Clean Air Act in 1990, and is generally regarded as an environmental and economic success.[19] The cap-and-trade system for industrial emitters of greenhouse gases, established by the European Union in response to the Kyoto Protocol has been less effective.[20] In the EU system the price of carbon emission permits collapsed as a result of the granting of permits to industrial GHG emitters well in excess of actual emission levels at the time of the establishment of the system.[21] Attempts are now being made to redesign the system to address these shortcomings.

Voluntary Instruments

A third type of policy instrument, which became highly prevalent in Canada in the 1990s, is voluntary initiatives. For public policy purposes, these instruments are typically characterized by public challenges to industry by governments to reduce their emissions of pollutants in exchange for public recognition of their performance or, alternatively, avoidance of future regulatory requirements. Voluntary initiatives dominated Canadian environmental policy in the 1990s, with two programs—the Accelerated Reduction and Elimination of Toxics (ARET) launched in 1994 and the Voluntary Climate Registry (VCR) initiated in 1995—constituting the federal government's principal initiatives on industrial sources of toxic substances and GHG emission respectively. Under the ARET program, industrial facilities were challenged to reduce their emissions of persistent, bioaccumulative, and toxic substance emissions by 90 per cent and emissions of all other toxic substance emissions by 50 per cent by the year 2000.[22] The VCR encouraged industry, business, and government to make public commitments and to develop and implement voluntary action plans for reducing their greenhouse gas emissions.

Voluntary initiatives have been highly controversial. Governments and industry actors have argued that voluntary action avoids the developmental and administrative costs of regulations and promotes a more cooperative approach to achieving environmental policy goals. Critics of voluntary initiatives as the foundation of public policy strategies on major environmental issues take the view that they are likely to be ineffective due to the lack of consequences for failures to achieve policy goals, particularly where there is no credible underlying threat of regulatory action in the event of such outcomes; their vulnerability to 'free rider' problems, where firms or organizations who decline to participate in a voluntary initiative avoid the costs incurred by their competitors who do partake; and the lack of effective monitoring and reporting systems. Concerns were also raised regarding the potential for voluntary initiatives to reintroduce the closed door, industry–government bipartiate bargaining[23] model that defined the early stages Canadian environmental policy formulation, with industrial actors preempting the establishment of more vigorous policy goals by 'volunteering' to pursue less ambitious goals.[24]

The use of voluntary instruments has been less controversial on a smaller scale, particularly when dealing with highly specialized situations where deployment of the full range of coercive and economic tools available to governments may not be necessary or appropriate. The widespread implementation of changes in practices in Canadian dentists' offices to prevent the release of mercury contained in waste dental amalgam into municipal sewer systems, for example, was initiated through a voluntary memorandum of agreement signed between the Canadian Dental Association and Environment Canada,[25] although requirements for waste dental mercury capture were also ultimately established through municipal by-laws and provincial regulations.[26]

Informational Instruments

Although governments have collected environmental data and information from the beginnings of the establishment of government agencies concerned with the management of natural resources and the environment, the gathering and dissemination of environmental information really only came into its own as an instrument for achieving specific policy outcomes in the 1990s. The first pollutant release and transfer registry (PRTR), the United State's Toxic Release Inventory (TRI),[27] was established in 1987 in the aftermath of the Bophal chemical plant disaster in India. Under these systems, facilities are required to report annually on their releases and off-site disposal of specified lists of pollutants. The information is then made available to the public. By the mid-1990s, the emerging World Wide Web and developments in web server technologies offered enormously enhanced public access to the information collected through pollutant release inventory systems, and opened major new possibilities for the use of this information. Customized user designed data searches and the combination of pollutant release data with geographic, demographic, and economic information became possible.[28] Canada was the second country in the world to establish a pollutant release inventory, the National Pollutant Release Inventory (NPRI), in 1992.[29]

The direct impact of the release of PRTR data on facility environmental behaviour remains a matter of debate. Claims have been made that PRTRs have outperformed regulatory initiatives in driving reductions in pollutant releases.[30] While there is anecdotal evidence of changes in individual facility performance in response to rankings as large sources of pollutant releases and transfers in PRTR reports, the impact of public PRTR data releases *per se*, versus other factors, such as regulatory initiatives, at the aggregate level, is much less certain.[31] On the other hand, the value of PRTR data in the identification of leading sources of priority pollutants, evaluations of program and policy instrument effectiveness, and raising community and facility awareness of emissions that otherwise would not be identified, is more firmly established.[32]

Public Outreach and Education

Environmental education and awareness initiatives have generally been regarded as the 'softest' or least coercive of the substantive environmental policy instruments available to governments. Like voluntary initiatives, education and awareness programs only encourage rather than require action and do not provide direct economic incentives for changes in behaviour. In practice, education and awareness initiatives can provide a number of important functions as parts of overall strategies for environmental sustainability. Formal (i.e., school classroom) and informal educational initiatives are central to building constituencies for policy action both in the present and future.

Education and awareness strategies are also essential to motivating and sustaining behavioural changes at the individual and household level. In Canada, the widespread participation of households in increasingly ambitious waste diversion activities, transitioning in some communities, like the City of Toronto, from a simple process of taking bags of garbage to the curb every week, to sorting household wastes into six or seven streams,[33] resulting in waste diversion rates from disposal exceeding 40 per cent,[34] with little or no direct economic incentive or regulatory enforcement, highlights the potential impacts on behaviour of effective education and awareness initiatives.

Other Types of Policy Instruments

Although regulatory, economic, informational, voluntary, and educational tools are the focal points of current discussions of instrument choice in Canadian environmental policy, they do not constitute an exhaustive list of policy instruments available to governments.[35] Governments may employ procedural instruments with more indirect effects, focusing on modifying decision-making processes with respect to policies and projects that may affect the environment, rather than directly changing the behaviour of individuals or firms.[36] Environmental impact assessment processes, for example, which are intended to evaluate the potential overall environmental effects of projects and assess their rationale and the availability of alternative ways of meeting identified needs, before they proceed, have been established at the federal and provincial levels in Canada.[37]

Organizational tools, like the creation of specific agencies within or outside of government to act as focal points for policy development, implementation and evaluation, or to provide specific services have also been widely employed. Environmental commissioner's offices were created in the mid-1990s at the federal level and in Ontario. The federal Commissioner for Environment and Sustainable Development (CESD)[38] and the Environmental Commissioner of Ontario,[39] are mandated to report publicly to Parliament and the Ontario legislature respectively, on the effectiveness of environmental policies and the overall environmental performance of federal and Ontario governments. The commissioners' offices were intended to strengthen the overall level of effort put into addressing environmental issues by governments by establishing permanent independent public evaluation and reporting mechanisms.

Combinations of Instruments and Regimes

Although academic discussions of policy instruments tend to make sharp distinctions between regulatory, economic, voluntary, and other types of instruments, in practice it is rare for any type of instrument to be used in isolation. In fact, the most effective environmental policy strategies have used combinations of instruments to achieve their goals. The successful strategies pursued by Canadian governments with respect to acid rain control in the 1980s and water pollution from the pulp-and-paper sector in the early 1990s, for example, employed a combination of regulatory requirements to reduce emissions and discharges, and substantial subsidies to the effected industries to assist them with the installation of new equipment to meet the new requirements.[40]

One of the best examples of a highly integrated strategy employing a variety of policy instruments comes from the US state of California in the area of energy efficiency. Over the past 30 years, following a successful 1976 proposition[41] that no new nuclear power stations be built until a solution is found for the management of waste nuclear fuel, it is estimated that the state has reduced is peak demand for electricity by more than 12,000 megawatts relative to what it would have been under business as usual conditions.[42] This amounts to a reduction in electricity demand comparable to the output of three nuclear power stations the size of Ontario's Darlington facility, the largest in Canada. The reductions were achieved in the context of a rapidly growing population and economy.

The aggressive use of standards and codes (i.e., regulatory instruments) to push low energy efficiency products like older models of air conditioners and refrigerators out of the marketplace has been one of the foundations of California's strategy. The state has adopted a cycle of updating its energy efficiency standards every three years, a practice now followed in 16 other states, creating an expectation of continuous improvement in the energy efficiency performance of products, buildings, and services.[43] In California, the standards and codes upgrading system was integrated with a host of other instruments, including pricing energy to ensure that it reflects the real costs of energy production, financial incentives for the adoption of energy efficient technologies and practices, investments in research on energy efficient technology design and program evaluation, aggressive outreach and education programs on energy efficiency carefully targeted at specific audiences and markets, and sophisticated monitoring and information systems to provide feedback on program effectiveness into an overall strategy.[44] At the same time, it is important to note that the California system was not implemented as a complete strategy from the outset. Rather the system has evolved incrementally, through a process of experimentation, feedbacks, and modification over three decades, with the California Energy Commission playing an integrative role.

Strategies that rely on single instruments or simple combinations of instruments, like regulation and subsidy, can be adequate when the policy goals being sought are relatively limited, such as the reduction of emissions of a specific pollutant from a specific industrial sector. The achievement of deeper structural, economy-wide changes in behaviour is more likely to require the use of an integrated regime that uses a combination of different instruments. California's strategy, for example, is intended to produce permanent long-term changes in the state's overall patterns of energy use and in its markets for energy consuming products, as opposed to obtaining marginal adjustments to a very limited range of existing activities.

Approaches to Choosing Policy Instruments

Given the range of potential options available to them to address a given problem or goal, the question arises of how governments make decisions about what tools to employ. Typically, either implicitly or explicitly, a number of criteria are taken into consideration.

Effectiveness

Perhaps the most basic consideration is the question of whether a particular instrument will be effective in achieving the desired policy outcome. Certainty of the results is particularly important where human health and safety are directly at risk. The timeliness of the result can also be an important consideration. Economic instruments, such as environmental taxes and charges, may well result in the required changes in behaviour but the timeframes within which consumer responses to the higher prices that result from such strategies will occur may be uncertain. Regulatory instruments, when backed with a credible expectation of enforcement, are generally seen to offer relatively high certainty of outcomes,[15] and generally set the timelines within which these results need to be achieved.

Efficiency

A second factor likely to be considered by policymakers is the potential efficiency of different options. In the context of competing demands on the resources of government and society, governments will generally seek to achieve their policy goals at the lowest possible cost, with the intent of maximizing the resources available to address other problems. Efficiency can be defined in terms of a number of different dimensions. These aspects include the achievement of the desired result at minimum cost to society as a whole, to the government agencies that will have to implement and administer the chosen instruments, and to the individuals and organizations whose behaviour will be affected. Governments facing significant resource or financial constraints, for example, may tend towards the use of lower-cost instruments like voluntary initiatives, despite the fact that they may be less effective than options like regulation; the latter are seen to be associated with higher administrative costs.[46]

The regulatory policies adopted from time to time by Canadian governments have generally defined efficiency in purely economic terms. These policies have required that the environmental and health benefits of regulatory initiatives in particular be demonstrated to exceed their costs to governments and the economy as a whole.[47] These types of requirements have presented significant barriers to the use of regulatory instruments because it is generally easier to assess the cost of installing additional pollution prevention and control equipment at industrial facilities than to establish the economic value of the environmental and health effects that will be avoided as a result of the adoption of new technologies or practices.[48]

The apparent relative inefficiency of regulatory strategies in terms of the costs related to their development, administration, and enforcement, and the degree to which they may limit innovation in the responses of the affected firms and individuals, has been a central feature of critiques of these tools. In contrast, it has been widely argued that economic instruments offer means of achieving policy goals at lower costs, in part by permitting the affected actors to make their own choices about how to respond to the price signals provided by such instruments.[49]

Distribution and Fairness of Costs and Benefits

A third consideration is the likely distribution of the costs and benefits of a given strategy. In general, it is seen to be difficult to use relatively more coercive (and potentially effective) tools, such as regulatory and economic instruments, where the resulting costs will be concentrated among a small number firms or sectors, and the benefits widely spread. Those who would suffer the costs of such strategies have strong incentives to resist them strongly, while the benefits may be so widely distributed that no specific constituency emerges to argue for action.[50]

The fairness of the distribution of the costs and benefits of a given choice of instruments within society must also be considered. Is the strategy consistent, for example, with the widely accepted polluter pays principle[51] that those who generate the pollution should internalize the resulting environmental costs? Does the strategy impose disproportionate costs on vulnerable sectors of society, or conversely offer disproportionate benefits for other members of society? The problem of free riders has been central to critiques of the use of voluntary instruments in Canadian environmental policy.[52] The option of free riding is typically much more difficult where economic or regulatory instruments are employed. Fairness concerns have also been raised with respect to the impacts of emission trading systems on the release pollutants, such as smog precursors or heavy metals (e.g., mercury), that are likely to have impacts in the vicinity of emitting facilities. Facilities may 'buy' their way out of emission reduction requirements by purchasing emission permits rather than actually reducing their emissions. As a result, the communities who are most heavily affected by the pollutants may experience no benefit from reductions in the overall reduction in releases.[53]

Political and Policy Factors

In addition to these considerations inherent in a particular instrument and in relation to a specific environmental problem, a number of other factors are likely to enter into the decision-making process. In addition to being effective, efficient, and fair, policy instruments must be seen to be politically acceptable by decision-makers. These considerations can have a major impact on instrument choice.

During the 1980s and 1990s, neo-conservative, or more appropriately neo-Liberal, ideas about the role of governments dominated at the federal and provincial levels. These models emphasized the reduction of governmental interference in private sector economic activity. Instead, the role of markets as the most efficient mechanisms for allocating access to resources, including environmental resources, was highlighted, with the state's role being focused on the facilitation of the efficient functioning of markets.[54]

One of the practical manifestations of the prevalence of these ideas was the establishment at the federal level and in many provinces of increasingly elaborate 'regulatory management' systems. In some cases these systems incorporated explicit biases against the use of regulatory instruments and typically established extensive analytical and procedural tests, such as requirements of cost–benefit analyses demonstrating that there would be 'net' economic benefits from environmental, health, or safety initiatives that applied when government agencies did propose the use of regulatory tools. The effect of these approaches—reflected, for example, in Government of Canada's regulatory policies adopted in 1986, 1994, and 1999, and in the work of the Red Tape Commission that existed in Ontario between 1995 and 2003[55]—was to make the use of regulatory instruments in environmental policy virtually impossible. These policies were a major factor in the apparent enthusiasm of Canadian environmental agencies for voluntary, non-regulatory approaches in the 1990s.

In a democratic society, the public acceptability of different options is also a key consideration. There is, for example, strong evidence that a carbon tax could be a highly effective policy instrument for combating climate change.[56] However, concerns over the public acceptability of the higher energy prices that would result from such a tax led Canadian political leaders, including former Prime Minister Jean Chrétien to explicitly rule out the option. Instead, federal and provincial climate change strategies throughout the 1990s and the early years of the current decade emphasized voluntary action, subsidies for GHG emission reduction technologies and initiatives, and public education and outreach efforts.[57]

Other factors may also enter the equation. International trade agreements, like the North American Free Trade Agreement (NAFTA) and the World Trade Organization (WTO) Agreements, to which Canada is party, impose important restrictions on the instruments that may be employed to address environmental problems that might also affect international trade. In addition to requiring that any policies adopted be demonstrated to be 'necessary' and treat domestically produced and imported goods equally, the 'least trade restrictive' (as opposed to most effective, efficient, and fair) approach to achieving policy objectives is to be taken. The investor–state provisions contained in Chapter 11 of the NAFTA may further increase the reluctance of government agencies to pursue the use of regulatory instruments.[58] Successive federal regulatory policies, including the 2007 Cabinet Directive on Regulatory Streamlining, have placed a very strong emphasis on the need for compliance with international trade rules in the selection and design of policy instruments with respect to health, safety, and the environment.[59] Much less emphasis is placed on compliance with other international commitments related to human rights, health, safety, security, and the environment.[60]

Federal–provincial relations may be an additional consideration in instrument choice, particularly at the federal level. Traditionally, provincial governments have strongly opposed the use of regulatory tools by the federal government in the environmental field. Rather, provinces have preferred that they be the primary regulator of industrial sources of pollution and that the federal government restrict itself to a supporting role, principally through the use of fiscal instruments to assist firms in installing additional pollution prevention and control technologies.[61]

Combinations of instruments can be employed to overcome political and policy barriers to particular strategies. As noted earlier, subsidies have often been employed to address objections from particular regions or sectors to the implementation of significant regulatory initiatives. At the same time, there can be very strong disincentives to attempt implementing more sophisticated integrated regimes or to employing a number of different policy instruments simultaneously in the absence of overwhelming political support. Such approaches not only require much greater policy development capacity on the part of the government agencies advancing such approaches,[62] but also face increased risk of blockage within the governmental decision-making process given the number of specific components to which challenges may be raised inside or outside of government.

The Canadian Environmental Policy Experience

Regulatory tools have been the primary environmental policy instrument used by Canadian governments from the time of the initial emergence of public health concerns related to pollution in late nineteenth century.[63] Regulatory instruments have provided the foundation of provincial and territorial legislative regimes for the management, prevention and control of pollution (particularly from industrial sources), and the management of natural resources. Regulation has also been the dominant instrument used by the federal government when it has intervened in relation to pollution from particular sectors or in relation to specific substances of concern.

In the Canadian experience, regulatory instruments have demonstrated a record of high effectiveness when employed vigorously. Regulatory tools provided a structure for addressing the most egregious individual industrial sources of air and water pollution in the early stages of environmental policy formation in Canada.[64] More targeted uses of regulatory instruments in the 1980s and early 1990s led to major reductions in industrial emissions causing acid rain, as noted above, and in water pollution from the pulp-and-paper sector. In the latter case, new federal and provincial requirements established in the early 1990s resulted in reductions in discharges of chlorinated dioxins and furans of nearly 99 per cent, while releases of biological oxygen demand materials fell by 94 per cent and releases of total suspended solids decreased by 70 per cent between 1987 and 2000.[65] Regulatory tools were also instrumental in the elimination of lead from virtually all gasoline in Canada by the early 1990s;[66] leaded gasoline had been a major source of atmospheric lead pollution.

Regulation has always been the favoured response to environmental problems by the public.[67] However, by the mid-1990s a combination of factors came together to significantly reduce the enthusiasm of governments for regulatory measures. In the context of worsening economic conditions, the status of the environment as a top-of-mind public concern went into steep decline. At the same time, major reductions in the budgets and, as a result, capacities of environmental agencies, driven by concerns over the overall fiscal situation of Canadian governments, were implemented. The increasing dominance of neo-liberal perspectives on the role of government and, at the federal level, a crisis of federalism flowing from the outcome of the 1995 Québec referendum, completed a near 'perfect storm' against the use of regulatory instruments in Canadian environmental policy.[68]

Rather, at the federal and provincial levels the emphasis shifted to a focus on promoting voluntary action by industry to address environmental problems. Two high-profile, voluntary, non-regulatory initiatives—ARET and the VCR—dominated Canadian environmental policy during the late 1990s. Indeed, environmental policy discussions in Canada came to be defined by the regulation versus voluntary instruments debate.[69] By the early years of the new millennium, however, the empirical evidence of the failures of the high profile voluntary initiatives like the VCR and ARET were becoming increasingly obvious. In the case of the VCR, by 2002 participants in the program only accounted for 55 per cent of industrial GHG emissions, and barely 20 per cent of those participants were actually reporting their GHG emissions. More than half of those reported major increases in their GHG emissions since 1990.[70] ARET had sought a 90 per cent reduction in emissions of listed persistent bioaccumulative toxic substances between 1994 and 2000. The actual reduction achieved by reporting firms was 52 per cent, with the bulk of the reductions coming from the base metal smelting and pulp-and-paper sectors. Interestingly these sectors had been the subject of major *regulatory* initiatives in the late 1980s and early 1990s,[71] with the implication that responses to those requirements, rather than the ARET program, were the primary driver of the reported emission reductions.

Public interventions by medical professions regarding the health consequences of the failures of existing, largely voluntary, approaches on air quality issues[72] further reinforced the case for the use of more vigorous tools in the achievement of policy goals. The final blows to voluntarism as a central pillar of Canadian environmental policy came from the judicial inquiries into the drinking water contamination disasters that occurred in Walkerton, Ontario and North Battleford, Saskatchewan in May 2000 and April 2001 respectively. Seven people died and more than 2,300 became seriously ill in Walkerton; between 5,800 and 7,100 people were affected in North Battleford.

In both cases the inquiries highlighted the role of 'voluntary compliance' in failures by the relevant provincial governments to act on evidence of poor drinking water system management practices before the disasters.[73] In the case of Walkerton, the role of the province's policies against the adoption of new regulatory requirements that might have prevented or mitigated the impact of the disaster was also highlighted.[74]

By the middle of the current decade, Canadian governments were signalling a much greater willingness to employ regulatory instruments in environmental policy. In the context of the re-emergence of high levels of concern over environmental issues, particularly climate change,[75] proposals for voluntary action by governments are now clearly seen as indications of a lack of seriousness about taking action. Even the federal government of Prime Minister Harper, which was initially strongly adverse to significant action on climate change, has proposed both new legislation and an extensive package of regulatory initiatives to address both climate change and air quality issues, especially those from industrial sources.[76] Whatever the shortcomings of the specifics of these proposals,[77] they make it clear that governments now perceive the need to employ regulatory measures to respond to the public's expectations of action on environmental issues. At the same time, it is important to note that various 'smart regulation' initiatives set in motion at the federal and provincial levels in the early years of this decade have continued to enhance 'regulatory management' regimes and the barriers that they imply with respect to the use of regulatory instruments by governments.[78]

In comparison to the roles of regulatory and voluntary tools in the actual implementation of Canadian environmental policy, there has been extensive discussion in Canada of the potential roles for economic instruments in environmental policy since the 1992 World Conference on environment and development but, until very recently, almost no application of these tools. In fact, international assessments of Canada's environmental policy performance have highlighted Canada's failure to employ environmental taxes and charges, particularly in relation to water resources,[79] but this criticism applied in virtually all areas. Where environmental charges had been imposed in Canada, they had been employed for administrative cost recovery purposes, rather than being set at levels high enough to motivate changes in behaviour.[80]

The introduction of, first, a modest carbon tax in Québec in the fall of 2007,[81] and then a much more substantial and comprehensive carbon tax regime in British Columbia in July 2008,[82] may indicate a shift in the willingness of Canadian governments to employ environmental taxes and charges. At the same time, many provinces and territories, particularly those with strongly resource-based economies—Alberta, Saskatchewan, and the northern territories—have objected strongly to the carbon tax concept.[83] The defeat of the federal Liberal Party, which had made a major ecological fiscal reform initiative, including a comprehensive carbon tax, a central element of its election platform[84] in the October 2008 federal election may cause other Canadian governments to hesitate to pursue such initiatives.

Discussions of cap-and-trade systems for large final emitters of GHGs have been central to Canada's debates on climate change policy over the past decade.[85] However, as of mid-2008, only Alberta had actually adopted such a system. The Alberta initiative has been subject to widespread criticism for its focus on reducing the *intensity* of GHG emissions per unit of economic output, rather than implementing a 'hard' cap on total emissions, and as being likely to facilitate continued growth in the province's emissions as a result.[86] Experiments with cap-and-trade systems for pollution have otherwise been limited to the creation in 2001 of a trading system for sulphur dioxide and nitrogen oxides (smog and acid rain precursors) from large sources in Ontario.[87] However, the Ontario system has been widely criticized as a flawed design,[88] and in the context of the province's withdrawal from a market model for its electricity system very few trades have actually occurred.[89]

Canada was initially a leader in the use of informational instruments in environmental policy, establishing the world's second comprehensive PRTR, the National Pollutant Release Inventory (NPRI).[90] After an initial period of expansion, including the addition of criteria for air pollutants and the lowering of reporting thresholds for priority toxic substances, development of the NPRI has stalled and the program is now said to be 'under review'.[91] Launched in 2001, Ontario's own industrial air emission reporting program, which had included a range of pollutants beyond those covered in the NPRI, including GHGs, was effectively terminated in 2006.[92]

Public education and outreach strategies have been ubiquitous in Canadian environmental policy, dominating, for example, along with the VCR, federal and provincial climate change strategies over the past decade. The effectiveness of these tools in achieving environmental policy goals in the absence of other instruments has always been the subject of debate, although some cases, such as municipal waste diversion, suggest that they have been more useful than widely thought.

Conclusions

Reflecting on the Canadian environmental policy experience, a number of observations are possible regarding Canadian governments' approach to the selection and use of policy instruments. Perhaps the most striking feature, particularly in comparison to practices in Europe and the United States has been, until very recently, the relatively limited range of tools that have actually been employed by Canadian governments in an environmental policy context. Regulatory instruments, occasionally supplemented by fiscal instruments in the form of subsidy, have dominated the Canadian experience. The major experiments with voluntary instruments in the 1990s largely ended in failure. While there have been extensive discussions around the use of a range of economic instruments, particularly environmental taxes and charges and cap-and-trade initiatives, it has only been in the last year that there has been serious movement towards actual implementation of these types of instruments. Even then, the widespread employment of environmental taxes and charges in Canada remains in doubt, particularly in light of the defeat of the federal Liberal's 'Green Shift' proposal in the 2008 federal election.

A second outstanding feature of the Canadian experience has been the tendency of Canadian governments to employ policy instruments individually, or in simple combinations, typically the regulation plus subsidy approach, rather than to integrate the full range of available tools into comprehensive regimes along the lines of, for example, California's approach to energy efficiency or some of the approaches to climate change seen within the European Union. The apparent unwillingness of Canadian governments to employ a fuller range of potentially effective instruments, or to bring combinations of instruments together in overall strategies, represents a serious barrier to the achievement of the deeper changes in economic structure and social behaviour, such as economy-wide reductions in the use of fossil fuels, which are needed to advance environmental sustainability.

This Canadian experience can be explained by a number of factors. At the level of the selection of specific policy instruments, it is apparent that a broader range of policy and political factors enter into the discussion than the 'rational' considerations of effectiveness, efficiency, and fairness in relation to the achievement of stated policy goals. Formal regulatory policies, international trade rules, public opinion, non-governmental actors, and federal–provincial relations all influence instrument choice at least as much as the inherent characteristics of the available tools. The effect of these factors is to frequently drive decisions away from the potentially most effective approach and instead in the direction of the least political and administrative resistance. The result can be both to discourage innovation and experimentation, particularly involving regulatory, economic, and informational instruments and, more broadly, attempts to implement comprehensive regimes except in rare cases where there is very strong political support for such approaches.

More systemic explanations for lack of innovation and employment of integrated regimes in Canada also need to be considered. In general, Canadian governments have tended to seek a comparatively limited range of goals through their environmental policy initiatives. The focus of environmental policy has been relatively narrow, attempting to reduce, for example, emissions of particular pollutants from specific sectors and sources. Conventional regulatory instruments, or simple combinations of tools (e.g., regulation plus subsidy), may be entirely adequate and indeed have been highly effective when employed with vigour in relation to such goals.

What Canadian governments have generally not done is to seek the kinds of broader, systemic policy outcomes that jurisdictions who have employed more innovative, integrated, and ambitious regimes have attempted to achieve. California's approach to energy efficiency for example, is not motivated by a desire to improve the energy efficiency performance of individual products *per se*, but rather is an effort to achieve long-term structural changes throughout the state's economy and society to increase its energy efficiency and reduce the need for new energy sources. It is precisely this kind of broad, long-term policy objective that Canadian governments have been reluctant to embrace with respect to environmental policy.

Herein may lie the real explanation for the lack of innovation and integration in instrument choice in environmental policy by Canadian governments. The problem is not so much one of a lack of imagination and innovation in selecting and implementing policy instruments, but rather a lack of ambition in terms of the policy goals being sought by governments in the first place. The basic range of tools employed by Canadian governments has been appropriate for the kinds of environmental policy goals being sought. The weakness with this approach is that while it may produce successes in relation to specific problems, it does little to alter the overall trajectory of Canada's economy and society in relation to sustainability. Climate change in particular presents an especially serious problem with respect to Canada's conventional approach to environmental policy. An effective response to climate change, reducing Canada's absolute GHG emissions on the scale and timeframes required by Canada's international obligations, will require changes in technology and behaviour throughout the economy. Canada's business-as-usual approach to environmental policy is unlikely to be able to produce such outcomes. A more ambitious and integrative approach to both the establishment of environmental policy goals and their implementation will be needed.

Although such a departure from conventional approaches to environmental policy in Canada faces serious challenges, the recent initiatives of some provincial governments, such as the carbon tax and broader climate change strategies being introduced by British Columbia and Québec suggest that there is some willingness to embrace these kinds of more ambitious policy goals and employ more comprehensive and integrated strategies for achieving them. The fate of these initiatives in the face of increasing resistance will be indicative of the likelihood of serious Canadian progress towards sustainability over the next few years.

Questions for Review

1.   What are the main policy instruments that Canada's governments have traditionally used to respond to environmental issues?
2.   How useful or effective are regulatory approaches by governments for achieving environmental policy goals?
3.   Does voluntarism have any role to play in an effective environmental policy regime?
4.   Should Canada's governments put more or less emphasis in environmental policy on educational and information strategies?

Notes

1. On the 'policy cycle' concept see M. Hessing, M. Howlett and T. Summerville, *Canadian Natural Resource and Environmental Policy: Political Economy and Public Policy*, 2nd ed. (Vancouver: UBC Press, 2005), 102–34.
2. Commissioner for the Environment and Sustainable Development *2006 Report* (Ottawa: Minister of Supply and Services, 2007); 'The Commissioner's Perspective', accessed at http://www.oag-bvg.gc.ca/domino/reports.nsf/html/c20060900ce.html, 22 November 2007.
3. See for example, M. Bramley, *The Case for Deep Reductions: Canada's Role in Preventing Dangerous Climate Change* (Ottawa: Pembina Institute and David Suzuki Foundation, 2005).
4. See, for example the Ontario *Environmental Protection Act* R.S.O. 1990, Chapter E-19, s.14.
5. Ontario *Environmental Protection Act*, s.9.
6. Canadian Environmental Protection Act, 1999, (1999 c-33) ss.272-274.
7. See, for example, K. Webb, 'Between Rocks and Hard Places: Bureaucrats, the Law and Pollution Control', in R. Paehlke and D. Torgeson, eds, *Managing Leviathan* (Peterborough: Broadview Press, 1990), 201–28.
8. See, for example, M. Winfield and G. Jenish, *Ontario's Environment and the Common Sense Revolution: A Four-Year Report* (Toronto: Canadian Institute for Environmental Law and Policy, 1999), Figure 1.3.
9. Environment Canada, 'Acid Rain: What's being done, what has Canada done?', http://www.ec.gc.ca/acidrain/done-canada.html, accessed 12 October 2006. Although the program emission reduction goals were achieved, it subsequently became apparent that further emission reductions would be necessary to halt the environmental and health impacts of acid rain.
10. See for example, Organization for Economic Cooperation and Development *Economic Instruments for Environmental Protection* (Paris: OECD, 1989). See also J. Anthony Cassils *Exploring Incentives: An Introduction to Incentives and Economic Instruments for Sustainable Development* (Ottawa: National Round Table on the Environment and Economy, 1993).
11. For a summary of the Swedish program, see the Pembina Institute, available at http://www.fiscallygreen.ca.
12. See http://www.ecoaction.gc.ca/ecoenergy-ecoenergie/index-eng.cfm, accessed 25 January 2008.
13. See http://www.powerauthority.on.ca/SOP/, accessed 25 January 2008.
14. *The Great Lakes Water Quality Agreement/Promises to Keep: Challenges to Meet* (Toronto: Alliance for the Great Lakes, Biodiversity Project, Canadian Environmental Law Association and Great Lakes United, December 2006), avaiable at http://cela.ca/uploads/f8e04c51a8e04041f6f7faa046b03a7c/553GLWQA_promises.pdf, accessed 2 July 2008.
15. K. Harrison, *Passing the Buck: Federalism and Canadian Environmental Policy* (Vancouver: UBC Press, 1996), 103.
16. For an overview of the EFR concept, see http://www.fiscallygreen.ca/efr.html.
17. For a summary of the Swedish program, see the Pembina Institute, available at http://www.fiscallygreen.ca.
18. See, for example, 'The Regulation of Sulphur Dioxide', in G. Bruce Doern, ed., *Getting it Green: Case Studies in Canadian Environmental Regulation* (Toronto: C.D. Howe Institute, 1990), 129–54.
19. See, for example, C. Carlson, D. Burtaw, M. Cropper, and K. Palmer, 'Sulphur Dioxide Control by Electric Utilities: What are the gains from Trade?' (Washington: Resources for the Future, 2000), available at http://www.rff.org/Documents/RFF-DP-98-44-REV.pdf, accessed 8 February 2008.
20. For an overview of the European Union Emission Trading System see *EU Action Against Climate Change: EU Emission Trading* (Brussels: European Communities, 2005), available at http://ec.europa.eu/environment/climat/pdf/emission_trading2_en.pdf, accessed 24 October 2007.

21. 'What price carbon?', *The Economist*, 15 May 2007.

22. See http://www.ec.gc.ca/nopp/aret/en/index.cfm, accessed 8 February 2008.

23. See G. Hoberg, 'Environmental Policy: Alternative Styles', in M. Atkinson, ed., *Governing Canada: Institutions and Public Policy* (Toronto: Harcourt Brace, 1993), 307–42.

24. See K. Harrison, 'Voluntarism and Environmental Governance', in E.O. Parsons, ed., *Governing the Environment* (Toronto: University of Toronto Press, 2001), 207–46.

25. http://www.ec.gc.ca/CEPARegistry/documents/agree/daw.cfm, accessed 18 June 2008.

26. For a description of these types of measures in Ontario see Canada and Ontario, *Canada-Ontario Agreement Respecting the Great Lakes Ecosystem – 2003-2003 Biennial Progress Report* (Toronto: Ontario Ministry of the Environment and Environment Canada, 2004), http://www.ene.gov.on.ca/en/publications/water/index.php#4, accessed 12 December 2008.

27. http://www.epa.gov/tri/.

28. See M. Winfield, 'North American Pollutant Release and Transfer Registries', in D.L. Markell and J.H. Knox, eds, *Greening NAFTA: The North American Commission for Environmental Cooperation* (Stanford: Stanford University Press, 2003), 38–56.

29. http://www.ec.gc.ca/pdb/npri/npri_home_e.cfm, accessed 25 January 2008.

30. See, for example, A. Fung and D. O'Rourke, 'Reinventing Environmental Regulation from the Grassroots up: Explaining and Expanding the Success of the Toxics Release Inventory', *Environmental Management* 25 (2000): 115–27.

31. See for example, K. Harrison and W. Antweiler, 'Environmental Regulation vs. Environmental Information: A View from Canada's National Pollutant Release Inventory', unpublished working paper, Department of Political Science, and Faculty of Commerce and Business Administration, January 2001.

32. OECD Environment Directorate, *Presentation and Dissemination of PRTR Data: Practices and Experiences/Getting the Words and Numbers Out* (ENV/JM/MONO(2000)17), 30 January 2001, 17.

33. Recyclable metals and plastics (blue box), paper and paper products (grey box), household organics (green bin), leaf and yard wastes, household hazardous wastes, residual wastes, and in some households, disposable diapers.

34. City of Toronto, 'Residential Diversion Rate', http://www.toronto.ca/garbage/residential-diversion.htm, accessed 24 October 2007.

35. For an overview of policy instruments see, C. Hood, *The Tools of Government* (Chatham, NJ: Chatham House Publishers, 1986).

36. On the concepts of substantive and procedural instruments see M. Howlett, 'Policy Instruments and Implementation Styles: The Evolution of Instrument Choice in Canadian Environmental Policy', in D.L. VanNijatten and R. Boardman, eds, *Canadian Environmental Policy: Context and Cases*, 2nd ed. (Toronto: Oxford University Press, 2002), 26–7.

37. See T. Meredith, 'Assessing Environmental Impacts in Canada', in B. Mitchell ed., *Resource and Environmental Management in Canada* (Toronto: Oxford University Press, 2004), 465–96.

38. http://www.oag-bvg.gc.ca/internet/English/oag-bvg_e_46.html.

39. http://www.eco.on.ca.

40. Harrison, *Passing the Buck*, 103.

41. i.e., Referendum.

42. A.H. Rosenfeld (Commissioner, California Energy Commission), 'Energy efficiency for California, the US the World No.1 in the California "Loading Order"'. Presentation to the Manatt Forum on 28 September 2007, http://www.energy.ca.gov/papers/index.html, accessed 24 October 2007.

43. See R. Peters, A. Ballie, and M. Horn, *Successful Strategies for Energy Efficiency* (Ottawa: The Pembina Institute, 2006) for a discussion of US state approaches to energy efficiency standard setting.

44. See generally, S. Hall, R. Peters, and M. Winfield, *A Quick Start Energy Efficiency Strategy for Ontario* (Toronto: Pembina Institute, 2006).

45. See D. Maconald, 'Coerciveness and the selection of environmental policy instruments', *Canadian Public Administration* 44, 2 (2001): 161–87.

46. Howlett, 'Policy instruments and implementation styles', 28–9.

47. See, for example, Government of Canada, *Government of Canada Regulatory Policy* (Ottawa: Treasury Board Secretariat, 1999).

48. For a general critique of the use of cost benefit analysis in environmental policy see Herman E. Daly and John B. Cobb, Jr, *For the Common Good: Redirecting the Economy Toward Community, the Environment, and a Sustainable Future* (Boston: Beacon Press, 1989); Paul Craig, Harold Glasser, and Willett Kempton 'Ethics and Values in Environmental Policy', *Environmental Values* 2, 2 (1993): Summer.

49. On these debates see D.M. Driesen, 'Is emission trading an economic incentive program?: Replacing the command and control/economic incentive dichotomy', *Washington and Lee Law Review*, Spring 1998. See also Robert W. Hahn and

Robert N. Stavins, 'Incentive-Based Environmental Regulation: A New Era from an Old Idea?', *Ecology Law Quarterly* 1, 3 (1991).

50. See generally James Q. Wilson, *The Politics of Regulation* (New York: Basic Books, 1980).

51. Organisation for Economic Cooperation and Development, *The Polluter Pays Principle* (Paris: OECD, 1975).

52. Harrison, 'Voluntarism and Environmental Governance'.

53. Chinn, L.N., 'Can the Market be Fair and Efficient? An Environmental Justice Critique of Emissions Trading', *Ecology Law Quarterly* 26, 1 (1999): 80–125.

54. See, for example, A. Kranjc, 'Wither Ontario's Environment: Neo-Conservatism and the Decline of the Ministry of the Environment', *Canadian Public Policy* January 2000. See also D. Eberts, 'Globalization and Neo-Conservatism: Implications for Resource and Environmental Management', in Mitchell, ed., *Resource and Environmental Management in Canada*, 54–79.

55. On the role and mandate of the 'Red Tape Commission' see The Hon. D. O'Connor, *Report of the Walkerton Inquiry: The Events of May 2000 and Related Issues* (Toronto: Queen's Printer for Ontario, 2002), 462–65.

56. See, for example, National Round Table on the Environment and Economy, *Getting to 2050: Canada's Transition to a Low Carbon Economy* (Ottawa: National Round Table on the Environment and the Economy, 2007).

57. On the evolution of federal climate change policy see Winfield and Macdonald, 'The Harmonization Accord and Climate Change Policy: Two Case Studies in Federal–Provincial Environmental Policy', 274–80.

58. Eberts, 'Globalization and Neo-Conservatism: Implications for Resource and Environmental Management'.

59. http://www.regulation.gc.ca/directive/directive00-eng.asp, accessed 14 February 2008.

60. See M. Winfield, *The Federal Cabinet Directive on Streamlining Regulation Commentary from the Pembina Institute* (Toronto: The Pembina Institute, 2007), http://www.pembina.org/pub/1421, accessed 14 February 2008.

61. See generally, Harrison, *Passing the Buck*, Winfield and MacDonald 'The Harmonization Accord and Climate Change Policy'.

62. M. Howlett, 'Enhanced Policy Analytical Capacity as a Prerequisite for Effective Evidence Based Policy Making: Theory, Concepts and Lessons from the Canadian Case', *Canadian Public Administration* (forthcoming).

63. On the early evolution of Canadian environmental and natural resources policy see M. Howlett, 'Policy Instruments and Implementation Styles', 30–1.

64. On the impacts of the early environmental regulatory regime in Canada see D. Macdonald, *The Politics of Pollution* (Toronto: McClelland and Stewart, 1991), 131–200.

65. Environment Canada, 'Implementing Sustainable Practices in the Pulp and Paper Industry: A 10-year Path to Success', Backgrounder, 6 June 2003, http://www.ec.gc.ca/press/2003/030606_b_e.htm, accessed 12 October 2006.

66. See the Gasoline Regulations (SOR/90-247).

67. See, for example, S. Bennett, 'Canadian Opinions on Environmental Policy: Patterns and Determinants', in A. Frizzell and J.H. Pammett, eds, *Shades of Green: Environmental Attitudes in Canada and Around the World* (Ottawa: Carleton University Press, 1997), Table 2, page 21. See also Environics, *The Environmental Monitor*, 1995–2000, various studies accessed at the Canadian Opinion Research Archive at http://www.queensu.ca/cora/.

68. On these developments see M. Winfield, 'Governance and the Environment in Canada: From Regulatory Renaissance to Smart Regulation', *JELP* 17 (2007): 72–3.

69. See generally R.B. Gibson, ed., *Voluntary initiatives and the new politics of corporate greening* (Peterborough: Broadview Press, 1999).

70. M. Bramley, *The Case for Kyoto: The Failure of Voluntary Corporate Action* (Ottawa: Pembina Institute, 2002).

71. Review Branch, Environment Canada, *Evaluation of the ARET Initiative* (Ottawa: Environment Canada, 2000).

72. Most notably, see Ontario Medical Association, *The Health Effects of Ground Level Ozone* (Toronto: Ontario Medical Association, 1998).

73. See the conclusions of the resulting public inquires: The Hon. D. O'Connor, *Report of the Walkerton Inquiry: Part 1* (Toronto: Queen's Printer for Ontario, 2002); The Hon. R. Laing, *Report of the Commission of Inquiry into matters relating to the safety of drinking water in North Battleford, Saskatchewan* (Regina: Queen's Printer for Saskatchewan, 2002).

74. O'Connor, *Report of the Walkerton Inquiry: Part 1*, Chapter 10, 367–402.

75. The environment re-emerged as the leading top of mind public concern in April 2007. See Angus Reid strategies, *National Political Landscape: Focus on the Environment*, 23 January 2007. Also see Decima Research, *Environment on the Agenda*, 4 January 2007.

76. Environment Canada, *Turning the Corner: An Action Plan to Reduce Greenhouse Gases and Air Pollution* (Ottawa: Ministry of Supply and Services, April 2007).

77. See, for example, M. Bramely, *Analysis of the Government of Canada's April 2007 Greenhouse Gas Policy Announcement* (Ottawa: The Pembina Institute, 2007), http://climate.pembina.org/pub/1464, accessed 14 February 2008.
78. On 'smart regulation' initiatives in Canada see Winfield, 'Governance and the Environment in Canada: From Regulatory Renaissance to "Smart Regulation"'.
79. Organisation for Economic Cooperation and Development *OECD Environmental Performance Reviews: Canada* (Paris: OECD, 2004).
80. For an overview of the use of economic instruments in Canadian environmental policy see http://www.fiscallygreen.ca.
81. For an overview of recent provincial level climate change initiatives in Canada see M. Winfield, C. Demerse, J. Witmore, 'Climate Change and Canadian Energy Policy', in S. Bernstein, J. Bruttee, D. Duff, and A. Green, eds, *A Globally Integrated Climate Change Policy for Canada* (Toronto: University of Toronto Press, 2008).
82. See http://www.fin.gov.bc.ca/scp/tp/climate/carbon_tax.htm, accessed 26 June 2008.
83. B. Curry and N. Scott, 'Northern premiers assail Liberal green plan', *The Globe and Mail*, 30 June 2008.
84. See *The Green Shift* (Ottawa: Liberal Party of Canada, 2008).
85. On the evolution of federal policy regarding large final emitters of GHGs see Commissioner for Environment and Sustainable Development *2006 Report* para 1.46-1.87, http://www.oag-bvg.gc.ca/domino/reports.nsf/html/c20060901ce.html#ch1hd4c, accessed 1 February 2008.
86. See, for example, M. Bramley, *An Assessment of Alberta's Climate Change Action Plan* (Ottawa: Pembina Institute, 2002).
87. See http://www.ene.gov.on.ca/envision/air/etr/index.htm, accessed 1 February 2008.
88. See, for example, J. Wellner, 'Comments on Emissions Trading And NO_x And SO_2 Emission Limits for the Electricity Sector', 30 August 2001 on behalf of Pollution Probe et al., http://www.pollutionprobe.org/Happening/etletteraug30.htm, accessed 1 February 2008.
89. Forty-two trades were recorded in 2008 as of 12 December 2008. Of these all but six were internal to Ontario Power Generation. See http://www.oetr.on.ca/oetr/search/view_cur_transactions.jsp, accessed 12 December 2008.
90. See http://www.ec.gc.ca/pdb/npri/npri_home_e.cfm.
91. Allen Woods, 'Tories seek clean slate on fresh air policies: commission own studies', *National Post*, 4 May 2006.
92. See Ontario Regulation 127/01, as amended.

5

Defining Effective Science for Canadian Environmental Policy Leadership

Stephen Bocking

The complex and contested terrain of science and governance is evident wherever Canadians have transformed their environment. For example, on the Pacific coast, salmon are raised in pens for market. Some see this industry as environmentally sustainable and economically essential; others consider it a threat to wild salmon stocks, commercial and sport fisheries, and coastal cultural identity. Both sides invoke scientific arguments to support their claims. On the Prairies, computer models predict worsening drought as climate change takes hold and oil sands plants and irrigated agriculture demand more water. This exemplifies how scientific knowledge can add larger meaning to everyday observations, like those of shrinking glaciers in the Rocky Mountains. In southern Ontario and Quebec, cities expand across the landscape, swallowing ecosystems in a region that, biologists say, possesses more endangered species than any other area of Canada. And in laboratories and industrial facilities across the country, an expanding array of products incorporate nanotechnologies, coatings, powders, and structures engineered on the atomic scale, that promise novel benefits, as well as health and environmental risks both unknown and largely unexamined by scientists.

As these instances illustrate, science plays essential roles in environmental governance; it shapes how we understand, argue over, and choose to protect or to exploit our environment. These roles are evident in every sector. Regulatory agencies frame their objectives in terms defined by science, with contaminants measured in the parts per billion, and the status of endangered species evaluated in terms of population and ecosystem ecologies. Industries hire scientists to assess impacts, defend their interests, and develop 'green' technologies. Activist groups assemble scientific information to strengthen their arguments for environmental protection. All these activities build on research accomplished by scientists in universities, government laboratories, and other institutions, in Canada and elsewhere.

But these roles also exemplify the challenges encountered in applying science to the pursuit of environmental leadership. Debates about the science of salmon farming have often distracted from efforts to resolve the conflicting visions of coastal communities and ecosystems. The implications of water scarcity in Alberta have been obscured by scraps over energy and provincial autonomy. Efforts to apply science-based planning to biodiversity conservation struggle against the economic benefits of converting ecosystems to subdivisions. Research into nanotechnology products attracts heavy investment, but study of their consequences is almost ignored.

In these examples, as in many other instances, the status and contributions of science are fiercely contested, revealing as a fantasy the notion of scientific knowledge as merely the objective, rational foundation of wise policy. Occasionally, these contests come to public attention. In the late 1980s and early 1990s, for example, controversy was ignited in Alberta when the environmental assessment of a paper mill on the Athabasca River was manipulated to correspond to provincial preferences. In British Columbia the federal government suppressed scientific data relating to the proposed expansion of an Alcan facility on the Nechako River. A few years later, fisheries scientists attributed mismanagement of the Newfoundland cod fishery to, among other factors, political interference with their advice.[1] Meanwhile, back in Ottawa, the Liberal government of the day imposed severe cuts on environmental science, exacerbating the gap between needs and resources that has been evident since the early days of Environment Canada.[2] And most recently, concerns have been expressed regarding the Conservative government's attitudes towards science, as evidenced by cutbacks to wildlife science, the muzzling of Environment Canada scientists, abolition of the post of National Science Advisor, and a continuing failure to respond effectively to the scientific consensus on climate change.[3]

Effective environmental policy relies on science for several essential functions. It provides the anticipatory function of identifying emerging environmental problems such as climate change. It contributes to the formation of new environmental policy (for example, the designation of ecological integrity as the basis for national parks management). It guides the use and management of environmental resources, such as forests and fish, by evaluating the impacts of harvesting and the state of the resource. And, finally, it provides a basis for adjudicating conflicting uses or values regarding the environment.

These functions are an essential basis for environmental leadership. Actually fulfilling them requires, at least, addressing the problems noted above: avoiding undue interference in research and the communication of its results, assuring steady funding, and paying attention to new information as it becomes available. But leadership must go beyond these minimal requirements. Scholars in several disciplines have identified a variety of other obstacles to effective science in policy contexts, including competing interpretations of scientific information, failures to weigh scientific evidence in relation to economic or political imperatives, and an absence of necessary research on environmental hazards. Their analyses have also generated insights into the essential challenge of science in environmental governance: connecting knowledge to visions of natural and social well-being. As a result, various practical efforts aimed at ensuring science can play effective roles in governance are underway. These approaches are grounded in the awareness that environmental leadership demands knowledge that is scientifically sound and relevant to actual problems, credible to all parties, and politically legitimate. Producing such knowledge, in turn, depends on a new model of scientific practice and application, as well as a broader commitment to diverse strategies for generating environmental knowledge.

Surveying Environmental Science

Environmental science today is the product of an accretion over time of knowledge from diverse sources: federal and provincial agencies, universities, industry, environmental organizations, and also citizens. This knowledge has been produced for a similarly wide range of purposes, including resource management (and its critique), basic research, meeting regulatory requirements, and understanding local environmental concerns. The consequences of this pluralistic research landscape include the incorporation of a broad range of forms of knowledge in policy-making and related debates, conflicts over contrasting scientific interpretations, and a consequent questioning of the assumptions regarding the practices, objectives, and application of science. Science thus plays roles in governance that, while essential, are nothing like the ideal often invoked of a rational process in which scientists determine the neutral facts regarding an environmental problem, which are then matched with an optimal solution by policymakers knowledgeable about both the science and the relevant regulatory or policy tools. Instead, science is itself deeply implicated in politics, making this political character a necessary consideration in determining how science can play effective roles in policy. Ethical and political possibilities and preferences are implicated in the practice of science itself: in scientists' choices of research methods, scales of inquiry, standards of proof to be applied to evidence, and strategies for managing uncertainties. Far from being a neutral arbitrator of environmental disputes, both scientific knowledge and the practice of science itself embody particular ideas about nature and human conduct, with consequences that may be oppressive for local communities or ecosystems.[4]

This entanglement of science and politics is evident not just within science itself, but also within the relation between science and broader political priorities.[5] For example, while a chief goal of Canadian federal and provincial science policy is to encourage the development and commercialization of innovative environmental technologies, achieving these goals depends as much, if not more, on effective environmental regulation—which creates a demand for these technologies—as on specific policies for guiding scientific activities.[6] Similarly, shifts in the focus of scientific research often depend on changes in policy. Thus, while Natural Resources Canada laboratories, have in recent years, begun to examine environmental dimensions of resource extraction, their continuing focus on oil sands and other developments of questionable environmental rationality reflects the larger departmental mandate of service to the resource industry.[7] Political and economic preferences also have wider implications for science. How the goals of environmental policy are defined in terms of human health, intact ecosystems, or sustainable resource use determines what forms of expertise are considered most relevant. Questions of governance—about the relative roles of government and the market, and the importance of public versus private goods—also help determine how science will be structured and applied.

These implications become especially evident in debates over the definition of an issue as a matter of science or of politics. It is often argued that environmental decisions should be made through reference to 'sound science', which is presented as an objective, rational alternative to political considerations. Yet this position itself has political implications. It implies that action must wait until scientific standards of proof have been satisfied; this is why agendas of deregulation have often invoked the need for basing decisions on science. It also accords an advantage in environmental debates to those with the most scientific (and often, economic) resources, removing agency from communities and individuals, particularly indigenous peoples. And finally, defining a contested issue as a matter of science tends to distract attention from the political preferences or economic structures that may be at the root of environmental problems. Such has been the case in natural resource management, where a commitment to science-based decisions has long reinforced a preference for industrial transformation of nature. In practice, therefore, insistence on the need for 'sound science' may be less about rational policy than about shifting the debate towards more powerful interests.

Over the last several decades, the complex relations between science and politics have been especially evident in international affairs. Canada's contribution and vulnerability to climate change and long-range transport of contaminants, Canadian scientists' leadership in understanding these phenomena, and the application of knowledge from elsewhere to domestic environmental issues, exemplify the porous nature of national borders, at least where environmental science is concerned. This international dimension is also evident in continental and global trade agreements, where standards of evidence based on 'sound science' frame disputes over barriers to trade.[8]

Four Models of Science

But how can we move beyond this description, and construct a more analytical perspective on the place of science in environmental governance? Several partial efforts are useful, but they also suggest a need for a more comprehensive view.[9] One such view might be framed in terms of various models of science: that is, sets of ideas that guide the relation between science and governance. Through these models, it is possible to understand the diversity of ways in which science relates to environmental governance, their shortcomings, and, more generally, the assumptions about society and nature that are embedded in the ideas and practice of science, where they serve as unnegotiated social prescriptions.[10]

For several decades *basic research* has been closely associated with universities and some federal laboratories. In this model, scientific disciplines define scientists' agendas, with research problems framed in terms of those considered most interesting within the discipline, as well as in terms of strategic areas set by the Natural Sciences and Engineering Research Council (NSERC), or by policy-oriented programs such as the Canadian Foundation for Climate and Atmospheric Sciences. Underlying this model is the view that useful knowledge can be best obtained through research that is directed by scientists themselves. Such research has, in fact, often generated highly useful knowledge, as was evident in, for example, the formation of an understanding of the mechanisms of long-range transport of contaminants, and the identification of the role of CFCs (chlorofluorocarbons) in damaging the stratospheric ozone layer. These and other episodes illustrate how the contribution of research to governance can often be entirely unexpected, as problems are examined within the scientific community, building intellectual capital to be drawn on when attention becomes focused on an emerging crisis.

Yet basic research cannot alone fulfill all the roles of science in environmental governance. It tends to neglect environmental challenges that lack theoretical significance or that require long-term monitoring or other practices that are of less interest to scientists. The disciplinary structure of science can also impose a limited vision. For example, Canadian atmospheric scientists, most trained in physical meteorology, were slow to identify the changes in atmospheric chemistry that were eventually recognized as acid rain. Such episodes also illustrate how interdisciplinary research is essential; however, the departmental structure of many universities presents obstacles to such work (although interdisciplinary programs are now growing rapidly).

Environmental administration has an insatiable appetite for knowledge, generating research activities known as *regulatory science*. This research encompasses everything from estimating tree growth as part of a forest harvesting regime, to studying the toxicity of contaminants in order to set water quality standards. Regulatory science is perhaps the largest component of environmental research in Canada. For example, 72 per cent of Environment Canada's science budget covers 'related scientific activities'—a category that encompasses regulatory science. These activities, while essential, often attract little attention. Environmental monitoring by the Water Survey of Canada is a case in point.

Long-term knowledge of water quality and quantity is an essential public good, yet it is collected almost entirely outside the public eye, and with modest funding.[11] Regulatory research is conducted within federal and provincial agencies, and by university faculties of applied science. Industry, including consulting firms, is also a major player, in part in response to regulatory requirements, but also because federal policy encourages the private sector to contribute to funding research. Collectively, these activities fulfill their role by transforming knowledge into distinct arenas of professional practice, imparting the authority of expertise to decisions made by administrative agencies and regulated industries.

While essential, regulatory science has its own shortcomings. Because industry often pays the bills, the results are often proprietary and closed to public scrutiny. Beyond the challenge of assuring the quality of private information, this can hinder regulators' efforts to protect the public interest, reinforce obstacles to public participation in decision-making, and accentuate concerns regarding the close ties between regulators and private interests. A related concern is that the information generated may be relevant only to immediate government or industry priorities. For example, forestry studies often focus strictly on tree growth and fail to assess the health of the entire ecosystem. This research has also been criticized for failing to accommodate local conditions, whether in nature or in human communities. The tacit prescriptive commitments embedded in scientific knowledge may be inconsistent with local attitudes towards nature and, as a result, this knowledge is often perceived as irrelevant to, or even a deliberate misunderstanding of, the places in which people live.[12]

Most fundamentally, by defining issues as strictly technical, regulatory science, like the assumptions of administrative rationalism that underpin it, focuses debate not on ends (about which it is assumed all agree) but on efficiency of the means. In doing so it discourages public attention to the political dimensions of environmental issues, implicitly justifying the existing order. The consequences include a failure to challenge the assumptions of conventional risk assessment and natural resource management, an acceptance of dominant ideas regarding how nature should be used, and a reinforcing of the tendency of bureaucratic organizations to resist learning, favouring delivery of standardized programs over efforts to understand the unexpected, or to experiment with alternative approaches.

In the last two decades *advocacy science* has emerged as a significant phenomenon in environmental governance, often challenging the assumptions and practice of regulatory science. Citizens and environmental organizations have become significant consumers and, to some extent, producers of scientific knowledge. Experience shows that if an issue is perceived to have a direct impact on a community, people will actively acquire technically sophisticated information, often sufficient to challenge professional expertise. Community groups may seek volunteer expertise at local universities, while larger groups hire scientists to review issues and prepare position papers. Nongovernmental organizations have also emerged as knowledge brokers, relating information to policy options and acting as conduits between scientists, the media, and the public. For example, in the Great Lakes region advocacy organizations such as Great Lakes United have used scientific information to build a cross-border consensus on protecting the lakes. More recently, the Pembina Institute has contributed by explaining how climate change science relates to energy efficiency, development of the oil sands, and other policy issues.

Other organizations seek to influence the research agenda itself, by providing funding or facilities for researchers, or by conducting research in areas of special relevance. Smaller groups may do community-based monitoring of environmental resources, while larger groups have their own scientists or commission research. For example, the World Wildlife Fund supports studies of endangered species; the Raincoast Research Society provides facilities for research on the implications of salmon farms for marine ecosystems; and conservation groups urging protection of transboundary natural areas have coordinated wildlife research, demonstrating capacities in these areas beyond those of provincial, state, or federal governments.[13]

These activities share with regulatory research the view of science as essential to the policy process. But they also embody challenges to policy agendas, to the structures of environmental governance (including the close relations between government and industry), to the status of these actors as the dominant providers of knowledge, and even to conventional definitions of the issues. Such challenges are essential because they entail a necessary broadening of both the policy agenda and participation in the policy process. But advocacy science has its own shortcomings, some of which stem from the political context of this research. A frequent outcome of communicating science in the context of controversy is increased polarization, as advocates accept whatever evidence is consistent with their own views, and discount contrary information. Advocacy science can also exacerbate controversy by focusing attention on conflicting interpretations of knowledge. And finally, as in regulatory science, advocates in a controversy can evade responsibility for their value choices by hiding behind the protective veil of science, with the consequence that debate shifts from whatever political, economic, or moral values or interests may be at stake to focus instead on scientific issues.

During the last decade a fourth model of science has gained prominence. In the environmental field, as in other policy realms, *innovation science*—usually defined in terms of the pursuit of marketable technologies—has become a chief focus of federal and provincial science policies. The motivation is economic; technology is seen as underpinning greater prosperity. Innovation policies are founded on the view that economic benefits are not the inevitable outcome of research, but instead depend on careful attention to the ecology of research, particularly active collaboration between scientists, industry, and policymakers.[14] Such a view is evident in the federal innovation strategy released in January 2002. It can also be seen in, among other initiatives, an emphasis by federal granting agencies (including NSERC and Genome Canada) on partnerships between scientists and industry, so as to ensure that research is focused on the most relevant, commercially viable opportunities. These partnerships are usually encouraged by requirements for matching funding from industrial or other sources. In the environmental field, the innovation agenda is evident in efforts to facilitate commercialization of 'green' technologies, both to improve the environmental performance of conventional industry and to build an environmental industry. These objectives are pursued, for example, by the three Canadian Environmental Technology Advancement Centres (in western Canada, Ontario, and Quebec); by Sustainable Development Technology Canada (a federal foundation that works in partnership with the private sector to support development of innovative technologies); and, at the provincial level, by the Ontario Research Fund and the British Columbia Research and Innovation Strategy. Some support for innovation science is also focused on specific sectors; an example is the Technology Early Action Measures (TEAM) of the federal Climate Change Action Fund. With the Obama administration intending to greatly increase investment in research on clean energy technologies, Canadian governments may follow suit.

Viewed as a means of combining environmental and economic priorities, innovation research has been adopted by federal and provincial governments alike as a chief strategy for sustainability. As such, it makes an essential contribution to reducing the impacts of economic activities, particularly by reaching into decision-making processes within firms that would be otherwise inaccessible to regulatory action or advocacy pressures. Its shortcomings, however, reflect its reliance on commercialization potential and market forces as the basis for determining research priorities. Given this reliance, innovation research tends to neglect research on topics that lack economic potential, including the study of emerging and long-term concerns, or species and habitats that lack economic significance. It also tends to shortchange contributions to the scientific basis for public policy, and, more generally, the building of environmental knowledge that is accessible to all. For example, the Canadian Biotechnology Strategy has always emphasized promotion of this technology, neglecting balanced assessment of its environmental risks and benefits. A similar pattern appears to be emerging with nanotechnology; research on environmental implications remains patchy and uncoordinated. There is also reason for concern regarding the potential for universities—recipients of considerable innovation funding over the last decade—to be distracted from their public service roles.[15] And as is the case with regulatory science, links between science and economic interests raise concerns regarding access to proprietary knowledge, as well as the problematic nature of research that serves economic interests, and yet is presented as acting in the service of a single, undifferentiated public— disallowing questions regarding who does and who does not gain from these investments. Finally, there is the problematic view of technology itself as the solution to environmental problems. This view often motivates political leaders to neglect other dimensions of environmental challenges.

As this review of models of science and environmental governance illustrates, the landscape of Canadian environmental science reflects responses to a multiplicity of motivations and circumstances. While certain sectors are most closely associated with certain models—universities for basic research, environmental organizations for advocacy science—the diversity of relations between institutions and models of science makes such generalizations risky. In particular, the federal government pursues research that conforms to several models. For example, the Environmental Technology Centre contributes to understanding air pollution through both regulatory and innovation research. In contrast, the National Wildlife Research Centre adheres to a basic research model with few, if any, links to the private sector. It is ironic that this diversity often remains unrepresented in public presentations of research, particularly those of the federal government. These instead tend to emphasize innovation science because, as a model, it fits more readily within the federal storyline of science in the service of prosperity. In contrast, much less attention is directed to 'public good' science, including that devoted to providing a basis for regulation.[16] That research tends instead to become visible only at times of crisis, such as when cod stocks are forced to near-extinction or when a potentially hazardous contaminant is identified.

This review also illustrates that this diversity is essential to leadership in environmental policy. Only by applying a variety of models can science respond effectively to diverse requirements for environmental knowledge. This becomes especially evident if we consider how environmental challenges can become evident through a variety of means, including basic research, evolving public concerns, or routine monitoring. Responses to these challenges—through regulation, incentives, education, or other approaches—can similarly depend on a variety of strategies, including discipline-oriented basic research, targeted regulatory science, studies and communications by environmental organizations, or better technologies.

These research models can also give us a sharper understanding of the challenges involved in applying science to environmental governance. Environmental knowledge is often uncertain or contested, tied to powerful interests or committed advocates, inaccessible to the public, neglectful of essential political requirements, or heedless of demands for participation in decisions involving its production. As a result, widespread skepticism has emerged regarding the veracity of scientific information. Other challenges are also evident. Environmentalists find that science cannot provide the support they expect. Regulatory agencies find that science provides only fragmentary grounds on which to base their decisions. Parties to controversies find that scientific evidence does not resolve divisions but instead exacerbates them. Those who oppose environmental initiatives invoke—and sometimes exaggerate—scientific uncertainties, a practice most evident today in climate change debates, but one that dates back to at least the 1920s, when evidence of the health effects of leaded gasoline began to emerge. (It was more than 60 years before we actually shifted to only unleaded gas.) And beyond the shortcomings of each model of science lies the uncertainty and ignorance prevalent in all but the simplest issues, stemming from incomplete theoretical understanding, insufficient research, or the complexity of natural and human systems. In such contexts, a single answer is rarely possible. Often there may be no answer at all, particularly in complex policy areas that push scientific inquiry to the outer edge of accepted facts.

This reality of knowledge and practice—often uncertain or incomplete, embodying objective authority but incorporating subjective values and attitudes, providing not one single 'truth' but multiple partial perspectives—defines the essential challenge of science in environmental governance. How, then can it be possible to ensure that science provides the knowledge we need to achieve environmental leadership?

Science and Environmental Leadership

At least two key issues must be considered. One relates to the agenda of science, and the need for a stronger emphasis on shaping scientific priorities in response to perceptions of the overall public good. A second issue concerns how science relates to the changing landscape of environmental governance, and particularly to the need to resolve debates over contentious environmental challenges. Both issues relate to shortcomings in the four models that frame contemporary Canadian environmental science.

As we have seen, each of these models emphasizes a particular agenda: the disciplinary priorities of basic research, the information requirements of regulatory agencies, the demand for knowledge for advocacy, or the potential for innovative commercial technologies. All are important, and yet collectively, these agendas neglect some urgent knowledge needs. Consider, for example, the study of agriculture and its environmental implications. The overwhelming emphasis in Canadian agricultural science is on higher yields through intensive laboratory-based practices, including genetic engineering. The ultimate objective is to create marketable innovations, such as seed varieties and chemical products. But as some critics have pointed out, this emphasis neglects research on alternative strategies, including organic agriculture, as well as other approaches that emphasize resilience over maximum production, and that produce public, rather than private, intellectual property.[17]

An even more significant gap between existing research and emerging challenges is evident in energy technologies. In recent years a number of observers have argued that, even with appropriate pricing of energy through a carbon tax or other measures, market forces alone will not call into existence the technologies required for a drastic reduction in carbon emissions.[18] A massive expansion of research on these technologies is also required, and yet public investment in solar, wind, and other forms of alternative energy has not kept pace. This gap between what research is needed and what is being funded parallels the gap between research as a public good (as in, for example, basic research on climate change) and research on innovative technologies. Scientists can project, at least roughly, the climate that will result from various scenarios of carbon emissions. However, existing research agendas, including those of innovation science, fail to fulfill an analogous anticipatory function with respect to technologies, and especially those that may not yet be commercially viable, but that could be in the future in the context of a supportive economic and regulatory environment.

The requirement, in short, is for a research agenda that combines the practical imperatives of innovation research with the anticipatory capacity of environmental science, generating technologies that address not just possibilities for commercialization, but the public good. Defining a new environmental research agenda thus requires identifying and bridging the gaps between the models that today govern science in Canadian environmental affairs.

These considerations regarding the agenda of research can also provide some insight into new approaches to doing science that can overcome obstacles to effective science, particularly in the context of controversy. These obstacles include unavoidable uncertainties and areas of ignorance in our knowledge of nature. As a result, science is only rarely able to provide a single best option for action. This is particularly the case because our judgements, while informed by science, must also incorporate myriad political differences, with these differences generating contrasting views even when our search for guidance must turn away from science, and instead pursue a deeper understanding of the social, political, and cultural dimensions of our relationship with the environment.[19]

The requirement for new approaches also stems from the evolving nature of scientific activity. An everyday reality for many, if not most, scientists is that research is a highly pluralistic activity, with extensive networks of collaboration among scientists who are often within numerous distinct institutions and sectors. Thus, the boundaries between scientific institutions are blurred, with scientists in governments, universities, industry, and advocacy organizations working (if not always smoothly) together. For example, the federal Environmental Technology Centre studies and formulates policies relating to air pollution through a network of researchers in federal and provincial departments, industry, and academia.[20] Such arrangements reflect the requirements of the research itself—including the technical capabilities required to study all aspects of air pollution, and the partnerships that are often required for effective delivery and practical application of research results.

An additional consideration is that scientific activity is embedded in processes of environmental governance that are themselves evolving. This evolution encompasses a shift from conventional 'end-of-pipe' regulation, towards—for all but the simplest environmental problems—extensive collaboration. Governance thus requires attention to not just the substance of policy, but the procedural mechanisms required for networks of actors to be guided towards sustainability, including dissemination of information, reflexive regulation, and partnerships.[21] Such mechanisms, in turn, require careful design if they are to be considered legitimate, including ample consultation and other forms of participation.

These aspects of change in science and governance imply new requirements for scientific practice beyond those customarily associated with science, such as mastery of the theoretical literature and rigorous technical procedures. Foremost among these is the building of a capacity for effective communication and collaboration. This, in turn, imposes requirements relating to the conduct and content of science.

The need for more effective communication of science is widely acknowledged. But there are multiple challenges involved in actually achieving this, particularly in the context of controversy. It is a truism that the specialized journal article—the traditional medium for conveying scientific information, and one that remains the basis for advancement in basic research—is often ineffective in communicating knowledge to those who might apply it. Neither is the news media always able to communicate science effectively, both because of its shortcomings relating to the framing and simplification of issues, and because of its tendency to present issues as more contentious than may be justified by the actual scientific consensus (a problem most evident with respect to climate change).[22] It is, at least in part, in response to these shortcomings that various interests—both industrial and environmental—are increasingly employing the Internet to communicate directly to selected audiences.

More generally, the obstacles to communicating science to decision-makers are both structural—relating to where scientists are situated within government departments and other institutions—and substantive, reflecting the divergent objectives, communication strategies, and relations of trust between scientists and those who use scientific information. Communication practices for science are evolving rapidly in response to these challenges. This evolution has become particularly evident in diverse issue-specific fora for discussion and consensus-building across institutions and sectors (for example, with respect to aquaculture, the Speaking for the Salmon process conducted by Simon Fraser University), as well as in formal expert committees, such as the Committee on the Status of Endangered Wildlife in Canada (COSEWIC).[23] These fora, and effective communication generally, depend on building relationships of trust between scientists and those who use scientific information, reflecting how communication is affected not just by its format but also by evaluations of the institution or individual that is communicating. Such communication, furthermore, must be in both directions, that is, a true dialogue, ensuring that research is not only relevant but is communicated in ways consistent with public and institutional concerns and priorities.

Yet both scholarship and experience are also indicating that effective roles for science, and therefore environmental leadership itself, depends on more than communication.[24] The networked character of science implies ambiguities regarding the purpose and orientation of research: who will apply the results, and whether the knowledge will be considered public or private. This is particularly the case in the context of controversy where the conduct of science must be considered acceptable to all parties if it is to contribute to resolving differences. As a result, just as policy is being evaluated in terms of both content and process, so is science now being evaluated in terms of knowledge, and how that knowledge was obtained and applied. In other words, there is a convergence underway in how policy and science are being received and evaluated by environmental actors.

This convergence can be understood in terms of three aspects of scientific practice. The first relates to evaluations of scientific credibility. Peer review—familiar in basic research, and also now often used in regulatory and advocacy contexts—plays an important role in these evaluations. Peer review is not infallible, especially in practical contexts, but its value can be enhanced by understanding that it serves best not simply by assuring the truth of scientific results, but by 'witnessing' research, helping to ensure its quality and rigor. This function, in turn, implies reconsidering the structure of the review process: relying less on individual reviewers than on groups of independent experts, and widening participation beyond the scientific community, to include, for example, holders of local knowledge. Scientific credibility also depends on aspects of the process of science that are less accessible to peer review, such as the relations between scientists and economic or other interests, and the perceived openness of scientists to considering other perspectives and forms of knowledge.

A second aspect of scientific practice relates to relevance. Effective science that is able to solve problems and advance the policy agenda must fulfill a diversity of roles, from anticipating emerging issues to understanding the basis of persistent conflicts. This, in turn, requires a broad definition of relevance, implemented through a pluralistic research strategy that draws on a diversity of participants in setting the research agenda.[25]

The third aspect of effective science is legitimacy. It depends, in part, on transparency regarding the objectives of research and its consequences for all interests. This can be assured through open arrangements for funding science and determining research objectives. It also requires open, inclusive negotiation of the relation between knowledge and action—whether, say, action on a problem can be taken on the basis of a weight of evidence approach, or must wait until there is absolute proof of the need for action. Explicit articulation of how decisions using uncertain or incomplete evidence will be made is also required: will it be by, say, balancing benefits and risks, or by invoking the precautionary principle? Such requirements acknowledge that the legitimacy of research is achieved not through universal norms of scientific conduct but through a context-dependent process that takes into account local interests and concerns.[26] Legitimacy also poses particular challenges for science and its relation to other ways of thinking about nature; it requires defining which questions may be addressed by science, and which require other approaches, while acknowledging that science is only one of several ways of knowing the world.

These requirements relating to credibility, relevance, and legitimacy imply a new model of science as the basis for environmental leadership. This model might be described as *modest science*—that is, science that contributes distinctive knowledge but is cognizant of the value of other forms of knowledge, and is also mindful of democratic imperatives and the boundaries between science and other perspectives. Essential to this model are transparent, consensual approaches to distinguishing between those questions that can be answered by science and those that, while perhaps illuminated by scientific knowledge, depend for resolution on political, economic, or moral considerations.

A chief implication of this new model of science is that institutions framed in terms of conventional models of science are not sufficient for science to be fully effective. Neither science that is insulated from the policy world, as in basic research, nor science that is fully integrated within this world, as in regulatory or advocacy science, can provide the information required. Science that fails to relate effectively to pressing environmental problems risks irrelevancy. Science too closely enmeshed in politics risks becoming itself the focus of dispute, distracting attention from genuine political, economic, and moral differences. Such an outcome has been too commonly encountered, as is evident in issues ranging from climate change to salmon aquaculture.

Instead, new forms of institutions for science, that are able to integrate scientific and non-scientific considerations, are required. One of the more promising innovations are 'boundary organizations': that is, organizations that, rather than insisting on a clean demarcation of science and policy, straddle the boundary between them, and thus provide the basis for stabilizing this boundary. Experience has shown that such organizations (the Intergovernmental Panel on Climate Change is a well-known example), are able to synthesize knowledge and contribute to setting the research agenda, while achieving agreement on consensual knowledge, even across diverse interests and scientific disciplines.[27] Other innovations in institutional design, such as learning organizations that embody the capacity to adapt to changing conditions and to new knowledge, suggest further possibilities.

These new kinds of institutions and the networked character of science and governance generally, have implications for various sectors, and particularly for government. It is becoming increasingly evident that agencies that have both policy and scientific responsibilities need to evolve from serving as the primary source of scientific information, to facilitating the use of science from a diversity of sources. Acting as reliable, trusted knowledge brokers, these agencies could fulfill such tasks as disseminating information, and facilitating dialogue among diverse actors. While some agencies are beginning to acknowledge the importance of these tasks, the often widespread distrust of these agencies, founded on histories of lack of transparency and perceptions of conflict of interest (as when an agency both regulates and promotes an industry), also exemplifies the challenges involved in fulfilling this role.

Canadians have learned a great deal about their natural environment through scientific research (although many uncertainties and areas of ignorance remain). This knowledge should be able to provide the basis for environmental leadership. But for it to do so, research must go beyond those models that have traditionally guided its pursuit, instead embracing approaches to scientific practice and related institutional structures that promise to encourage formation of knowledge that all parties will consider credible, relevant, and legitimate.

Questions for Review

1. What has been the role of science and of scientists in the making of Canadian environmental policy? Should they have greater influence in policy processes?
2. What should be the balance between scientific, economic, social, and other concerns and interests in Canadian environmental policy?
3. To what extent is science culturally relative? Are there blind spots towards local communities, traditional knowledge, and the perspectives of non-scientists, and if so what are the consequences?
4. What are the differences between basic science, regulatory science, advocacy science and innovation science? What are the ways in which each of these contributes to or acts as a constraint on environmental policy activism?

Notes

1. Mary Richardson, Joan Sherman, and Michael Gismondi, *Winning Back the Words: Confronting Experts in an Environmental Public Hearing* (Toronto: Garamond Press, 1993); Bev Christensen, *Too Good to Be True: Alcan's Kemano Completion Project* (Vancouver: Talon Books, 1995); J.A. Hutchings, Carl Walters, and Richard L. Beamish. 'Is Scientific Inquiry Incompatible with Government Information Control?', *Canadian Journal of Fisheries and Aquatic Sciences* 54 (1997): 1198–1210.
2. Bruce G. Doern and Thomas Conway, *The Greening of Canada: Federal Institutions and Decisions* (Toronto: University of Toronto Press, 1994).
3. Peter Calamai, 'The Struggle over Canada's Role in the Post-Kyoto World', in G. Bruce Doern, ed., *Innovation, Science, Environment: Canadian Policies and Performance, 2007–2008* (Montreal and Kingston: McGill-Queens University Press, 2007), 32–54; Hannah Hoag, 'Canada abolishes its national science advisor', *Nature* 451, 31 (January 2008): 505. In December 2008 Environment Canada forbid a leading government climate scientist to attend the United Nations climate conference in Poznan, Poland. At the same meeting GermanWatch, an advocacy group, ranked Canada second to last (out of 60 countries) in its climate performance and policies.
4. S. Bocking, *Nature's Experts: Science, Politics, and the Environment* (New Brunswick, NJ: Rutgers University Press, 2004), 25–44.
5. S. Jasanoff, *Designs on Nature: Science and Democracy in Europe and the United States* (Princeton University Press, 2005).
6. Bert Backman-Beharry and Robert Slater, 'Commercializing Technologies through Collaborative Networks: The Environmental Industry and the Role of CETACS', in G. Bruce Doern, ed., *Innovation, Science, Environment: Canadian Policies and Performance, 2006–2007* (Montreal and Kingston: McGill-Queens University Press, 2006), 169–93.
7. Bruce G. Doern and Jeffrey S. Kinder, *Strategic Science in the Public Interest: Canada's Government Laboratories and Science-Based Agencies* (Toronto: University of Toronto Press, 2007), 94–116.
8. Bruce G. Doern, 'The Martin Liberals: Changing ISE Policies and Institutions', in G. Bruce Doern, ed., *Innovation, Science, Environment: Canadian Policies and Performance, 2006–2007* (Montreal and Kingston: McGill-Queens University Press, 2006), 3–34.
9. See, for example, Bruce G. Doern and Ted Reed, eds., *Risky Business: Canada's Changing Science-Based Policy and Regulatory Regime* (Toronto: University of Toronto Press, 2000); W. Leiss, *In the Chamber of Risks: Understanding Risk Controversies* (Montreal and Kingston: McGill-Queens University Press, 2001); Doern and Kinder, *Strategic Science*.

10. Bocking, *Nature's Experts*.

11. Doern and Kinder, *Strategic Science*.

12. B. Wynne, 'Public Understanding of Science', in Sheila Jasanoff, et al., eds, *Handbook of Science and Technology Studies* (Thousand Oaks, CA: Sage Publications, 1995), 361–88.

13. J.N. Sanders and P. Stoett, 'Extinction and Invasion: Transborder Conservation Efforts', in P. LePrestre and P. Stoett, eds, *Bilateral Ecopolitics: Continuity and Change in Canadian-American Environmental Relations* (London: Ashgate, 2006), 157–77.

14. Bruce G. Doern, 'The Reshaping of an Agenda for Innovation, Science, and Environment (ISE)', in G. Bruce Doern, ed., *Innovation, Science, Environment: Canadian Policies and Performance, 2007–2008* (Montreal and Kingston: McGill-Queens University Press, 2007), 3–31.

15. M.G. Bird, 'Harmful Distraction: The Commercialization of Knowledge at Canada's Public Universities', in G. Bruce Doern, ed., *Innovation, Science, Environment: Canadian Policies and Performance, 2007–2008* (Montreal and Kingston: McGill-Queens University Press, 2007), 281–98.

16. Doern and Kinder, *Strategic Science*, 117–165, 201–2.

17. See, for example, E. Ann Clark, 'Has Ag Biotech Lived Up to Its Promise? (and what should the scientific community do about it?)'. Lecture, 25 November 2004.

18. See, for example, J. Sachs, *Common Wealth: Economics for a Crowded Planet* (New York: Penguin, 2008).

19. S. Jasanoff, 'Technologies of Humility', *Nature* 450, 1 (November 2007): 33.

20. Doern and Kinder, *Strategic Science*.

21. Michael Howlett and Jeremy Rayner, '(Not so) "Smart regulation"? Canadian shellfish aquaculture policy and the evolution of instrument choice for industrial development', *Marine Policy* 28 (2004): 171–84.

22. Bocking, *Nature's Experts*.

23. R. Routledge, Patricia Gallaugher, and Craig Orr, 'Convener's Report—Summit of Scientists on Aquaculture and the Protection of Wild Salmon', Simon Fraser University, 2007; D.L. Vanderzwaag and J.A. Hutchings, 'Canada's Marine Species at Risk: Science and Law at the Helm, but a Sea of Uncertainties', *Ocean Development and International Law* 36, 3 (2005): 219–59.

24. Dan M. Kahan, et al., 'Biased Assimilation, Polarization, and Cultural Credibility: An Experimental Study of Nanotechnology Risk Perceptions', *Project on Emerging Nanotechnologies*, Brief No. 3. 2008.

25. Bocking, *Nature's Experts*.

26. See, for example, C.A. Miller, 'Challenges in the Application of Science to Global Affairs: Contingency, Trust, and Moral Order', in Clark A. Miller and Paul N. Edwards, eds, *Changing the Atmosphere: Expert Knowledge and Environmental Governance* (Cambridge: MIT Press, 2001), 247–85.

27. David H. Guston, ed., 'Special Issue: Boundary Organizations in Environmental Policy and Science', *Science, Technology, and Human Values* 26, 4 (2001): 399–500. On the significance of boundary organizations and analogous mechanisms in an interjurisdictional context see D.L. VanNijnatten and W. Henry Lambright, 'North American Smog: Science-Policy Linkages across Multiple Boundaries', *Canadian-American Public Policy*, 45 (2001).

6

The Struggle of the Canadian Federal Government to Institutionalize Sustainable Development

Glen Toner and James Meadowcroft

Environmental policy is usually reactive. It involves creating recovery plans for species once they are threatened; adopting regulations to govern the use of toxic substances that endanger human and animal life; cleaning up sites contaminated by industrial activity; studying, monitoring, and documenting the decline in natural capital and ecological systems inflicted by human activity, and the like. Development is the activity that humans engage in every day when they get out of bed and contribute to economic and social life in a multitude of ways. For the past two centuries or so this development process has become increasingly unsustainable in that it has made it difficult for nature to sustain the natural capital upon which life depends. Recognition in the 1980s that this human development process had to shift from unsustainable to sustainable had a profound impact on public policy discourse in national governments and international organizations. While environment policies were geared up to contain and fix increasingly serious problems imposed by industrial activity, sustainable development policies were intended to address the root causes of the problems by altering the corporate and governmental decision-making processes that triggered the unsustainable practices of human systems.

Our Common Future, the 1987 report of the World Commission on Environment and Development (WCED) made the following prescient observation: '. . . in the end, sustainable development is not a fixed state of harmony, but rather a process of change in which the exploitation of resources, the direction of investments, the orientation of technological development, *and institutional change* are made consistent with future as well as present needs.'[1] William Ruckelshaus, former head of the United States Environmental Protection Agency, clarified the transformative nature of the shift required in human thinking and practice when he said

[c]an we move nations in the direction of sustainability? Such a move would be a modification of society comparable in scale to only two other changes: the Agricultural Revolution of the late Neolithic, and the Industrial Revolution of the past two centuries. The revolutions were gradual, spontaneous, and largely unconscious. This one will have to be a fully conscious operation, guided by the best foresight science can provide. If we actually do it, the undertaking will be absolutely unique in humanity's stay on earth.[2]

Hence, sustainable development is about changing, in a fundamental way, the human development trajectory. Government policies which shape, trigger, or influence human activity at the level of the firm, the community, and the individual are a key part of the development experience. Since 1987, various Canadian federal governments have formally committed to this transformation by introducing sustainable development policies, institutions, and practices. Indeed, in the 1990s Canada was considered an innovator and leader in this 'change process'. Few would say that this is the case today. This chapter will assess the scope and dynamics of this institutional change process within the federal government over the past 20 years.[3]

Interestingly, in early 2008 the Parliamentary Standing Committee on Environment and Sustainable Development considered a private member's bill (Bill C-474) to create a *Federal Sustainable Development Act*, which among other things would require the development and updating every three years of a national sustainable development strategy for the federal government.[4] Both authors of this chapter, independently, were invited to testify before the Committee on C-474. The content of and debate on the bill (which received Royal Assent on 26 June 2008) will act as a reference point for this chapter as they reveal many of the structural challenges that the sustainable development institutionalization process has confronted in Canada since the introduction of the Mulroney Conservative Government's 1990 Green Plan. Given the transformative agenda of sustainable development it is not surprising that this period has been characterized by both breakthroughs and setbacks. In reference to the change process it described above, the WCED added the profound insight that, '[w]e do not pretend that the process is easy or straightforward.'[5] Indeed, it has not been.

It may appear paradoxical that C-474 was introduced by the Liberals while in opposition when the bill would significantly alter processes and institutions they introduced while in power. Or, is this an example of 'institutional learning' as experience has revealed the shortcomings of the Liberal's original innovations? And, why did the Conservatives appear reluctant to change institutions and processes introduced earlier by their partisan rivals? The chapter will assess the empirical record of both the Liberal and Conservative governments by exploring five major areas of contestation which together have constrained the ability of the government to engage in policy innovations that lead to real progress. The first constraint is Canadian federalism and partisan politics, which together make it difficult to create meaningful national policies and institutions. The second constraint focuses on the difficult challenge of introducing new thinking in the form of sustainable development ideas and instruments into the hidebound federal policy system. The third constraint is the institutional politics that resists structural or policy limits on the executive in the Canadian system. The fourth constraint flows from organizational design problems created by previous attempts at innovation. The final constraint is the bureaucratic inertia that has led to much resistance to change at the level of departments. But before we turn to these constraints it is necessary to say something more generally about the challenge sustainable development presents to contemporary governments.

The Scale of the Sustainable Development Change Agenda

As formulated by the Brundtland Commission, and elaborated subsequently in a series of international meetings (such as the Rio Earth Summit in 1992), sustainable development has come to represent an emergent international norm that has been absorbed increasingly into domestic political discourse. It emphasizes the protection of global life support systems, equity within and between generations, the importance of meeting basic human needs, and public participation in environment and development decision-making.[6] The idea was formulated as a 'bridging concept' to draw together concerns of rich and poor countries and to denote a new form of development that would be both more equitable and more sensitive to environmental limits.

Thus, sustainable development entails a fundamental change in the way environment and development decisions are made; the idea is to draw together the two domains so that instead of environmental policy struggling to clean up the consequences of ill-conceived economic advance, the economic, social, and environmental dimensions are considered from the outset. It is about altering the 'quality' of growth so that change leads to authentic societal progress.

There is no doubt that institutionalizing sustainable development represents a real challenge. This is not so much because the term can be interpreted in different ways, or invoked by specific actors to justify very different courses of action, although one often encounters this complaint. The constructive ambiguity of sustainable development is typical of normative terms (think of other examples such as 'freedom', 'equality', and 'democracy') which have a clear core meaning and play a central role in political life, but about which we argue continuously. But it does mean that sustainable development cannot be invoked as a mechanical formula, which will crank out a specific policy recommendation in any given context. Rather it must be applied to particular circumstances, and it inevitably involves value choices about the sort of development we want to encourage and the kind of society in which we want to live.[7] Think of the suburban sprawl debate. The real difficulty is that sustainable development implies a radical shift from business-as-usual; it disrupts bureaucratic routines and established ways of doing things, and it demands new thinking and changed behaviour.

Conventional governance structures evolved over centuries of political experimentation and struggle, as societies tried to find acceptable ways to manage their affairs. Elements such as a written constitution; responsible government; periodic elections; the party system; individual civil, political, and social rights; and civil service neutrality are the results of generations of innovation, trial and error, reform, counter-reform, and adjustment. But the history of the second half of the twentieth century has revealed an emerging set of societal problems which our inherited governance institutions proved ill-equipped to manage. For while the industrial countries have proven relatively successful in promoting economic growth and building a social policy welfare net, much of this advance has been purchased at the cost of a rapidly deteriorating global environment, while many billions of people remain in poverty in the developing countries.

As compared to conventional approaches, governance for sustainable development implies a longer term perspective—one that considers consequences two, three, or more generations in the future. It deals with issues that cut across established jurisdictions and have implications at multiple scales, from the local community to the global commons. It requires integration of economic, social, and environmental considerations and the breaking down of the traditional partitions among government departments responsible for different dimensions of policy. Governance for sustainable development requires decision-making in conditions of acute uncertainty. And it requires public officials to interact with many societal actors because the solutions are not just in the hands of government but depend on innovation at all levels in society. Moreover, although it is usual to emphasize collaboration and consensus, the transition towards more sustainable ways of living is likely also to involve acute struggles as those who gain from existing (unsustainable) patterns of living resist the transition to more ecologically sound ways of doing things.

Sustainable development is often described in terms of three 'pillars'—the economic, social, and environmental—but in a rich country like Canada it is the environmental pillar that has been systematically neglected, and it is the integration of the environmental dimension into develop-ment decision-making that is so critical. Environmental integration implies a re-conceptualization of what 'growth', 'development', and 'the public good' imply. And it points towards a dramatic transformation of key economic sectors (energy, transport, agriculture, construction, and so on) to reduce the environmental impacts of production and consumption.[8] Some indication of the scale of the necessary changes is made evident by climate change. Scientific evidence now suggests that in the developed countries greenhouse gas emissions will have to fall by more than 80 per cent by mid-century if we are to avoid dangerous disturbance of the global climate system. Such a reduc-tion implies radical changes to existing patterns of energy use. But unsustainable societal practices are manifest in many other areas including land use, biodiversity loss, the (mis)management of biophysical resources, and chemical release.

Let us turn now to the constraints that have held back federal engagement with this sustainable development challenge.

Federalism, Politics, and Voters

Over the past 20 years federal–provincial entanglements and partisan politics have hindered consis-tent and sustained federal governmental engagement with sustainable development. International experience suggests that geographically-extensive federal states face particular challenges articulat-ing a coherent response to sustainable development, but in Canada the situation seems especially acute. Here, the constitutional division of powers, federal–provincial tensions over energy resources, longstanding regional sensitivities, and nationalist feelings in Québec have combined into a particu-larly potent brew. With respect to sustainable development, the pathologies of Canadian federalism have played out in different ways: jurisdictional complexities make the organization of co-operative action essential but intrinsically difficult and time consuming; politicians may be reluctant to take up issues because of a fear of jurisdictional entanglements; and the temptation to duck responsi-bility and blame others can be overwhelming. Moreover, provincial governments provide political representation for locally entrenched economic interests and claims about jurisdiction often serve as a proxy for distributive conflicts.[9]

Such problems have been particularly manifest in climate change policy where different regional resource endowments, economic structures, energy systems, and levels of affluence have under-pinned very different perspectives on the question. Vacillating between a deferral to provincial sensibilities and unilateral action that ignored previous commitments, the federal government has failed to provide consistent leadership and to establish the fruitful interactions with provincial and municipal governments required to advance this file.

Partisan disputes have also taken their toll: the Liberals abandoned the Green Plan which had been initiated by their Conservative rivals; and the Conservatives shut down Liberal climate programs as soon as they returned to power, only to resurrect similar initiatives a year later. Even inner-party rival-ries contributed to the climate change fiasco as, for example, when Paul Martin refused to endorse the Liberal government's Kyoto plan as he jostled to succeed Jean Chrétien as Prime Minister.

Political infighting is a staple of representative democracy, but it can certainly cause difficulty for files like sustainable development which try to set decision-making in a longer time perspective and demand cooperation across a range of traditionally distinct policy areas. Thus, the polarized polit-ical style associated with the Westminster model and first-past-the-post electoral systems, such as we have in Canada, may present something of a challenge. Most democratic states now incorporate some form of proportional representation which generates more balanced assemblies, encourages cross party collaboration, and favours coalition governments. Moreover, such mechanisms facilitate entry into the legislature of parties championing new ideas that have significant, but geographically distributed, support (such as the Green Party), rather than the regionally-based currents (such as the Bloc Québécois and the former Reform Party) which under the Westminster model can more easily convert popular support into seats. In the debate on C-474, both the Conservatives and Bloc exaggerated provincial sensitivities. This fixation with jurisdictional questions has handicapped the Bloc, which is normally sensitive to both environmental and sustainable development issues, from acknowledging the immense independent impact that cities will have on the twenty-first century sustainability challenge and the federal role in shaping these impacts.

Yet, it is possible to exaggerate the operation of these features. The Canadian government would never have been considered a leading sustainable development innovator at one time if there were not significant drivers of change also operating in Canada. Constitutional complexities and jurisdictional tensions are simply facts of doing politics in Canada. When there is enough pressure for action, solutions are usually found. Indeed, in some circumstances the federal distribution of power can favour innovation, as governments are able to move ahead with reforms in their areas of authority even when others are unwilling to act. Consider, for example, the carbon tax initiative in British Columbia. Moreover, substantial regional autonomy should, in principle, allow sustainable development policies to be better adjusted to local conditions. It is also true that features of the electoral and party systems which may have hampered substantive engagement with sustainable development at the federal level might, in other circumstances, have the opposite effect. The Liberal's 1993 electoral manifesto outlined during the campaign many of the innovations they would later introduce. Strong majority governments of the type typically produced by first-past-the-post electoral systems can provide the authority to drive forward change. Arguably, this was the case in the late 1980s and early 1990s when pioneering sustainable development efforts were introduced by the Mulroney Conservatives and the Chrétien Liberals.

Hence, the priorities of politicians and electorates, rather than characteristics of the political system, deserve a more important place in the story. One can argue, for example, that over the last few decades Canadians and their political leaders have been confronted with tough issues relating to free trade, deficit reduction, periodic recessions, and the Québec referendum which have made it a challenge for concerns about sustainable development to hold their ground. And yet governments everywhere face difficult issues, and there is evidence that in some countries sustainable development has found a more important place on the political agenda.[10] For example, in the 1990s Sweden faced serious economic difficulties that threatened its established welfare state model, but the government placed sustainable development at the core of its political program, calling for efforts to build a 'green welfare state'. Today, Sweden has institutionalized an impressive system of national environmental goals. Over the past decade, the United Kingdom has shed its image as an environmental laggard, contributing positively on the climate change front, most recently with the institutional innovation of regular 'carbon budgets', presented to Parliament and assessed by a panel of independent experts.

One cannot deny that Canadian political leaders have episodically shown leadership when they believed that there was substantial pressure from the electorate for more fundamental change.[11] The general assumption by politicians, journalists, and other analysts, it appears, is that Canadian voters want to protect the environment but do not understand the economic consequences of their desires and are unwilling to pay for the measures that would be required to deal with the major environmental problems. Consequently, politicians lost interest in environmental innovation once the voters' attention shifted back to other issues. In part, this is because environmental policies have traditionally been portrayed as a 'cost' to society and commerce. Sustainable development policies, however, highlight improved health outcomes for citizens and ecosystems, as well as economic efficiency gains as a way of underscoring the opportunities and benefits of the sustainable development change agenda. The challenge in Canada has always been in carrying through at the operational level during the low periods of public interest, the innovations introduced with rhetorical flourish during periods of high public interest. The 2008–9 'recession' is another test of whether Canadians have made this transition in their thinking, of whether concerns about climate change have fundamentally altered our understanding.

New Ideas and Instruments

Despite the rhetorical endorsement of sustainable development by political leaders, such new thinking has not penetrated deeply into the core of government activity in Canada. Politics and the public service remain largely in a traditional mind-set—with established production-oriented and distributional issues at centre stage. For politicians, time horizons are typically short, with an emphasis on regional trade-offs, the concerns of key economic sectors, the management of day-to-day crises and embarrassments, and partisan point-scoring. To some extent, all of this has been exacerbated by recent minority governments as every political act is assessed in terms of its putative electoral impact.

Climate policy provides an obvious example of a failure to embrace new thinking, where a decade of debate was largely dominated by short-term issues around Kyoto ratification and implementation, and governments continuously put off hard decisions. The basic insights that climate change is going to impact much of what government does, that adaptation will require major adjustments to existing policy frameworks, and that the scale of the emissions reductions required over the next half century will imply a radical transformation of the way we produce and consume energy, have simply not sunk in.[12]

That is not to say there has been no progress. The adoption of the *Canadian Environmental Protection Act* (CEPA), the *Canadian Environmental Assessment Act* (CEAA), and the *Species at Risk Act* (SARA), has finally provided a broad federal legislative framework for environmental protection. Canada has also begun to implement a new approach to chemicals policy, and there is promise in the Conservative government's New Regulatory Framework for air emissions. But, for the most part, these initiatives remain anchored in a traditional environment/human health protection paradigm. Certainly, it can be argued that these legislative actions represent a catch-up in areas of environmental policy where Canada lagged behind other industrialized states. But what has not happened is the definition of broad and integrative long-term environmental goals, the horizontal and vertical coordination of policy to promote environmental, social, and economic advance, as well as the delineation of a new—and environmentally sustainable—development trajectory. The Green Plan and the Guide to Green Government, which came the closest to articulating such a vision, had difficulty maintaining influence in day-to-day decision-making.[13] One of the key innovations of the *Federal Sustainable Development Act* is the requirement that measurable goals and targets, and an implementation strategy for meeting each target, be introduced to bring real meaning to sustainable development goals, backed up by regulations and designated ministerial responsibility.

Over the past two decades a range of new approaches that challenge traditional ways of doing things have begun to be applied in developed states, including life-cycle assessment of products and projects; 'cradle-to-grave' management; environmental and sustainability certification; greening government operations (procurement, energy use, buildings, fleet management); ecological fiscal reform; sustainability planning; and so on.[14] But, in Canada at the federal level, the take-up of these ideas has been sporadic. Governments have toyed with innovative practices, commissioning studies and pilot projects, but rarely following through in terms of actions that really change the way government business is done. For example, in terms of ecological fiscal reform, until very recently senior officials at the Department of Finance have consistently resisted attempts to 'green' the tax system.[15]

In the area of societal participation and multi-stakeholder dialogues Canada was an acknowledged innovator. The idea was to bring together representatives from business, civil society, and governments in order to build understanding and drive change. But government often failed both to provide a reinforcing policy framework, and to support sustainable development innovators and leaders. Joint recommendations were seldom implemented and good will was squandered. Today, many business and environmental stakeholders are skeptical of federal politicians who talk up a storm but do not deliver. On the other hand, we see the federal government increasingly requesting advice on long-term climate change issues from the multi-stakeholder-based National Round Table on the Environment and Economy (NRTEE).[16] And in terms of further institutionalizing such multisectoral bodies in legislation, the *Federal Sustainable Development Act* requires the creation of a Sustainable Development Advisory Committee that includes representation from each province and territory, and from aboriginal, business, and environmental nongovernmental organizations, and from labour.

Institutional Politics

Although a number of mechanisms have been put into place to ensure that government activity is aligned with sustainable development objectives and takes account of environmental issues, they lack political and administrative salience. In other words, they relate more to the form than to the substance of government. For example, the process of 'strategic environmental assessment' established by cabinet directive (1990, 1999, and 2004) is conducted 'in house' with no opportunity for external stakeholders to influence proceedings. Since 2004, departments have been obliged to issue a statement on environmental effects on completion of the SEA. But documents prepared for cabinet are secret; the process remains remarkably opaque and appears to have little influence on the formulation of policy. After all, impacts very often can be portrayed as marginal (in comparison to accumulated burdens in any given category) or necessary (even if classed as significant) to secure other advantages. Internally, this process is widely seen as just one additional administrative hurdle to be negotiated before a policy (that is destined to go forward) receives formal approval.

Departmental sustainable development strategies, one of Canada's early innovations, have not become part of real business planning of departments. The strategies are typically prepared by well-meaning teams of relatively junior officials who compile lists of existing commitments and canvass colleagues for suggestions to include in the glossy publication. Commitments are typically process oriented—highlighting commitments to 'publish a plan', 'review existing practice', or 'bring forward a proposal' by such and such a date—rather than relating to the substantive goals of the agency or department. The real decisions continue to be made by senior staff with no reference to paper strategies. The absence of an overarching federal strategy that establishes government-wide priorities has left the departmental strategies unconnected.[17] The core purpose of the *Federal Sustainable Development Act* is to fill this now well-known gap with a legal framework for developing and implementing a Federal Sustainable Development Strategy to provide context and direction to departmental sustainable development strategies.

Moreover, oversight by central agencies of the sustainable development file has been highlighted as a major weakness in the Canadian model. And since senior departmental and central agency officials have known that this is not an issue on which careers are made or broken, they focused their attention on other problems. It remains basically true that sustainable development is seen as the purview of Environment Canada, with a little help from NRCan and Fisheries and Oceans. This is a truly outdated conceptualization of the problem; as unsustainable development is an industrial policy problem. While cabinet and DM committees have been established periodically to coordinate sustainable development initiatives, these have played no more than a temporary coordinating role. PCO has, to date, declined to assume an active supervisory stance, nor has sustainable development bulked large in the concerns of Finance or Treasury Board.[18] This fundamental weakness has not really been addressed in the *Federal Sustainable Development Act* as it creates a Sustainable Development Office within Environment Canada rather than the PCO, the department of the Prime Minister. The Act also creates a Committee of the Queen's Privy Council of Canada to 'have oversight of the development and implementation of the Federal Sustainable Development Strategy'.[19] How important its impact will be remains to be seen.

Above all, there has been political and bureaucratic resistance to structures and processes which are seen to constrain the Prime Minister's authority to organize the conduct of government as he or she sees fit. Of course, much of the history of the evolution of democratic governance has been the development of institutional mechanisms to control the political executive. Today, many rules and procedures which appeared originally as constraints on the prerogatives of the executive constitute cornerstones of democratic accountability. Consider the regular meeting of parliament, the presentation of annual accounts, freedom of information legislation, Treasury Board procedures, and so on. The independence of the central bank, for example, was long resisted by an executive that wanted to retain its freedom to manipulate monetary policy in the run up to an election. Of course, if sustainable development is only perceived as a 'constraint', if it is seen simply as a check on 'normal' decision-making, it will continue to struggle to be integrated into the vision and practice of the executive itself. It is no coincidence that the breakthroughs have happened when the issue has been embraced by the Prime Minister.

Organizational Design Issues

Canada has made some key institutional design innovations. Two departments of government—Industry Canada and Natural Resources Canada—have amended their core statutory acts to include sustainable development, and several pieces of foundational law have included sustainable development as a goal of the legislation. Interestingly, the most creative institutional innovations have been made outside of the executive branch. This shows that governments are capable of institutional innovation, but are inclined to do it in a way that minimally impacts the autonomy of ministers. The NRTEE was created in 1989 as an outcome of the World Commission on Environment and Economy's 1986 visit to Canada. It has always been an arms-length advisory organization designed to bring together a cross section of societal leaders from industry, labour, and academe to advise the Prime Minister on key issues.[20] Under the Harper government the reporting relationship has unfortunately been downgraded to the Minister of the Environment.[21] The International Institute for Sustainable Development is headquartered in Winnipeg and is now largely autonomous of the government; it has developed a financial base that is no longer primarily reliant on federal funds. It is a highly respected research-based organization that works on both Canadian and international issues. Sustainable Development Technology Canada is also an arms-length agency.[22] It invests funds provided by the federal government in innovative clean technology developments in order to leverage private sector capital in innovation.[23] While each of these organizations has carved out an interesting and valuable niche in the panoply of sustainable development institutions in Canada, none are directly involved in the day-to-day decision-making process of government which influences the development trajectory of the country.

The fourth institutional innovation, the Commissioner of Environment and Sustainable Development (CESD), has proven to be the most controversial. This is perhaps not surprising because it is also the closest to the day-to-day operations of government. The CESD was created by the Chrétien government in 1995 in fulfillment of a commitment made in the 1993 election campaign to create an environmental auditor general.[24] The idea for an environmental auditor general was introduced by the environmental community during the development stage of the Green Plan,[25] but rejected by the Conservatives. The House of Commons Standing Committee on Environment and Sustainable Development, in its 1994 deliberations on the structure and functions of such an office, recommended the creation of a fully independent Commissioner who would report directly to Parliament. The combination of stiff resistance to the creation of an independent official by bureaucrats in the key line departments, and the offer from the Auditor General to house the new office within his existing apparatus resulted in the location of the CESD at a second-tier level within the Office of the Auditor General (OAG). This was a mistake in organizational design or, at the very least, in the naming of the new office. The OAG is a long standing and highly regarded audit office that reports directly to Parliament and has a legitimate proscription against commenting on policy. The transformative change agenda represented by sustainable development is inherently forward-looking and policy-oriented. Placing a Commissioner-type function within an audit office that is only allowed to look back and audit existing programs to ask if the departmental activity met its stated objectives was bound to come up against its inherent contradictions. While the CESD established, not surprisingly, a strong reputation for audit work over the period of 1997 to 2008, it was never really able to exercise the Commissioner functions expected of independent Commissioners like the Commissioner of Official Languages. Based on this decade-long experiment, the Liberals concluded that they had got it wrong initially and C-474 had a major section making the CESD independent of the OAG. This part of the Bill was ruled out of order by the Speaker of the House of Commons on technical grounds.

The Liberal government only modestly constrained the autonomy of the bureaucracy by choosing an odd model that required departments to create, and update every three years, departmental sustainable development strategies, while not requiring the government as whole to develop a government-wide strategy. This bottom-up approach was a unique experiment internationally, and after four rounds of strategies and a decade of practice, it is largely judged a failure. The 2007 Report of the CESD was the most recent of a devastating series of critiques of the departmental strategy process.[26] Most observers have come to the same conclusion.[27] As noted above, the Liberals who created both the CESD and the sustainable development strategy requirement were, by 2008, calling for a fundamental redesign. Ironically, the Conservative government is resisting the structural reforms to the institutions introduced over a decade ago by the Liberals, even though all parties are largely in agreement that the current arrangements have failed. The Conservatives appear concerned that an independent CESD would become an advocate of sustainable development within the parliamentary system, and that advocacy should only be excised by political parties and interest groups. This, interestingly, has never been a charge levelled at the Commissioner of Official Languages, who is an expected and respected advocate for the growth and development of both official languages in the practices of the federal government and across Canada.[28]

Bureaucratic Inertia

While politicians come and go in democratic political systems, the bureaucracy is the permanent custodian of long term problems. *Our Common Future* got to the heart of why bureaucratic inertia is such a powerful barrier to sustainable development:

> The objective of sustainable development and the integrated nature of global environment/development challenges pose problems for institutions . . . that were established on the basis of narrow preoccupations and compartmentalized concerns . . . The challenges are both interdependent and integrated . . . Yet most of the institutions facing these challenges tend to be independent, fragmented, working to relatively narrow mandates with closed decision processes. Those responsible for managing natural resources and protecting the environment are institutionally separated from those responsible for managing the economy. The real world of interlocked economic and ecological systems will not change: the policies and institutions concerned must.[29]

This is a poignant observation. The disaggregated Canadian experiment placing departmental strategies rather than a government-wide strategy at the centre of the change process strengthened the barrier of bureaucratic inertia. That is, with no vision to guide them, the creative interpretation of what sustainable development would comprise in policies and programs was largely left to departmental officials. The most they had to guide them was the 1995 Guide to Green Government and periodic consultations with departmental stakeholders. Given the paucity of direction or oversight from the central agencies, it is not surprising that the calibre and resilience of departmental strategies varied widely. Some departments did a decent job of integrating the three-year sustainable development strategies with the annual business planning process, but most did not. Some departments had engaged senior management and attempted to build SD capacity amongst staff, but most did not. Some departments developed serious ongoing management systems to monitor their own performance in terms of implementation of commitments, but most did not. Some allocated the financial resources required to support such changes within the departmental systems, but most did not. Because the central agency's accountability regime did not hold them accountable in any meaningful way, the senior management of most departments did not take the process seriously. The bureaucratic underlings noticed the attitudes of their superiors and the fairly junior officials tasked with leading were usually unable to overcome the inertia.

Indeed, the paucity of leadership and engagement by senior managers was one of the main barriers continually identified in a decade of reports from the CESD. PCO employed Deputy Ministers' coordinating committees as the primary instrument for coordinating horizontal issues across departments. However, there was virtually no cost to DMs for underperformance in this area.

That is one reason that the *Federal Sustainable Development Act* includes a clause creating the legal requirement for 'performance-based contracts' for senior officials 'for meeting the applicable targets referred to in the Federal Sustainable Development Strategy and the Departmental Sustainable Development Strategies'.[30] Simply put, someone in the system has to be held accountable for the 'implementation gap' identified ad nauseum by the CESD. The absence of such performance requirements in their contracts, and the lack of rigour associated with the SEA process in cabinet decision-making, led some DMs to conclude that the PM and cabinet were not serious about the rigorous implementation of the strategies. These suspicions of the motivation of cabinet ministers, combined with an inherent hostility to limits on departmental autonomy under the paradigmatic shift embodied by sustainable development, left many departmental senior management cadres unmotivated to undertake the types of changes that would provide traction. Retired Deputy Ministers Ian D. Clark and Harry Swain went so far as to categorize sustainable development as a 'utopian framework' entailing 'surreal management requirements'.[31] Because the disciplined application of a sustainable development approach would constrain bureaucratic autonomy and raise performance expectations, it was to be avoided because 'reality eventually prevails'. Given such attitudes, it is perhaps not surprising that the CESD would document a decade of policy and program failures and mismanagement as well as the inability of various iterations of DM's coordinating committees to influence colleagues.

Departmental rivalries and conflicts have been a significant barrier to achieving real progress on climate change policy in Canada. The inertia and inevitable implementation gap that flows from the current system is exemplified by the inability to make meaningful progress on greening of government's operations. As one of Canada's largest employers, purchasers, and landowners, the federal government can have a significant impact, and since the 1992 Code of Environmental Stewardship (A Green Plan program) it has been promising to be a leader in promoting SD management practices. Despite the expenditure of hundreds of millions of dollars on building retrofits, procurement program changes, and administrative innovations such as creating the Office of Greening Government Operations, the CESD still concluded in 2008 that '[t]he government's progress toward providing departments preparing sustainable development strategies with guidance on greening their operations is unsatisfactory.'[32] The explanation, in part at least, appears to reflect an unwillingness to impose system-wide constraints on departments with respect to key elements such as procurement. The result is a puzzling, though not surprising, inability to make progress on the relatively easy challenge of making the government a better environmental citizen. This, at the same time that governments are asking citizens to reduce their ecological footprint.

Conclusion

For more than 20 years, Canadian federal governments—both Liberal and Conservative—have made sporadic attempts to engage with the sustainable development agenda. Many specific reforms have born fruit but attempts to change the overall operation of government, to break the established pattern of Canadian politics, or to shift the traditional development trajectory, have been half-hearted and, to this point, unsuccessful. Today, Canada has a set of institutions for environmental governance, and a policy orientation that places it well back from the international sustainability innovators. On some issues, such as climate change, Canada's performance is simply disgraceful. But the sheer abundance of Canada's natural endowments and the relatively small size of its population have provided us with a relatively good environmental quality and a prosperous life-style. To some extent Canadians have been shielded from the true impacts of their profligate habits. It remains to be seen whether Canadians will awake from their complacent ways.

With the passage of the *Federal Sustainable Development Act*, a new chapter has begun. Canada will finally have a federal sustainable development strategy, and formal structures and systems to put in place national priorities, to improve co-ordination across the federal family, to fix appropriate policies, and to more carefully measure and monitor what has been accomplished and what remains to be done. But to what extent will things really change? That, of course, remains to be seen. Because after a certain point what matters is not formal procedures, but the political spirit that animates them. Simply put, if the political leadership and electorate are really committed to change, then progress can be made. If not, even the most impressive array of structures and procedures can rapidly degenerate into rhetoric and box-ticking, while in the corridors of power it remains business-as-usual.

Questions for Review

1. What kinds of changes are needed to put Canada on a path towards sustainable development?
2. What new policy approaches and instruments have been used by Canada's governments, and how effective have these been?
3. What institutional or organizational changes are required in the federal bureaucracy?
4. To what extent does the new Federal Sustainable Development Act signal a change in the federal approach?

Notes

1. World Commission on Environment and Development (WCED), *Our Common Future* (Oxford; Oxford University Press, 1987), 9 (our emphasis).
2. As quoted in David Suzuki Foundation, *Sustainability within a Generation* (Vancouver: David Suzuki Foundation, 2004).
3. Both authors have monitored this change process domestically and internationally over this period. See for example, G. Toner, 'Canada: From Early Frontrunner to Plodding Anchorman', and W. Lafferty and J. Meadowcroft, 'Patterns of Governmental Engagement', in W. Lafferty and J. Meadowcroft, eds, *Implementing Sustainable Development: Strategies and Initiatives in High Consumption Societies* (Oxford: Oxford University Press, 2000), 53–84 and 337–421. The authors co-organized a major conference reflecting on this period and projecting forward in celebration of the twentieth anniversary of the publication of *Our Common Future*. See Proceedings of *Facing Forward looking Back: Charting Sustainable Development in Canada 1987–2007*, Ottawa, 18–19 October 2007.
4. The bill introduced by MP John Godfrey was inspired in part by T. Gunton and C. Joseph, *Toward a National Sustainable Development Strategy for Canada* (Vancouver; David Suzuki Foundation, 2007).
5. WCED, 9.
6. W. Lafferty, 'The Politics of Sustainable Development: Global Norms for National Implementation', *Environmental Politics* 5 (1996): 185–208; J. Meadowcroft, 'Sustainable Development: A New(ish) Idea for a New Century?', *Political Studies* 48 (2000): 370–87.
7. See, for example, J. Meadowcroft, 'Who is in Charge Here? Governance for Sustainable Development in a Complex World', *Journal of Environmental Policy and Planning* 9 (2007): 299–314.
8. B. Masterson, 'From Eco-efficiency to Eco-effectiveness: Private Sector Practices for Sustainable Production', in G. Toner, ed., *Sustainable Production: Building Canadian Capacity* (Vancouver: UBC Press, 2006), 27–41.

9. See G. Toner and F. Bregha, 'Institutionalizing Sustainable Development: The Role of Governmental Institutions', in G. Toner and J. Meadowcroft, eds, *Innovation, Science and Environment: Special Edition—Charting Sustainable Development in Canada 1987–2027* (Montreal: McGill-Queen's University Press, 2009).

10. Consider P. Dreisen and P. Glasbergen, *Greening Society: the Paradigm Shift in Dutch Environmental Poilitcs* (Dordrecht: Kluwer Academic, 2002); L. Lundqvist, *Sweden and Ecological Governance* (Manchester: Manchester University Press, 2004); W. Lafferty, *Governance for Sustainable Development: The Challenge of Adapting Form to Function* (Cheltenham: Edward Elgar, 2004); and J. Meadowcroft, 'National Sustainable Development Strategies: A Contribution to Reflexive Governance?', *European Environment* 17 (2007): 152–63.

11. Mark Winfield has shown that environmental concerns have topped the polls only intermittently in Canada. See M. Winfield, 'Polls, Politics and Sustainability', in G. Toner and J. Meadowcroft, eds, *Innovation, Science and Environment: Special Edition—Charting Sustainable Development in Canada 1987–2027* (Montreal: McGill-Queen's University Press, 2009).

12. See J. Simpson, M. Jaccard, and N. Rivers, *Hot Air: Meeting Canada's Climate Change Challenge* (Toronto: McClelland and Stewart, 2007).

13. For more detailed analyses of the Conservative's and Liberal' governance innovations see G. Toner, 'The Green Plan: From Great Expectations to Eco-Backtracking to Revitalization?', in S. Phillips, ed., *How Ottawa Spends 1994–95: Making Change* (Ottawa: Carleton University Press, 1994), 229–60; G. Toner, 'Environment Canada's Continuing Roller Coaster Ride', in G. Swimmer, ed., *How Ottawa Spends 1996–97: Life Under the Knife* (Ottawa: Carleton University Press, 1996), 99–132; L. Juillet and G. Toner, 'From Great Leaps to Baby Steps: Environment and Sustainable Development Policy Under the Liberals', in G. Swimmer, ed., *How Ottawa Spends 1997–98: Seeing Red—A Liberal Report Card* (Ottawa: Carleton University Press, 1997), 179–209; G. Toner and C. Frey, 'Governance for Sustainable Development: Next Stage Institutional and Policy Innovations', in G.B. Doern, ed., *How Ottawa Spends 2004–2005: Mandate Change in the Paul Martin Era* (Montreal: McGill-Queen's University Press), 198–221.

14. See G. Toner and D.V.J. Bell, 'New Century Ideas and Sustainable Production', in G. Toner, ed., *Sustainable Production: Building Canadian Capacity* (Vancouver: UBC Press, 2006), 2–23.

15. For early assessments in the Canadian context see National Round Table on the Environment and Economy, *Ecological Fiscal Reform and Urban Sustainability: An Analysis of Federal Policies* (Ottawa, 2002) and *Toward a Canadian Agenda for Ecological Fiscal Reform: First Steps* (Ottawa, 2002).

16. See National Round Table on Environment and Economy, *Advice on a Long-term Strategy on Energy and Climate Change* (Ottawa, 2006) and *Interim Report to the Minister of Environment* (Ottawa, 2007).

17. Francois Bregha, 'Missing the Opportunity: A Decade of Sustainable Development Strategies', in G. Toner, ed., *Innovation, Science and Environment: Canadian Policies and Performance 2008–2009* (Montreal: McGill-Queen's University Press, 2008), 30–52.

18. Commissioner of Environment and Sustainable Development, 'The Commissioner's Perspective—2005', *2005 Report to the House of Commons* (Ottawa, 2005), 9–13.

19. See Canada, *Federal Sustainable Development Act*, Clause 6, 26 June 2008.

20. For the source of the NRTEE's intellectual origins see National Task Force on Environment and Economy, *Report* (Downsview, 1987).

21. For an overview of the development of the NRTEE see S. Boutros, 'A Child of Brundtland: The Institutional Evolution of the National Round Table on the Environment and Economy', in G. Toner and J. Meadowcroft, eds, *Innovation, Science and Environment: Special Edition—Charting Sustainable Development in Canada 1987–2027* (Montreal: McGill-Queens University Press, 2009).

22. For a discussion of the contributions of IISD see L. Hayward, 'The Best of Brundtland: The Story of the International Institute for Sustainable Development', in G. Toner and J. Meadowcroft, eds, *Innovation, Science and Environment: Special Edition—Charting Sustainable Development in Canada 1987–2027* (Montreal: McGill-Queens University Press, 2009).

23. For an analysis of the work of SDTC see A. Montambault, 'Building a Sustainable Development Infrastructure in Canada: The Genesis and Rise of Sustainable Development Technology Canada', in G. Toner and J. Meadowcroft, eds, *Innovation, Science and Environment: Special Edition—Charting Sustainable Development in Canada 1987–2027* (Montreal: McGill-Queens University Press, 2009).

24. Liberal Party of Canada, *Creating Opportunity: The Liberal Plan for Canada* (Ottawa, 1993), 64.

25. Greenprint for Canada Committee, *Greenprint for Canada: A Federal Agenda for the Environment* (Ottawa, 1989).

26. Commissioner of Environment and Sustainable Development, 'Sustainable Development Strategies', *2007 Report to the House of Commons* (Ottawa, 2007).

27. For a discussion of the development of the CESD see L. Smallwood, 'Advocate or Auditor? The Conflicted Role of the Commissioner of Environment and Sustainable Development', in G. Toner and J. Meadowcroft, eds, *Innovation, Science and Environment: Special Edition—Charting Sustainable Development in Canada 1987–2027* (Montreal: McGill-Queens University Press, 2009).

28. G. Toner, 'The Harper Minority Government and ISE: Second Year-Second Thoughts', in G. Toner, ed., *Innovation, Science and Environment: Canadian Policies and Performance 2008–2009* (Montreal: McGill-Queen's University Press, 2008), 3–29.

29. WCED, 9.

30. *Federal Sustainable Development Act*, Clause 12.

31. I. Clark and H. Swain, 'Distinguishing the Real from the Surreal in Management Reform: Suggestions for Beleaguered Administrators in the Government of Canada', *Canadian Public Administration* 48, 4 (Winter 2005): 453–76.

32. Commissioner of Environment and Sustainable Development, 'Greening of Government Operations', *2008 Report to House of Commons* (Ottawa, 2008), 2.

PART

III

Environmental Governance at Multiple Levels

7

The North American Context: Canadian Environmental Policy and the Continental Push

Debora L. VanNijnatten

There can be no doubt that Canada's environmental policy landscape has changed significantly over the past decade, particularly in regard to developments in our own backyard. In fact, our backyard seems to have become simultaneously deeper and longer. While the United States still looms large in terms of our environmental policy strategies, the country is now seen less as a monolithic, unitary actor which exerts pressure on its northern neighbour and more as a loose collection of voices loudly conveying different messages vis-à-vis environmental matters. Over the course of the Bush administration, Canadians watched as many American states, reacting against a national agenda that was decidedly anti-environmental, tried to force action through the federal courts while also forging ahead with ambitious policies in their own jurisdictions. In many cases, Canadian jurisdictions have been asked to cooperate in these ventures.

At the same time, 'North America' has become a more concrete entity for Canadian environmental policy-makers and policy analysts. After years of debate about the impacts of NAFTA on the environment, we are gradually arriving at a more nuanced and broader view of environmental policy dynamics in a liberalized, continental trade context. Careful convergence studies have found little compelling evidence of a generalized race-to-the-bottom in environmental standards and there are some examples of upward harmonization. We have even come to realize that Canadian environmental performance is often not what we would wish to race 'up' to, given our rather mediocre standards in many areas. Yet, we have also acquired a greater awareness of the yawning development gap on the continent, the challenge this poses for future sustainability, and the need for governance frameworks which will allow us to *jointly* address these challenges. In fact, we now have in place some very basic architecture for trilateral environmental collaboration, most notably in the form of the North American Commission for Environmental Cooperation.

This chapter considers North American influences on Canadian environmental policy-making and policy. The first section of the chapter outlines the mechanisms by which North American ideas and actors influence Canadian environmental policy at multiple governance levels: bilateral, trilateral, and cross-border regional. It sets out the argument that the North American dynamic has changed; whereas bilateral interaction between the Canadian and American national governments dominated until the early 1990s, now the most significant interactions over the past decade or so have been between subnational governments, namely states and provinces, working together at the cross-border regional level. Interestingly, while under the previous bilateral regime the Canadian government was often the initiator of cooperation, at the subnational level it is American states who are pushing for more ambitious transborder environmental action. Further, there have been noteworthy initiatives at the trilateral level which have served as a supportive backdrop for subnational activities.

A key concern of this chapter, in keeping with the theme of this volume, is whether this changed North American dynamic is likely to constrain or encourage environmental policy leadership in Canada. There is some preliminary evidence indicating that the new dynamic is influencing Canadian environmental policy-making by changing the manner in which policy agendas are set and goals adopted, and also by encouraging the consideration of alternative, especially market-based, policy instruments. This, in turn, has created opportunities for environmental policy leadership, perhaps even for innovation in terms of policy instrument choice in Canada. At the same time, however, the cross-border regional dynamic has thus far served to reinforce the differences in environmental policy approach which already exist among provinces, and between the provinces and the federal government; this complicates even further the primary task outlined in the Introduction to this volume— namely, building a more comprehensive and integrated environmental policy regime in Canada.

The North American Dynamic: From a Bilateral to a Continental Portrait of Environmental Governance

North American influences are understood here as being generated in a context that includes governance at three levels: bilateral, trilateral, and cross-border regional. The reader will note that the term *governance* has been used, rather than *government*. While we associate the term 'government' with the exercise of authoritative decision-making within a particular political unit (e.g., Canada or Ontario), 'governance' can be understood more broadly as the activity of making authoritative public choices.[1] As noted in the Introduction, conventional political institutions, such as cabinet and parliament, are increasingly supplemented, and in some cases supplanted by, other 'sites' of governance. And, it is just a short step from there to envisioning governance sites which are primarily transboundary, involving actors from different governments and from outside these governments. Moreover, these governance sites do not tend to emerge organically; rather, officials at one level take the lead in defining and implementing policy activities.[2]

Bilateral Governance

Analysts of Canadian environmental policy are most familiar with the Canada–US bilateral relationship although, paradoxically, governance at this level has become the least significant in terms of environmental policy activity. Those studying the Canada–US environmental relationship in the 1980s, who emphasized the importance of bilateralism and diplomacy, would have been surprised at such a statement. As Maxwell Cohen noted in 1983: 'Canada and the United States occupy and inevitably have to jointly manage a vast continental region . . . some five thousand miles of boundary [that] are the major fact of sovereign life for both countries.'[3] John Carroll, in setting out the framework for his ground-breaking volume—the first comprehensive, cross-case analysis of Canadian–American environmental relations entitled *Environmental Diplomacy*—chose his cases on the basis of their 'diplomatic importance and relevance to the overall bilateral relationship'.[4] In their detailed analyses of the development of Great Lakes pollution and acid rain regimes, Don Munton and Geoffrey Castle concluded that, '[t]hough both Canada and the United States still enjoy legal sovereignty and substantial political autonomy in formulating their environmental policies, . . . the structures within which they operate are, increasingly, artifices of the emerging bilateral regime.'[5]

Bilateral environmental interactions have certainly produced valuable institutions and important policy actions. The International Joint Commission (IJC), established under the *1909 Boundary Waters Treaty*, has been the most prominent bilateral institution operating in Canada–US environmental relations, perhaps the most prominent bilateral environmental institution on the continent. Operating under the general guidance of six Commissioners—three Canadian and three American, all political appointees—the IJC provides an umbrella for numerous advisory and management boards. In addition to managing water use and levels, the IJC has become engaged with issues relating to pollution of shared waters.[6] This engagement resulted in the *Great Lakes Water Quality Agreement* (signed in 1972, updated in 1978), a binational agreement that highlighted areas within the Lakes experiencing severe environmental degradation and provided a framework for addressing these. On the west coast, the Pacific Salmon Commission was established under the *Pacific Salmon Treaty* in 1985 to set and implement long-term goals for the joint management of the salmon fishery. The Treaty established a framework to prevent overfishing and to allocate the resource between various interests in the two countries. When this framework broke down in the 1990s, the Treaty was renegotiated and the Commission now plays a more active role in resource conservation. In addition, when the highly-politicized conflict between the two countries over acid rain came to a conclusion with the 1991 passage of the *Canada–United States Air Quality Agreement*, this led to the creation of another bilateral institution, the Canada–US Air Quality Committee. Effective cooperation and diplomacy by the Air Quality Committee (and its subcommittees) has resulted in binational 'annexes' to reduce the flow of acid rain precursors and ground-level ozone.[7] An annex for particulate matter is currently under negotiation.[8]

These binational institutions have had a fair degree of success in managing more narrowly defined environmental disputes, but less success in taking a longer-term sustainability perspective along the shared border. One of the reasons for this lack of a longer-term view is that, by their very nature, Canada–US binational institutions have been constrained by the politics of sovereignty and territorial integrity. The IJC can be an effective mechanism for mediating disputes regarding the management and use of shared water resources. However, in recent decades it has encountered significant difficulties in dealing with the Canadian and American national governments, as well as domestic agencies in the two countries. While many stakeholders had hoped that the IJC would be a forceful advocate for transboundary environmental quality, the two national governments have stymied attempts—whether originating inside or outside the Commission—to assign to the IJC a more independent role in studying and adjudicating border issues. Munton, for example, has observed that, '. . . . by the very nature of its unique and rather anomalous position vis-à-vis the governments, the IJC remains a vulnerable institution with limited capabilities and authority . . . less than an equal match for the sovereign will of the two governments which created it.'[9] The Pacific Salmon Commission finds itself treading carefully among various and conflicting proprietary interests in a resource that is allocated according to nationality—indeed, over-allocated among the two countries. Recent efforts to protect chinook stocks, which involve the 'sale' of fishing rights between the two countries, is a case in point.[10] For its part, the Canada–US Air Quality Committee has had some high-profile successes, but precisely because it has restricted its engagement to reducing specific pollutants, one at a time, and in such a way that actions taken remain firmly within the restricted mandates of domestic agencies.[11]

Moreover, bilateral environmental institutions and initiatives along the border have been susceptible to the changing policy and thus financial priorities of governments, and environmental agencies which provide much of the support for bilateral programming have not fared well. The early 1990s appeared to be the high point of environmental engagement by Canada and the US, with commitments made domestically, bilaterally, and at the international level. However, in the mid-1990s in Canada, deficit reduction through 'program review' exercises became the primary concern and Environment Canada lost almost one-third of its budget and one-quarter of its staff. In the US, the Republican-dominated Congress blocked Clinton's environmental initiatives with its de-regulatory Contract with America. After the election of George W. Bush in 2000, the political agenda became even more explicitly anti-environmental, this time directed from the White House. US EPA programs also underwent cuts beginning in 2002–3 as a result of the Bush administration's attempts to address a sizable budget deficit. In both countries, cuts encouraged a retreat to the fulfillment of core regulatory responsibilities, and funding for transboundary projects became less imperative. Moreover, with the increased focus on domestic and border security post-9/11, the two countries (but especially the US) have shifted their focus to other security-related, as opposed to environmental, border issues and federal monies have been diverted to associated programs and technology.

Trilateral Governance

At the same time that environmental policy energy was fading at the national level in Canada and the United States, the Canadian–American environmental relationship was increasingly being supported by a trilateral framework. Beginning in the mid-1990s, academic attention focused on such issues as the effects of the North American Free Trade Agreement (NAFTA) on the environment and the influence of new supranational mechanisms, including those established under the North American Agreement on Environmental Cooperation (NAAEC). NAFTA and the NAAEC 'promised to transform a hitherto almost exclusively bilateral relationship into a new trilateral community, by making many issues, processes, and institutions into a new trilateral structure'.[12] By the end of the decade, it was argued that the NAAEC's institutional offshoot, the Commission on Environmental Cooperation (CEC), had 'brought trilateralism in an intense and permanent way to North America and to Canada–US environmental governance'.[13] The CEC has a mandate 'to promote trinational cooperation for sustainable development, conservation, and environmental protection' through the provision of 'tangible services, in the form of activities and outputs'.[14] CEC program managers run seminars, workshops, and exchanges to promote technical training; develop methodologies, tools and databases to support policy formulation; and fund community-based projects in the three countries. More controversially, the CEC, through its citizen submission process and its powers to undertake research on specific environmental policy problems, can also act as an 'environmental watchdog' to ensure that governments are enforcing their own environmental laws.

The implementation of these key tasks by the CEC has been hampered by both a lack of political support and inadequate resources, however. The NAAEC and CEC bear the scars of their highly political origins; the NAAEC was the price Canada and Mexico had to pay for US congressional approval of the NAFTA, and they sought to limit both their own commitments under the agreement and the CEC's powers. Viewed with suspicion by many national and agency officials in all three countries, attempts by the CEC Secretariat to be ambitious in its undertakings or, some would argue, even to fulfill the basic requirements of its mandate, has been met with resistance—not unlike national governments' treatment of the IJC. Indeed, the autonomy of the Secretariat has been constrained at numerous points by the involvement of national executives in the Secretariat's program operations and attempts to restrict the scope of the citizen submission process provided for under the NAAEC.[15] Interestingly, the CEC has been directed by the governments to stay away from climate change policy, clearly a politically volatile environmental issue for all three countries. A lack of political support for the CEC's activities is likely also linked to the meager budget provided to the Secretariat by the three national governments—$3 million US from each government. Given that the CEC's budget has not changed since 1994, its real value has declined by almost 20 per cent.[16]

Yet, in its 2004 evaluation of the CEC, the Ten-year Assessment and Review Committee stated that the CEC's most notable accomplishment 'may be the creation of a trilateral North American community joining the governments and the public'.[17] Indeed, there can be no doubt that the CEC has increased the number and range of contacts among government officials at different levels and their various stakeholder groups. Kirton notes with respect to the CEC that, although the organization's autonomous political impact is limited by its lack of formal policy advisory responsibilities, it has nevertheless exerted influence through 'the scientific credibility it has commanded and the broader support base and epistemic community it is fostering through the many expert groups, study teams, and consultations it has created. . .'.[18]

And it is through these networks and epistemic communities that the CEC has been able to accomplish a great deal in particular areas. For example, thanks to the CEC, reporting on toxic releases into the environment now occurs in all three countries using comparable methodologies. The CEC has also facilitated the establishment of North American Regional Action Plans (NARAPs) for reducing persistent and toxic chemicals such as PCBs, dioxins and furans, and mercury on the continent. In addition, the CEC has shown considerable tenacity in terms of keeping power plant emissions on governments' agendas, releasing regular reports on transboundary flows, environmental impacts, and the links between energy policy choices and air pollution. And, the CEC has undertaken a number of targeted initiatives in terms of biodiversity protection, with programming focused on migratory birds and marine mammals. All of these initiatives serve to broaden the perspective of governments and foster dialogue on shared environmental objectives, while providing some (albeit minimal) support for implementation.

A more recent trilateral initiative, the 2005 Security and Prosperity Partnership of North America (SPP), is also likely to exert some influence over environmental activity on the continent, although the direction and scope of this influence is difficult to foresee at this time. The SPP originated with Canadian and Mexican concerns that continental trade flows were being damaged by an American obsession with security; it is the most significant trilateral initiative since NAFTA and represents the most current thinking on trilateral cooperation. Notably, the SPP also undertakes a 'quality of life' agenda, which includes a commitment to 'joint stewardship of the environment'. At the present time, the SPP's environmental approach is decidedly ad hoc, disjointed, and unambitious, consisting mainly of repackaged, 'end-of-pipe' initiatives already being undertaken by various levels of government (including bilateral institutions and the CEC), in the areas of air quality, water quality, invasive species, migratory wildlife and oceans issues.[19] These initiatives are being overseen by an Environment Working Group staffed by agency representatives from the three countries which reports regularly to the three governments on progress.[20]

Yet, the existence of an Environment Working Group under the auspices of the SPP indicates a slightly greater openness to pursuing environmental collaboration within North America or, perhaps more realistically, to highlighting or reinvigorating cooperation that is already ongoing. It is also an acknowledgment of the links between trade, economic growth, and environmental sustainability, although this link is by no means operationalized in programming. Potentially more far-reaching in this regard are the attempts, since the trilateral Leaders' summit in Montebello, Québec in August 2007, to link the continental energy and climate change agendas by jointly pursuing opportunities for lower-carbon technologies and thus reducing greenhouse gas emissions within North America.[21] These attempts run the gamut from 'nuts and bolts' initiatives such as harmonizing energy efficiency standards for consumer products and sharing information on vehicle fuel efficiency, to broader proposals for constructing a 'joint vision of biofuels for transportation by 2020' and achieving comparable air emissions inventories as well as emissions estimation methodologies for power plants.[22] In addition, an agreement for the exchange of information for clean energy has been signed by the three leaders. These types of initiatives are likely to continue under the increasingly institutionalized 'Leaders' Summits', which appear to be replacing the publicly unpopular SPP.

Subnational and Cross-border Regional Governance

To make matters more interesting, not to mention more complex from an analytical perspective, the bilateral and trilateral aspects of North American environmental governance do not represent the whole governance picture, or even the most colourful part. Indeed, case study work over the past decade indicates that it is subnational governments, particularly US states and to some extent Canadian provinces, often acting through cross-border cooperative mechanisms, that have been the primary locus of environmental policy initiative and innovation to address transboundary problems.[23] This literature shows that subnational cross-border interactions have become more formalized and increasingly multilateral or regional in orientation, as well as more ambitious in terms of the projects undertaken.[24]

In fact, recent empirical work by this author provides evidence that distinct 'environmental cross-border regions'—possessing observable boundaries and capable of autonomous action—are developing on the Canada–US border.[25] Three different approaches were employed to discover the boundaries of these environmental cross-border regions (CBRs). First, one might expect that environmental CBRs are built primarily upon or contain major ecological features which provide some kind of impetus for joint action. In the Pacific Northwest the transboundary relationship is anchored by the Georgia Strait–Puget Sound Basin, the Cascades, and the 'Crown of the Continent', the montane cordillera landscape connecting Yellowstone to the Yukon. The Red River Basin straddling Manitoba, North Dakota, and Minnesota requires attention to shared watershed management challenges. In the Canada–US heartland, the Great Lakes Basin is the dynamus for considerable cross-border interactions. And, in the Canada–US Northeast, the Appalachian landscape and the maritime reality, particularly the Gulf of Maine Basin, promotes a shared view of environmental challenges.

Second, and perhaps more telling, are the results of a recent elite survey targeting government, private sector, academic, and civil society representatives who work in a cross-border capacity.[26] Survey respondents generally agreed that there is such a thing as a cross-border region and that CBRs have states and provinces as their basic units.[27] They also agreed on the core state–province membership of cross-border regions: British Columbia and Washington state in the Pacific Northwest, Ontario and those states bordering the Basin in the Great Lakes–Heartland, and the New England states, New Brunswick and Nova Scotia in the East. Further, they agreed that the boundaries of cross-border regions should be based at least in part on ecological features. When asked which factors were most important in defining their CBRs, survey respondents rated 'shared ecosystems' and 'locational factors' quite highly, more highly than 'cultural similarities' or 'historical links'.[28] Moreover, although respondents emphasized concrete ecological boundaries in their understanding of cross-border regions, they also observed that environmental cooperation may encourage interactions beyond these boundaries. As one respondent noted, 'bigger is often better in terms of defining a cross-border region as so many environmental issues require a broader coordination of efforts.'[29] Thus, the membership of environmental cross-border regions can include jurisdictions on the periphery of the 'core'.

A third method of discovering the boundaries of CBRs is to trace the formal imprint of cross-border environmental governance. This author constructed a database of state–province environmental governance linkages along the Canada–US border[30] and found that linkages are regionally concentrated in the Pacific Northwest, Great Lakes, and New England/Maritime areas. The New England region has a smaller number of agreements and institutions but these are largely multilateral and involve most or all members of the region. In the Great Lakes, there is a combination of multilateral and bilateral activity; there are numerous mechanisms incorporating all Great Lakes jurisdictions but also a host of bilateral agreements between Ontario and its neighbours. In the Pacific Northwest, the picture is one of bilateralism, with the very close BC–Washington relationship at its core, although there are multilateral mechanisms dealing with coastal environmental and natural resource management.[31]

Overall, environmental CBRs appear to have boundaries that are firm enough to identify core membership in a region for most purposes but flexible enough so as to incorporate other relationships depending on the issue. We can identify three environmental cross-border regions that build upon distinct core clusters of subnational jurisdictions; the Pacific Northwest (encompassing British Columbia, Alberta, Washington state, Idaho, Oregon, and Montana); the Great Lakes–Heartland (including Ontario, Minnesota, Michigan, New York, Illinois, Indiana, Ohio, Wisconsin, and Pennsylvania); and New England (including Québec and the four Maritime provinces as well as Vermont, Maine, New Hampshire, Massachusetts, Rhode Island, and Connecticut). In addition, we can identify three smaller clusters of jurisdictions that straddle core cross-border regions and might be considered sub-regions characterized primarily by networks of bilateral (rather than multilateral) interactions: Québec–Northern New England (New York and Vermont); Manitoba, Minnesota, and North Dakota; and Alberta, Montana, and Idaho. The core clusters can radiate influence outward to draw in other states and provinces in the sub-regions or on the periphery for particular purposes. For example, though generally a northeastern jurisdiction in terms of its environmental policy activity, Québec does participate in certain Great Lakes initiatives.

The three environmental CBRs certainly show evidence of autonomous action. It is at the cross-border regional level that the most ambitious initiatives in North America exist. For example, while national governments have done relatively little on the climate file, either domestically or bilaterally, subnational governments, often working within cross-border regions, have undertaken a variety of initiatives, including a number of continental 'firsts': a 2001 Climate Change Action Plan by the Conference of New England Governors–Eastern Canadian Premiers (NEG/ECP) which includes greenhouse gas reduction targets as well as sector-specific initiatives to achieve these reductions; inventory and modelling work to support the launching of cap-and-trade programs (the Regional Greenhouse Gas Initiative in the US Northeast and the Western Climate Initiative in the US/Canadian West); and carbon taxes in Québec and British Columbia. In addition, states and provinces have undertaken far-reaching and broad-based initiatives with respect to watershed management (via the Great Lakes Charter), airshed management (in both the Northeast and Pacific Northwest), and toxics (such as the NEG/ECP 1998 Mercury Action Plan). Environmental cross-border regions are also establishing institutional supports to implement these regional goals, although there appear to be differences and asymmetries among environmental CBRs in this respect.[32]

An important aspect of the shift from bilateral to cross-border regional environmental governance is the accompanying shift in the locus of leadership. While under the previous bilateral regime the Canadian government was often the initiator of cooperation, at the subnational level it is American states who are pushing for more ambitious transborder environmental action. As noted elsewhere in this volume, provinces have not generally tended toward stringent and innovative environmental policy choices. And, as Bruce Lourie and Doug Macdonald point out in their chapters, neither does the Canadian Council of Ministers of the Environment (CCME), the main intergovernmental forum for national environmental discussions, seem to promote environmental zeal. Instead, the critical factor here has been environmental policy activism on the part of American states, many of whom have reacted to the gearing down of the federal environmental regulatory machine in the US under the Bush administration by moving ahead on their own, even in areas where it was not clear that they had the jurisdiction to do so. From air quality and climate change, to nonpoint source water pollution and habitat management, many states have committed to ambitious policy goals and experimented with new policy instruments to achieve these goals. The reasons for this activism are complex; states, particularly those in the Northeast and along the west coast, have been driven forward by a peculiar mix of electoral politics, interest group pressures, legacies associated with earlier legislative commitments and (ironically) federal support for capacity-building in the 1990s, as well as supportive state professional associations such as the Environmental Council of the States (ECOS).

This innovation and energy has been transferred northward; in most cases, it is states rather than provinces which have been the driving force behind some of the most ambitious cross-border regional initiatives. For example, it was the commitment by Massachusetts to a 'Zero Mercury Strategy' which helped to drive the NEG/ECP's Mercury Action Plan. The Western Climate Initiative emerged out of the energies of certain west coast US states; only when the Initiative was up and running did British Columbia and then other Canadian provinces become interested. The original impetus for the Great Lakes Charter was concern on the US side that there would be major demands on the basin's water resources in the future.[33] This creates 'peer pressure' on provinces, who meet regularly with their state colleagues in cross-border forums, to follow their lead.

Over the past decade or so, then, there has been environmental policy activity at all three governance levels—bilateral, trilateral, and cross-border regional. Yet, activity undertaken by subnational governments working within cross-border regional cooperative institutions has been the most frequent and ambitious, driven forward by activist American states, while bilateral activity has waned considerably. Trilateral initiatives are also significant in terms of providing a framework for dialogue among environmental policy-makers in the three countries, broadening their perspectives to take continental pollutant pathways into account, and encouraging them to set and pursue joint goals in particular areas.

A New Policy-making Dynamic

What, then, does continuing and often vigorous environmental cooperation in cross-border regions, along with a thickening framework of cooperation at the trilateral level, mean for environmental policy-making in Canada? At the same time, what are the implications of less bilateral environmental governance? There is some preliminary evidence to indicate that the new dynamic is changing the manner in which Canadian environmental policy agendas are set and goals adopted, and is also encouraging the consideration of alternative, especially market-based, policy instruments.

First, as provinces have become drawn into cooperative regional arrangements with their immediate American neighbours, this has contributed to a dynamic whereby the Canadian environmental policy agenda is increasingly set in subnational and cross-border regional forums—not by national officials or even in CCME discussions. One case study example is mercury pollution reduction.[34] National governments in the US and Canada had undertaken little in terms of mercury reduction during the 1990s. At the subnational level, however, the NEG/ECP adopted a comprehensive Mercury Action Plan in 1998 designed to reduce mercury in the region. Based on extensive research showing that mercury posed a health and environmental threat in the Northeast, the Governors and Premiers endorsed the long-term goal of virtual elimination of anthropogenic mercury releases in the region, with interim reduction goals of 50 per cent by 2003 and 75 per cent by 2007. In order to achieve these reductions, the NEG/ECP endorsed objectives for the reduction of mercury emissions from specific point sources (municipal solid waste combustors, medical waste incinerators, sludge incinerators, utility and nonutility boilers, as well as other industrial and area sources), for the source reduction and safe waste management of mercury and for research and continued monitoring of mercury in the environment.[35] A Mercury Task Force staffed by state and provincial officials was put in place to guide implementation.

Interestingly, the CEC had already been working on a North American Regional Action Plan on Mercury; mercury was selected as one of the first four priority substances for action as early as 1996 under the CEC's Sound Management of Chemicals program. A Phase I Action Plan on Mercury was accepted by officials in the three countries in November 1997, instructing the Parties to undertake actions with specific targets and timeframes. Thus, the CEC had created both an umbrella policy framework and an impetus for action. Moreover, an official from the CEC participated in the NEG/ECP discussions.[36] It was only later, in 2000, that the CCME endorsed Canada-wide standards for mercury air emissions, mercury-containing lamps, and mercury in dental amalgam after an intergovernmental negotiating process which included NEG/ECP representation. The Canada-wide standards then aided the Atlantic provinces and Québec in fulfilling some of their commitments under the 1998 Mercury Action Plan.[37]

Climate change is a more recent example of this dynamic. Canadian federal climate change policy is famous—inside and outside of the country—for its timidity; Douglas Macdonald's chapter in this volume provides considerable detail in this regard. Consisting entirely of 'soft' measures to encourage greenhouse gas reduction, including voluntary programs for industry emission reductions, incentives for science and technology development, and public education/suasion programs, successive federal 'action plans' have failed to make even a dent in Canada's Kyoto target. This target has, in any case, been publicly abandoned by the current Harper government. At the same time, however, subnational governments—particularly US states—have undertaken a wide range of 'harder' initiatives, including legislated targets for overall emissions reduction, aggressive mandates for alternative energy production by power producers, legislated automobile emissions targets, and as noted above, putting in place the policy and technical frameworks for cap-and-trade programs that have fed into regional cross-border discussions of climate change. One cap-and-trade program, RGGI, has now achieved operational status; 10 northeastern and Mid-Atlantic have undertaken to cap CO_2 emissions from the power sector, and the second auction of CO_2 credits has already been held. The Western Climate Initiative, a cross-sectoral program in the US/Canadian West covering stationary sources, energy supply, transportation, residential and commercial fuel use, industry, waste management, agriculture, and forestry is being phased in. British Columbia, following the lead of California, Washington state, and Oregon, has also committed in legislation to a hard cap on emissions.

This work at the subnational level on cap-and-trade systems is no doubt figuring into the very recent national discussions in the two countries on the appropriate tools to use with respect to a national climate change plan. Incoming President Barak Obama has committed to legislating greenhouse gas emission targets and to implementing a cap-and-trade program. With the ascent of Henry Waxman, a decidedly pro-environment Democrat from California, to the chairmanship of the House of Representatives Environment & Energy Committee, climate change legislation will be introduced sooner rather than later.[38] Meanwhile, the Harper government in Canada has shifted from opposing any such system to advocating a trading system based on less stringent intensity targets in the face of increasing numbers of Canadian provinces opting to join the American regional trading systems.[39] In fact, Harper announced the day after the US election, and reiterated in the 18 November 2008 Speech from the Throne, that Canada would be interested in joining a North America-wide cap-and-trade system.

Certainly, the absence of bilateral environmental leadership—until now—has played a key role in developments at the subnational level. When national governments undertake bilateral actions, they tend to mobilize provinces toward common goals as part of the diplomatic and negotiating processes. This can be seen in the case study example of the 2000 Ozone Annex to the 1991 *Canada–United States Air Quality Agreement*,[40] which in many aspects was a reprise of the acid rain negotiations of the 1980s. In an effort to get the Americans to agree to reduce transboundary flows of ground-level ozone from the US Midwest into Central Canada by setting a NOx reduction target for their midwestern power plants, Canadian federal officials needed to offer up their own reduction target, to have a 'clean slate', so to speak. This, in turn, required that provinces, which are responsible for actual point source reductions, mandate cuts in NOx. In what appeared to be classic two-level game dynamics, federal officials pressured the provinces, particularly Ontario, to agree to emission reductions so that pressure could then be placed on US states to make reductions—which would have a dramatic impact on ground-level ozone levels in Ontario.

The Ozone Annex, however, was one of the very few bilateral initiatives over the past decade. Where the Canadian and American national governments have engaged in joint initiatives, these have taken the form of MOUs focusing on protocols for increasing cooperation in science and technology, such as in climate change research. These do not require governments to undertake any new policy actions. The promotion of carbon capture technology by the two national governments is a rare example of federal officials galvanizing (limited) action within provinces.

Second, it seems likely that participation in cross-border regional initiatives has encouraged a greater openness on the part of provinces to alternative and particularly market-based policy instruments. US states which are participating in the NEG/ECP's Climate Change Action Plan were from the beginning of the program much more likely to adopt a range of policy instruments, including regulatory targets for greenhouse gas reductions, alternative energy generation and tailpipe emissions, incentives for energy conservation, and the RGGI emissions trading system for the electricity sector on the US side. By contrast, eastern Canadian provinces were more likely to rely on voluntary 'challenges' to encourage industry emissions reductions, negotiated emissions reductions agreements with industry which were not binding, as well as public education programs to encourage energy conservation.[41] There was initially little interest in regulated emissions reductions, alternative energy mandates or market-based instruments such as cap-and-trade regimes.

However, this is changing. Québec has formulated a comprehensive *2006–2012 Action Plan* for climate change that includes a duty on gasoline and other fossil fuels, new tailpipe emission standards (on the California model), alternative energy, and energy efficiency targets and emission reduction targets for various industrial sectors. The province has adopted a greenhouse gas reduction goal of six per cent below 1990 levels by 2012. Prince Edward Island passed a *Renewable Energy Act* in December 2005, which requires utilities to acquire at least 15 per cent of electrical energy from renewable sources by 2010. And, there are plans to substantially increase this mandate. British Columbia has instituted both a cap on emissions and a carbon tax. Ontario, Québec, Manitoba, and British Columbia are in the process of joining/have joined the US state-led Western Climate Initiative, and have called on other provinces to take part. In fact, Québec Premier Jean Charest has publicly mused that it is only a matter of time before all provinces and territories follow the US and unite behind a common strategy: 'I don't think we can look at this issue now without factoring in the change that's going to happen in the Unite States in the short term . . . we should lead and prepare for a cap-and-trade system.'[42]

One might argue that cross-border regional cooperation is in some ways unstable. Most cross-border regional programming relies on the high-level political support of all jurisdictions, which is difficult to maintain given varying patterns of governing party ideology and shifting political priorities; the recent shift in the fall of 2008 to economic policy concerns given the financial crisis is only the most recent example. Cross-border regional initiatives also rely on the personal interaction of officials within agencies in participating jurisdictions and their willingness to continue to commit time and resources; both are vulnerable in light of staff changes and tight budgets. However, North American forces, and particularly cooperation at the subnational level within cross-border regions, appear to have created opportunities in Canada for environmental policy action and leadership—and perhaps even some innovation in terms of policy instrument choice—at the provincial level that might not otherwise exist.

Divergence and Discord From Below?

While we have noted the positive potential of cross-border regional interaction, undergirded by the new trilateral framework, to provide opportunities for environmental policy action, there may also be some drawbacks. More specifically, these continental forces and trends have served to intensify the centrifugal dynamics already present in the Canadian environmental policy-making regime. This, in turn, complicates the already difficult task in Canada of building the comprehensive and integrated regime that is necessary to meet the challenge of sustainability.

Environmental policy-making in Canada, as many of the chapters in this volume attest, features a relatively weak federal government, by decision as well as by design,[43] forced to bargain with muscular provinces. The Canadian federal government has the constitutional jurisdiction to address transboundary pollution problems, through such means as the negotiation of international agreements (e.g., the Kyoto Protocol) although in most cases the provinces have been in the business of requiring point source emission reductions. For example, jurisdiction over the regulation of greenhouse gas emissions from industries, energy development and use, consumer goods, and the residential sector is shared but the political dynamics of Canadian federalism, infused as it is with concerns about Québec nationalism and province-building in other regions, encourages the federal government to tread lightly here. Where the federal government does wish to pursue national action, extensive consultation is necessary and generally takes place in the CCME, where provinces and the federal government negotiate 'Canada-wide standards' as equals. Yet, even where Canada-wide standards are agreed, the federal government cannot, strictly speaking, force provincial compliance.

Provincial room for manoeuvre is further facilitated by executive dominance over the policy-making process. Given the power of the governing party over both branches of government in a situation of majority control, as has most often been the case at both the federal and provincial levels, policy discussions and conflict are contained within the executive, and consist of exchanges between the senior bureaucracy, cabinet, and whichever societal or business interests are granted access to these discussions. It is here that the environment–economy trade-offs are made, and economic interests generally have the upper hand. The Canadian environmental policy legacy is, not surprisingly, one of mandates that allow for considerable executive discretion and are subject to quick changes or even reversal, depending on the proclivities of the party in power.

Both executive domination and provincial independence within the federal system are enhanced with cross-border environmental regionalism. In general, environmental CBR linkages are focused primarily around state-province executive actors and are transgovernmental in nature, i.e., involving transnational communication and cooperation between officials in related departments of participating governments. Cooperation is carried out via annual conferences of political leaders, whose discussion outcomes then provide direction to committees of senior-level officials (who have process and management responsibilities) and mid-level officials (who have project-specific tasks). Continued communication and work is carried out by these latter officials; there appears to be relatively little role for legislatures, or even interest groups, outside of government. Moreover, cross-border environmental cooperation is rooted in and tied to a broadening network of interactions, both economic and political, that draw provinces more closely into the orbit of their state neighbours.[44] In this context, subnational governments see themselves as linked to each other—not to their national governments—in the struggle to succeed in a global marketplace that is linked to particular environmental policy perspectives.

Federal disengagement from environmental policy over the past decade, when levels of concern for the environment were relatively low, did not seem to be regarded by federal actors as particularly problematic; indeed, federal governments seemed content to have subnational governments assume a leadership role and even provided support for such activities. The Georgia Basin–Puget Sound International Airshed Management Strategy, carried out under the auspices of the British Columbia–Washington state Environmental Cooperation Council, has benefited from considerable Canadian federal scientific and financial support.[45] Moreover, Environment Canada officials and representatives from the CEC also took part in discussions on the NEG/ECP's Mercury Action Plan and have been supportive of the initiative. Federal officials seemed to view themselves as supporting provincial action rather than as environmental policy leaders.

However, now that the Canadian federal government wishes to take on a more active role in accord with public opinion and the anticipated shift in the American national environmental policy approach, cross-border regional environmental cooperation has the potential to create conflict where federal and provincial policy preferences differ, such as in the very public debate about the role of emissions trading in national climate change policy and about whether Canada should adopt 'intensity' versus 'absolute' emission targets. This discord has thus far acted as a barrier to a more integrated national environmental policy approach. Provincial environmental policies are now tied to agendas and initiatives that have emerged out of north–south dialogue in shared institutions in ways they were not a decade ago.

Indeed, the analysis in this paper shows policy goal convergence in particular cross-border regions, yet diversity across regions in terms of those goals. In the case of climate change policy, for example, the NEG/ECP's *Climate Change Action Plan* commits members to reduce GHG emissions to 1990 levels by 2010, 10 per cent below 1990 levels by 2020 and to ultimately decrease emissions to levels that do not pose a threat to the climate. Further west, the Dakotas, Iowa, Minnesota, Manitoba, and Wisconsin have launched a Powering the Plains (PTP) initiative, which includes a consensus agreement to develop regional scenarios for reducing CO_2 emissions 80 per cent from 1990 levels by 2050, and a commitment to developing a 'regional energy transition roadmap' to help achieve this long-term goal. In the Pacific Northwest, British Columbia, Washington, Oregon, and California are committing to reduce greenhouse gas emissions by 33 per cent of current levels by 2020 under the auspices of the broader Western Regional Climate Action Initiative.

And, as discussed above, there are differences in terms of the climate change policy instrument preferences of provinces, differences that are likely to bear some relationship to their respective cross-border regional alliances. Certainly, this proposition merits much closer empirical scrutiny. Can convergence of state–provincial policy goals or even policy instruments be attributed to initiatives being undertaken within environmental CBRs? A case study conducted by this author in another policy issue area—mercury pollution reduction—may be indicative; it found that there is some clustering among the six New England states and the five eastern Canadian provinces with respect to policy instruments advocated in the NEG/ECP Mercury Action Plan.[46] Among the six New England states, clustering is very much in evidence; all six states have endorsed the reduction target and those states with air emissions sources tagged in the Action Plan (utility boilers, incinerators, etc.) have, for the most part, adopted limits more stringent than federal standards. There is also some clustering in terms of mercury-containing product restrictions, disposal objectives, and notification requirements among New England states. The Atlantic provinces also have endorsed the NEG/ECP target and have adopted some mercury policy instruments that are consistent with the Mercury Action Plan, although they not been quite as active as New England states. Atlantic provinces, like the six New England states, have been most active in regulating point sources associated with atmospheric mercury releases, and they have also adopted similar disposal and notification requirements.

Cross-border regionalism has thus created its own policy legacy in the form of public political commitments, action plans, technical and policy documents, reporting briefs, and programming infrastructure buttressed by (often) years of effort and preciously expended political will. And we know that, once established, policy legacies are notoriously difficult to change.

Observations

As the first decade of the twenty-first century draws to a close, then, to what extent has a broader understanding of 'North America' replaced 'the United States' as the key descriptor of Canada's transnationalized environmental policy context? Over the past 12–15 years, bilateral environmental engagement seems to have taken a backseat to interactions at other governance levels. The North American Agreement on Environmental Cooperation signalled a shift in our political and environmental perspective; we have been drawn into trilateral arrangements, such as the CEC, which have come to provide a broader policy umbrella for thinking about and addressing specific environmental challenges. Our perspective has been 'lengthened' to include the southern parts of the continent.

To a greater extent, however, it has deepened, and we note the large number of often ambitious environmental policy activities which are being carried out at the subnational and cross-border regional level. Thus, we now operate in an environmental policy-making environment where we need to look both 'up' and 'down' for the source of much environmental policy leadership.

The changes discussed in this chapter are real and have the potential to influence Canadian environmental policy; they carry the seeds of our future environmental policy choices and architecture. And one should not characterize this picture as bleak; certainly, the American influence seems to be a relatively positive one, encouraging more ambitious action and consideration of a wider range of policy tools to address environmental problems. Many of the US states which border Canada have been instrumental in terms of acting as environmental policy entrepreneurs, both for their own national government and for neighbouring provinces.

However, this cross-border regional dynamic comes at a price. It has served to reinforce the differences in environmental policy approach which already exist among provinces, and it seems to be, at the current time, contributing to a growing divergence and discord among the provinces and federal government. This divergence complicates even further the perennial problem of building a more integrated environmental policy regime in Canada. As of early 2009, all signs indicate that the Canadian and American national governments are poised to undertake more leadership on the climate file, including in bilateral forums. They will not be able to erase a decade's worth of policy activity at the subnational level; indeed, they will have to engage this differentiated but innovative legacy directly.

Questions for Review

1. How effective have been the traditional Canada–US binational frameworks, such as those focused on Great Lakes water quality or transboundary air quality?
2. What has been the significance of the North American Agreement on Environmental Cooperation and the North American Commission for Environmental Cooperation for Canadian environmental policy?
3. Why have American states and Canadian provinces become more important North American policy actors?
4. What impact does cross-border cooperation have on Canadian provincial and national environmental policies?

Notes

1. Lamont C. Hempel, *Environmental Governance: The Global Challenge* (Washington, DC: Island Press, 1996), 10.
2. Debora L. VanNijnatten, 'Cross-Border Environmental Governance in North America: Building from the Bottom-Up?' Paper prepared for the Conference: *National Solutions to Trans-border Problems? The Challenges for Building Cross-Border Governance Practices in Post-NAFTA North America.* First Meeting of Tri-national Academic Group for the Study of Emerging Governance Institutions in North America (TAGGINA), March 2008, Monterrey, Mexico.
3. Maxwell Cohen, Preface to John E. Carroll, *Environmental Diplomacy: An Examination and a Prospective of Canadian–U.S. Transboundary Environmental Relations* (Ann Arbor: The University of Michigan Press, 1983), ix.
4. John E. Carroll, *Environmental Diplomacy*, 3.

5. Don Munton and Geoffrey Castle, 'Air, Water and Political Fire: Building a North American Environmental Regim', in A. Claire Cutler and Mark W. Zacher, eds. *Canadian Foreign Policy and International Economic Regimes* (Vancouver: UBC Press, 1992), 333.

6. The Treaty, which dealt primarily with the 'levels and flows' of boundary waters, also included a strongly worded prohibition on the pollution of boundary waters: 'the waters herein defined as boundary waters and waters flowing across the boundary shall not be polluted on either side to the injury of health or property on the other.'

7. Debora L. VanNijnatten, 'Analyzing the Canada–United States Environmental Relationship: A Multi-Faceted Approach', *The American Review of Canadian Studies: Thomas O. Enders Biennial Issue on the State of the Canada–U.S. Relationship* 33, 1 (Spring 2003): 93–120.

8. The Embassy of the United States, Ottawa, 'U.S.–Canada Cooperation on Environmental: Air Quality Issues," Available at http://ottawa.usembassy.gov/content/textonly.asp?section=can_usa&subsection1=environment&document=environ ment_airquality (accessed 25 May 2008).

9. Don Munton, 'Paradoxes and Prospects', in Robert Spencer, John Kirton, and Kim Richard Nossal, eds, *The International Joint Commission Seventy Years On* (Toronto: University of Toronto, Centre for International Studies, 1981), 81.

10. Justine Hunter, 'Salmon deal sells out fishermen, B.C. trollers say', *Globe and Mail*, 24 May 2008. Available at http://www.theglobeandmail.com/servlet/story/LAC.20080524.BCTREATY24/TPStory/?query=pacific+salmon(accessed 24 May 2008).

11. Debora L. VanNijnatten, 'Negotiating the Canada–U.S. Ozone Annex: A Case Study in Transboundary Environmental Relations'. Global Affairs Institute Transboundary Case Program, Maxwell School for Citizenship and Public Affairs (New York: Syracuse University, 2001).

12. J. Kirton, 'The Commission for Environmental Cooperation and Canada–U.S. Environmental Governance', *The American Review of Canadian Studies—Red, White and Green: Canada–U.S. Environmental Relations* 27, 3 (Autumn 1997): 459.

13. Ibid., 481.

14. Stephen P. Mumme and Pamela Duncan, 'The Commission on Environmental Cooperation and the U.S.–Mexico Border Environment', *Journal of Environment and Development* 5, 2 (June 1996): 203.

15. John Kirton, 'The Commission for Environmental Cooperation', 474; Laura Carlsen and Hilda Salazar, 'Limits to Cooperation: A Mexican Perspective on the NAFTA's Environmental Side Agreement and Institutions', in C.L. Deere and D.C. Esty, eds, *Greening the Americas: NAFTA's Lessons for Free Trade* (Cambridge, MA: MIT Press, 2002), 224.

16. Ten-year Review and Assessment Committee, *Ten Years of North American Environmental Cooperation*, 19.

17. Ibid., 4.

18. J. Kirton, 'The Commission for Environmental Cooperation', 473.

19. Debora L. VanNijnatten, 'The SPP as an "Indicator Species" for the Emerging North American Environmental Regime', *Politics and Policy* 35, 4 (2007): 664–82.

20. SPP Home, 'SPP Prosperity Working Groups'.

21. Debora L. VanNijnatten, 'Cross-border Environmental Governance in North America'.

22. Security and Prosperity Partnership of North America, 'Key Accomplishments since August 2007'. Available at http://www.spp.gov/pdf/key_accomplishments_since_august_2007.pdf (accessed on 18 May 2008).

23. See, for example: Barry G. Rabe, *Statehouse and Greenhouse: The Emerging Politics of American Climate Change Policy* (Washington, DC: Brookings Institution Press, 2004); Debora L. VanNijnatten, 'The Constituent Regions of the Canada–United States Environmental Relationship', in George A. MacLean, ed., *Canada and the U.S.: A Relationship at a Crossroads?* Centre for Defence and Security Studies. Proceedings of the University of Manitoba Political Science Students Conference, 2006, Winnipeg, Manitoba; Debora L. VanNijnatten, 'Environmental Constituent Regions and the Canada–U.S. Relationship'. Paper prepared for the Linnea Terrarum: International Borders Conference, March 2006, El Paso, Texas; and, Debora L. VanNijnatten, 'Mercury Reduction in the United States and Canada: Policy Diffusion across Internal and International Borders'. Paper prepared for the Annual Meeting of the American Political Science Association, September 2005, Washington, DC.

24. See, for example: J. Alley, 'The British Columbia–Washington Environmental Cooperation Council: An Evolving Model of Canada–United States Interjurisdictional Cooperation', 53–71, in R. Kiy and J.D. Wirth, eds, *Environmental Management on North America's Borders*. (College Station: Texas A & M University Press, 1998); D.K. Alper, 'Transboundary Environmental Relations in British Columbia and the Pacific Northwest', *The American Review of Canadian Studies—Red, White and Green: Canada–U.S. Environmental Relations* 27, 3 (Autumn 1997): 359–84; D.K. Alper, 'Emerging Collaborative Frameworks for Environmental Governance in the Georgia Basin/Puget Sound Ecosystem'. Paper presented to the Association of Borderland Studies, April 2003, Las Vegas, Nevada; L.P. Hildebrand, V. Pebbles, and D.A. Fraser, 'Cooperative ecosystem management across the Canada–U.S. border: Approaches and experiences of transboundary programs

in the Gulf of Maine, Great Lakes and Georgia Basin/Puget Sound', *Ocean and Coastal Management* 45 (2002): 421–57; A. Springer, 'North American Transjurisdictional Cooperation: The Gulf of Maine Council on the Marine Environment', *Canadian–American Public Policy* (April 2002). Available at http://www.umaine.edu/canam/PublicPolicyJournal/titles. htm.

25. Debora L. VanNijnatten, 'Towards Cross-Border Environmental Policy Spaces in North America: Province–State Linkages on the Canada–U.S. Border', *AmeriQuests: The Journal of the Center for the Americas* 3, 1 (2006); Debora L. VanNijnatten, 'Environmental Cross-Border Regions and the Canada–U.S. Relationship: Building from the Bottom-Up in the Second Century?' Paper prepared for the authors' workshop on: *Transboundary Environmental Governance: The Second Century*, Barry Rabe and Stephen Brooks, eds (Washington, DC: Woodrow Wilson Institute, 8–9 May 2008).

26. As part of its *North American Linkages* research project, Policy Research Initiative (Government of Canada) researchers and three university academics (including this author) constructed a detailed 12-page Elite Survey, the purpose of which was to examine the nature of relationships and interactions at the cross-border level. Respondents were surveyed from the four cross-border regions outlined by the PRI and from a range of organizations—provincial–state governments, cities, nongovernmental organizations, think tanks, chambers of commerce, regional economic development agency, and associations. A total of 547 people were contacted and received the survey. One hundred individuals completed the survey for a response rate of 19 per cent. Surveys were completed between 20 July and 7 October 2005. This author acted as academic advisor in the formulation and implementation of the survey.

27. Emmanuel Brunet-Jailly, Susan E. Clarke and Debora L. VanNijnatten, 'I. The Results in Perspective: An Emerging Model of Cross-Border Regional Co-operation in North America', *Leader Survey on Canada-US Cross-Border Regions: An Analysis. North American Linkages Working Paper Series 012*, Government of Canada, Policy Research Initiative, February 2006.

28. Debora L. VanNijnatten, 'Environmental Cross-Border Regions and the Canada–U.S. Relationship'.

29. Phone interview with Daymon Trachsel.

30. As a first step in building the database, existing studies were consulted, such as Swanson (1976), Stein and Grenville-Wood (1984), Canada School of Public Service (2004), as well as the CEC Transboundary Agreements Database. Research was then conducted in order to determine whether additional linkages could be discovered. Preliminary lists of linkages—including the name, date of establishment, and membership—were then sent to each state and province for verification. Input from state and provincial officials resulted in deletions from the database, as additional linkages were declared inactive. A few additions also resulted from the verification process. Particular conditions were imposed for the inclusion of state–province linkages in the database. First, there must be some form of documentation on the linkage which provides evidence of its existence and nature and, second, states and provinces must be the primary agents of the linkage. The database is current to the end of 2005.

31. Debora L. VanNijnatten, 'Towards Cross-Border Environmental Policy Spaces in North America'.

32. Debora L. VanNijnatten, 'Environmental Cross-Border Regions and the Canada–U.S. Relationship'.

33. International Joint Commission, *Protection of the Waters of the Great Lakes: Final Report to the Governments of Canada and the United States*, February 2000.

34. Debora L. VanNijnatten, 'Mercury Reduction in the Canadian Provinces: Interprovincial vs. Cross-border Policy Diffusion'. Paper prepared for the Annual General Meeting of the Canadian Political Science Association, June 2006, Toronto, ON.

35. The Committee on the Environment of the Conference of New England Governors and Eastern Canadian Premiers, *Mercury Action Plan 1998*. New England Governors/Eastern Canadian Premiers, June 1998.

36. Debora L. VanNijnatten, 'Mercury Reduction in the Canadian Provinces: Interprovincial vs. Cross-border Policy Diffusion'. Paper prepared for the Annual General Meeting of the Canadian Political Science Association, June 2006, Toronto, ON.

37. C. Mark Smith and Stephanie D'Agostino, 'New England Governors and Eastern Canadian Premiers Mercury Action Plan: Where Do We Stand?' PowerPoint Presentation, 2004.

38. Jeffrey Simpson, 'What America's clean-air booster means for Canada', *Globe and Mail*, 22 November 2008. Available at http://www.theglobeandmail.com/servlet/story/RTGAM.20081121.wcosimp22/CommentStory/specialComment/.

39. Jonathan Fowlie, 'Three premiers say they'll bypass Harper, go with B.C. on climate change', *Vancouver Sun*, 30 January 2008. Available at http://www.canada.com/vancouversun/news/story.html?k=22306&id=382d49c8-04a1-4775-b652-dfc02aaddc67 (accessed 23 May 2008).

40. Debora L. VanNijnatten and W. Henry Lambright, 'Canadian Smog Policy in a Continental Context: Looking South for Stringency', in Debora L. VanNijnatten and Robert Boardman, eds, *Canadian Environmental Policy: Context and Cases*, 2nd ed. (Don Mills: Oxford University Press, 2002).

41. New England/Eastern Canada Climate Change Report Card Partners, *Third Annual Assessment of the Region's Progress Toward Meeting the Goals of the New England Governors/Eastern Canadian Premiers Climate Change Action Plan of 2001*. Available at http://www.newenglandclimate.org/Scorecard2006.pdf (accessed 12 August 2008).

42. Brian Laghi, 'Ottawa far behind provinces on climate change: Report', *Globe and Mail Update*, 26 July 2008. Available at http://www.theglobeandmail.com/servlet/Page/document/v5/content/subscribe?user_URL=http://www.theglobeandmail.com%2Fservlet%2Fstory%2FRTGAM.20080716.wclimate0716%2FBNStory%2FNational%2Fhome&ord=88314086&brand=theglobeandmail&force_login=true.

43. See Kathryn Harrison, *Passing the Buck: Federalism and Canadian Environmental Policy* (Vancouver: UBC Press, 1986); and Kathryn Harrison, 'Federal–Provincial Relations and the Environment: Unilateralism, Collaboration, and Rationalization', 123–44 in Debora L. VanNijnatten and Robert Boardman, eds., *Canadian Environmental Policy: Context and Cases*, 2nd ed. (Don Mills: Oxford University Press, 2002).

44. Debora L. VanNijnatten and Gerard W. Boychuk, 'Economic Integration and Cross-Border Policy Convergence: Social and Environmental Policy in the Canadian Provinces and American States', *Journal of Borderlands Studies* 19, 1 (Spring 2004): 37–58.

45. Debora L. VanNijnatten, 'Analyzing the Canada–United States Environmental Relationship: A Multi-Faceted Approach', *The American Review of Canadian Studies: Thomas O. Enders Biennial Issue on the State of the Canada–U.S. Relationship* 33, 1 (Spring 2003): 93–120.

46. Debora L. VanNijnatten, 'Mercury Reduction in the Canadian Provinces: Interprovincial vs. Cross-border Policy Diffusion'. Paper prepared for the Annual General Meeting of the Canadian Political Science Association, June 2006, Toronto, ON.

8

Sustaining Canadian Cities: The Silos and Systems of Local Environmental Policy

Mary Louise McAllister

Canadian local governments are constitutional creatures of the provinces and heavily dependent on property taxes for revenues. As such they are ideologically, institutionally, and financially constrained from promoting biophysical or socio-economic sustainability now, or for future generations. It is not surprising that promoters of healthy, resilient cities invariably find their agendas submerged by a tidal wave of property development plans—projects that are supported by the unceasing municipal quest for revenues required to support burgeoning societal demands. The property tax, originally designed to fund infrastructure and 'hard' services, is now being stretched to finance social, public health, and other 'soft' services. Local governments are seeking other sources of revenue, including fostering private sector partnerships, licensing, and fees for services.

Throughout the twentieth century, cities have been planned and governed according to principles that separated land uses and public services. 'Silos' in planning practice and city bureaucracies emerged to deal efficiently with incompatible uses and to govern more effectively. These approaches may have worked reasonably well throughout much of the twentieth century. That said, they are not effective tools for dealing with the complex interactions of valued biophysical and socio-economic ecosystems. Cities are becoming increasingly congested while public health concerns are mounting, along with the accumulating stresses on vital social and biophysical systems.

What is surprising, perhaps, is that Canadian cities are able to innovate in the environmental arena at all. In the twenty-first century citizens are pressuring for a more inclusive form of local governance, where members of the interested public are effectively promoting more sustainable cities. Lobbying by members of civil society, along with other demands on governments, has led to a number of provincial environmental laws, local by-laws, policies, and practices. Local policies are increasingly designed to recognize the value of ecological goods and services as well as their interrelationship with community health. Moreover, watershed-based approaches and initiatives promoting healthy communities are requiring municipalities to work together with members of the public. These projects transcend administrative and political jurisdictional boundaries in order to achieve more sustainable approaches to governance. Outcomes include innovations ranging from greenbelt preservation, to alternative energy projects, to ecosystem approaches to health.

Underpinning these developments is a growing theoretical body of literature that reconceptualizes what is meant by 'good' environmental policy. Historically, urban environmental concerns were viewed in terms of the city's bio-physical properties. To the extent that they were considered at all, they were managed through departments of public health and safety and, in time, through the use of zoning to separate incompatible uses. Today, decision-makers are beginning to recognize that environmental health will not be achieved through reductionist approaches and that 'good' environmental policy integrates both biophysical and socio-economic considerations. Healthy cities depend on knowing how to foster desirable, resilient socio-ecological systems. Growing recognition of this emerging paradigm requires a host of new administrative and policy responses. As a result, some institutional learning is taking place with respect to the long-term sustainability of Canadian urban areas. A review of a few of these initiatives indicates that some local decision-makers are beginning to test the turbulent waters of complex systems and integrated policy approaches in hopes of nudging Canadian cities in a more sustainable direction.[1]

Scientific Management and Property Development: Early Twentieth Century Approaches to the Environment

> *Health for Efficiency*
> *Efficiency for Production*
> *Production for Well-being*
> Slogan at 1924 Town Planning Institute of Canada Meeting[2]

The Canadian constitution allocated jurisdiction over local governments to the provinces. As a result, municipalities can pass only by-laws and levy taxes in conformance with provincial legislation and regulation. Jurisdictional limitations on local governments impose a number of constraints on their ability to devise effective environmental policy. Municipalities have been historically responsible primarily for providing hard infrastructure and services for the city. The major funding source of municipal governments is property tax, and even then, only a portion of that can be spent at their discretion. Canadian government revenues are split 50 per cent federal, 42 per cent provincial, leaving municipalities with only 8 per cent.[3] This constitutional and fiscal straightjacket has been accompanied by a particular set of historical circumstances that further restrained the decision-making authority of local governments.

At the turn of the twentieth century, much city activity was organized around individual economic interests. The job of local governments was to protect those interests and to maintain social order and public safety through the provision of services, such as sewers, fire protection, waste removal, and policing. With urbanization, the process of separating the rural from the urban, and distancing city dwellers from the resources they consumed and discarded, was taking place at a rapid rate. As Smith and MacKinnon have noted,

> It was the bourgeois reform movement of the late nineteenth century that banished livestock to the countryside; the campaign had been motivated in part by a proper concern for disease, but more so by obsessive tidiness. It was the poor who kept livestock, and the things that poor people did were deemed unsightly. It was another wedge separating people from their food.[4]

Local environmental policy, as such, was not on the political agendas of the day, although its precursors might be identifiable in two ways: a concern with urban public health, and a collective desire to foster attractive and appealing cities. An early urban reform movement generated by a growing middle-class to clean up cities led to some social assistance, housing, and improved health conditions for the poor. At the heart of the urban development initiatives was a dynamic business community that envisioned how public and social well-being could be advanced through the economic prosperity of the cities. Members of the business community frequently made up the majority of city council. When business interests did not have a personal interest, or where their priorities may have conflicted with other public concerns, there were visible environmental repercussions. Residents of early Canadian cities suffered from a toxic combination of noxious emissions from smokestacks, poisonous wastewaters, and untreated garbage when industrial enterprises intermingled with residential housing. The urban planning profession emerged to deal with these incompatible land uses through subdivision and zoning. The groomed 'city beautiful' approach was based on notions of efficient scientific planning and zoning. The policy goal stressed fostering the aesthetic beauty of a city so new residents and investors would be drawn to the community. Land developers, businesses, and homeowners whose views dominated municipal councils reinforced the value placed on private property. As one individual claimed, 'the real business of city government is property.'[5]

A few early radical thinkers recognized that planning should incorporate the goals of a healthy social, living, and natural environment. One of them, Thomas Adams, argued for a holistic planning approach with a strong government presence to ensure the well-being of the entire community.[6] In his conception, each neighbourhood would contain ample gardens, parks, a town centre, a library, and shops. Some elements of these ideas can be found in cities today, although other competing community goals and political realities have made it difficult to adopt anything but some general principles. In 1909, the federal Commission on Conservation was established as an advisory body to the Government of Canada. It included recognition of the link between urban planning and conservation. Thomas Adams was invited to join the Commission as Advisor on Town Planning.[7]

The rapid growth and public concern about a compromised quality of living and public health as a result of incompatible land uses led early twentieth-century decision-makers to undertake a more orderly and scientific approach to municipal planning. Beyond that, however, there was little room for policy considerations that did not fall within the priorities of local decision-making elites. Throughout the following decades, land development for the purposes of raising revenues became a pressing priority with little thought given to the impact on environmental goods and services. The unceasing quest for property-based revenues set the stage for a conflict between two communities of interest, a conflict that continues today. It consisted of opposing views held between those whose vision for sustaining cities was predicated on values of economic growth and land development, and those belonging to an emerging social and environmental movement whose ideas about sustainability were something altogether different.

Emerging Local Environmental Policy: Healthy Communities

They paved paradise and put up a parking lot
With a pink hotel, a boutique, and a swinging hot spot
                Joni Mitchell, 'Big Yellow Taxi', 1970

As has been frequently proclaimed, particularly by members of the 'baby boomer' generation, the 1960s and 1970s was a time of intense social activism. During this era, critics questioned municipal decision-making processes that promoted large real estate development projects over the objections of neighbourhood groups. Other citizens found support within a broader social movement sweeping North America—a movement that focused on human rights, environmental degradation, and poverty. Citizen groups, homeowners, and university students protested the disintegration of urban neighbourhoods, the 'blockbusting' techniques of various developers, and the lack of attention paid to alleviating the housing and health problems of the urban working class. Rapidly growing suburbs fuelled the demand for socio-ecologically and economically expensive infrastructure and services. Shopping centres, big box stores, and ultimately, power centres gobbled up land, resources, and retail dollars. In the early 1980s, the opening of the mammoth West Edmonton Mall offered one of the most prominent examples of the times. Christopher Leo claimed it to be the 'prime cause' of inner city Edmonton's stress.[8]

Healthy Communities

By the 1980s, recognition of the interconnections between social, economic, and biophysical health increasingly brought environmental concerns into the mainstream of local governmental policy and planning. One notable movement, Healthy Cities, rapidly gained public recognition first in Canada and then around the world. Canadian physician and public health planner Trevor Hancock developed a model that placed health at the centre of three overlapping rings containing community conviviality, environmental viability, and economic adequacy. The idea of Healthy Communities is based on a set of interdependent and mutually self-determining concerns with ethics, identity, and place.[9] In terms of governance, this model emphasizes a holistic approach that leads to new processes and political structures, including roundtables and consensus-building. These processes also lead to alternative avenues of influence that operate both inside and outside the formal structures of local governments. In 1986, one year before the Brundtland Commission's report, *Our Common Future*, the World Health Organization met in Lisbon to establish the Healthy Cities Project, an idea that originated in Toronto in 1984. As of 2007, the Healthy Cities or Healthy Communities movement included more than 7,500 cities and towns throughout the world.[10]

Socio-ecological Systems Perspectives

As the twentieth century drew to a close 'ecosystem' perspectives and approaches garnered policy attention. Ecosystems analyses include a broad spectrum of actors and variables operating at different scales in time and place. Catherine Dowling, for example, suggests that, '[a]n ecosystem approach can be characterized by six elements including natural environmental planning units, a holistic interdisciplinary approach, cross-scale considerations, inclusive multidisciplinary decision-making, adaptive and flexible management, and an underlying sustainability ethic.'[11] A sustainability ethic includes valuing social as well as biophysical ecological systems and recognizes the connections between them. While a few decades ago, ecosystem perspectives largely focused on biophysical health (e.g., water and air quality), they have evolved to include healthy social systems as an essential component of a resilient ecosystem.

Socio-ecological systems perspectives have led many to new prescriptions in local decision-making. One such approach is watershed-based planning that crosses local jurisdictional boundaries.

Yet decisions made to serve the needs of a political jurisdiction may run counter to the requirements of a sustainable ecosystem. This challenge led to the *bioregional* concept that suggests natural regions, rather than artificially constructed political regions, should be the organizing units of human activity.[12] Poverty, food insecurity, air pollution, groundwater contamination, overpopulation, and habitat fragmentation do not respect political jurisdiction and operate in multiple spatial and temporal scales. Decision-makers operating within narrowly defined boundaries are unable to transcend these boundaries. Alternative governance structures and processes that break down narrow conceptual and jurisdictional boundaries and their associated limitations are required.

One way of determining natural boundaries is to assess them on the basis of physical characteristics such as drainage patterns, landforms, vegetation, and climate.[13] As Hodge and Robinson point out, ecosystem approaches have been influencing the way in which theorists, planners, and practitioners are carrying out their work throughout the country.[14] The role of civil society is an important component of this approach. As noted by one activist and academic, an example of the civil society approach to bioregionalism would be one that can 'build influence for political and institutional change in the political sphere at the local level . . . supported by strong horizontal efforts to define new cultural watershed identities, develop norms of cooperation and civic solidarity and build networks of restoration activists.'[15]

A visible, influential application of this approach in the 1990s was that of the Royal Commission on the Future of the Toronto Waterfront. The Crombie Commission (established in 1988) was asked to come up with recommendations on how to deal with the contaminated waterfront and related lands in the face of 'jurisdictional gridlock'.[16] The commission initiated an extensive consultation process, which involved teams composed of developers, environmentalists, traffic engineers, landscape architects, scientists, community activists, federal and provincial public servants, and city officials. The commission's mandate covered the Greater Toronto Bioregion, extending from the Niagara Escarpment on the west, the Oak Ridges Moraine on the north and east sides, and Lake Ontario's shoreline.[17] Despite the mixed reviews about the extent to which the recommendations of the process were effectively implemented (much of it is still a work in progress), the process was successful on many levels. Robert Gibson and his colleagues observed that the Crombie Commission introduced Canadian decision-makers to the idea of ecosystem planning as an alternative to conventional planning. Conventional planning, they argued, is based on a belief in the need for economic growth. According to this view, environmental impacts of that growth would be managed through adjustments. In contrast, ecosystem planning 'rejects business as usual'.[18] It recognizes that not all economic growth is good; in fact, it can undermine the biophysical, social, and economic resilience of a community. Among many other principles, Gibson et al. suggested that ecosystem planning needed to be linked with other aspects of democratic change, social learning, community building, and environmental enlightenment.[19]

In the 1990s, while land use roundtables and public consultative initiatives across the country gained steam, many provinces were simultaneously engaged in slashing budgets and offloading responsibilities for environmental and social programs to the municipalities. In contrast, American governments were actively occupied with strengthening the 'liveability' of their cities. To that end, they were working on harnessing urban sprawl with investment in transit, green spaces, mixed-use developments, and downtown revitalization initiatives while engaging in collaborative community participation. These 'smart growth' approaches were adopted throughout the United States and, eventually, Canada where, in 1999, a non-profit group introduced Smart Growth BC.[20] The approach contains promising elements. As John Sewell notes, however, Smart Growth proponents face some fairly intractable challenges[21]: rapid growth continues to gobble up land in and around cities, the Canadian public relies heavily on cars to get around, and suburbs are inexorably munching their way through valued wetlands and other green spaces.

The last half of the twentieth century saw the emergence of diverse groups of social activists concerned with a range of urban ills including displacement of the poor, unbridled growth and development, and associated costs. Local governments were institutionally, fiscally, and ideologically ill-equipped to deal with the barrage of complex interconnected problems. The Healthy Cities project, the Crombie commission, and Smart Growth all signalled a recognition that escalating environmental problems required a different set of institutional responses to environmental policies, ones that could foster desirable socio-ecological urban systems. It was also becoming clear that the magnitude of the challenges ahead would require significantly more resources and tools than those readily available to Canadian municipal governments.

Resilient Cities: Local Innovations in the Twenty-First Century

> In seeking sustainability, we must look to the human potential for selective adaptability. We cannot afford to maintain outmoded nineteenth-century views of the dominance and invincibility of technological 'man'. . . . Success will be found and must be measured in terms of our ability to foster both urban and global systems of feedback that simultaneously detect and communicate threats to our ecological, social and economic systems.[22]

Conceptions of ecosystem approaches to governance continue to evolve. Currently, one of the most salient approaches in the literature is that which is based on resilience thinking. It is not new; it was the premise of all traditional societies immediately dependent on the land for survival.[23] In our predominantly urban society, however, it has been largely forgotten. The work of the Resilience Alliance—a solutions-oriented group—is becoming more widely known. Resilience thinking recognizes that 'socio-ecological systems are complex adaptive systems. . . . Its focus is on how the system changes and copes with disturbance. Resilience, a systems capacity to absorb disturbance without a regime shift, is the key to sustainability.'[24] If this type of thinking were adopted, new approaches to governing would be required. The following examples discuss some promising initiatives taking place in Canada and elsewhere that might succeed, given the right mix of incentives and factors.

Intergovernmental Cooperation: A Nested Approach

Sustaining valued socio-ecological systems requires a level of cooperation between municipalities that would have been unconceivable 100 years ago, when they actively competed with each other to attract businesses and industry to locate in their own cities. Yet, cooperation is now taking place at all levels. The national Federation of Canadian Municipalities (FCM) plays an important coordinating role between governments. For example, the FCM and the ICLEI—Local Governments for Sustainability (founded as the International Council for Local Environmental Initiatives)—have worked together to foster partnerships to combat the effects of climate change and reduce contributions to greenhouse gases. The Canadian organization, Partners for Climate Protection (a sub-group of ICLEI's international entity, Cities for Climate Protection) is comprised of 166 municipalities throughout the country.[25]

Nationally, after years of decreasing grant transfers to municipalities and intensive municipal lobbying, senior levels of governments have funded some new programs for local governments. Of particular note is the $33 billion federal infrastructure program taking place over 2007–2014. Half of that amount—funded through the municipal GST rebate and the gas tax fund—is directed towards the municipalities to invest in transit, local infrastructure, water, and waste and energy management systems, while encouraging conservation.[26] The serious global economic downturn at the end of 2008 could serve to accelerate federal infrastructure on local projects. The green infrastructural deficit is something else again. One of the more notable municipal 'federal to local' government programs in 2000 were two green municipal funds designed to encourage investment in innovative environmental projects. These funds included a $550 million endowment which operates through the Federation of Canadian Municipalities.[27] Despite these and other encouraging funding signs from senior levels of government, they fall far short of what is required to surmount urban environmental policy challenges. Moreover, increased funding and resources only go so far; what is needed are different approaches to governing sustainable communities.

Place-based Governance and Municipalities

Geographer Becky Pollock, among others, has developed the notion of a place-based alternative to governance predicated on more fluid boundaries than those dictated by political jurisdiction. The concept combines ecological and political interpretations of 'space', with social and cultural interpretations of 'place'.[28] To achieve this, a different view of what constitutes good local governance is required, one that contains a comprehensive understanding of the diverse individuals, communities, and interests residing within a particular place and knowledge about how these actors are affected by (and contributors to) local socio-ecological conditions.[29] In this context, good governance includes an informed and engaged public, along with trustworthy, supportive, and inclusive institutions capable of learning and promoting collaborative networks.[30]

With place-based governance, co-ordination takes place amongst municipalities and other local bodies in order to protect valued socio-ecological systems. Such a function could be facilitated through an organizational body such as a biosphere reserve. These reserves were first created over 30 years ago under the United Nations Educational, Scientific, and Cultural Organization (UNESCO) Man and the Biosphere program to help protect biodiversity on a global scale through local level initiatives. As of 2007, there were 529 reserves throughout the world, 15 of them in Canada.

Over time, much like environmental sustainability, the approach to these reserves has deepened and extended. The concept of a biosphere reserve has evolved beyond a primary preoccupation with conservation, research, and education to include concerns such as sustainable livelihoods and development practices. It is recognized that in order to sustain biodiversity, the quest for biophysical integrity of desired ecosystems must be coupled with governing systems that promote social equity and community development. Biosphere reserves can be considered a 'global through local' governance mechanism. In Canada, their initial designation is typically championed locally in initial planning and organizational stages.[31] The biosphere reserve model is an example of collaborative governance across nested scales. Local landscape and place-based initiatives serve as learning and demonstration sites, and provide tools for governments at all levels to implement more sustainable decision-making.[32] Global, national, and regional biosphere reserve networks serve as vehicles for the exchange of knowledge, skills, and experiences of local practitioners and citizens, thereby providing a supportive framework for more localized sustainability initiatives. All of Canada's biospheres face serious challenges, as municipalities within or adjacent to them struggle to achieve the often competing objectives of socio-economic and biophysical sustainability. Moreover, the limited financial base and the heavy reliance on volunteers make it difficult to maintain momentum.[33] On the positive side, collaborative governance is becoming increasingly accepted by government institutions. In the Canadian spring 2008 federal budget, this work was recognized through the allocation of $2 million for use in capacity building for biosphere reserves.[34]

While the biosphere reserves offer an attractive conception for fostering participatory, watershed-based co-operation, other place-based approaches are also supported by local, provincial, and federal governments. Examples include community forests, conservation areas, protected greenbelt areas, and watershed-based initiatives.

From Grey to Green Infrastructure (Eco-infrastructure)

Along with federal–provincial and inter-municipal cooperation, are the intra-municipal initiatives that can be taken within the city itself. One of the primary responsibilities of local government has always been the provision of infrastructure to service property. Infrastructure has been defined as 'the substructure or underlying foundation, especially the basic installations and facilities on which the continuance and growth of a community or state depends'.[35] Increasingly, proponents are suggesting that the so-called 'green' or 'eco-infrastructure' approach should be used as a counter-approach to traditional, centralized grey-infrastructural approaches to energy, transportation, water, and waste systems.

Green infrastructure has been defined as 'an integrated infrastructure *system* with a reduced ecological footprint over its life cycle, and with significant benefits for the community economy and quality of life.'[36] It can also be viewed as the biophysical natural life support systems. These closed-loop, or soft path, approaches look to regenerate natural systems and focus on 'augmenting the self-design of natural flows, or perhaps, mimicking these flows with engineered designs that nevertheless allow natural flows much scope for taking their own course'.[37] The goals are to foster resilience; reliance on renewable, smaller, dispersed, flexible systems with lower lifecycle costs; and responsiveness to local social and physical conditions. Some funding for such green initiatives has been provided by governments at all levels—local, provincial, and federal, including Infrastructure Canada. Green infrastructure covers a wide range of initiatives including the installation of green roofs on municipal buildings, energy conservation programs, improved transit systems, community gardens, and green spaces as well as projects that encourage a community sense of place and stewardship.

Food security is one example that is rapidly garnering attention. Xuereb and Desjardins suggest food security in a community is present when 'all residents have access to, and can afford to buy safe, nutritious, and culturally-acceptable food that has been produced in an environmentally-sustainable way and that sustains our rural communities.'[38] Examples of food security initiatives throughout Canada include the widespread adoption of municipal food charters which address all steps of the food production and distribution process in order to achieve a number of goals. The emphasis is on reducing the reliance on fossil foods (reducing food miles) as well as encouraging a local food economy, community economic development, social justice, and ecological health.[39]

While city by-laws and zoning can be huge obstacles to the development of green infrastructure approaches, changes to by-laws and zoning do follow as those approaches gain legitimacy on public agendas and are incorporated into local policy. One example of the shifting perspective, and of a decision that has some important implications for municipal autonomy, was a 28 June, 2001 ruling in which the Supreme Court of Canada upheld the right of the city of Hudson, Québec 'to pass a by-law which banned the cosmetic use of pesticides within municipal boundaries'. It deemed that such by-laws were acceptable as long as they did not conflict with legislation at the provincial or federal levels. This issue pitted the Canadian Environmental Law Association (also representing nine other environmental groups) against two companies that used pesticides. The companies were appealing the right of the city to pass a by-law that controlled the use and application of pesticides. Many of the intervenors represented organizations with national scope or anti-pesticide groups in other communities.[40]

There are other interesting aspects to the case. Jerry DeMarco has noted that most provincial municipal acts (including Québec) allow for the passing of by-laws that promote general welfare or the environment. The court decision cited international law emphasizing the precautionary principle and upholding the right of local governments to take preventative action to stop environmental harm. Noting an emerging institutional trend that gives some recognition to municipal autonomy, DeMarco, quoted the following sections of the Supreme Court ruling:

[para 3] The case arises in an era in which matters of governance are often examined through the lens of the principle of subsidiarity. This is the proposition that law-making and implementation are often best achieved at a level of government that is not only effective, but also closest to the citizens affected and thus most responsive to their needs, to local distinctiveness, and to population diversity. . . . The so-called 'Brundtland Commission' recommended that 'local governments [should be] empowered to exceed, but not to lower, national norms' [para 49]. A tradition of strong local government has become an important part of the Canadian democratic experience. This level of government usually appears more attuned to the immediate needs and concerns of the citizens.[41]

As with the case of the no-smoking by-law, a decision taken in one municipality can catch on quickly in another. Subsequent to Quebec's 2006 pesticide bans, the Ontario government passed a bill in 2008 to ban the use and sale of pesticides that may be used for cosmetic purposes. Other provinces were considering similar action.[42]

Telecommunications and Intelligent Cities

Cities and various forms of human interaction are being fundamentally altered by the rapid adoption of information technology in all aspects of life. With good reason, the application of technology in environmental circles has often been discussed in a critical way when observing the perils of introducing innovations in the absence of a broad understanding of their socio-ecological implications. Yet the potential of information technology to reduce the consumption of non-renewable resources or to stimulate local economic development is an area of inquiry that needs closer policy attention from those interested in sustainable cities. For example, the Internet is fostering the growing use of telecommuting, which could reduce the amount of time commuters spend on the road and the demand for more highways. The Internet could also be used to provide local information exchanges for the purpose of bartering services or used goods, or to stimulate environmental education between communities, thereby speeding up the pace of the adoption of green ideas. Information technology is also being used to introduce smart-metering, whereby utilities can encourage water and electricity conservation by measuring the amount and time of usage.

The Governing Challenges of Complex Systems and Administrative Sylos

All of these eco-developments frequently require resources and authority that local governments do not possess. This is particularly the case in Canada where the central and provincial governments wrangle for resources while cities have been largely left out of the debate, lacking as they do any constitutional legitimacy. Transformative institutional learning and political will is needed to overcome global political, economic, and societal expectations and practices. Ecosystem perspectives are now beginning to inform the way in which some government decision-makers, such as planners, view their cities.

Sometimes, these ideas are introduced into public consultative processes, particularly when local decision-makers are engaged in community 'visioning' exercises. Such perspectives may even be nibbling at the edges of established assumptions about the kinds of values that should drive a city's future. As yet, however, these perspectives do not appear to have resulted in restructured government administrations and policy processes in a manner that might reverse the burgeoning pressures on socio-ecological life support systems. The concept of sustainable or healthy communities seems to be well-entrenched among activists and a few other communities of interest. The means, mechanisms, and political desire needed to effectively implement those concepts, however, are far from being realized in daily local government decision-making.

This situation is partly attributable to the building blocks of governing structures. Government institutions are established in a way that allows them to maintain social control. Institutional structures offer a means to impose order and organize civil society in a complicated environment. The more intricate the problems, the more risk adverse organizations become. As environmental concerns become more imperative, governments react in crisis mode and are less able and less willing to explore innovative models for governance. Ann Dale observes that, '[w]hen one is stuck in a spiralling pattern of exploitation and conservation, systemic learning cannot take place, and reactive rather than proactive policy choices become the norm.'[43]

Moreover, those who have a vested interest in maintaining the status quo support bureaucratic, hierarchical structures. There are few built-in incentives for changing existing practices and venturing into a much less certain decision-making environment. Holistic approaches to decision-making require adaptive management techniques, long-range decision-making, the relinquishment of control, the sharing of information, consensus-building exercises, and the abandoning of long-held world views revolving around notions of rationality, efficiency, and effectiveness. The sheer magnitude and complexity of the task provides ample reason for decision-makers who yearn for a simpler world to reduce problems to a few simple resolvable objectives. At the local level, one of the primary historic objectives has been to provide services in the most economically efficient manner assessed in today's dollars rather than in tomorrow's ecological costs. Governments are well acquainted with the cost–benefit exercises associated with providing hard services delivered through bureaucratic structures. They have few tools that would allow them to weigh the relative costs of development and economic growth against the very real, but difficult to assess, environmental and social costs. This reliance on old methods of assessing costs and benefits through a simple economic indicator fails to recognize that a viable economy rests on the resilience of the natural and human systems on which it depends. Moreover, systems approaches could further serve to obscure lines of accountability and responsibility. These goals are important in a representative democracy as well as to the functioning of any large bureaucratic organization.

Despite these constraints, local governments have established a number of environmental committees that include members of the interested public. Usually, however, these committees and their related activities fall under the jurisdiction of a particular department that deals primarily with physical landscapes or biophysical equality, such as Parks or Waste Management and they are often issue- or location-specific. Applying an ecosystem approach is something altogether different and not readily applied to practical situations. Quite apart from needing the political will and initiative, it is a challenge to craft policies that can accommodate numerous variables, including various spatial and time scales and appropriate boundaries of sub-systems and larger systems. Nevertheless, as George Francis suggests, 'collective capabilities to act must extend over a much wider range of spatial and time scales than is commonly considered if certain non-sustainable human activities are to be reversed.'[44] In this view, the degree to which desired local ecosystems (including human systems) are healthy constitutes the single most crucial factor in determining the long-term future of cities. The ability to plan on an ecosystem basis is a prerequisite of sustainability as well as preventing environmental crises from happening. A striking example of governance failure would be the environmental tragedy which occurred in 2000 in Walkerton, Ontario, where seven people died and 2,300 were sickened as a result of E. coli contamination in the water supply, and the speed with which political actors were forced to respond after the fact.[45] As Ann Dale notes in her thoughtful analysis:

> It would . . . be prudent for human activity systems to reconcile methods of production with the rehabilitation and maintenance of ecosystems that provide the essential services for all life. We need a common language and an adequate conceptual framework within which to work, institutional reform based on a convergence of human and natural system cycles. . . .[46]

Urban planners, such as Patsy Healey, observing these institutional constraints, suggest that new collaborative processes are required 'where territorial political communities can collectively address their conflicts and maximize their chances to shape their places and their future'.[47] Collaborative planning, Healey argues, serves a valuable 'countervailing force to functional service delivery logics for organizing government'.[48]

Conclusion

Effective local policy that can counter the cumulative environmental effects of unsustainable urban living calls for transformative institutional and social learning and adaptation, at all scales, from international organizations to local neighbourhoods. It is, without doubt, a daunting task. Political will is required. Local governments and their citizens need to have the means and authority to make changes happen. They require a much more meaningful degree of self-governance than is currently the case in Canada. Scale is important. Just as bureaucracies require tasks to be broken down into manageable pieces, problems that are most readily dealt with are smaller and closer to home, what systems thinkers refer to as tight feedback loops. Natural processes need to once again be visible, tangible, and meaningful to the public.

To be sure, steps are being taken. Soft paths to energy and water consumption are now being seriously investigated as is green infrastructure. Naturalized gardens are springing up in place of 'bowling green' lawns. Mixed residential and affordable housing has become an important policy goal. Neighbourhood markets and community gardens are blossoming in abandoned lots. And, in some places, the chickens, banned for 100 years, are returning to the coop in urban backyards. Yet, for such initiatives to be more than entertaining human interest stories for the local media, they need to take place within the context of wide-sweeping structural and policy change that represents socio-ecological imperatives.

Diverse members of the public also would have to be encouraged to engage in civic discussions if there are to be healthy communities. The extent to which council and staff take public participation seriously is a measure of the openness and responsiveness of the local government. In addition, the ability of the local government to incorporate biophysical, social, and economic considerations into its political institutions and processes reflects its relative level of adaptability to complex ecosystem requirements. Openness, responsiveness, and adaptability are adjectives that do not mesh readily with bureaucracy, administration, and hierarchy, all hallmarks of established organizations. Nevertheless, municipal governments are taking tentative steps in this direction, in their attempts to incorporate principles of sustainability into local decision-making. As the above examples suggest, it is often at the local level of government and activity that environmental innovation can happen. Their diversity and comparatively smaller size (relative to provincial and federal governments) grants them the flexibility to introduce changes and respond to problems that are less tractable at a larger scale of decision-making. As with the no-smoking by-laws, pesticide bans, or food security, municipalities and provincial governments can learn from each other, observing diverse examples of local innovation throughout the country and then adapt and adopt those ideas in their own communities and provinces.

The journey towards healthy, sustainable communities follows a winding, frequently diverging, and always elusive path. Nevertheless, despite numerous constraints at work in public institutions, the functions and practices of local governments are dynamic; as institutions, they do learn and evolve. Possibilities do exist, opportunities arise, and the collective environmental costs of retaining the status quo are becoming painfully apparent. The urgent need for institutional change that can produce effective local environmental policies is an imperative that is increasingly difficult for decision-makers to ignore.

Questions for Review

1. In what ways are Canada's local governments important environmental policy actors?
2. What are the factors that might constrain environmental policy activism on the part of local governments and what factors might serve to encourage such activism?
3. What is the Healthy Communities model? What measures have our major cities taken to move closer to the Healthy Communities model?
4. How might the activities of major cities and smaller local governments differ as regards environmental policy?

Notes

1. Portions of this chapter are based on Mary Louise McAllister, *Governing Ourselves? The Politics of Canadian Communities* (Vancouver: UBC Press, 2004).
2. Thomas I. Gunton, 'The Ideas and Policies of the Canadian Planning Profession, 1909–1931', in Alan J. Artibise and Gilbert A. Stelter, eds, *The Usable Urban Past: Planning and Policies in the Modern Canadian City* (Toronto: Macmillan and Co., 1979), 182.

3. Mike Harcourt, 'From Restless Communities to Resilient Places: Fixing our Municipal Fiscal Imbalance', in *Special to Globe and Mail Update*, 2007. Globe and Mail.com.

4. Alisa Smith and J.B. MacKinnon, *The 100-mile Diet: A Year of Local Eating* (Toronto: Random House Canada, 2007), 75.

5. James Lorimer, *A Citizen's Guide to City Politics* (Toronto: James, Lewis and Samuel, 1970), 4.

6. Gerald Hodge, *Planning Canadian Communities: An Introduction to the Principles, Practices and Participants* (Toronto: ITP Nelson, 1998), 108.

7. Alan J. Artibise and Gilbert A. Stelter, 'Conservation Planning and Urban Planning: The Canadian Commission of Conservation in Historical Perspective', in C. Gaffield and P. Gaffield, eds, *Consuming Canada: Readings in Environmental History* (Toronto: Copp Clark, 1995), 152–69; Kent Gerecke, 'The History of Canadian City Planning', in James Lorimer and Evelyn Ross, with the editors of *City Magazine*, eds, *The Second City Book: Studies of Urban and Suburban Canada* (Toronto: James Lorimer, 1977), 151.

8. Christopher Leo, *The Subordination of the Local State: Development Politics in Edmonton* (Winnipeg: University of Winnipeg, Institute of Urban Studies, 1995).

9. Trevor Hancock, ed., *Healthy Sustainable Communities: Concept, Fledgling Practice, and Implications for Governance* (Gabriola Island, BC: New Society Publishers, 1997).

10. Ontario Healthy Communities Coalition, 2007. Available at http://www.healthycommunities.on.ca/ohcc.htm.

11. Catherine Dowling, 'Ecosystem Management: Meeting the Challenges of Community Initiatives' (University of Ottawa: Institute for Research on Environment and Economy, 1995).

12. Mike Carr, *Bioregionalism and Civil Society: Democratic Challenges to Corporate Globalism* (Vancouver: UBC Press, 2004).

13. David Crombie [Hon.], Royal Commission on the Toronto Harbourfront, *Regeneration: Toronto's Waterfront and the Sustainable City: Final Report* (Toronto: Minister of Supply and Services Canada, 1992).

14. Gerald Hodge and Ira M. Robinson, *Planning Canadian Regions* (Vancouver: UBC Press, 2001).

15. Carr, 2004, 287

16. Crombie, 1992, 1–2.

17. Hodge and Robinson, 2001, 330.

18. Robert B. Gibson, Donald H.M. Alexander, and Ray Tomalty, 'Putting Cities in Their Place: Ecosystem-based Planning for Canadian Urban Regions', in Mark Roseland, ed., *Eco-City Dimensions: Healthy Communities, Healthy Planet* (Gabriola Island, BC: New Society Publishers, 1997), 25–40.

19. Ibid.

20. Deborah Curran and Ray Tomalty, 'Living It Up', *Alternatives* 29, 3 (2003): 10–18; Ann Dale, *At the Edge: Sustainable Development in the 21st Century* (Vancouver: UBC Press, 2001), 11.

21. John Sewell, 'Breaking the Suburban Habit', *Alternatives* 29 (2003): 22–9; Smith and MacKinnon, 2007.

22. Robert Woollard and William Rees, 'Social Evolution and Urban Systems: Directions for Sustainability', in J.T. Pierce and Ann Dale, eds, *Communities, Development, and Sustainability across Canada* (Vancouver: UBC Press, 1999), 27–45.

23. B.H. Walker and David Salt, *Resilience Thinking: Sustaining Ecosystems and People in a Changing World* (Washington: Island Press, 2006).

24. Ibid., 38.

25. Federation of Canadian Municipalities. 'The Green Municipal Fund: Investing in Leadership, Inspiring Change', 2008. Available at http://www.sustainablecommunities.fcm.ca/GMF/.

26. Infrastructure Canada, 'Building Canada', 2008. Available at http://www.buildingcanada-chantierscanada.gc.ca/index-eng.html?wt.ad=infc-eng.

27. Federation of Canadian Municipalities, 2008.

28. Rebecca Pollock, 'Place-based Governance for Biosphere Reserves', *Environments* 32, 3 (2004): 27–42.

29. Sara Edge and Mary Louise McAllister, 'Place-based Local Governance and Sustainable Communities: Lessons from Canadian Biosphere Reserves', *Environmental Planning and Management*. Forthcoming.

30. Patsy Healey, 'Collaborative Planning in Perspective', *Planning Theory* 2, 2 (2003): 101–23; Gerald Hodge, *Planning Canadian Communities: An Introduction to the Principles, Practice, and Participants* (Toronto: ITP Nelson, 1998); M. Raco and J. Flint, 'Communities, places, and institutional relations: Assessing the role of area-based community representation in local governance', *Political Geography* 20 (2001): 585–612.

31. Canadian Biosphere Reserve Association, 2007. Available at http://www.biosphere-canada.ca.

32. UNESCO, 'People, Biodiversity and Ecology'. Available at http://www.unesco.org/mab/. Updated 8 August 2008.

33. Edge and McAllister, 2008.

34. Department of Finance, Canada, 'Budget 2008', 2008. Available at http://www.budget.gc.ca/2008/plan/chap4a-eng.asp.

35. Elisa Campbell and The Sheltair Group, Inc., 'The Five W's of Green Infrastructure', in *FCM Sustainable Communities Conference* (Ottawa: Federation of Canadian Municipalities, 2002).

36. Campbell, 2000.

37. Brian Milani, *Designing the Green Economy: The Postindustrial Alternative to Corporate Globalization* (Lanham, MD: Rowman & Littlefield Publishers, 2000), 103.

38. Marc Xuereb and Ellen Desjardins, *Towards a Healthy Community Food System for Waterloo Region* (Waterloo: Public Health, 2005), 24.

39. Vancouver Food Policy Council, 'Vancouver Food Charter: Context and Background', City of Vancouver, January 2007. Available at http://www.city.vancouver.bc.ca/COMMSVCS/socialplanning/initiatives/foodpolicy/tools/pdf/Van_Food_Charter_Bgrnd.pdf.

40. Jerry DeMarco, 'Overview of the Hudson Decision', in *FCM Big City Mayors' Caucus*, 2001; Catherine Dowling, 'Ecosystem Management: Meeting the Challenges of Community Initiatives' (Ottawa: University of Ottawa, Institute for Research on Environment and Economy, 1995).

41. Ibid.

42. Ontario, Ministry of the Environment, 'Ontario Lawns and Gardens Go Green: McGuinty Government Plans Ban on Cosmetic Pesticides', *News Release*. 22 April 2008. See also 'Taking Next Steps in Pesticide Ban', *News Release*. 7 November 2008.

43. Ann Dale, *At the Edge: Sustainable Development in the 21st Century* (Vancouver: UBC Press, 2001).

44. George Francis, 'Exploring Selected Issues of Governance in the Grand River Watershed', *Canadian Water Resources Journal* 21, 3 (1996): 303–9.

45. Dennis R. O'Connor, (Hon.), 'Part 1: A Summary: Report of the Walkerton Inquiry: The Events of May 2000 and Related Issues' (Toronto: Ontario Ministry of the Attorney General, Queen's Printer, 2002).

46. Dale, 2001, 58.

47. P. Healey, 'Building Institutional Capacity Through Collaborative Approaches to Urban Planning', *Environment and Planning A* 30 (1998): 1531–46, 1531.

48. Healey, 2003: 116.

9

Aboriginal People and Environmental Regulation: The Role of Land Claims Co-management Boards in the Territorial North

Graham White

As recent attention to issues of global warming has brought home, the fragile environment of Canada's far North is especially vulnerable to damage wrought by human activity. The North is rich in natural resources, particularly non-renewable natural resources such as oil, gas, diamonds, gold, uranium, and iron ore, but their exploitation often comes at significant environmental cost. The Aboriginal people who call the North home and who constitute an overwhelming proportion of the population in most northern communities, have a special relationship—both spiritual and economic—with the land that renders them acutely sensitive to the potential environmental consequences of resource development.

This mixture creates a difficult setting for establishing environmental policy which would allow for exploitation of the North's non-renewable resources—the principal hope for much-needed economic development—in an environmentally sensitive manner and which would take fully into account the perspectives and preferences of the local Aboriginal people. No clearer illustration could be found of what is termed in this volume's Introduction the struggle 'with the operationalization of sustainable development in the context of advanced capitalism'.

For most of the twentieth century, as evidenced by two prominent features of the present-day landscape, protection of the environment was of negligible concern in northern resource development projects and other activities. Rivers in the central Yukon remain massively disfigured by seemingly endless miles of dredge tailings, enormous mounds of gravel dug up from riverbeds from the early 1900s to the 1960s by huge placer mining barges in search of gold. To the east, throughout Nunavut the tundra is littered with rusting oil drums, abandoned machinery, and PCB-laden ground left from the construction of the DEW Line in the 1950s and other defence or mining projects. These and other environmental depredations occurred in no small measure because of the complete exclusion of local Aboriginal people from governmental institutions and decision-making processes, which in turn meant that their experience, insights, and wishes were all but completely ignored.

More recently, as elsewhere in Canada, strong concern for the environment has come to the fore in the North. The last few decades have also witnessed remarkable changes in the political-governmental complexion of the North, not least in the prominent role that Aboriginal leaders and political organizations have come to play. Among the most far-reaching of these changes has been the settlement of 'comprehensive land claim agreements' across most of the territorial North. The myriad governance provisions of these constitutionally protected modern-day treaties include the establishment of a host of 'co-management' boards designed to include Aboriginal people and their perspectives in public policy decisions relating to wildlife management and environmental regulation.

The chapters in this book demonstrate that, overall, Canadian governments have been neither ambitious nor innovative when it comes to environmental policy. The creation of these claims boards appears to be an exception. The boards are new, unique institutions within the Canadian federation. They are not extensions of the federal government or of the provincial/territorial governments; nor are they species of Aboriginal self-government. Rather, they exist at the intersection of the three orders of government. That they are new and distinctive, however, is not to say that they are effective; assessing their effectiveness is a central objective of this chapter.

The chapter looks at the environmental regulatory boards created under the land claims agreements in the territorial North. It examines their operations and processes, paying special attention to the extent to which Aboriginal peoples participate in and influence their activities. Though comprehensive claims have been finalized in three provinces—Québec, British Columbia, and Newfoundland and Labrador—the chapter will specifically examine only the claims boards existing in the three territories—Yukon, the Northwest Territories (NWT), and Nunavut—with the lion's share of the analysis focused on boards in the NWT. Following a brief overview to set the comprehensive land claims and the territorial governments in context, the chapter sets out a description of the principal environmental regulatory boards in the Mackenzie Valley of the NWT and examines their role in the regulatory process. It then looks at various aspects of Aboriginal participation in environmental regulation through the claims boards—highlighting a few especially notable decisions arising from board reviews—and surveys some of the shortcomings of the boards.

Background: Comprehensive Claims and Territorial Governments

In much of southern Canada, the Aboriginal peoples who occupied the land before the coming of the Europeans signed treaties with the British government, and later the Canadian government, between the eighteenth century and the 1920s. While fundamental disagreements exist about the nature and intent of these treaties, and about the Canadian government's record in fulfilling its obligations under them, the historic treaties provide, at least, a legal basis for the control exercised by the Canadian state over the lands they cover.[1] Across great swaths of the country, however, the Aboriginal people were never conquered militarily nor did they sign treaties with British or Canadian authorities, thereby agreeing to accept the sovereignty of the Canadian state. Nonetheless, their lands were subsumed into Canada and their longstanding status as self-governing nations dismissed by Canadian governments. By the early 1970s, however, the federal government, spurred on by the landmark Calder decision of the Supreme Court of Canada acknowledging that 'unextinguished Aboriginal title' might still exist in areas without treaties, had accepted the need to settle the outstanding claims of the Aboriginal peoples who had never signed treaties.[2]

Thus, the federal government embarked on a program of settling 'comprehensive land claims agreements', which the Government of Canada acknowledges are 'modern treaties', in the areas without historic treaties. Since the mid-1970s, claims have been finalized covering all of Nunavut,

Northern Quebec, most of Yukon, and the Northwest Territories,[3] and parts of Labrador and British Columbia. Negotiations are still underway on other claims across the North and in British Columbia. Finalized land claims agreements are complex, highly detailed legalistic documents which, once ratified by vote of the affected Aboriginal people and by acts of Parliament and the relevant provincial or territorial legislature, achieve constitutional protection under section 35 of *The Constitution Act, 1982*. They are thus far, far more than simple contracts or policy statements, not least in that their provisions supercede those of ordinary laws.[4]

Each comprehensive claim is unique, but all share common features. In return for giving up title to their traditional lands (but not other Aboriginal rights), the Aboriginal people receive a substantial cash payment, fee simple ownership of selected parcels of land (including some with subsurface rights), and other economic benefits. As well, each claim involves a range of far-reaching governance provisions, including co-management boards to manage wildlife, regulate the environment, and carry out related functions (e.g., land-use planning).

Because this chapter is exclusively devoted to claims boards in the Northern territories, a word about the territories and their governments is in order. Constitutionally, territories lack the status of provinces. For example, the federal government has the technical power to abolish or rearrange the territories at will, though it is inconceivable that it would do so. More significantly, their jurisdictional scope, though substantial, is not as broad as that of the provinces. The territorial governments exercise many of the key powers that provinces wield, including jurisdiction over health, education, social welfare, local government, civil law, local and regional transportation, and so on. Ottawa, rather than the territorial governments, has jurisdiction over a few fields which 'south of 60' fall under provincial control; most are of minor consequence but one is of central importance, both in overall terms and for purposes of this paper.

Elsewhere in Canada, Crown land is owned and controlled by the provinces; in the territories the federal government still retains ownership and thus, in important ways, control of Crown land (as it did in the Prairies until the 1930s). Since the vast bulk of land in the three territories is Crown land, this has huge economic implications; the hundreds of millions of dollars in royalties generated by the diamond mines of the NWT and Nunavut, for example, accrue to Ottawa rather than to the territorial treasuries. As well, it effectively means that most issues of environmental policy and regulation fall within the federal, rather than the territorial, government's ambit. An important qualification to this overall picture pertains to the Yukon, where an extensive devolution agreement in 2003 saw Ottawa transfer administrative responsibility for—though not actual ownership of—lands and nonrenewable resources to the territorial government. Accordingly, the Yukon territorial government takes the lead in setting and implementing environmental policy, including matters coming before the claims boards.

Much could be said of the geographic, economic, demographic, and political characteristics of the territories. For present purposes let us simply highlight a few key points:

- The territories have distinctive demographic profiles, most notably in the predominance of Aboriginal people: Aboriginal people constitute roughly 20 per cent of the population in the Yukon, 50 per cent in the NWT, and 85 per cent in Nunavut. Overall figures are misleading. Because the non-Aboriginal population is heavily concentrated in a few larger centres, most communities have large Aboriginal majorities.
- The territorial governments are fully democratic: Members of the Legislative Assembly (MLAs) are elected by universal franchise and operate according to the familiar tenets of British-style

'responsible government'. Territorial governments are headed by premiers and cabinets, though political parties are absent in both the Nunavut and NWT legislatures.

- While they may lack the full array of provincial powers, the territorial governments are large, professional organizations of critical everyday importance to their residents.
- In all three territories, the Aboriginal political organizations—governments in a very real sense—are integral to the system of governance to an extent unimaginable in most of southern Canada.

Claims Boards in the Mackenzie Valley

A great many variations are evident in environmental regulatory boards established by and under the six settled claims across the territorial North (one in Nunavut, four in the NWT, and one in the Yukon[5]), in terms of structure, mandate, budget, process, effectiveness, and the like. No point would be served in enumerating these variations; instead the balance of this discussion will focus on two of the largest, most active boards: the Mackenzie Valley Land and Water Board (MVLWB) and the Mackenzie Valley Environmental Impact Review Board (MVEIRB), with occasional reference to boards in the Yukon and Nunavut.

Under the provisions of the 1992 Gwich'in and 1993 Sahtu land claims in the northern NWT (as well as the subsequent Tlicho agreement in the central NWT), the federal government was required to establish a series of co-management boards to deal with land-use planning and environmental protection in the Mackenzie Valley (essentially the entire NWT south of the delta of the Mackenzie River[6]). After some delay, which led to Ottawa finding itself in court over unfulfilled treaty obligations, the MVLWB and the MVEIRB were created under the federal *Mackenzie Valley Resource Management Act* (MVRMA), which was passed by Parliament in 1998. This might suggest that a simple act of Parliament could substantially alter or indeed abolish these boards, with the implication that their existence and influence rests precariously on the favour of the federal government. However, this is true only in a technical sense. Were Ottawa to do away with the boards, it would immediately be faced with a constitutional obligation to create replacement boards with similar mandates and composition.

The organization of the MVEIRB is relatively straightforward. The board, whose mandate covers the entire Mackenzie Valley, is composed of eight members who serve on a part-time basis and a Chair, who effectively works full-time on board business. Operating on a budget of roughly $3.2 million a year, it has a dozen full-time professional staff and routinely hires consultants to provide technical expertise that board staff may lack. Its office is in the territorial capital, Yellowknife. Structurally, the MVLWB is far more complex. Three regional boards, the Gwich'in, Sahtu, and Tlicho land and water boards, were established under the comprehensive land claims in these areas. These boards are responsible for projects which affect only their regions. The MVLWB is responsible for applications coming from what are termed the 'unsettled areas'—the parts of the southern NWT where claims have yet to be finalized—plus projects which might affect the environment in more than one region or which might be 'transboundary' in nature, that is, with implications for an adjacent province or territory. All members of the regional land and water boards belong to 'the big board' (the MVLWB) and, with additional members from the unsettled areas, at full strength it has 19 members (including the Chair). The staff complement and budget of MVLWB are similar to those of the MVEIRB and its office is also in Yellowknife. The regional land and water boards are headquartered in their own regions and together they have roughly 20 staff.

A fundamentally important feature of these boards is their co-management nature. 'Co-management' is a term widely used in resource management to denote various forms of power sharing between government and other organizations or individuals.[7] In this instance, it refers primarily to the all-important composition of board membership. Decisions about who will be appointed to government boards are typically made exclusively by government, though they sometimes consult with important stakeholders about possible members. Under the MVRMA (as stipulated in the claims), although the federal government formally makes most appointments to the Mackenzie Valley boards, half the members are nominees of government (two each from the federal government and the Government of the Northwest Territories [GNWT]) and half are nominees of Aboriginal organizations and governments. In virtually all instances, Ottawa appoints whoever the GNWT and the Aboriginal organizations nominate; in the case of members from its region, the Tlicho Government makes the appointments itself, without requiring approval from Ottawa. Since the Aboriginal organizations and governments almost always nominate Aboriginal members, and many territorial government nominees and some federal appointees are also Aboriginal, the result is that a majority of board members, often a strong majority, are Aboriginal. This is enormously important.

The boards and their members are required to be independent—like judges, they are to make decisions based on their best judgment without direction or influence from outside entities, be they government or Aboriginal organizations. It is important to appreciate that the parties are careful to nominate only persons whose views they find compatible. Moreover, the elemental fact of a strong Aboriginal presence on the boards is of huge importance in determining how the boards operate and the decisions they reach.

The Environmental Regulation Process

All but the tiniest construction, infrastructure, or resource extraction projects require land use permits and/or water licences, which specify in great detail what project proponents may or may not do to the geophysical environment, as well as what measures they must take to ensure against potential (as opposed to actual or predictable) environmental damage, plus remedial actions to restore the environment once the project is completed. Thus, anyone—governments included—proposing anything—from a major pipeline, road, or diamond mine, to a culvert over a small creek—must secure formal government approval based on environmental acceptability. It is mainly the land and water boards and the MVEIRB that determine whether proposed projects meet environmental standards and that impose conditions on them to ensure that the environment is protected.

The MVRMA is long, highly complex, and replete with barely comprehensible legal language. So too, board processes are convoluted and confusing (a simplified schematic diagram setting out basic processes fills an entire page). Very much simplified, the process unfolds as follows.[8]

Applications from project proponents are screened by various governmental bodies, usually a land and water board. If the screener believes the potential environmental impact to be minimal, either because the project is very small or because the applicant has identified and committed to specific detailed measures to mitigate possible environmental damage, it will issue the requisite licences or permits or, in the case of certain larger projects, recommend to the federal Minister of Indian and Northern Affairs that the project be approved.[9] If the screener concludes, in the words of the act, that the proposed development 'might have a significant adverse impact on the environment or might be a cause of public concern'[10] it refers the application to the MVEIRB for a thorough environmental assessment (EA). Only a small proportion of projects are sent for EA. The MVEIRB can also decide to conduct an EA on a project even if none of the screening bodies has sent it forward, but only rarely does so.

An EA is a prolonged, formal process that typically involves public hearings; detailed reviews of technical data; and extensive exchange of information and opinion among the MVEIRB, government agencies, the project proponent, and the people and communities in the potentially affected area. It can easily take a year or more. All documents generated in this process become part of the public record, readily accessible via the public registry on the board's website.

Once the information has been assembled and analyzed and all those potentially affected by the project—including the local Aboriginal communities—heard from, the board issues a report to the federal minister recommending that the project be approved as is, that it be rejected entirely, or that it be approved subject to specific measures to mitigate possible environmental damage. Recommended measures are often extensive and detailed. Approval of the federal minister (who responds on behalf of other federal departments, as well as territorial departments which may be involved) is required to confirm the board's recommendation. Once ministerial approval is received, the application is sent to the appropriate land and water board for issuance of the detailed licences or permits.

This summary might suggest that the boards are purely advisory and that the final analysis decisions rest with Ottawa, which would in turn raise questions about Aboriginal influence and about 'co-management'. In a strictly legal sense, the final decision on most large or controversial applications is made by the federal minister, though many routine decisions on smaller projects are made by the land and water boards without federal approval. Since Ottawa in general and the Indian and Northern Affairs Canada (INAC) minister in particular are eager to facilitate large economic development projects such as pipelines and mines, it might be supposed that the apparent federal control of the decision might produce less stringent environmental conditions on proposed projects than the boards would recommend. In terms of real world politics and policy, however, such a reading greatly underestimates the boards' power and influence.

In the first place, the boards' reports are thorough and professional, based on extensive review of relevant technical data and expert opinion, and thus carry significant credibility and political weight. In addition, virtually the entire process is carried out in public[11] and all documents—including the formal response from the minister to the EA report and its recommendations—are public. This transparency adds to the credibility of the board and its reports and requires Ottawa to justify any objections it may have to board recommendations.

More significantly, the MVRMA itself makes it difficult for the federal minister to simply reject recommendations from a MVEIRB EA report and all but impossible to substitute his or her conditions for those proposed by the board. The only route open to a minister who wishes to reject an EA report is to refer the matter to an Environmental Impact Review (EIR) but this is an unpalatable option since EIRs are more formal, extensive, costly, and time-consuming than EAs (and thus disagreeable and frustrating to proponents). Not surprisingly, no federal minister has chosen this route. Ottawa may negotiate with the board about revising its recommended conditions through an informal 'consult to modify' process. Many disputes between the federal minister and the board are resolved this way, though the process can take considerable time. If this process fails to resolve differences, stalemate ensues; without board agreement to modify its recommendations the minister cannot impose his preferred conditions, but without ministerial approval, no licenses or permits may be issued and the project cannot proceed. Such standoffs are not common, but nor are they unknown; in one case differences between the board and the federal minister over recommendations in an EA report issued in February 2005 (on an application initiated in October 2003) remained unresolved (and the project in limbo) in January 2009.[12]

The expansive mandates of the Mackenzie Valley boards under the MVRMA significantly enhance their clout and the influence of Aboriginal people in the environmental assessment process. Nor was this accidental; 'in many instances the language of the legislation was kept deliberately broad to ensure maximum involvement for Indigenous people, and to ensure that all uses of land that could have an impact would be subject to proper environmental assessment.'[13] A crucial illustration relates to the definition of the 'environment', which the boards are to protect against adverse impacts. It includes not only the geophysical environment—the land, water, air, and the flora and fauna—but also 'the social and cultural environment . . . [and] heritage resources'.[14] This broad remit gives the Mackenzie Valley boards (and the Yukon Environmental and Socio-economic Assessment Board, whose act contains a similar provision), significantly wider leeway to examine issues relating to the human environment than other agencies conducting EAs elsewhere in Canada. For example, under the *Canadian Environmental Assessment Act*, the federal statute operative in most other parts of Canada, socio-economic concerns are considered only under specific circumstances;[15] no such limitations constrain the Mackenzie Valley Boards.

Moreover, as noted above, the land and water boards are to send applications to EA if they perceive that the proposed project 'might have a significant adverse impact on the environment or might be a cause of public concern'. Since nowhere in the act or the regulations supplementing it are such key terms as 'significant', 'adverse', or 'public concern' defined, the boards are left with wide discretion in interpreting them. This ambiguity serves to enhance the boards' ability to establish the ground rules in their efforts at protecting the environment.

A final important point about the boards' legal mandates: in keeping with one of the MVRMA's guiding principles—enhancing the well being and preserving the way of life to the Aboriginal peoples of the Mackenzie Valley—the act explicitly sets the 'traditional knowledge' (TK) of the Aboriginal people on an equal footing with Western 'scientific knowledge'.[16] This noteworthy provision is examined more extensively below.

Aboriginal Involvement and Influence on Claims Boards

Two separate characteristics of claims boards make for significant Aboriginal influence on the boards involved in environmental regulation (as indeed on other claims boards). One is the substantial number of Aboriginal board members, the other is the requirement for extensive, genuine consultation with local communities—which are typically overwhelmingly Aboriginal—potentially affected by proposed developments.

As noted above, the boards were explicitly designed on a co-management basis, in the sense of guaranteed representation by the nominees of Aboriginal governments and organizations on the boards, and not in token numbers. A recent analysis found that across the three territories between 40 and 90 per cent of claims board members were Aboriginal; at the MVLWB, 67 per cent of all those who served on the board from its creation to early 2008 were Aboriginal; the figure for the MVEIRB was 53 per cent.[17] That board members—Aboriginal and non-Aboriginal—act independently and do not take instructions from the parties which nominated or appointed them does not mean that Aboriginal sensibilities are left behind. Consider the following episode concerning Gabrielle Mackenzie-Scott, a Dene member (and later Chair) of the MVEIRB, during a public hearing on a proposed diamond drilling project:

> . . . a Dene woman stepped forward, pleading with the board to protect the area because her baby teeth were buried there.
>
> 'A lot of people would have found that to be strange, but I could relate to the woman,' says Mackenzie-Scott, 'She was about my age and I too had the experience of having my baby teeth buried in a ceremony. This was an important moment in life for both me and my mother. I know where my baby teeth are buried. Many people have sacred places like this.'[18]

As the specific board decisions outlined below illustrate, Aboriginal board members bring their distinctive worldviews to bear when evaluating the environmental consequences of projects they review.

Not only are Aboriginal people involved as decision makers, they participate in the process via consultations and public hearings. The Mackenzie Valley boards are required by the MVRMA to ensure that the people who stand to be affected by proposed projects are taken into account in environmental reviews. Nor are these pro forma consultations. Guidelines set out by the MVLWB make it clear that project proponents are required to engage in extensive and sincere interaction with local communities about their projects, and to do so before submitting an application. Tellingly, the guidelines refer to 'involvement' rather than 'consultations' and would-be applicants are warned that they 'will be asked to demonstrate the extent of community involvement as part of the formal application and to provide an indication of how a specific proposal was modified or prepared to reflect the regional community concerns.'[19]

Once an application is received, the Board informs local communities, Aboriginal organizations and governments, and other potentially affected groups and actively solicits their views. Should a project be sent for EA—often on the basis of 'public concern'—the MVEIRB process is likely to entail public hearings in which community representatives, officials of Aboriginal organizations, and local people are invited to appear and to address the Board. Not only do they have the right to speak, they have the right to question representatives of the companies or governments and to ask them to explain or justify their plans and assertions—all in public.

In all phases of their activity, boards strive to include Aboriginal TK in environmental decision-making. A widely cited definition of TK describes it as, 'a cumulative body of knowledge, practice and belief, evolving by adaptive processes and handed down through generations by cultural transmission about the relationship of living beings (including humans) with one another and with their environment.'[20]

In practice, giving voice to TK entails such things as giving as much credence to information and opinion provided by Aboriginal elders with decades of experience on the land as is accorded to that offered by professional consultants and biologists with university credentials. Aboriginal people with daily experience of the location, numbers, and behaviour of wildlife; of long- and short-term changes in the health and spatial distribution of plants and trees; of patterns of water movement in rivers, lakes, and the like may have a better understanding of the complex interrelationships of the myriad elements of the natural environment than those trained in Western science, whose focus is typically more narrow and lacks long-term perspective. Aboriginal hunters and elders, with generations of observation and experience to draw on, may be better placed to predict the consequences of putting a road across a caribou migration route than Western scientists. This is not to say that TK is necessarily at odds with the findings of Western science—indeed they often complement one another—but to emphasize the involvement of Aboriginal people and their experiences and perspectives in the process. Prior to the advent of the Mackenzie Valley boards, TK played a far less significant role in environmental regulation in the NWT and certainly had no legal status, as it does under the MVRMA.

Notable Board Accomplishments

Given the number, range, and complexity of the proposed projects which the boards have screened and reviewed in the decade since the MVRMA came into effect, it is possible only to highlight a small number of specific illustrations of the boards' contribution to environmental protection in the Mackenzie Valley. The mammoth, multi-billion dollar Mackenzie Gas Project, the centrepiece of which is the proposal to construct a pipeline from the Arctic Ocean, through the Mackenzie Valley, to northern Alberta, might be thought an obvious case study for illuminating the role of Northern claims boards and the influence of Aboriginal peoples through them. And while it is certainly of great intrinsic import and has much to say about the regulatory process for megaprojects in the North, it is not examined in this section, for several reasons. Although the Mackenzie Valley claims boards are involved, because the proposed pipeline would pass through the Yukon, the Inuvialuit Settlement Region (which, under the Inuvialuit claim has its own regulatory apparatus), the Mackenzie Valley (as defined by the MVRMA), and Alberta, a host of regulatory agencies, including the National Energy Board are also involved. Accordingly, the process is staggeringly complex and thus not easily summarized and, moreover, by its very nature is unique and not necessarily illustrative of either claims boards in general or the Mackenzie Valley boards in particular. Finally, at the time of writing, the process was still underway and the final resolution of the issue clearly some time away.

Early in 2005, the MVEIRB issued its EA report on a proposal for a small exploratory diamond drilling project at Drybones Bay, roughly 45 kilometres south-east of Yellowknife on Great Slave Lake. The actual biophysical environmental effects of the proposed drilling were relatively minor but the Board unanimously recommended that the project be rejected in its entirety because of a 'cultural impact so severe it could not be mitigated . . . the cultural groups that have long utilized Drybones Bay consider it to be of utmost importance—as a spiritual place, as a gathering place, as a burial grounds, as a place of rest and respite, as a learning place, and as a harvesting place.'[21] After an initial hesitation, the federal government accepted the Board's recommendations, killing the project. This was an unusual occurrence not only because it was the first time the Board had recommended complete rejection of a project, but also because the Board has subsequently recommended approval, with appropriate mitigation measures, for similar projects in the vicinity of Drybones Bay. Nonetheless, it serves to underline both the Board's clout and the influence, via the boards, of the Aboriginal people's holistic appreciation of 'the environment' on decision making.

A more far-reaching episode was the disposition of an application by a mining company to explore for uranium at Screech Lake in the watershed of the upper Thelon River, some 80 kilometres south of the Thelon Game Sanctuary, which spans the NWT–Nunavut border. The MVLWB had referred the project to EA on the basis of concerns expressed by the people of the small Dene community of Łutsël K'e, the closest community to the proposed development (though more than 200 kilometres distant). At the MVEIRB's public hearing in Łutsël K'e, community members expressed profound disquiet at the prospect of uranium mining in this pristine and ecologically sensitive area central to their traditions and lifestyle. In its May 2007 EA report, the Board noted that 'at the heart of this issue is the belief that the Upper Thelon is a spiritual place that must be protected from any type of desecration . . . the Review Board agrees that the potential for industrial development of the area is incompatible with the aboriginal values of this spiritually significant cultural landscape'[22] and recommended that the project be rejected. In short order the INAC minister accepted the recommendation.

These outcomes are unusual in that they involved the outright rejection of proposed projects. More common are board recommendations leading to mitigation measures designed to protect and preserve the geophysical and cultural environment for projects given the go-ahead. By way of illustration, the Boards routinely recommend—and the federal and territorial governments accept—such measures as reduction in the number and size of 'seismic lines' (clearings in the bush to accommodate seismic exploration); limitation on times and seasons where drilling and other activities may take place, so as not disturb wildlife; more stringent water quality standards and monitoring than project developers proposed; extensive baseline studies to document the size, nature, and health of fish and wildlife stocks in potentially affected areas; strict conditions, and sometimes outright prohibitions, on location of access roads and camp sites; involvement of local Aboriginal elders in determining the location of archeologically or spiritually important sites to be avoided in exploration and exploitation activities. These and other measures are designed to strike a balance between environmental protection and resource development, with substantial emphasis on the importance of maintaining and respecting Aboriginal culture and lifestyle. To be sure, such measures may fall short of what some—both Aboriginal and non-Aboriginal—think necessary to protect and preserve the environment, but by the same token they are often significantly more extensive than development proponents would put in place. It is also worth bearing in mind that, as board approaches and policies become better known across the Mackenzie Valley, would-be developers include tougher environmental protection measures in their initial proposals in anticipation of board recommendations.

Shortcomings

Although the MVEIRB EA process has been described as 'exemplary', especially in light of the typical failings of such processes to give adequate voice and influence to Aboriginal people,[23] the regulatory regime of the Mackenzie Valley claims boards has significant shortcomings. Some, such as the lack of intervenor funding and limits to the incorporation of TK into board processes, relate directly to Aboriginal participation and influence. Other failings affect Aboriginal influence less directly but are no less important. These include the complexity of the process; limits on the recourse to TK; problems of enforcement; and concerns about board independence, mostly but not entirely arising from statements and activities of the federal government.

While Aboriginal organizations and communities fully appreciate the importance of being involved in the process through participation in public hearings and submission of written documents, they often lack the capacity—the human and financial resources—to take on the myriad issues confronting them, only some of which involve environmental assessments of projects proposed for their lands. The Mackenzie Valley boards have long argued that without intervenor funding, Aboriginal organizations and communities are often unable to make their views and concerns known. (Intervenor funding refers to money made available to organizations and groups to enable them to participate effectively in regulatory processes. It could be used to enable staff to prepare submissions, to hire consultants and other experts to provide evidence to support their case, to defray travel costs for representatives to attend hearings and meetings, and so on.)

As highlighted above, the boards take TK seriously in gathering and evaluating information and in reaching recommendations. Genuine as these efforts are, criticisms are sometimes heard that TK is not always given the same respect as Western science or that board staff (who tend to be non-Aboriginal and typically have university backgrounds) and proponents will always ensure that information acquired and analyzed according to the Western science paradigm will be presented to the boards, whereas TK may not be as readily available. Additionally, while it is clear that boards make sincere and extensive efforts to utilize TK in their deliberations, it is equally clear that certain spiritual-cosmological aspects of TK, involving for example ethical understandings of how humans should relate to one another, are simply incompatible with the worldviews of the Western bureaucratic state in which the boards are embedded.[24]

A particularly weak link in the Mackenzie Valley environmental regulatory regime is enforcement. The claims boards have no enforcement authority or capacity. They must depend entirely on the staff of the federal government to inspect projects once they are licensed and to enforce the conditions of licenses and permits. The oftentimes substantial gap between conditions imposed by the boards and compliance, as enforced by INAC inspectors and other officials, has long been a sore point. A recent appeal for action from the chairs of the MVEIRB and of all the Mackenzie Valley land and water boards to the senior INAC official in the NWT estimated that 'only about 46% of the [MVEIRB's] measures accepted by the Minister of INAC are being implemented by regulatory authorities and that, of those, less that [sic] 50% are actually inspected for purposes of compliance or enforcement. At best, only 25% of the Review Board's measures are having any affect [sic] on the impacts they were designed to mitigate.'[25] It does not necessarily follow that conditions set out in permits and licenses are being ignored, but without systematic inspection and follow-up to ensure compliance, the effectiveness of the regime is cast into some doubt. In response, INAC contends that many of the conditions that the boards argue it is not enforcing are either beyond the boards' mandates or are too imprecise to make enforcement possible.

The effectiveness of the boards is heavily contingent on their independence from government, especially the federal government. And while the boards, especially the MVEIRB, have not been reluctant to criticize the INAC or to issue reports or take other actions unwelcome in Ottawa, the question of board independence is never far below the surface. Every penny of the boards' funding comes from Ottawa. Although their core funding is secure, the number, scope, and thus the cost of the EAs, public hearings, and other activities the boards will be required to conduct in any given year is unpredictable and largely funded through special transfers which have to be negotiated every year. Ottawa has thus far provided the boards with adequate funding—though never as much as the boards argue they need to fulfill their mandates properly—and has not used its financial upper hand over the boards to attempt to influence their decisions and recommendations. Nevertheless, the boards, as well as those who interact with them, remain acutely aware of 'the golden rule of politics': he who has the gold, rules.

Board independence also stands to be affected by the appointment process. As noted above, Ottawa usually appoints persons nominated by the GNWT and by the Aboriginal organizations and governments, but on occasion has shown itself willing to use its appointment—and dismissal—powers to promote its interests. Isolated instances have occurred of Ottawa refusing to appoint other parties' nominees (apparently for reasons other than the nominees' failure to pass the requisite security and criminal background checks).[26] The most noteworthy example of the federal government using its political muscle to affect board membership involved its abrupt and questionable removal of a veteran member of the MVEIRB who had vigorously opposed the board's Chair on the grounds that his actions were motivated by subservience to the federal government and its priorities.[27]

To be fair, delays on Ottawa's part—often long, disruptive delays—in making appointments to board vacancies has been more of a concern than federal attempts at influencing boards through its appointment prerogative. The potential for high-handed intervention by Ottawa in this fashion, however, remains a concern.

It is also clear that the federal government, especially but not exclusively under the Harper Conservative administration, is desirous of reining in some of the boards and rendering environmental protection processes in the NWT less time-consuming and less complex. Industry has long complained about the delays, expense, and uncertainty of environmental regulatory processes, and of course about some of the conditions imposed by the boards. Former Conservative INAC Minister Jim Prentice complained vigorously about what he termed the 'spider's web' of regulatory processes in the NWT and vowed improvements.[28] His successor, Chuck Strahl, appointed a 'special representative' (a former Deputy Minister of Justice in Alberta and later head of the Alberta Energy and Utilities Board) to review the regulatory regime in the NWT and to make recommendations for reform. The McCrank Report, published in July 2008, agreed with some of industry's criticisms about the complexity and unpredictability of the regulatory system in the Mackenzie Valley. It proposed both sweeping changes to the boards and their operations and piecemeal recommendations. At the same time, the report was at some pains to emphasize that 'this is not an attempt to diminish or reduce the influence that Aboriginal people have on resource development in the North.'[29] The only certainty about the disposition of the report's recommendations was that, at best, they would not be easily or quickly realized.

Nor should it be thought that challenges to board independence come solely from Ottawa (or, under devolved regimes, the territorial capitals). A recent disturbing episode from Nunavut illustrates that Aboriginal organizations and governments may also threaten board independence. An application for a water licence for a gold mine had been languishing for some time at the Nunavut Water Board, which exercises similar functions to the Mackenzie Valley land and water boards. Pressing for quick approval, in order to create jobs and economic opportunities, were the Kitikmeot Inuit Association and other, largely Inuit-dominated, political and business organizations. When board staff issued a long detailed critique of the proponent's most recent revision of its application, the board summarily fired its long-serving and highly respected executive director, whereupon the board's entire technical staff resigned in support, citing blatant political interference.[30]

Conclusion

Environmental policy encompasses a good deal more than processes relating to regulation of resource extraction and infrastructure projects, extending for example to reduction of harmful emissions, recycling and waste disposal practices, sustainable economic activity, and green energy production. For Canada's far North, however, many of these issues are largely beyond local control since to a considerable degree they originate in southern Canada and elsewhere. Where local Northern people can influence policy on important environmental issues directly affecting them is on economic development projects such as mines, roads, and oil and gas wells and pipelines, which are both substantial in number and potentially far-reaching in their environmental consequences. Especially given the economic, cultural, and spiritual significance of the land to the Aboriginal people, its protection looms as a critically important environmental issue. Accordingly, having in place stringent processes for environmental regulation for resource extraction and infrastructure projects, processes which afford the Aboriginal people of the North meaningful involvement and influence, is crucially important.

The regulatory boards created to fulfill the Northern comprehensive land claims, such as the MVLWB and the MVEIRB, were designed to provide just such processes. The environmental protection regime established under the claims is an exemplar of the Second Generation policies identified by the editors in the Introduction as taking 'a more holistic, "place-based" approach which is concerned with the health of ecosystems'. To be sure, the boards have their shortcomings, but overall their record—both in maintaining a high-quality regime of environmental impact assessment and of imposition of mitigation measures and in assuring that the concerns and the approaches of the local Aboriginal people are taken into account in decision making—is one of solid accomplishment. In this instance, just as the whole notion of comprehensive land claim agreements represents an innovative restructuring of the relationship between the Canadian state and Aboriginal peoples, the board regime—even if it remains a work in progress—qualifies as innovative and ambitious.

Questions for Review

1. What are the main environmental issues in Canada's North?
2. How important are environmental considerations in the policies of governments with responsibilities in the North?
3. What should be the role of traditional aboriginal knowledge in environmental policy?
4. Why do the roles, powers, and composition of co-management boards matter for environmental policy?

Notes

1. On the nature and importance of the historic treaties and the controversies surrounding the adequacy of the government's fulfilment of its treaty obligations, see Royal Commission on Aboriginal Peoples, *Final Report* Volume II (Ottawa: Supply and Services Canada, 1996), ch. 2.
2. Christa Scholtz, *Negotiating Claims: The Emergence of Indigenous Land Claim Negotiations in Australia, Canada, New Zealand, and the United States* (New York: Routledge, 2006), ch. 4.
3. Much of the current NWT was covered by Treaty 8 (1899) and Treaty 11 (1921) but the government's policy tacitly accepts that in areas, such as the NWT, where existing treaties were fundamentally flawed, comprehensive land claims could be negotiated.
4. Bernard Funston, 'Canada's North: Barren Lands or Blind Spot', in Ian Peach, ed., *Constructing Tomorrow's Federalism: New Perspectives on Canadian Governance* (Winnipeg: University of Manitoba Press, 2007), 87.
5. In the Yukon, an Umbrella Final Agreement sets out an overall framework covering the entire territory. Individual First Nations negotiate their claims and self-government agreements within this framework. As of early-2009, 11 of 14 Yukon First Nations had settled claims.
6. An earlier claim, the 1984 Inuvialuit Final Agreement, created a series of boards with responsibility for the northern part of the Mackenzie Delta and the portions of the Arctic coast and the Arctic islands within the NWT.
7. Fikret Berkes, P.J. George, and R.J. Preston, 'Co-management: The Evolution of Theory and Practice of the Joint Administration of Living Things', *Alternatives* 18, 2 (1991): 12.

8. Any number of nuances, exceptions and complications are ignored in this overview. For a somewhat more detailed plain-language account of the process, see SENES Consultants Limited, *Northwest Territories Environmental Audit 2005, Main Report* (Yellowknife, 2005), 4-1–4-3 and 5-1–5-12; for a more extensive, formal account see MVEIRB, *Environmental Impact Assessment Guidelines* (Yellowknife, 2004), 5–41.

9. Because of the territories' constitutional status, Indian and Northern Affairs Canada (INAC) takes the federal lead in policy areas which elsewhere in Canada would be the responsibility of other departments, such as the Department of the Environment.

10. Mackenzie Valley Resource Management Act, *Statutes of Canada 1998*, c. 25 [henceforth MVRMA], s.125.1 (b).

11. The principal exception is that, as required by the act, the various boards meet behind closed doors to formulate their reports and decide on recommendations.

12. The MVRMA process is entirely unique. The process established under the Yukon Environmental and Socio-economic Assessment Act, which has broadly similar objectives, is very different. For example, once the YESA Board makes a recommendation, in most cases, if government does not take explicit action within a relatively short time span, the recommendation is automatically approved.

13. Graham White, Vern Christensen, and Alan Ehrlich, 'Involving Canada's Indigenous Peoples in Environmental Impact Assessment: Co-management through the Mackenzie Valley Environmental Impact Review Board'. Paper presented at the Annual Conference of the International Association for Impact Assessment, Seoul, Korea, June, 2007, 5.

14. MVRMA, s 115.

15. Alan Ehrlich, 'Comparative Overview of EIA across Selected Jurisdictions', Mackenzie Valley Environmental Impact Review Board, November 2001, 20.

16. MVRMA, s 60.1 (b).

17. Graham White, '"Not the Almighty": Evaluating Aboriginal Influence on Northern Claims Boards', *Arctic*, 61 Suppl. 1 (2008), Table 1, page 75.

18. Ed Struzik, 'Guardian of Sacred Place', *Edmonton Journal*, 24 February 2008.

19. MVLWB, 'Public Involvement Guidelines for Permit and Licence Applications to the Mackenzie Valley Land and Water Board', October 2003, 1.

20. Fikret Berkes, *Sacred Ecology: Traditional Ecological Knowledge and Resource Management* (Philadelphia: Taylor and Francis, 1999), 8.

21. Mackenzie Valley Environmental Impact Review Board, 'Further Considerations of the Ministers' Questions'. Attachment to a letter from Gabrielle Mackenzie-Scott, Chairperson of the MVEIRB to Hon. Andy Scott, Minister of Indian Affairs and Northern Development, 23 June 2005, 4.

22. *Idem*, Report of Environmental Assessment, Ur Energy Exploration Project, May 7, 2007, 4. Complete documentation of the Drybones Bay and Screech Lake projects may be found in the public registry on the MVEIRB website at http://www.mveirb.nt.ca, by searching under the names of their proponents, New Shoshoni Ventures and Ur Energy.

23. Lindsay Galbraith, Ben Bradshaw and Murray B. Rutherford, 'Towards a new supraregulatory approach to environmental assessment in Northern Canada', *Impact Assessment and Project Appraisal* 25 (March 2007), 33, 36; see also White, Christensen and Ehrlich, 'Involving Canada's Indigenous Peoples'.

24. Graham White, 'Cultures in Collision: Traditional Knowledge and Euro-Canadian Governance Processes in Northern Land-Claim Boards', *Arctic* 59 (December 2006), 401–14.

25. Letter from Mackenzie Valley board chairs to Trish Merrithew-Mercredi, Regional Director General, INAC, Yellowknife, 11 December 2007.

26. On the rare occasions when Ottawa declines to appoint a nominee it does not provide reasons for its decisions.

27. Bob Weber, 'Nault Muzzling Regulatory Agency, Critics Say', *Globe and Mail*, 11 October 2003, A14.

28. Hon. Jim Prentice, 'Notes for an Address to the Canadian Energy Pipeline Association Annual Dinner'. Calgary, 23 May 2006.

29. Neil McCrank, *Road to Improvement: Report to the Honourable Chuck Strahl, 'The Review of the Regulatory Systems across the North'*. Ottawa: Indian and Northern Affairs Canada, May 2008, 13.

30. John Thompson, 'Technical Staff Quits in Protest', *Nunatsiaq News* 13 April 2007.

10

Canadian Environmental Policy in the Global Context: Obligations and Opportunities

Robert Boardman

Canada's environmental problems are influenced in various ways by what happens outside North America. Therefore, thinking internationally has to be an integral part of Canadian environmental policy. How big that part is, however, has varied over time. Furthermore, there is often wide disagreement on what Canada should do in response to international developments. For example, all countries will be affected in coming decades by the decisions taken by Brazil, Russia, India, and China (the BRIC countries) that determine their respective greenhouse-gas (GHG) emissions. These emissions may increase by over 40 per cent by 2030.[1] Should Canada wait until there is firm evidence of significant mitigation commitments on their part, or would it be more appropriate to engage sooner in a long-term course of tougher self-restraint in climate change policy? Other problems arise from the large development orientation of much of the environmental work of the United Nations and its associated organizations. How extensive should Canada's commitments be to international activities whose primary beneficiaries are other countries?

There are several reasons for taking international environmental policy seriously. First, some Canadian problems are inherently international. Acting alone, or even in collaboration with US partners, Canada cannot make effective policies that will safeguard its interests in relation to the ozone layer, global biological diversity, the management of international fish stocks, problems of the transnational spread and regulation of toxic chemicals, and protection of the Arctic environment. Secondly, Canada gains from the gradual spread of sound international legal and administrative arrangements on matters such as the trade in endangered species and marine pollution. Thirdly, even if the benefits are not tangible or immediate, there is value in participating in international processes, in being part of global conversations. Fourthly, this participation reinforces the traditional benefits to Canada of pursuing an outward-looking, multilateralist approach to foreign policy. Finally, international activities have direct consequences for domestic environmental policy. Sometimes these reinforce and augment what governments are doing anyway, as is the case for the Canadian networks of protected wetlands and heritage sites. And, sometimes new and unanticipated value is added, for example, in the way that Canada's adherence to the Convention on Biological Diversity was a factor leading eventually to federal legislation on endangered species (see Chapter 14 by Stewart Elgie).

However, the international level of environmental governance also has limitations as a driver of policy leadership and innovation. Canada's is only one voice in a world of some 190-plus sovereign states. Even when there is political will for change on the part of Ottawa, opting for international lead roles—as Canada has done at different times on the protection of the ozone layer, climate change, the circumpolar Arctic environment, and forests—requires a substantial mobilization of scientific and diplomatic resources, and luck. Global governance is fragmented. Multiple forums exist, even in the same issue-area; effective collaboration among international organizations is often elusive; and there is no clearly identifiable authoritative body on the environment like the World Trade Organization (WTO) on trade issues. Participation rights at international venues are restricted. Environmental nongovernmental organizations have some access points, but for many activities the main participants are government agency officials. Much of what goes on in intergovernmental forums seems, at first sight, to be repetitive, legalistic, and inconclusive. Most such events are not reported in the news media. Private-sector critics detect undercurrents of regulatory interventionism and anti-business sentiment. Support for environmental multilateralism has been steadily eroded by factors unrelated to the environment, such as a general disenchantment with UN-style cooperation, the Harper government's preference for consolidating Canada–US ties, the appeal of classical-liberal ideas of the small state and trade liberalization, and competition for priority from energy supply issues and traditional notions of security.

The internationalist reflexes of many of Canada's environmental policy actors—governmental and private—nonetheless remain resilient. Traces of many international environmental agreements are embedded in Canadian law and public administration. To assess the significance of the international level of governance for environmental policy leadership and innovation, this chapter looks first at trends in the workings of environmental multilateralism, and then focuses on Canadian experiences in relation to three policy arenas: international environmental protection in the Arctic, the transnational spread of toxic chemicals, and governance developments in the global biological economy.

Canada and Environmental Multilateralism

Choice and Interests in the Global System

Environmental governance comprises many agreements and institutions. Several hundred international agreements deal with environmental topics. About 230 are primarily environmental, and of these around 40 are identified by the UN as core conventions.[2] The rules of international law define convention processes. Complex negotiations, if successful, produce a document open for signature by states; the agreement enters into force internationally when a certain number of states, defined in the text, have both signed and ratified it. Several key conventions generate subsidiary agreements such as protocols. Some institutions, for example, the International Maritime Organization (IMO), initiate the processes leading to such agreements, while others, including Conferences of the Parties (COPs) to conventions, are set up by them. Many produce additional bodies. According to one US official speaking in Montreal in 2001, the international environmental calendar is now filled with 'a blizzard of ministerials, COP meetings, and meetings of other subsidiary bodies as well as ad hoc gatherings'.[3]

Global environmental governance reflects a four-decade history of diplomatic routine and cautious progress punctuated by bursts of innovation. There were significant advances in the first half of the 1970s (a period which saw major agreements on wetlands, heritage, the international trade in endangered species, marine pollution, and other topics) and from the mid-1980s to the early 1990s (during which negotiations were completed on landmark instruments on the ozone layer, biological diversity, chemicals, and climate change). Many processes are lengthy. The IMO's London protocol on dumping and marine pollution (a comprehensive updating of a 1972 agreement) was finalized in 1996 and, following ratifications by Mexico and other countries, entered into force in 2006.

Not all of these agreements and institutions affect Canada. Crucial choices concern the extent to which commitments should be made to international activities in particular issue-areas. Much can be done inside Canada without investment of scarce resources at the international level. While the debates on Kyoto have led some critics to advocate a deeper commitment to a strengthened multilateralism, oriented to human security, others have drawn from its weaknesses the lesson that traditional multilateralism is not up to the task of engineering creative environmental policy change. The search for climate change alternatives has promoted activities by NGOs, corporate initiatives, and action by municipalities and provincial and territorial governments.[4] While Canada is almost inevitably drawn into some international issues because of its geography and natural resources (for example, on issues of coastal and marine environmental protection, the Arctic, ozone layer protection, transboundary pollution, boreal forest issues, and climate change) governments still face critical choices at multiple points in these processes.

Canada's actions can help to marginalize or inflate the importance of particular governance settings. It can, to some extent, 'shop around' for sympathetic forums. Analysts have used various terms—lead and veto states, for example, forerunners and followers, pushers and bystanders, supporters and resisters—to describe the spectrum of responses of countries to global developments. Canada was an early critic and non-signatory of the Convention on Migratory Species (CMS). This important 1979 agreement was viewed as problematic for Canada's fishing interests, and as an innovation that overlapped with existing agreements. By contrast, Canada took a lead in relation to such measures as the UN fish stocks agreement, which entered into force in 2001, the London marine dumping agreement of 1996, chemicals issues confronting Arctic and other international bodies, and activities from the mid-1980s on the protection of the ozone layer.

Such choices are influenced by a variety of factors. Consideration of the economic impacts of policy options has been increasingly persuasive for Ottawa. International trade questions directly and indirectly influence many environmental policy areas. The free trade agreement between Canada and Peru, signed in May 2008, is one of several that are associated with environmental cooperation agreements. Canada agreed, among other things, to help strengthen the protection of biological diversity in Peru, and to assist Peru in encouraging corporate social responsibility (CSR) and environmental best practices by its companies.[5] The WTO acknowledges the importance of environmental policies for member-states. Its trade liberalization goals, however, make it alert to the risk that some policies may hide protectionist impulses or may have other trade distortion effects. The problem has given rise to lively debates among economists on the impacts of environmental regulations and multilateral environmental agreements (MEAs) on trade flows. Key cases in WTO processes have recognized the validity of national environmental regulation, but have defended fundamental trade law principles such as non-discrimination.[6]

The various framings of environmental issues affect and are shaped by the roles and interrelations of government agencies. Environment Canada is responsible for Canadian activities on a core group of international environmental agreements, including the Ramsar convention on the protection of wetlands. The rise of climate change as a 'high-politics' mainstream issue, signalled by its presence in international forums such as the G8 meetings in Toyako, Japan in 2008, has reinforced the role of Foreign Affairs and International Trade Canada on some aspects. Health Canada has responsibilities on many international chemicals management issues, for example through its collaboration with the International Program on Chemical Safety (IPCS) on endocrine disruptors. Indian and Northern Affairs Canada (INAC) is the important player on many Arctic questions, and Transport Canada maintains the link with the IMO and its agreements on marine pollution.

At the international level there is no institution with authority comparable to that of the WTO on trade issues (though there is a long history of debate on the possible establishment of a World Environmental Organization [WEO]). Instead, tasks are splintered among numerous agreements and institutions in a constantly shifting mosaic of governance fragments, each with varying support, policy reach, compliance demands, and powers. Environmental NGOs can get observer status in some organizations (for example, the UN environmental mega-conferences); generally they do not have access to trade institutions, though some have recently been able to put arguments into the WTO dispute settlement process.[7]

Transnational Problem-solving

While limited, this complex global architecture is nonetheless vital to the tasks of environmental problem-solving. The Commissioner for Environment and Sustainable Development wrote in 2004 that:

> In Canada, the quality of our environment depends not only on what we do at home but also on activities outside our borders. Our domestic actions alone are often insufficient to protect our environment, our resources, and our health. We need to work with other countries to develop common solutions to international problems that impact us directly.[8]

In addition to participating in intergovernmental arrangements, this search for 'common solutions' also involves cross-jurisdictional attentiveness and learning. Ideas and instruments seep through borders, both from and into Canada, for example on good laboratory practices relevant to environmental regulation. Processes of diffusion are assisted by international agreements. The policy approaches and styles of forerunner countries on environmental policy, including the Scandinavian countries and Germany on several issues, become a focus of policy discussion in other jurisdictions.[9] Canadian policy innovations on protected areas have been influenced by debates in the International Union for the Conservation of Nature (IUCN).[10] Studies of particular chemical compounds circulate routinely among policy communities in different countries. Health Canada's consideration in 2008 of the hazards of bisphenol A (BPA) was aided by the results of parallel risk assessment processes undertaken by the European Food Safety Authority, the US Food and Drug Administration, and the National Institute of Advanced Industrial Science and Technology in Japan.

Some comparisons between Canada and other countries are handy tools for critics. Canadians have historically performed worse on issues of residential waste and water and energy use than citizens of Germany and other European countries. The Paris-based Organisation for Economic Cooperation and Development (OECD), of which Canada is a member, has been a key institution lobbying for stronger policy performance by its member-states, for example through determining the optimal mix of policy instruments in environmental policy.[11] In its 2004 evaluation of Canada, it urged a more 'aggressive' pursuit of climate change policies and their implementation, greater monitoring capabilities for oil spills and other marine pollution problems, and the continued phasing out of ozone-depleting substances.[12] Transnational politics cross boundaries and levels. Canadian practices on a wide variety of topics from seal hunts and asbestos exports, to oil sands development and Kyoto non-compliance have been among the topics eagerly taken up by environmental critics in Europe. Jeffrey Simpson of the *Globe and Mail* has pointed to the United Kingdom's record of reducing greenhouse-gas (GHG) emissions and has contrasted governmental and corporate attitudes there with the 'deep denial' of climate change he finds in Canada.[13]

Transnational environmental processes are closely connected with problems of multi-level governance.[14] Referring to developments in the UN and in international law as a 'level' of government is misleading if it implies there are authoritative institutions in these arenas. Rather, there are multiple interactions among levels. Through its treaty-making power, the federal government is the key player but many issues touch on the interests of the provinces. Multi-level governance in Canada has been described as 'the outcome of the games played within and across a particular combination of institutional incentive structures'.[15] Looking at policy processes in this way began with studies of the European Union (EU), but the approach is of increasing relevance for understanding Canadian environmental policy. Given the facts of globalization, regionalization, and continentalization, as well as the constitutional basis for the environmental and resource policy roles of the provinces, analytical approaches that neglect multi-level politics are limited. Global economic change has reshaped the map of institutions and governance processes, and international actors and forums have become a normal part of Canadian environmental policy-making.

Networks of Obligations

A third feature of international developments is that these create a complex network of commitments for Canada. Ratification of the Convention on Biological Diversity (CBD) of 1992 meant acceptance of an obligation to produce the Canadian Biodiversity Strategy. It also helped to launch the protracted process that culminated in the federal Species at Risk Act (SARA) of 2002 although, as Stewart Elgie argues in Chapter 14, there was initially an argument in Ottawa that this obligation was met by existing federal and provincial practices. Adherence to the Convention on International Trade in Endangered Species (CITES), implemented in Canada through the Wild Animal and Plant Protection and Regulation of International and Interprovincial Trade (WAPPRIITA), has enhanced Canada's capacities to act against the illegal wildlife trade, for example, imports of African elephant ivory and the queen conch (a threatened Caribbean shellfish). Participation in the Ramsar convention likewise strengthens the Canadian framework of protection of wetlands, of which 37 sites have been listed.

Significant procedural obligations follow from many international agreements. A typical requirement is for the submission of regular reports; discussion of these forms an important element in the compliance procedures of many international agreements. Following Canada's ratification of the Kyoto protocol, for example, the federal government had to submit reports on progress (the first was submitted in March 2007), and also to put in place a national registry designed according to Kyoto specifications to record emissions permits and related matters, which it concluded in 2008.

There is also a politics of obligations. Obligations can be evaded by steering clear of institutions or spinning avoidance strategies within them, or they can be created by signing and ratifying agreements. Many obligations, like the preparation of reports and participation in COPs, are not politically or economically onerous. This still leaves a lot of room for manoeuvre. Critics took Ottawa to task in the 1990s for failing to implement key provisions of the Canadian Biodiversity Strategy, produced as an obligation of CBD membership. Critics of the Harper government, including environmental groups and, in 2008, the Parliamentary Commissioner, have reasonably argued that the collapse, eventually acknowledged, of the possibility of meeting Canada's Kyoto targets means that Canada is not only incurring heavy international reputational costs but is legally in violation of its commitments under that agreement. The federal government denied the latter point in federal court in March 2008 in a case launched by the group Friends of the Earth, in part on the grounds that the penalties built into the Kyoto agreement for non-compliance are not legally binding. This interpretation is doubtful in international law, but more importantly it does not address the real criticism.

International agreements vary considerably in the specificity of the commitments that states take on by joining them. The Montreal protocol on the protection of the ozone layer and the Kyoto protocol on GHGs imposed quantitative targets and timetables on parties. This contrasts with the vaguer and more open-ended Ramsar commitment to protect by international listing Canadian wetlands of international significance. Both kinds of agreements are valuable. Obligations accepted by other countries are also relevant to Canadian goals. In international meetings in Montreal in September 2007, for example, agreement was reached on the quicker phasing out, particularly in developing countries, of a traditional group of ozone-layer-threatening compounds (hydrochlorofluorocarbons [HCFCs]).

There is also a range of more vague 'soft-law' understandings. These include the ideas embedded in resolutions passed by international conferences. The precautionary principle calls for environmental protection measures even in the absence of 'conclusive' scientific evidence of harm. It can be found in many international statements and in several international agreements that Canada has joined, such as the 1985 Vienna convention on the protection of the ozone layer and the London marine dumping protocol. Its presence in the Cartagena Protocol on Biosafety (the main instrument for managing trade involving genetically modified organisms [GMOs]) reinforced criticisms of that agreement by both Canada and the US. The precautionary principle has wide international acceptance, and is embedded in several European jurisdictions, but it still has an uncertain place in Canadian environmental law.[16]

Multi-level Governance and the Global Environment: Three Canadian Experiences

The Circumpolar Neighbourhood: Canada and the Arctic Council

The Arctic environment has self-evident significance for Canadians. Canadian interests in the region are also grounded in economic, energy, resource, and security concerns. As several Arctic nations have a stake in the broader circumpolar region, however, some kind of multilateral framework is essential for the effective promotion of Canadian values and interests. Canada has taken a lead role on many questions, often bilaterally in association with Arctic partners.

This is a region of primary security interest for the US. Ottawa has diverged in the past on several points from US positions, and there is an historic disagreement over ownership of the Northwest Passage. Washington has traditionally been skeptical at best about the need for an effective regional intergovernmental organization with environmental policy power, and has resisted framing the Arctic Council in this way. Before this was set up (by Canada and six other Arctic states in 1996), the US was reluctant even to participate in the modest Arctic Environment Protection Strategy (AEPS), and only joined after determined lobbying by the Canadian government.[17] US officials have also been alert to the risk that Arctic forums might be used by multilateralists to sneak Kyoto-style precedents in through a back door.

Canadian approaches to environmental policy in the region thus nestle within a complex mix of security and economic concerns. Canada's interest in Arctic environmental protection in the late 1960s stemmed, in part, from the political calculation that this was a way to gain international support for its position on sovereignty over the Northwest Passage.[18] Issues of concern to Ottawa have included polar bear protection (the subject of a five-nation agreement in 1973), contaminants affecting wildlife habitats and human health, Arctic haze, and environmental problems involved in the decommissioning of cold war military bases. Climate change later increased the profile of the Arctic environmental agenda. It raised the prospect of a future warmed Arctic with an economy driven by a natural resources boom and changing transportation technologies. The post-cold war revisiting of Arctic tensions was epitomized by Russia's controversial claim in 2007 to large stretches of the seabed, including the North Pole, on the grounds that these areas form a geological extension of the Lomonosov ridge. The measures outlined by Prime Minister Harper in the throne speech in October 2007 included plans for a new port and a commitment to systematic arctic seabed mapping.

The Arctic Council promotes cooperation on a variety of environmental issues. In addition there is continuing scientific work through the 1973 polar bear agreement, still the only regional 'hard-law' environmental agreement, and there are references to the Arctic environment in several other international agreements.[19] The Council built on previous arrangements, particularly the AEPS, which had developed on the basis of initiatives by Canada and Finland. Canadian scientists and officials take part in the complex networks that underpin Arctic Council tasks, including bodies on the Conservation of Arctic Flora and Fauna (CAFF) and the Protection of the Arctic Marine Environment (PAME), and the Arctic Monitoring and Assessment Program (AMAP). Arctic governance is characterized by significant levels of aboriginal participation. Inuit and other organizations have been active in pressing for more effective actions on toxic chemicals. The Arctic Athabaskan Council (AAC) has urged reforms to achieve these and other goals, and greater publicity to counter a widespread lack of public awareness in the north of the work of the Arctic Council.[20]

Chemicals problems, climate change, resource development, and polar bear protection have consistently been high environmental priorities for Canada in multi-level Arctic settings. In the 1980s, Canadian scientists identified several compounds, and groups of compounds such as persistent organic pollutants (POPs), in the Arctic environment. These findings drove the search for effective multi-level frameworks, including the Arctic Council and the chemicals regime discussed in the next section of this chapter.[21] Although some recent evidence has suggested that levels of contaminants in mother's milk are diminishing,[22] these issues remain a high priority. Research on related environmental health issues in northern communities are an important focus of Canada's current national program for the International Polar Year.

Climate change debates have highlighted multiple risks in the Arctic, particularly in view of the projections of the Arctic Climate Impact Assessment (ACIA), which in 2004 anticipated significant declines in sea-ice cover in the next three decades. In the early 2000s, scientists from Canada and Iceland worked in the PAME framework on strategic planning on pollution. In 2002 Arctic governments decided to produce a detailed assessment of the implications of intensified activities in oil and gas and minerals. The assessment, announced at the Arctic Frontiers conference in Tromsø, Norway, in early 2008, drew attention to the likely growth of resource activities in the Mackenzie Delta, Beaufort Sea and other areas, and the implications for oil spills and other marine threats.

Polar bears are also affected by climate change. They are dependent on sea-ice platforms and are vulnerable to the implications of Arctic warming processes. However, some of Canada's polar bear populations have remained stable. This has led the government of Nunavut to defend a strong position on the need for expanded hunting quotas. Like their counterparts in Alaska, Nunavut officials were highly critical of the US federal decision in May 2008 to list the polar bear under endangered-species law. Polar bear management draws on complex interactions among multiple levels from local communities and game committees, through provincial, territorial, aboriginal and federal governments, to the international scientific cooperation sponsored through IUCN since the early 1970s.[23] Work on polar bears overlaps with, but takes place mostly outside, the formal structures of the Arctic Council. However, the Council has, through CAFF, been active in monitoring and debating policy options for birds and other wildlife species. Canada has been a target of conservationist criticism in this forum on issues such as the traditional Newfoundland murre hunt.[24]

Chemicals across Borders: Canada and LRTAP

The convention on Long-Range Transboundary Air Pollution (LRTAP) is primarily a Europe-centred agreement. Canada has made extensive use of it as a means of promoting international consideration of toxic chemicals issues, particularly those relating to northern regions.[25] In addition to chemicals questions, other persistent issues on LRTAP agendas include several with a high priority for Canada: Arctic haze, for example, the effects of air pollution on forests, and the acidification of rivers and lakes.

LRTAP grew out of scientific research in the 1970s on air pollution. Canada ratified it in 1981. Ottawa's interest grew with appreciation of the potential of its capacities for generating subsidiary agreements. This protocol-making process provided Canada with a means of securing international recognition of several transborder pollution issues. These issues were already a priority focus of research on Arctic communities and wildlife, particularly through the Northern Contaminants Program (NCP). This program—set up in 1991 in association with the Arctic Environmental Strategy—produced a major report in 1997 on the persistence of POPs and other compounds in the Arctic. Research on POPs in the Great Lakes during the 1980s also fed into these processes. Canada and Sweden took lead roles in the early 1990s in proposing that LRTAP negotiate a POPs protocol and undertook the groundwork for this. Canadian scientists and officials were active in the processes that led in 1998 to protocols both on POPs and on heavy metals. (A separate and more fully international POPs agreement, also with Canada as an active supporter, was concluded in Stockholm in 2001.) The LRTAP system has grown steadily over time. Six other protocols were negotiated in the period 1984–99, including agreements on sulphur, nitrogen oxides, and volatile organic compounds (VOCs).

In addition to its substantive policy concerns, much of LRTAP's strength as an environmental governance device, and its attractiveness to Canadian participants, lies in its combination of policy-oriented scientific deliberations and its compliance mechanisms.[26] Technical evaluations of specific compounds are central to its processes. Like the Montreal protocol of 1987 on the ozone layer and the Kyoto protocol, LRTAP procedures are designed to elicit compliance by governments. With the accumulation of protocols, increasingly stringent quantitative targets in relation to particular compounds have been built into the overall LRTAP process.[27] Reporting obligations are a primary means of achieving this goal. Canadian officials have been elected at various times to the important implementation committee. This identifies and publicizes national gaps, and monitors follow-up steps taken by governments. For example, it has recently pointed to problems in Greece and Spain in relation to nitrogen oxides and Norway on VOCs. Canada has generally fared well under this kind of scrutiny.[28] Even so, this falls short of being a fully effective enforcement mechanism. Effectiveness is elusive in any intergovernmental organization, and in practice LRTAP procedures are sensitive to the particular problems facing national governments and are not conducive to confrontational politics.

LRTAP processes connect with multiple Canadian governments and agencies. Important biomonitoring research related to LRTAP objectives was carried out during the 1980s by the Canadian Wildlife Service, the Department of Fisheries and Oceans, and other federal agencies. Links with northern and Arctic issues bring in Indian and Northern Affairs Canada, Environment Canada, and Health Canada. There are contaminants committees in each of the territorial governments. Several aboriginal organizations, including the Inuit Circumpolar Conference (Canada), the Inuit Tapirisat of Canada, organizations representing the Dene Nation, and the Council of Yukon First Nations, regularly monitor LRTAP work. The ICC in particular was active nationally and internationally in promoting the POPs and heavy metals protocols, for example by publicizing research indicating the high levels of POPs from fish consumption in northern Canadian mothers and children.

Processes are watched closely by industry associations. Indeed, one complaint of US chemicals producers has been that the absence of the US from LRTAP means that industry concerns in relation to particular chemicals are not articulated effectively. International settings form an important part of broader transnational processes on toxic chemicals. In 2004, for example, Norway raised the issue of pentabromodiphenyl ether (PeBDE), a chemical mixture used as a flame retardant. The LRTAP technical process concluded that it was persistent in the environment at levels exceeding its guidelines, that it was not easily biodegradable, and that according to LRTAP criteria on bioaccumulation and toxicity it had the potential to adversely affect human health.[29] Also in 2004, the US halted manufacture of the commercial mixture. Over the next two years, Environment Canada listed the mixture and several of its component chemicals under CEPA; there was agreement on its phasing out in 2005, and it was banned from 2006. Pressure on Ottawa from the US manufacturers of a related flame-retardant mixture, deca-PBDE, and also from car manufacturers in Canada, led Ottawa in 2008 to confirm a ban on its manufacture in Canada but to allow its continued import and use.[30]

In another case, the industry association representing North American chlorinated paraffins producers lobbied against the inclusion on the LRTAP POPs list of some of these compounds (short-chain versions or SCCPs), arguing that significant adverse effects, even in the Arctic, could not be demonstrated.[31] The American Chemistry Council similarly made a submission to Health Canada in 2008 in connection with Ottawa's evaluation of the risks from bisphenol A (BPA), widely used in food and drink containers. It welcomed the agency's draft assessment in April 2008 that concluded that on balance there were minimal risks to consumers.[32]

The Global Biological Economy: Canada and the CBD

At first an enthusiast, Canada signed and ratified the Convention on Biological Diversity (CBD) in 1992. It hosts the secretariat in Montreal. However, the country's overall orientation changed over time. The multilateralist reflexes dominant in the early 1990s gave way to more considered and interest-based analyses of the costs of compliance. In particular, Ottawa later backed away from the CBD's Cartagena protocol on biosafety.

Unlike some of the previous international conventions that Canada had signed on to, such as CITES and the Ramsar convention, the CBD put issues of biodiversity conservation firmly in a context of economic development and the use of natural resources. Its provisions were as much economic as biological. Through its focus on 'the issue of who owns, controls and profits from the genetic information stored in species', the CBD had far-reaching implications for agriculture, forestry and the biotechnology and pharmaceuticals industries.[33] GMOs quickly became central issues in the workings of the CBD regime. Pitted against the European view of the appropriate use of the precautionary principle, and of the information to be given to consumers of agricultural and other products through labelling, was the US view, and from the early 1990s increasingly the Canadian view, that biotechnology is an integral part of broad strategies of sustainable development and not an appropriate target for excessive regulation.[34]

The CBD has a complex governance system.[35] Canada is obliged to produce national reports, structured around answers to questions from the CBD secretariat, and to attend conferences of the parties (COPs). The ninth of these (COP 9) was held in Bonn, Germany, in 2008. Its large scope indicates the ambitious range of CBD concerns: agricultural biodiversity and biofuels, global issues of plant protection, invasive species, forest biodiversity, the use of ecosystem approaches, and (an important CBD goal defined in 2002) how best to reverse or minimize biodiversity loss by 2010. The Cartagena protocol generates its own continuing exchanges through regular meetings of the parties (MOPs).

The fusion of economic and biological issues in the CBD makes the question of effectiveness contentious. Different actors appraise it differently. There has been modest administrative progress. International shipping practices, for example, have been gradually adapting to the requirements of the Cartagena protocol.[36] The CBD's implementation body, however, meeting in Montreal in 2005, concluded that 12 years after the convention entered into force there was still a 'lack of significant progress' towards the goal of building state implementation capacities. It also pointed to a lack of awareness of key biodiversity issues, for example on the part of donor countries in their relations with developing countries, and a lack of political will to build these into project planning. Only just over one-half of the parties had produced national biodiversity strategies and action plans.[37]

Canada's participation in the CBD also reveals many of the features of multi-level governance. The Canadian Biodiversity Strategy addressed CBD objectives in general terms but failed to provide for enhanced mechanisms for coordination among Canada's governments. In 2001 the federal/provincial/territorial biodiversity working group tried to push collaboration further. The *Biodiversity Outcomes Framework for Canada* was designed in 2006 as a means of improving the coordination and monitoring of Canadian CBD-related activities. However, the persisting difficulties were acknowledged in Canada's Third National Report to the CBD. This emphasized the challenges posed by the existence of multiple governments, including Aboriginal self-governance institutions, and multiple stakeholders, including the 'large interest' in biodiversity issues on the part of citizens, communities, groups, and industry. Together with the size and regional variations of Canada these circumstances 'create a challenge when asked to answer questions from a comprehensive "national" perspective'.[38] Many Canadian activities relevant to the pursuit of CBD objectives have a multi-actor/multi-level character, for example in relation to several northern rivers and the Moose river basin in Ontario.[39]

The CBD thus serves as both a catalyst for new, and a reinforcer of existing, courses of action. As noted earlier it was a factor in Canada's progress towards federal endangered species legislation. Together with species recovery programs this legislation has been central to Canadian claims of progress towards the CBD's 2010 biodiversity goals. Canadian scientists have also been active in the Global Taxonomy Initiative, a CBD-supported international project to identify and document the world's biological resources.[40] Relevant, too, are a wide variety of other activities undertaken by multiple Canadian institutions, for example, on marine conservation, the integration of traditional knowledge into conservation thinking, problems of forest biodiversity (through the Canadian model forest network and other initiatives in relation to the boreal forest), threats from invasive species, and, more generally, the use of ecosystem approaches to the conservation and management of biological resources.

Conclusions

International and domestic environmental policies are mutually supportive. Canadian officials have, at times, taken leading roles in international bodies and made major contributions to international initiatives. International agreements reinforce Canada's domestic environmental regime. However, the relationship between the international and the domestic spheres has changed over time. Both have declined. A systemic timidity has overtaken Ottawa's approach to many international issues. Greater concern for economic factors in evaluations of international agreements was evident from the mid-1990s onward, as was enhanced attentiveness to the skepticism of the more environmentally cautious provinces. The post-9/11 re-emergence of traditional notions of security has diminished the prospects for a multilaterally-oriented foreign policy, an orientation that had historically bolstered Canadian actions in international environmental forums. The major international environmental negotiations of the 1990s—particularly on Kyoto and Cartagena—had substantial implications for Canadian economic interests, making them politically contentious at home. Government cutbacks throughout these years steadily undermined Canada's abilities to act internationally. This weakening was symbolized by the abolition in 2006 of the position of Ambassador for the Environment.

Yet even the few examples discussed in this chapter indicate a continuing record of modestly successful international activities. Many have worked best where constellations of actors—scientists and federal officials, with their counterparts in other countries and officials from the secretariats of intergovernmental organizations—have collaborated on specialized tasks. There has been more prospect for leadership and innovation where there is a clear nexus between environmental and health concerns, as with Arctic contaminants, and also where environmental policy exchanges are designed primarily to complement trade liberalization goals, as in Canada's relations with the EU and with its free-trade partners in Latin America. The site-listing approach of an earlier generation of international agreements, such as Ramsar, has flourished in part because of its minimalism and voluntarism, and, from a post-Kyoto retrospective, its negligible intrusions into economics.

Could good (or good enough) Canadian environmental policies be put in place without international actions? In theory this could be done: Canada's multiple governments could tend their respective environmental policy turfs and collaborate on national policy frameworks. However, it is difficult to imagine a scenario in which this trick could be performed well without the opportunities that participation in international forums provides for learning lessons and transmitting ideas, strengthening policy frameworks, being alert to opportunities for innovation, responding to global problems that affect Canada, and enlivening the voices of critics.

The global parts of the problem mix are set to expand during the next two decades. We will confront continuing pressures on the climate change agenda and on the problems of restructuring fossil fuel dependent energy economies, the continued rise of China, South and South-east Asia, and Latin America, a still more competitive race for the world's resources, mounting threats to biological diversity, and the transformation of the Arctic. There will be deepening interactions between environmental problems and those of global food security, natural disasters, human rights, and ethnic conflicts. On all these fronts, Canadian and global problems interact. These large-scale challenges require new forms of leadership, greatly improved capabilities for governance, and vastly expanded knowledge bases. Currently, Canada is only partially equipped for these tasks.

Questions for Review

1. What resources does Canada have to effect changes in the international governance of environmental issues?
2. How important are international developments for Canadian environmental policy?
3. Should Canada's development assistance programs be more oriented to environmental concerns?
4. Should Canada be a more active global player?

Notes

1. On trends see *OECD Environmental Outlook to 2030* (Paris: OECD, 2008).
2. Michael E. Kraft, *Environmental Policy and Politics*, 3rd ed. (New York: Pearson Longman, 2004), 265. Useful links to agreements can be found at www.ecolex.org.
3. J.F. Turner, in '4th Meeting of the Open-ended Intergovernmental Group of Ministers on International Environmental Governance, Nov. 30–Dec. 1, 2001, Montreal.' Available at http://www.state.gov/g/oes/rls/rm/699.7htm.
4. Matthew J. Hoffmann, 'The Global Regime: Current Status and *quo vadis* for Kyoto', in Steven Bernstein, Jutta Brunnée, David G. Duff and Andrew J. Green, eds, *A Globally Integrated Climate Policy for Canada* (Toronto: University of Toronto Press, 2008), 143–51.
5. Foreign Affairs and International Trade Canada, 'An Agreement on the Environment Between Canada and the Republic of Peru'. Media statement, 29 May 2008. Available at http://www.international.gc.ca.
6. Josh Ederington and Jenny Minier, 'Is Environmental Policy a Secondary Trade Barrier? An Empirical Analysis', *Canadian Journal of Economics* 36, 1 (2003): 137–54; Theodore H. Cohn, *Global Political Economy: Theory and Practice*, 4th ed. (Toronto: Pearson Longman, 2008), 202–8.
7. Robyn Eckersley, 'A Green Public Sphere in the WTO? The *amicus curiae* Interventions in the Transatlantic Biotech Dispute', *European Journal of International Relations* 13, 3 (2007): 329–56.
8. Commissioner of the Environment and Sustainable Development, *2004 Report* (Ottawa: Office of the Auditor-General of Canada, 2004), para. 1.5.
9. Kerstin Tews, Per-Olof Busch and Helge Jörgens, 'The Diffusion of New Environmental Policy Instruments', *European Journal of Political Research* 42, 4 (2003): 569–600.
10. Paul Kopas, *Taking the Air: Ideas and Change in Canada's National Parks* (Vancouver: UBC Press, 2007), 55.
11. OECD, *Instrument Mixes for Environmental Policy* (Paris: OECD, 2007).
12. OECD, *Environmental Performance Review of Canada* (Paris: OECD, 2004), Annex.
13. Jeffrey Simpson, 'On the Cusp of a New Revolution—a Green One', *Globe and Mail*, 26 October 2007, A11; and Jeffrey Simpson, Mark Jaccard, and Nic Rivers, *Hot Air: Meeting Canada's Climate Change Challenge* (Toronto: McClelland and Stewart, 2008).
14. Jenny Fairbrass and Andrew Jordan, 'Multi-level Governance and Environmental Policy', in Ian Bache and Matthew V. Flinders, eds, *Multi-level Governance* (Oxford: Oxford University Press, 2004), 147–64.
15. Rianne Mahon, Caroline Andrew, and Robert Johnson, 'Policy Analysis in an Era of "Globalization": Capturing Spatial Dimensions and Scalar Strategies', in Michael Orsini and Miriam Smith, eds, *Critical Policy Studies* (Vancouver: UBC Press, 2007), 50.
16. Mary Durfee and Mirit Shamir, 'Can the Great Lakes of North America Survive Globalization?', in Philippe Le Prestre and Peter Stoett, eds, *Bilateral Ecopolitics: Continuity and Change in Canadian–American Environmental Relations* (Aldershot: Ashgate, 2006), 154–5.
17. Rob Huebert, 'Canada–United States Environmental Arctic Policies: Sharing a Northern Continent', in Le Prestre and Stoett, eds, *Bilateral Ecopolitics*, 124.
18. Ibid., 119–21.
19. Melissa Verhaag, 'It is Not Too Late: The Need for a Comprehensive International Treaty to Protect the Arctic Environment', *Georgetown International Environmental Law Review* 15, 3 (2003): 555–7.

20. Arctic Council, *Meeting of Senior Arctic Officials, 12–13 April 2007, Tromsø, Norway. Final Minutes* 11, para. 10.1; and Arctic Athabaskan Council, *Improving the Efficiency and Effectiveness of the Arctic Council: A Discussion Paper* (Yukon: AAC, 2007). See also Igor Krupnik and Dyanna Jolly, eds, *The Earth is Faster Now: Indigenous Observations of Arctic Environmental Change* (Fairbanks: Arctic Research Consortium of the US, 2002).

21. Northern Contaminants Program, *Canadian Arctic Contaminants: Assessment Report II* (Ottawa: Indian and Northern Affairs Canada, 2003), xi.

22. Bob Weber, 'Contaminant Levels Dropping Among Arctic Mothers, Blood Studies Show', *Globe and Mail*, 29 September 2007, A10.

23. Robert Boardman, 'Polar Bears and the Canadian Arctic: Local Communities in a Globalizing World', in Chris Gore and Peter Stoett, eds, *Environmental Challenges and Opportunities: Local–Global Perspectives on Canadian Issues* (Toronto: Emond Montgomery, 2009), chapter 12. In general, see Martin Papillon, 'Canadian Federalism and the Emerging Mosaic of Aboriginal Multilevel Governance', in Herman Bakvis and Grace Skogstad, eds, *Canadian Federalism: Performance, Effectiveness, and Legitimacy*, 2nd ed. (Toronto: Oxford University Press, 2008), 291–313.

24. Robert Boardman, *The International Politics of Bird Conservation: Biodiversity, Regionalism and Global Governance* (Northampton, MA: Edward Elgar, 2006), 178–9.

25. Kirsten Hillman, 'International Control of Persistent Organic Pollutants: The UN Economic Commission for Europe Convention on Long Range Transboundary Air Pollution, and Beyond', *Review of European Community and International Environmental Law* 8, 2 (1999): 105–12.

26. Göran Sundqvist, Martin Letell, and Rolf Lidskog, 'Science and Policy in Air Pollution Abatement Strategies', *Environmental Science and Policy* 5, 2 (2002): 147–56. On the background to the Stockholm convention see David L. Downie and Terry Fenge, eds, *Northern Lights against POPs: Combating Toxic Threats in the Arctic* (Montreal: McGill-Queen's University Press, 2003).

27. M.A. Fitzmaurice and C. Redgwell, 'Environmental Non-compliance Procedures and International Law', *Netherlands Yearbook of International Law* (2001): 37–8; and Alexander E. Farrell and Terry J. Keating, 'Dissent and Trust in Multilateral Assessments: Comparing LRTAP and OTAG', in Alexander E. Farrell and Jill Jäger, eds, *Assessments of Regional and Global Environmental Risks: Designing Processes for the Effective Use of Science in Decision-making* (Washington, DC: Resources for the Future, 2005), 72–4.

28. UN Economic Commission for Europe, *Executive Body for the [LRTAP], 25th session, Geneva, 10–13 December, 2007: 10th Report of the Implementation Committee*, doc. ECE/EB.AIR/2007/3, 4–13.

29. UN Economic Commission for Europe, *Summary of Peer Technical Review Comments on Pentabromodiphenyl Ether and Perflurooctane Sulfonate Dossiers Submitted Under the UNECE-LRTAP POPs Protocol* (Geneva: ECE, 2005), 1–3.

30. Martin Mittelstaedt, 'Environment Canada Places Partial Ban on Flame Retardant', *Globe and Mail*, 12 July 2008, A7.

31. Chlorinated Paraffins Industry Association, *Regulatory Update 2007*, 1. Available at http://www.regnet.com/cpia/regulatory.htm.

32. Martin Mittelstaedt, 'Studies that Support Use of Bisphenol A Called into Question', *Globe and Mail*, 5 April 2008, A11; and ACC, 'Health Canada draft assessment supports safety of bisphenol-A', 18 April 2008. Available at www.americanchemistry.com/s_acc/sec_news_article.asp?CID=206&DID=7256.

33. Desirée McGraw, 'The CBD: Key Characteristics and Implications for Implementation', *Review of European Community and International Environmental Law* 11, 1 (2002): 17.

34. Peter Andrée, *Genetically Modified Diplomacy: The Global Politics of Agricultural Biotechnology and the Environment* (Vancouver: UBC Press, 2007), 112–13, 157–8.

35. Philippe G. Le Prestre, 'The Operation of the CBD Convention Governance System', in Philippe G. Le Prestre, ed., *Governing Global Biodiversity: The Evolution and Implementation of the Convention on Biological Diversity* (Aldershot: Ashgate, 2002), chapter 4.

36. Ahmed Djoghlaf, 'Introductory Message', *Biosafety Protocol News* 2, 3 (December 2007): 1.

37. CBD, 'Progress Towards Implementation of the Convention and Its Strategic Plan: Follow-up to the Recommendations of the Ad Hoc Open-ended Working Group on the Review of Implementation of the Convention. Note by the Executive Secretary', doc. UNEP/CBD/COP/8/15, 20 December 2005, 2–3.

38. *Canada: Third National Report*, 3. Available at www.cbd.int/doc/world/ca/ca-nr-03-en.pdf.

39. Ibid., 8–12.

40. Canadian Biodiversity Information Network, 'Global Taxonomy Initiative' (CBIN, 2005). Available at http://www.cbin.ec.gc.ca/issues/taxonomy/cfm?lang=e.

11

The Failure of Canadian Climate Change Policy: Veto Power, Absent Leadership, and Institutional Weakness

Douglas Macdonald

During the past decade, climate change has become the most salient Canadian environmental issue, eclipsing forerunners such as toxic chemicals, acid rain, or Walkerton-style pollution of drinking water by infectious disease. Unlike those issues, however, Canadian climate policy to date has not achieved even marginal success. There are three indicators of the current failure of Canadian climate policy. Firstly, while the Canadian target set out in the 1997 Kyoto Protocol to the United Nations Convention on Climate Change (UNFCCC) is to reduce greenhouse gas (GHG) emissions to six per cent below the 1990 level by 2012, the government of Canada reported in 2007 that emissions had increased 27 per cent between 1990 and 2004.[1] Secondly, not only are emission levels rising rather than falling, Canadian federal and provincial governments are no longer even trying to achieve the Kyoto six per cent reduction goal and deadline (see Table 11.1). Of the five jurisdictions shown in Table 11.1, only Québec has kept a six per cent reduction by 2012 as a policy objective). Of particular importance because of its potential ability to play a national leadership role, the federal government, led by Prime Minister Stephen Harper, has explicitly abandoned the Kyoto goal, albeit without taking what would seem to be the logical next step: to formally withdraw from the Kyoto regime. Thirdly, since Canada ratified the Kyoto Protocol in 2002 the national policy process itself has disintegrated into a shamble of uncoordinated and wildly different objectives, policy instruments, and programs.

We have no coherent national policy, we have given up on Kyoto, and emissions continue to rise. Clearly, of all the issues examined in this volume, climate change is the 'hard case' of Canadian environmental policy; it requires commitment, leadership, and policy innovation far beyond any seen to date. How do we explain this failure? How can Canada reverse this trend? The purpose of this chapter is to attempt to answer both questions.

To do that, the chapter first sets out the basic challenge which climate change poses for policy-makers. The article then reviews the evolution of Canadian policy to date and sets out the conclusions which can be drawn from that history regarding the factors which have precluded the implementation of effective policy. There are four such factors: (1) the large regional variations in the cost of emission reductions and associated differences in provincial interests; (2) applying

Environmental Policy Cases

terminology used for the study of international environmental regimes, the presence of a highly motivated veto state, in the form of the province of Alberta; (3) the absence of a motivated lead state, either a province or, more importantly, the federal government; and (4) the weakness of the institutional structure for federal–provincial environmental policy-making, which means there is no forum for addressing the first factor above, the need for a national agreement on sharing the overall cost of action amongst regions and provinces. Other factors, such as public opinion and the relative political power held by environmentalists and the business interests that have worked to stall progress are also relevant for understanding climate policy failure. They are included in this analysis, but as secondary factors, contributing to the second and third factors above (for instance, had public opinion consistently been at the high level of concern it reached in 2007 and had environmentalists been possessed of more political power, then the emergence of a motivated lead state would have been more likely). The chapter concludes with thoughts on how Canadian policy might overcome each of these four barriers.

Climate Change as a Policy Issue

The term 'climate change' refers to changes in the concentration levels of carbon dioxide, methane, nitrous oxide, and other gases (collectively referred to as 'greenhouse gases') within the global atmosphere.[2] Carbon dioxide is the most significant of the greenhouse gases and '[t]he global increases in carbon dioxide concentrations are due primarily to fossil fuel use and land use change, while those of methane and nitrous oxide are primarily due to agriculture.'[3] This change in the global atmosphere affects the balance of solar energy received and emitted by the planet, increasing average annual temperatures. Effects associated with climate change include alterations to ecosystem habitats, with implications for species extinction and vector-borne infectious disease; modified agricultural growing seasons; melting of polar ice caps; sea-level rise; changes in water availability; and severe weather events, such as hurricanes, drought, and heat waves. Changes to land use, such as deforestation and the associated release of the carbon stored in trees and to agriculture related to methane released by farm animals, are important aspects of the issue. The most important, however, is the carbon dioxide released during the burning of fossil fuels such as coal, oil, and natural gas. To reduce greenhouse gas emissions, humans must reduce their total demand for energy and switch to energy sources which do not emit carbon dioxide. In Canada, energy use by three industrial sectors—oil and gas, electricity, and manufacturing, collectively referred to as the 'Large Final Emitters'—accounts for roughly half of total emissions. Energy used by other industries, transportation, and the heating and cooling of buildings accounts for a large part of the other half. Climate change is, at heart, an energy issue, with approximately 80 per cent of Canadian greenhouse gas emissions coming from energy production and use.[4]

   This energy issue is also a true global collective action problem. No one country can eliminate climate change effects within its borders by acting unilaterally to reduce its own emissions. Unlike regional air issues such as acid rain, it is impossible for science to establish a causal connection between effects felt in one location and emission sources in another. Effects felt in any one country, even the largest GHG emitters such as the US and China, result not only from that country's own emissions but also the sum of all global emissions. For that reason, no state is logically motivated to act alone, without regard to what is being done by other countries. Because acting alone would cause a significant loss of trade competitiveness, each country must be assured that others are taking comparable action. In the current state of global governance, that assurance, weak though it may be, can only come if countries successfully conclude a multilateral environmental agreement. A major barrier to effective global action is the understandable reluctance of industrializing countries like India and China to place constraints on their development, constraints which were not experienced by the Organisation for Economic Co-operation and Development (OECD) nations during the past 100 years, and which they are so patently reluctant to take on now. At the heart of the global climate change problem is the question of how the total cost of emissions reductions will be divided between the developing south and the industrialized north. Exactly this same problem of regional allocation of the cost of action lies at the heart of Canadian policy.

History of Global and Canadian Climate Policy

As noted, the UNFCCC was negotiated in 1992 with the general goal of stabilizing emissions by 2000. The Convention was then strengthened in 1997 when the Kyoto Protocol assigned specific national objectives. Recognizing the differing historic responsibility for climate change, referred to above, through the principle of 'common but differentiated responsibility' the Convention and Protocol require more significant action from the OECD nations than from developing countries such as India and China. The US withdrew from the regime in 2001 and has since worked with Australia, Japan, India, Canada, South Korea, and China to establish a competing regime, the Asia–Pacific Partnership, which has no specific emissions objectives overall or nationally but instead aims generally to expand investment and trade in clean technologies. By 2005, enough nations had ratified the Kyoto Protocol for it to take legal effect. Since then, member countries have been working to negotiate a subsequent agreement to cover the period after 2012 when the Kyoto regime expires.[5]

Within Canada, the Mulroney government was an enthusiastic supporter of the UNFCCC both as it was negotiated prior to the 1992 Rio Conference and then afterward; Canada became one of the first countries to ratify the convention. By 1995, however, when the first Canadian national program was announced, the Chrétien government had come into power and the realities of resistance by the oil and gas industry and the oil-producing provinces, most notably Alberta, had become apparent. During that three-year period, the federal and provincial governments had established a process consisting of collaboration between the Canadian Council of Ministers of Environment (CCME) and Council of Energy Ministers (CEM), referred to as the Joint Meeting of Ministers (JMM). Committees of federal and provincial environment and energy officials consulted with relevant stakeholders and made policy recommendations at the periodic JMM meetings. There, the decision-making process was not majority rule, but rather consensual—just as in the case of international regimes such as the UNFCCC, giving each participant a potential veto power and leading most often to lowest-common-denominator results. The term refers to the dilemma facing lead states as they negotiate with veto states; the former know the effectiveness of the agreement will be diminished if veto states do not sign, but can only keep them in the process by agreeing to the low standards acceptable to the veto states.

The 1995 federal–provincial program relied primarily upon voluntary action by greenhouse gas sources, with no use made of law or tax to motivate reductions.[6] Prime Minister Chrétien had previously ruled out the use of a carbon tax; Alberta and industry were lobbying for voluntary programs; and within the lead federal government departments—Environment Canada and Natural Resources Canada—officials recognized that neither the Canadian public or business had any appetite for the coercive policy instruments being called for by environmentalists. At the time, a voluntary program was the only one possible.[7] To achieve the six per cent reduction objective agreed to at Kyoto in 1997, the federal and provincial governments then again used the JMM process, in consultation with all relevant stakeholders, to negotiate a second national program, announced in 2000. It, too, relied primarily upon voluntary action, still reflecting the lowest-common-denominator nature of the process. In 2002, over the vociferous resistance of industry and a number of provinces, the Chrétien government ratified the Kyoto Protocol.[8]

Ratification marked two significant changes in the evolution of Canadian climate policy. First, it shattered the consensual federal and provincial policy process. Unable to reconcile the differences which had been highlighted by ratification, the environment and energy ministers no longer met to co-ordinate their policy; the JMM process collapsed and has never been restarted. Secondly, the federal government abandoned voluntarism as a policy instrument and replaced it with two others: spending, for research and development and as a carrot to broker a series of bilateral agreements with willing provinces; and law, first in the sense of quasi-legal contracts with the large emitting firms and then as regulation using the authority of the Canadian Environmental Protection Act. Both are out of step with the norms of Canadian environmental policy. Although individual federal–provincial agreements have been signed in the past, national programs such as the 1985 national acid rain program and 1998 Harmonization Accord were developed through a multilateral federal–provincial process.[9] Similarly, regulation of private firms has been done almost exclusively by the provinces, using provincial law, whereas the federal government has done the science and worked to co-ordinate policy, but only rarely itself acted as regulator.[10]

In the months prior to the ratification vote in the House of Commons on 10 December 2002, as it was becoming clear that the multilateral federal–provincial policy process was going to be replaced by direct federal regulation, the Chrétien government entered into private negotiations with the oil and gas industry. The results were made public in a letter from the Natural Resources Minister to the Canadian Association of Petroleum Producers (CAPP) dated 18 December 2002: any costs borne by the industry to comply with GHG emission standards greater than $15 a tonne would be paid by the federal government.[11] That same figure was carried forward into the Conservative government climate plan released in April 2007.[12] In that plan, firms out of compliance with regulatory standards could avoid prosecution by paying $15 a tonne for all emissions above the standard. In effect, successive federal governments have capped industry GHG emission reduction costs at $15 a tonne.

Between 2003 and the time the Paul Martin government fell in late 2005, the federal government, led by then-Environment Minister Stéphane Dion, used its spending and law instruments to implement policy which ostensibly was intended to achieve the Kyoto target. Rather than rely on the JMM process, it attempted to cobble together a national program by negotiating a series of bilateral federal–provincial agreements, working to motivate provinces by offers of federal funding. Six such bilateral agreements were negotiated; however, Alberta was not included in that number.[13] Although the steps taken were small, more progress was being made under unilateral federal policy than had been the case with the multilateral JMM process.

That changed when the Harper government took minority-government power in January 2006. The Conservative election platform had given no priority to the climate issue or offered any policy specifics, saying only that, if elected, a Conservative government would, '[a]ddress the issue of greenhouse gas emissions, such as carbon dioxide (CO_2), with a made-in-Canada plan, emphasizing new technologies, developed in concert with the provinces and in co-ordination with other major industrial countries'.[14] The new government felt that urban smog was an issue of more pressing concern, and proceeded to bundle together the energy issue of climate and the toxic pollution issue of smog and indoor air quality under the common rubric of air issues. The new Conservative Environment Minister, Rhona Ambrose, shortly after taking office stated flatly that it was impossible for Canada to meet the Kyoto six per cent below 1990 target by 2012.[15]

By that time, however, public opinion polling on unprompted questions, such as 'What is the most important issue facing Canada today?' showed the environment had replaced the usual lead issues of health and education.[16] Although climate change had not figured as an election issue and was not included in its list of five government priorities, this movement in public opinion caused the Harper government to decide it needed to show some sort of policy response.[17] Minister Ambrose announced a package of climate and air pollution measures in October 2006 which shifted the GHG reduction target from six per cent below 1990s levels to 45–65 per cent below 2003 levels (already at least 25 per cent above 1990 levels) by 2050 and said that new regulatory standards would be negotiated with industry over the next three years.[18] The Harper government also abandoned any attempt to broker a national package of bilateral federal–provincial agreements, and instead simply gave the provinces funding allocated on a per capita basis.

The news media reported prominently on the denunciations of the October 2006 plan by environmentalists. In response, the Prime Minister moved Minister Ambrose out of the environment portfolio and replaced her with John Baird, presumably because he could both more effectively defend the Conservative program and attack the failure of the previous Liberal climate policy (something he never tired of doing). Minister Baird announced a new program in April 2007, which was essentially a return to the Liberal government policy but with weaker objectives and longer time-lines.[19] As set out in Table 11.1, the plan aims to reduce emissions by 20 per cent from 2006 levels by 2020 and requires that the three LFE industrial sectors reduce the intensity of their emissions—that is the ratio of emissions to production, by 18 per cent by 2010. As noted, if unable to do so, a firm could pay $15 for each out-of-compliance tonne into a technology development fund.

In the spring of 2008, the pattern of the Canadian policy process changed yet again when British Columbia, at the time of ratification a vocal opponent of effective action, took two unprecedented (within Canada) policy actions. The first was to impose a revenue-neutral carbon tax, increasing the price of fossil fuels and reducing by a corresponding amount other tax revenues.[20] The second was to announce plans to bring in 'hard-cap' law, which would set standards for GHG in absolute quantities which must be met regardless of increases in production.[21] This contrasts with the 'intensity' standards of the Martin and Harper governments, which regulate only the ratio of emissions to production, and thereby allow emissions to increase as the firm's production increases. The carbon tax has not proven popular with BC voters, particularly as the economy has moved toward recession, and may be repealed if the NDP wins the 2009 BC election.

At the time, it seemed this BC action might initiate a race-to-the-top and thus significantly change the pattern of Canadian policy development. Two subsequent events, however, have made that less likely. In the early fall of 2008, the Liberal Party, led by Stéphane Dion, went into the federal election campaign promising to bring in a carbon tax comparable to that of BC (the infamous 'Green Shift' plan). Neither the plan nor Dion himself sparked the imagination of voters. The Harper government was re-elected, albeit still on a minority basis and shortly afterward Dion was replaced as party leader by Michael Ignatieff. It is unlikely the Liberals will again campaign on the promise of a carbon tax. The second event, in November 2008, was the election of the Obama administration in the United States, followed by clear signs the new President planned to take policy action on climate change. As discussed below, this sparked another evolution in the Harper government's climate-change policy.

On 5 November 2008, the day after the US election, the Harper government announced that it would propose to the Obama administration a bilateral climate-change agreement, in order to harmonize policy in the two countries and—the essential element—guarantee that the US would not shut out imports of 'dirty oil' from the Alberta tar sands.[22] At the time of writing, it was clear that the desire to harmonize with US policy, in order to guarantee continued energy export access to the US market, was the major influence on Government of Canada climate-change policy.

Since 1992, each step in this process has been accompanied by the sound and fury of studies, reports, conferences, ministers' meetings, and plans, with increasing attention paid by the news media. All of this activity, however, has produced only fragmented, failed policy, as shown in Table 11.1.

Analysts explain this failure by pointing to the fact that the only policy instruments used to date, primarily appeals for voluntary action and government spending, have exerted no coercive pressure to reduce emissions.[23] This is true, but tells us very little. We need to go to the next level of analysis, to understand why governments to date have chosen to use only ineffective instruments. If Canada wishes to move from the current trajectory of failure to one of effective action, we must understand what fundamentals need to be changed. To that end, we now turn to discussion of each of the four factors contributing to Canadian policy failure.

Table 11.1 Climate Plans of Five Canadian Governments as of January 2009

Jurisdiction	Target	Plan date: Instrument/focus
Canada	2020 20% below 2006	2007 plan • industry regulation; 18% intensity reduction by 2010 or pay $15 tonne
BC	2020 33% below current	2008 plan • revenue neutral carbon tax developing industry cap-and-trade system
Alberta	2020 stabilize 2050 14% below 2005	2008 plan • carbon capture 70% • energy efficiency 12% • clean technology 18% 2007 law • large industry intensity reduction 12% by 2010; or pay $15 tonne
Ontario	2014 6% below 1990 2020 15% below 1990 2050 80% below 199	2007 plan • phase out coal plants for 44% of reduction needed • other measures, no law
Québec	2012 6% below 1990	2006 plan • hydroelectric and wind • voluntary industry • surcharge petroleum industries, not a real carbon tax

Sources: Environment Canada Turning the Corner Action Plan Controls on Industry, April 26, 2007; BC Ministry of Environment, Environmental Quality Branch, Climate Change; Alberta Ministry of Environment, Alberta's Climate Change Strategy; Ontario Ministry of Environment, Go Green, Ontario's Action Plan on Climate Change, August, 2007; Ministère du Développement durable de l'Environnement et des Parcs du Québec (2006). Plan d'action 2006–2012. Le Québec et les changements climatiques. Un défi pour l'avenir. Québec, Gouvernement du Québec.

Four Factors Explaining the Failure of Canadian Policy

Nature of the Issue

The fact that climate change is an energy issue is significant for Canadian policy success for two reasons. The first is the magnitude of the challenge. The quantity and type of required behaviour change is an order of magnitude different from that associated with such things as toxic chemical pollution or wilderness preservation. In those cases, societal goals and the physical and institutional infrastructures used to achieve them can remain unchanged, with modification needed only at the margins. The costs of a firm's environmental management system or a province's parks system are a very small percentage of total spending. In this case, however, we must fundamentally change what Podobnik refers to as the 'energy system'—'the interconnected network of production, transportation and consumption that delivers . . . energy resources to people for use in their daily lives'.[24] He describes the nineteenth-century implementation of the global coal-based system and the way in which that system was then supplemented and largely replaced during the past century by the current oil-based system, accompanied by enormous social transformations.[25] Now those two fossil fuel systems must be replaced by something else again, implying a behaviour change at least as great as that we have seen since Sherlock Holmes rode in a horse-drawn brougham cab through the gas-lit streets of London.

All industrialized states face this challenge. The challenge is magnified for Canada, however, not only because of this country's long distances and cold winters, but because of immigration-driven population growth, economic growth largely driven by oil and natural gas exports, and the structural importance of both oil and gas and motor vehicle manufacturing for the Canadian economy. The result is that stabilizing and then reducing GHG emissions is more difficult here than in the EU states which have, to date, led in the development of effective policy.[26]

This is less significant, however, than the aspect of the issue discussed above—the very different economic incentives facing the oil and natural gas producing provinces of Alberta, Saskatchewan, and Newfoundland compared to BC, Manitoba, and Québec, all three of which have access to hydroelectric power. Both Alberta government revenues and the economic well-being of the province as a whole are tied directly to the fortunes of the oil and gas industry. Albertans remember clearly what they saw as the federal tax grab of the 1980s National Energy Policy and the difficult days which followed when world oil prices, and Alberta revenues, collapsed. Québec, on the other hand, would not suffer to the same extent in a carbon-constrained North America, and might even find new opportunities to export hydro-electricity. Because energy is so central to modern economies, these different motivations are very strong indeed, so much so that it is almost fair to say the challenge of developing coherent national climate policy is comparable to that of the most intractable Canadian issue, also based in differing provincial motivations, the place of Québec in the confederation. This basic issue of strongly held differing regional and provincial incentives underlies each of the other three factors discussed here.

Presence of a Motivated Veto State

Chasek, Downie, and Brown give this description of a state whose economic interests will be harmed by imposition of a given environmental regime and for that reason works to delay the process and weaken the outcome:

For every global environmental issue there exists one state or group of states whose co-operation is so essential to a successful agreement for coping with the problem that it has the potential to block strong international action. When these states oppose an agreement or try to weaken it, they become veto . . . states.[27]

From the beginning, Alberta has played that role, consistently working to weaken the effectiveness of Canadian climate policy. With the oil and gas industry, it lobbied against the climate provisions of the Mulroney government 1990 Green Plan.[28] It then lobbied for voluntary action instead of law or economic instruments during the process of developing the 1995 program. Tellingly, when Prime Minister Chrétien publicly ruled out possible use of a carbon tax in 1994, he was speaking to a Calgary oil-industry audience.[29] The Alberta Premier protested loudly when Canada signed the Kyoto Protocol in 1997. During 2002, as the federal government moved toward ratification, Alberta led the provincial resistance and studied the possibility of a constitutional challenge to federal regulation.[30] Once it became clear that it had lost the ratification battle, rather than staying to fight the federal government in court, Alberta simply left the national process and implemented its own climate law (the first Canadian jurisdiction to legislate on the issue) which explicitly eschewed the Kyoto goal. As set out above, its 2008 climate plan continues to ignore Kyoto. Since the Stephen Harper Conservative government is based in Alberta, it seems fair to assume that Alberta, along with the oil and gas industry, had significant influence on the Conservative 2007 policy, particularly given its similarity to the Alberta program (thus eliminating the need for a court challenge). Finally, Alberta continues to veto effective Canadian policy, regardless of whether it is lobbying the federal government or other provinces, simply by its refusal to curtail the increase in emissions from its own oil industry. The Alberta refusal to act negates the possibility of Canada reaching the Kyoto goal.

Absence of a Motivated Lead State

'A lead state has a strong commitment to effective international action on the issue, moves the process of negotiations forward by proposing its own negotiating formula as the basis for an agreement, and attempts to win the support of other state actors.'[31] Given the resistance of Alberta, and to a lesser extent the resistance of other oil-producing provinces, the national process could only have succeeded had there been at least one government strongly committed to effective policy. Within the US respecting air quality, such leadership has come from the sub-national level; California has consistently exerted upward pressure on federal and state standards by the power of its example. As noted, the possibility exists in Canada that British Columbia might in the future play a similar role for climate policy. In the past, however, no province has taken the lead in pushing for effective national policy.[32] Furthermore, the Council of the Federation—an annual meeting of provincial premiers with no federal government representation—has tried several times to negotiate common policy, to date without success.

A greater problem is the fact that since 1992, successive federal governments have given only erratic leadership at best. The Mulroney government worked internationally to put the issue on the global policy agenda, unilaterally committed to stabilize emissions in 1990 and then, as noted, supported the Convention at Rio and ratified it early at home. It appeared this federal leadership would continue when in 1993 the Progressive Conservative government was replaced by that of Jean Chrétien, whose Liberal Party had been elected on a strong environment platform. After taking office, however, the Chrétien government failed to keep those promises.[33] Prime Minister Chrétien directly intervened in the climate change policy process twice, at the time of the Kyoto meeting in December, 1997 and in the fall of 2002 to unite his cabinet and caucus in favour of ratification. Ratification was undeniably a display of leadership, but it was a one-time event rather than a fundamental change in federal government direction. Prime Minister Martin's administration of 2004–05 achieved no particular success, either in developing its own direct regulatory program or pulling the provinces into a coherent national program. As noted, under the Harper government policy has moved backward, with the abandonment of the Kyoto goal.

The most telling indication of the lack of leadership which has been displayed by the Chretien, Martin, and Harper governments comes from a comparison of their climate change and energy policies. The former, as we have seen, has been marked by considerable rhetoric but only fitful action. Federal government policy respecting extraction and export of coal, oil, and natural gas, on the other hand, has been remarkably consistent. Here, we have seen leadership, as the federal government has worked to maximize the benefits to the Canadian economy of fossil fuel exports—in Prime Minister Harper's words, turning Canada into an 'energy superpower'.[34] Winfield states that 'federal environmental assessment or other environmental approvals processes have been applied as weakly as possible to major energy projects'[35] and estimates the value of annual federal government subsidy for the oil and gas industry to be $1.4 billion.[36]

The failure of successive federal governments to play a lead role on the climate file and thereby counter the Alberta veto role can be explained by a number of factors. The first is the structural basis of the Canadian economy. The fact that over three-quarters of Canadian exports go to the US market means that throughout this period it would have been difficult for Canadian policy to differ markedly from that of its trading partner. This structural factor, as discussed above, will in future likely lead to *more effective* Canadian policy, now that the inactivity of the George W. Bush administration has been replaced by the policy action of his successor. But even if it does, we still will see an absence of federal government leadership. Speaking on 20 January 2009, federal Environment Minister Jim Prentice said his government sought 'one shared commitment [in the global regime] from Canada and the US akin to the collective commitment of the European Union'.[37] In other words, Canadian policy would be made in Washington.

The other structural factor is the importance of the fossil fuel and motor vehicle industries. The regional concentration of these industries in the west and Ontario highlights another explanation for this history of weak federal leadership. Since the Québec Quiet Revolution of the 1960s, the Canadian federal system has evolved in such a way that federal government accommodation of strongly stated provincial desires has become the norm.

A third factor is party ideology. As a centrist party more interested in power than principle, the Liberals fashioned their 1993 platform to fit current public opinion but then had no ideological commitment to implement the platform once public support for environmental action waned. Although it had considerably watered down its right-wing ideology in order to gain power, the Conservative government elected in 2006 was still at least marginally more principled than its predecessor. Those principles, however, did not include action on climate change. The Harper government did not include climate change as one of its initial five priorities. In response to changing public opinion, Prime Minister Harper added the issue to his list in 2007 but, as described above, took no significant policy action.

Public opinion is the fourth factor which explains the lack of federal leadership. Opinion polls showed relatively weak support for environmental action from roughly 1992 to 2006, and the issue of climate change was not prominent in any of the federal elections held during that period.[38] Successive federal governments had no strong electoral incentives to act. Finally, we must look to the ongoing resistance of business. As we have seen, industry led the push for voluntary action rather than regulation in the 1990s, waged a public battle against ratification, brokered a private deal limiting the effectiveness of federal regulation and has since engaged in slow-paced negotiation of regulatory details. For all of these reasons, the federal government has not played a consistent lead-state role.

Weakness of the Federal–Provincial System

The history recounted above shows that one major reason for the failure of Canadian climate policy to date is the weakness of the system used to develop and implement that policy. The JMM process, which functioned during the decade prior to its collapse in 2002, was never strong enough to force the federal and provincial governments to stay at the table and hammer out an agreement on the critical issue of how they would share the overall cost of emissions reduction. Instead, each government was free to leave the table any time it chose.

The Québec government, for reasons related to the Parti Québécois separatist agenda rather than climate policy, refused to participate in the 1995 program and instead submitted its own plan to the UNFCCC. Prior to the 1997 third UNFCCC meeting at Kyoto, the JMM process reached agreement that the Canadian position should be stabilization by 2010. The federal government, however, then left the table and ignored that decision, instructing its diplomats that the Canadian position (initially) was three per cent below 1990.[39] At the JMM meeting in March 2000 Québec, which had by then rejoined the national process, walked out of the meeting and refused to sign the final communiqué;[40] in October 2000 Québec stayed but Ontario refused to sign;[41] in May 2002, because the other provinces refused to formally consider its proposed national plan, Alberta refused to sign and the Alberta Minister resigned as co-chair of the federal–provincial committee;[42] and then, at the last meeting before the JMM dissolved, in October 2002, the federal government refused to consider the request by the provinces to convene a First Ministers' meeting on the issue.[43]

Thus, we see that at various times the federal government (twice), Québec, Alberta, and Ontario all refused to abide by the negotiated outcomes generated by the process. Since all participating governments knew they could leave at any time, with no adverse consequences imposed upon them either by other governments or their own electorates, the process inevitably could produce only the weakest of outcomes. The institutional system lacked the necessary power to force participants to engage with one another and then accept the negotiated outcome. This is why the two national programs generated by the JMM process, in 1995 and 2000, were centred on the ineffective policy instrument of voluntarism, with no use made of the more coercive instruments of law or taxation.

Since 2002, as outlined above, there has been *no* formal system in place. The Martin government attempted to use a system of bilateral negotiation with individual provinces, but that effort was abandoned by the Harper government. Government officials undoubtedly speak to one another regularly, but no public, formal process for national policy development has been put in place to replace the JMM. In 2009, the Harper government speaks of harmonizing Canadian and American policy, but has made no specific suggestions for ways of first harmonizing policy *within* this country.

Conclusion

How can these barriers be overcome? With respect to the first, Canadians must recognize the magnitude of this policy challenge, which is the 'hard case' of all the environmental challenges facing this country, greater than any addressed over the past 50 years. Environmentalists, governments, and business must stop pretending that we can have our cake and eat it too. Canadian citizens, despite global recession and their rejection of the Dion carbon tax, must acknowledge the need to pay a price for the carbon they emit. More importantly, policy-makers must recognize and explicitly address the fact that significantly reducing GHG emissions will impose greater costs on some parts of the country than others; this simple fact is what underlies the Alberta veto-state position. At a rhetorical level, that fact was recognized at the time of Kyoto ratification and in theory has informed policy since. 'The [2002 federal government] Plan reflects the commitment made by First Ministers in 1997 and the principle reiterated by the provincial and territorial statement on climate change policy issued in Halifax on October 28, 2002, that no region or jurisdiction should be asked to bear an unreasonable burden in the realization of our climate change goals.'[44] To date, however, the federal and provincial governments have made no serious attempt to implement that principle.

This basic need to reach agreement on who will pay what portion of the total cost *has* been explicitly addressed, on the other hand, both at the international level and within the European Union. From the start, the UNFCCC regime has addressed the issue of cost-sharing between north and south. Explicit allocation of cost amongst the OECD nations was decided by a process of bargaining at the 1997 third Conference of Parties in Kyoto which resulted in different targets for different countries. Currently, the countries of the world are again negotiating allocation of cost for the post-2012 period. Similarly, in 1998 the member countries of the European Union reached agreement on which of them would bear what portion of the cost (ranging from a 25 per cent reduction target for Germany to a 27 per cent increase for Portugal) of meeting the overall EU target of reducing to 8 per cent below the 1990 level.[45] Prior to the 1997 Kyoto meeting, the parties to the UNFCCC had agreed that the EU could participate as though it were a single state accepting a single overall target. This meant there was an internal debate within the EU, both over the position it should take going into the Kyoto negotiations and how that overall cost should be shared amongst member states. Lead states such as Germany and the Netherlands recognized they could only reach agreement if others such as Portugal and Greece were allowed emission increases, to be compensated for by their own willingness to make significant reductions. The result, achieved both through technical analysis of each country's potential for reductions and political negotiation, was the 1998 Burden Sharing Agreement.[46]

The Canadian federal and provincial governments have recognized the need for an internal burden sharing agreement, through adoption of the 'no unreasonable burden' principle referred to above. They have never, however, explicitly, formally, and publicly discussed allocation of the overall Canadian cost. The international and EU examples suggest this is because there has never been a Canadian leader pressing for action and recognizing, perforce, the need to bargain with the laggards.

Turning to the second factor, what will be required to move Alberta from a veto-state role to one of willing participant in Canadian national climate policy? Ultimately, that depends upon internal Alberta politics. The political dynamic within that province must change sufficiently that any Alberta government seeking re-election will know that it can only achieve that goal by putting in place credible, effective policy to reduce Alberta emissions. The history of Québec separatism, which similarly is a decision that at the end of the day can only be made by Québec voters, suggests there is little the rest of Canada can do to influence the internal Alberta dynamic. Nevertheless, the federal and provincial governments should do what little they can. As they have been doing with Québec for 40 years, they must begin to bargain with Alberta. This can be done through the force of moral argument, offers to negotiate a cost-sharing agreement, and persuasion based in science to show that Alberta's own environmental, economic, and social interests can best be met by emissions reductions.

Such external pressure may also come from the United States. The 2007 US Energy Security and Independence Act prohibits federal agencies from buying fuels produced from oils, such as the Alberta tar sands process which generate more greenhouse gas emissions than conventional oil.[47] In the same vein, it is likely that US environmentalists will increasingly pressure their governments to take legislative action against imports of 'dirty oil' from the tar sands. As discussed above, this is what has prompted the Canadian government to propose a bilateral Canada–US climate-change agreement. If that were to happen, the Alberta government would find itself in a new and very different policy context, no longer facing only absent federal leadership and indifferent Canadian provinces, but instead powerful external pressures from south of the border.

For the third factor, prompting the federal government to play a consistent lead role may be only a little less difficult than inducing a reversal of Alberta policy. Public support for effective policy, as measured by opinion polls, has dropped from its 2007 level, making unlikely any significant increase in the political power of environmentalists. More possible is a change in business interests and accompanying change in the lobbying influence exerted on the federal government. On 1 October 2007, the Canadian Council of Chief Executives (CCCE) released a position paper on climate change which contained the followed statement:

> We know enough about the science of climate change to recognize that aggressive global action is required. The scale of the challenge is enormous, but it offers immense opportunities for Canada. We share the goal of slowing, stopping and reversing the growth of global greenhouse gas emissions (GHG) over the shortest time that is reasonably achievable.

The position paper offered no specific policy recommendations. Instead, it called for a national plan to replace the current patchwork of uncoordinated government policies; funding for new energy technology development as the central policy focus; emission reduction targets that 'recognize competitive realities' and 'ensure that firms are not arbitrarily penalized' (CCCE, 2007: 6); and use of either cap-and-trade or carbon tax instruments. This may be a sign of the phenomenon noted by Layzer (2007) with respect to business lobbying against climate policy in the US Congress: once regulation appears likely, firms drop their policy stance of outright opposition because they want to be in the room when the regulatory standards are set.[48] Furthermore, as the renewable energy sectors expand, they will certainly take what political action they can to further their economic interest in expanding their market share at the expense of fossil fuels.

Perhaps, however, we should not look inside Canada for the force which will prompt federal leadership. It might instead come from a *deus ex machina*, President Obama swinging on to the stage to play an active role and giving us the leadership we cannot find within ourselves. Debora VanNijnatten, in this volume, documents the growing influence of cross-border state–provincial groupings, such as the Western Climate Initiative, of which BC is a member. The leadership and institutional structure which prompted the BC carbon tax and industry hard-cap regulation were American. US policy, as noted, is beginning to change. Given the close economic integration of the two countries, and the Canadian tradition of following the US lead in environmental policy, the lead-state actor Canada so badly needs may soon appear dressed in stars and stripes.

Overcoming the fourth barrier, the weakness (or, since 2002, absence) of the process by which the federal and provincial governments develop coherent, co-ordinated policy raises issues basic to Canadian federalism. The facts of regionalism and differing language identities mean it is unrealistic to expect full coherence in any policy field. That said, it is clear that the national process for developing climate policy is weaker and produces less coherent policy than that used for other environmental issues, such as toxic pollution.[49] The climate policy process has to be made at least as robust as other national policy processes. How might that be done?

A necessary pre-condition is the existence of a motivated federal government, as discussed above. During his years as Prime Minister, Pierre Trudeau wanted more than anything else to give Canada a Charter of Rights and Freedom, which meant he had no choice but to make the First Ministers system as effective as possible. A Prime Minister similarly motivated on the climate file would have to revive the JMM process and, if necessary, supplement it with First Ministers meetings as needed. The federal government would then have to play a very different role from that it has to date—accepting outcomes rather than abandoning the process as it did in 1997 and again in 2002. By the same token, it would have to demand that as the price of admission all the provinces, as well as the federal government, give an initial commitment to stay at the table and accept the final negotiated outcome. Only once such a system was in place could the federal government then use its spending power and diplomacy to draw the provinces into agreement on effective policy.

Secondly, the federal and provincial governments might be motivated to stay with the process by external accountability pressure. Just as the Auditor General and Commissioner of Environment and Sustainable Development play institutionalized watch-dog roles, a new arms' length agency might be created to monitor and regularly report on the effectiveness of the federal–provincial climate process. That kind of visibility in the eyes of their voters would, at least marginally, increase the political price by a government thinking it might disengage from the national process.

As we have seen, the barriers which have prevented effective action since 1992 are formidable. There are signs of change: public opinion forced the Harper government to reverse its policy; for the first time, some provinces are starting to act; business may be coming to accept the inevitability of regulation; and changing US policy may indeed provide the leadership we so badly need, saving us from ourselves. Alberta, however, is not changing course and the need to negotiate a national burden sharing agreement is not part of the policy discourse. The four basic factors which have precluded effective policy must still be addressed.

Questions for Review

1. Why has Canada's climate change policy not achieved its stated goals?
2. Is a carbon tax an appropriate and effective instrument of climate change policy? Are voluntarist or regulatory strategies more effective for securing industry compliance with climate change objectives?
3. What steps could be taken to encourage the federal and provincial governments to adopt stronger agreed policies on climate change?
4. To what extent is Canada's climate policy set in Washington?

Notes

1. Canada, *The Cost of Bill C-288 to Canadian Families and Business* (Ottawa: Her Majesty the Queen in Right of Canada, 2007), 9.
2. IPCC, 'Summary for Policymakers', in *Climate Change 2007: The Physical Science Basis. Contribution of Working Group 1 to the Fourth Assessment Report of the Intergovernmental Panel on Climate Change* (Cambridge: Cambridge University Press, 2007).
3. IPCC, 'Summary', 2.
4. Canada, 'The Cost', 8.
5. Pamela S. Chasek, David L. Downie, and Janet Welsh Brown, *Global Environmental Politics* (Boulder, CO: Westview Press, 2006), 115–28.
6. Heather A. Smith, 'Stopped Cold', *Alternatives Journal* 24 (4).
7. Douglas Macdonald, David Houle, and Caitlin Patterson, 'L'utilisation du volontarisme afin de contrôler les émissions de gaz à effet de serre du secteur industriel'. Unpublished paper, 2008.
8. Douglas Macdonald, *Business and Environmental Politics in Canada* (Peterborough, ON: Broadview Press, 2007).
9. Mark Winfield and Douglas Macdonald, 'The Harmonization Accord and Climate Change Policy: Two Case Studies in Federal–Provincial Environmental Policy' in Herman Bakvis and Grace Skogstad, eds, *Canadian Federalism: Performance, Effectiveness and Legitimacy* (Don Mills, ON: Oxford University Press, 2008).
10. G. Bruce Doern and Thomas Conway, *The Greening of Canada: Federal Institutions and Decisions* (Toronto: University of Toronto Press, 1994); Kathryn Harrison, *Passing the Buck: Federalism and Canadian Environmental Policy* (Vancouver: UBC Press, 1996).
11. Macdonald, *Business and Environmental Politics*.
12. Environment Canada, 'Canada's New Government Announces Mandatory Industrial Targets to Tackle Climate Change and Reduce Air Pollution'. News Release, 26 April 2007.
13. Winfield and Macdonald, 'The Harmonization Accord and Climate Change Policy', 2008, 278.
14. Conservative Party of Canada Federal Election Platform, 2006, 37.
15. Jeff Salot, 'Kyoto Plan No Good, Minister Argues', *The Globe and Mail*, 8 April 2006.
16. Douglas Macdonald, 'Climate-change Policy-making by the Stephen Harper Government: A Case Study of the Relationship Between Public Opinion and Environmental Policy'. A paper delivered at the annual meeting of the Canadian Political Science Association, UBC, 6 June, 2008.
17. Elizabeth May, 'The Saga of Bill C-30: From Clean Air to Climate Change, or Not', *Policy Options*, 28, 5 (May 2007).
18. Environment Canada, 'Canada's Clean Air Act Delivered to Canadians'. News Release. 19 October 2006.
19. Jeffrey Simpson, Mark Jaccard, and Nic Rivers, *Hot Air: Meeting Canada's Climate Change Challenge* (Toronto: McClelland and Stewart, 2007); Douglas Macdonald, 'Explaining the Failure of Canadian Climate Change Policy', in Hugh Compston and Ian Bailey, eds, *Turning Down the Heat: The Politics of Climate Policy in Affluent Countries* (New York: Palgrave Macmillan, forthcoming).
20. BC Ministry of Finance, *Balanced Budget 2008*, 19 February 2008.
21. BC Ministry of Environment, 'B.C. First Province to Legislate Cap-and-Trade', 3 April 2008.
22. S. McCarthy and Campbell Clark, 'Ottawa Swoops in with Climate-change Offer', *The Globe and Mail*, 6 November 2008.
23. Nic Rivers and Mark Jaccard, 'Canada's Efforts Towards Greenhouse Gas Emission Reduction: A Case Study on the Limits of Voluntary Action and Subsidies', *International Journal of Global Energy Issues* 23 (2005): 307–23; Simpson, Jaccard, and Rivers, *Hot Air*, 2007.
24. Bruce Podobnik, *Global Energy Shifts: Fostering Sustainability in a Turbulent Age* (Philadelphia: Temple University Press, 2006), 3.
25. Ibid.
26. Simpson, Jaccard, and Rivers, *Hot Air*; Kathryn Harrison and Lisa McIntosh Sundstrom, 'The Comparative Politics of Climate Change', *Global Environmental Politics* 7, 4 (2007): 1–18.
27. Chasek, Downie, and Brown, *Global Environmental Politics*, 2006, 14. Emphasis in original.
28. Doern and Conway, *The Greening of Canada*, 98.
29. Terence Corcoran, 'Good-bye Carbon Tax, Hello Sanity', *The Globe and Mail Report on Business*, 1 June 1994.
30. Douglas Macdonald, 'The Business Campaign to Prevent Kyoto Ratification.' A paper delivered at the annual meeting of the Canadian Political Science Association, Dalhousie University, 31 May 2003.

31. Chasek, Downie, and Brown, *Global Environmental Politics*, 42.

32. Barry Rabe, 'Moral Super-Power or Policy Laggard? Translating Kyoto Protocol Ratification into Federal and Provincial Climate Policy in Canada'. Paper delivered at the Annual Meeting of the Canadian Political Science Association, London, Ontario, 2 June 2005.

33. Luc Juillet and Glen Toner, 'From Great Leaps to Baby Steps: Environment and Sustainable Development Policy under the Liberals', in Gene Swimmer, ed., *How Ottawa Spends, 1997–98* (Ottawa, ON: Carleton University Press, 1997).

34. Cited in Ian Rowlands, 'Integrating Climate Policy and Energy Policy', in Steven Bernstein, Jutta Brunnée, David G. Duff, and Andrew J. Green, eds, *A Globally Integrated Climate Policy for Canada* (Toronto: University of Toronto Press, 2008), 301.

35. Mark Winfield with Clare Demerse and Johanne Whitmore, 'Climate Change and Canadian Energy Policy', in Steven Bernstein, Jutta Brunnée, David G. Duff, and Andrew J. Green, eds, *A Globally Integrated Climate Policy for Canada* (Toronto: University of Toronto Press, 2008), 261.

36. Ibid, 261.

37. J. Prentice, Minister of the Environment, Speech to the Canadian Council of Chief Executives, 20 January 2009.

38. Macdonald, CPSA, 2008.

39. Winfield and Macdonald, 'The Harmonization Accord and Climate Change Policy', 275–6.

40. Andrew Bjorn, et al., *Ratification of the Kyoto Protocol: A Citizen's Guide to the Canadian Climate Change Policy Process* (Toronto: Sustainable Toronto, 2002), 80.

41. Ibid, 80.

42. Ibid, 81.

43. Macdonald, 'The Business Campaign'.

44. Government of Canada, *Climate Change Plan for Canada*, undated. Released November 2002, 9.

45. Nuno S. Lacasta, Suraje Dessai, Eva Kracht, and Katharine Vincent, 'Articulating a Consensus: The EU's Position on Climate Change', in Paul G. Harris, ed., *Europe and Global Climate Change: Politics, Foreign Policy and Regional Cooperation* (Cheltenham: Edward Elgar, 2007).

46. Ibid.

47. Barry McKenna and David Parkinson, 'U.S. Law Puts Chill on Oil Sands', *The Globe and Mail*, 24 June 2008, B8.

48. Judith A. Lazer, 'Deep Freeze: How Business Has Shaped the Global Warming Debate in Congress', in Michael E. Kraft and Sheldon Kamieniecki, eds, *Corporate Interests in the American Political System* (Cambridge, Massachusetts: The MIT Press, 2007), 93–125.

49. See Winfield and Macdonald, 'The Harmonization Accord and Climate Change Policy' for a comparison of the climate policy process with the Harmonization Accord process used for other environmental issues.

12

Renewable Electricity: The Prospects for Innovation and Integration in Provincial Policies

Ian H. Rowlands

While access to electricity services in Canada has been critical to the promotion of human well-being, it is nevertheless also accepted that the traditional arrangement of electricity systems—large, centralized power plants fuelled by fossil fuels, uranium, or large-scale dams—is not sustainable. It has led to a variety of environmental and social problems: air pollution at various scales (smog, acid precipitation, and global climate change), waste management challenges, and community disruption are but some examples.[1] In response, the increased use of renewable resources (for example, solar and wind) is often presented as an integral component of a sustainable energy strategy.[2]

The purpose of this chapter is to examine Canadian policies to promote the increased use of renewable resources in electricity supply systems. After briefly reviewing the structure of electricity systems in Canada, and highlighting the role of renewable resources therein, the range of conceivable policy options is presented. It is thus shown that strategies to promote increased use of renewable resources have, to varying degrees, relied upon government targets/obligations, competitive procurement, market mechanisms, and/or consumer initiatives to respond to economic incentives. These sample structures are then used to guide the exploration of policies in place across Canada. With provinces playing the lead role in efforts to promote the increased use of renewable electricity, this survey reviews activities under four headings: (1) government targets coupled with wind power procurement in major hydropower provinces, (2) broader 'requests for proposals' and 'renewable portfolio standards', (3) consumer demand for 'green power', and (4) 'feed-in tariffs'. After this review, the level of policy innovation evident in Canada is determined by comparing the national experience with global benchmarks.

Of course, the motivation for innovation in renewable electricity policy in Canada has been relatively muted. There has been no urgency in any proponents' calls for increased use of renewable resources in electricity supply: the traditional low price for electricity in this country, coupled with the relatively-low levels of emissions associated with its generation, have provided little support for these renewable electricity advocates.

Nevertheless, there has still been some relatively innovative thinking about the development of renewable electricity policy, most of which has revolved around broader ideas about 'integration'—more specifically, integration across policy approaches (using a variety of regulatory, taxation, and market mechanisms in combination, for example) and integration across issue-areas (recognizing the fact that electricity policy is effectively sustainability policy, because it potentially has implications across a range of economic, social, and environmental areas). While it is clear that there are some instances in which Canadian ideas have served to advance the broader set of policy discussions, at least in a North American context, it is equally evident that more innovation is still required.

Looking towards the future, the rising costs of conventional sources and the mounting pressure to de-carbonize our society mean that the demand for policy innovation will inevitably increase. As such, the experiences in Canada currently being developed, along with the growing global record, will be needed in order to stimulate proposals for additional strategies to promote the increased use of renewable electricity.

Canada's Electricity Supply Systems

Canada's electricity supply structures have arisen (largely) along provincial lines. Encouraged by a constitution that assigns individual provinces the responsibility for the 'development, conservation and management of sites and facilities in the province for the generation and production of electrical energy' (Section 92A(1c) of *The Constitution Act, 1867*), these sub-national governments have traditionally worked to develop secure, reliable, and economical means of supplying electricity to their citizens (in their homes as well as their workplaces) and, as appropriate, to export markets as well. At the national level, 2005 figures from the International Energy Agency reveal that almost 58 per cent of the electricity produced in Canada was from hydropower facilities (the vast majority of them of the 'large-scale' variety); coal provided almost 17 per cent, and nuclear energy almost 15 per cent. Other resources played a relatively modest role: natural gas just under six per cent, oil just over three per cent, and biomass at approximately 1.5 per cent. No other resource contributed more than one-quarter of one per cent.[3] There are, however, significant differences between provinces. Hydropower dominates some provinces, while others have a more balanced supply portfolio. Table 12.1 provides additional details.

Depending upon how 'renewable' is defined (and this definition is often contested),[4] Canada can be considered to already have significant renewable resources in its supply portfolio. However, take note of the hydropower figure cited above. If one restricts the category to the so-called 'new renewables'—often defined in terms of low-impact renewable resources, like solar, wind, small hydro, and biomass[5]—then the contribution to the supply portfolio across Canada is much more modest. In addition to the hydropower noted above (though recognizing that only a small portion of that would be included in this 'new' category), a similar observation could be made about the aforementioned biomass category; only some of it is generated in a sustainable manner. Further to these observations, and continuing to use the same data as referenced above, note that wind supplied approximately 0.23 per cent of Canadian electricity production in 2005, tidal approximately 0.005 per cent, and solar photovoltaics approximately 0.003 per cent.[6] With wind being the most significant of these three, it is worth noting here (as laid out in Table 12.2) the distribution of installed capacity across the country. Further information about different provinces' respective wind power portfolios are explored later in this chapter.

Table 12.1 Percentage of Electricity Generation by Utility Companies, by Province and Energy Source, 2005

Province	Hydro (including small amounts of wind and tide)	Nuclear	Coal	Natural gas	Heavy fuel oil (including petroleum coke)	Other (including manufactured gases, other petroleum products, other fuels and station service)
Newfoundland and Labrador	96.6	0.0	0.0	0.0	3.4	0.0
Nova Scotia and Prince Edward Island	10.0	0.0	71.7	1.9	15.8	0.6
New Brunswick	18.8	21.6	18.0	5.2	36.1	0.2
Québec	96.4	2.8	0.0	0.2	0.7	0.0
Ontario	22.3	50.2	19.7	7.3	0.6	0.0
Manitoba	98.8	0.0	1.2	0.0	0.0	0.0
Saskatchewan	24.0	0.0	55.8	20.1	0.0	0.1
Alberta	5.4	0.0	81.7	12.8	0.0	0.1
British Columbia	94.3	0.0	0.0	5.7	0.0	0.1
Yukon, Northwest Territories and Nunavut	70.6	0.0	0.0	0.0	0.0	29.4

Source: Statistics Canada, 'Percentage of electricity generation by utility companies, by province and energy source, 2005', http://www.statcan.ca/english/research/11-621-MIE/2007062/tables/table4.htm.

Table 12.2 Provinces' Installed Capacity, Wind Power, 2008*

Province	Installed capacity
Ontario	781 MW
Québec	531 MW
Alberta	524 MW
Saskatchewan	171 MW
Manitoba	103 MW
Prince Edward Island	72 MW
Nova Scotia	61 MW

* Includes only those provinces with at least 5 MW of reported installed capacity

Source: Canadian Wind Energy Association, 'Canada Becomes 12th Country in the World to Surpass 2,000 MW of Installed Wind Energy Capacity', http://www.canwea.ca/media/release/release_e.php?newsId=51.

Government Policies to Promote Increased Use of Renewable Electricity

During the past 10 years, there has been increased attention to the ways in which different policies could be used to promote the increased use of renewable resources in electricity supply systems. Much of this debate has had a trans-Atlantic flavour to it, with European preferences for the so-called feed-in tariff often contrasted with American tendencies to use the so-called renewable portfolio standard (RPS).[7] Given the attention accorded each, brief descriptions are appropriate here.

A feed-in tariff, in its most basic form, is a payment (usually at a premium to the market price for conventional electricity) to renewable electricity facilities for every unit of electricity generated, guaranteed for a number of years by a contract between the generator and some public and/or utility authority. Payment levels may be differentiated by technology, or even by facility location. Feed-in tariffs have been widely credited with spurring the original development of Denmark's wind industry and, more recently, Germany's and Spain's world-class renewable electricity industries.[8]

By contrast, a renewable portfolio standard reserves a portion of the broader electricity market for renewable resources by obliging market participants to ensure that a pre-determined share of their total electricity supply is provided by qualifying facilities. This pre-determined share may gradually 'ramp up' over time. Fulfillment of this obligation on the part of all electricity generators within the market may be facilitated by the use of some kind of 'tradable renewable energy certificates'. Renewable portfolio standards have been credited with spurring renewable electricity development in a number of states in the United States; Texas, for example, is an oft-cited success story.[9]

A third alternative often identified is the 'tendering scheme'. In this system, requests for proposals for renewable electricity are made at intermittent intervals; often a capacity quota is assigned to each of a variety of technologies. The bidder with the lowest price is then given a long-term contract, usually by some kind of government procurement institution, to supply renewable electricity. The United Kingdom implementation of the 'Non-Fossil Fuel Obligation' is often identified as one of the first tendering systems.[10]

Others have identified voluntary approaches, or instances in which consumers, themselves, make the choice to purchase green power. Financial subsidies/tax incentives aimed at reducing the initial capital costs of renewable energy technologies; and regulatory approaches which generate policies to place emission reduction obligations on electricity producers are additional categories.[11] Moreover, there are a number of variations on these themes. A recent Canadian categorization, for instance, had four distinct divisions: subsidies, price guarantees, regulated quantities, and taxes.[12] Another highlighted eight of the 'most common policies' from around the world: research and development, renewable portfolio standards, tendering, net-metering, feed-in tariff, other fiscal policies, green procurement, and green power programmes.[13] The structure used in this survey of Canadian policies at the provincial level uses the divisions most commonly found in the literature, influenced by the particular record of Canadian experience to date. More specifically, we examine, in turn, provinces that have government targets coupled with wind power procurement against a primarily hydropower core, broader requests for proposals and renewable portfolio standards, consumer demand for green power, and feed-in tariffs.

Provincial Policies in Canada

As we explore policies across Canada it should be noted that this review is not comprehensive, that is, not every policy in place is reviewed. For one, the focus of this section is, justifiably, on the provincial level. Consequently, federal and municipal policies, modest as they are, are not covered explicitly.[14] Moreover, a number of provinces have pursued different policy strategies, sometimes concurrently. Ontario, for example, initially left its policy strategies to be guided by consumer demand. The province then followed this with a renewable portfolio standard, transforming this into a request for proposals strategy, and then introduced a feed-in tariff; the result is that a variety of policies ended up being implemented.[15] In this chapter, however, we focus upon a 'significant' policy in each of the country's 10 provinces—that is, a policy that is both influential in renewable electricity outcomes in the province and useful in an exploration of the range of strategies in place in Canada. That exploration is undertaken in the following sections of this chapter.

Government Targets and Wind Power Procurement in Major Hydropower Provinces

As noted above, at the national level hydropower development dominates Canada's electricity production. And, interestingly, three of the four provinces that have such dominated systems have relatively similar renewable electricity development policies: Manitoba, Québec, and Newfoundland and Labrador have all set provincial targets and then had their dominant provincial utility develop procurement procedures for wind power; British Columbia has also let its utility take the lead in renewable electricity procurement, but it has aimed to solicit a broader range of resources. The experiences of the three former provinces are examined in this section, the one latter in the next.

With 99 per cent of its electricity generated by hydropower, Manitoba claims that most of its power is already 'green'. Nevertheless, it is also intent on diversifying its renewable electricity portfolio, particularly by means of wind power. A 2004 intention to develop 'up to 1,000 MW of wind power capacity over the next decade'[16] was strengthened into a 'commitment' in 2005. At that time, the Government of Manitoba laid out its 'very aggressive goal of developing 1,000 megawatts of wind power in Manitoba over the next decade'.[17] Indeed, in November 2005, the procurement process for wind power was initiated by Manitoba Hydro through a call for expressions of interest in developing potential wind power projects of more than 10 MW and up to 1,000 MW.[18]

Following the submission of these expressions of interest, the first request for proposals—for a total of 300 MW of capacity—was announced in September 2006.[19] Details followed from Manitoba Hydro in March 2007, with a July 2007 deadline for submissions.[20] In all, 17 potential developers submitted 84 proposals (some developers submitted multiple proposals) totaling more than 10,000 MW in capacity; individual projects had capacities ranging from 25.5 MW to 300 MW with locations spread throughout southern Manitoba.[21] Manitoba Hydro then evaluated these proposals on primarily economic criteria, though the utility reserved the right to bring other factors into consideration.[22] Manitoba Hydro subsequently invited seven developers considering 10 different locations (which ranged in size from 66 MW to 100 MW) to move to the next stage in the process. They were to provide 'best and final offers to develop and supply wind-generated energy to Manitoba Hydro'.[23] In March 2008, the utility announced that examination of the bids was continuing, with meetings to 'discuss further the feasibility of favoured projects'.[24] The Government had committed to three further allocations of 200 megawatts each between 2013 and 2018.[25]

Québec's electricity system is also dominated by large-scale hydropower resources; in this case, 96 per cent of the province's generation. The Government has displayed an interest not only in expanding its existing hydropower portfolio (more about that below), but also in diversifying its renewable resources with wind power. Similar to Manitoba, Québec's dominant utility—Hydro-Québec—has taken the lead in procuring wind power. Following government approval, Hydro-Québec launched a competitive bid process in May 2003 for 1,000 MW of wind energy. Interestingly, there was a requirement that 'all or most of the new wind turbines be installed in Québec's rural, windswept Matane and Gaspe peninsula regions, or on the Iles de la Madeleine'.[26] It was also required that the 'wind-turbine enclosures . . . be assembled in the region where they would be installed'.[27] Thirty-two proposals, totaling approximately 4,000 MW of capacity (from nine distinct bidders), were received. Contracts were awarded in October 2004 based on the lowest unit cost, including transmission, to two bidders: Cartier Wind Energy (six projects) and Northland Power (two projects). Together, the capacity totaled 990 MW.[28]

A second call was issued in October 2005. This time aiming for 2,000 MW of capacity, Hydro-Québec said 'at least 60% of the total cost of each wind farm must be incurred in Québec and a minimum of 30% of all wind turbine costs must be incurred in a region defined as the regional county municipality of Matane and the administrative region of Gaspésie–Îles-de-la-Madeleine.'[29] Further, in assessing the bids, Hydro-Québec announced that 'additional consideration will be accorded to projects promoting the development of Native or local communities, for instance through direct ownership. A balance is sought between the obligation to supply energy at the lowest possible price and a concern for partnering with local communities.'[30] In response, 66 proposals, totaling approximately 7,700 MW of capacity (from more than 25 distinct bidders), were received.[31] Contracts were awarded in May 2008, with 2,004 MW of new capacity selected from 15 proposals.[32]

While this process was unfolding, the Government of Québec, in 2006, released its energy plan, which highlighted its priorities for the coming decade. With respect to electricity, it highlighted the importance of hydropower as the continuing core of the electricity system, with the plan pledging to develop 4,500 MW of new capacity within the coming five years. This was to be supplemented by a secondary emphasis upon wind power. The 3,000 MW then being developed by Hydro-Québec through the two aforementioned requests for proposals were to be completed. Additionally, a longer-term goal of 4,000 MW by 2015 was articulated, though this was tempered by concerns about the cost-effectiveness of that supply. Indeed, it is worth noting that the two foremost priorities for the electricity system in the province were identified as 'energy supply security' and 'energy as a lever for economic development'. Nevertheless, coupled with plans for a third request for proposals focusing upon First Nations and municipalities, the Government of Québec was confident that it was on track to meet its year 2015 goal.[33]

Finally, let us consider the province of Newfoundland and Labrador, another hydropower intensive province. The province had a series of consultations on their electricity system in 2002. While attention was given therein to the extent to which different kinds of resources should meet future demand, there was no explicit focus upon any particular policy to encourage renewable resources.[34] Again, with the vast majority of the province's electricity generated by low-emission means, this is perhaps not entirely surprising.

Nevertheless, the province has shown a recent interest in wind power. In December 2005, it issued a request for proposals for 25 MW of wind power capacity.[35] After considering multiple submissions, an award of 25 MW was announced in October 2006.[36] A similar process unfolded the next year, when another 25 MW request for proposal was announced in October 2006;[37] a 27 MW award was issued in December 2007.[38]

Furthermore, the province also released its long-awaited energy plan during this period. A discussion paper in 2005 began to scope the issues, highlighting the importance of ensuring that the benefits of the province's vast natural resources were accrued by the province itself. (This, of course, is largely in reaction to the continued existence of a long-term contract regarding the Lower Churchill Hydroelectric Project, whose output is going to Hydro-Québec until 2041 at very low prices.) Indeed, the Upper Churchill Hydroelectric Project—deemed by many to be the continent's 'best' potential energy project—is the focus of much consideration in both the discussion paper and the subsequent plan (released in 2007) itself. Wind power received relatively little attention, with 80 MW being identified as an upper limit for capacity.[39] As we see above, however, the government has made considerable progress towards this level.

Requests for Proposals and Renewable Portfolio Standards

As is already evident from the experiences above, popular among Canadian provinces is a request for proposals strategy, with a target announced by the government but with the execution managed by the monopoly utility in the particular jurisdiction. Adding to the wind-focused experiences noted above, this section examines similar strategies that have been executed in other Canadian provinces. However, instead of focusing solely upon wind, the resource base is broader, at least in stated attention. Additionally, this section also examines experiences that self-identify as renewable portfolio strategies. The reader should note, however, that these particular experiences of policy development regarding renewable portfolio strategies—because they occur in electricity systems that have only modest levels of industry restructuring therein (and thus continue, for the most part, to be dominated by a single electric utility)—are quite close to what is described towards the beginning of this chapter as a tendering system (and what has come to be called, in the Canadian context, the request for proposals strategy). With those caveats, we turn now to the respective provincial experiences, beginning in the west with British Columbia, subsequently turning to Saskatchewan, and then focusing upon the three Maritime provinces.

In 2002, the intensity of the debate about the future of British Columbia's energy policy was beginning to grow, powered in no small part by the then just-past California electricity crisis, and the increasing reliance of British Columbia upon imports for its own electricity supply. A task force was convened to identify key issues and to begin to scope them out. Its discussion virtually began, as is often the case in Canada's hydropower-rich provinces, with a recognition that large-scale dams generate renewable (and, implicitly, desirable) electricity. With that starting point, the task force still recommended that portfolio standards for alternative energy be set, but nevertheless argued that the challenge was 'to develop achievable portfolio standards that also signal the need to diversify energy supply'.[40] To help achieve this goal, the Government, in its plan later that same year, established a 'clean energy goal': it would ask BC Hydro to ensure that '50% of new power supply over 10 years' was sourced from renewable resources other than large-scale hydropower.[41] This led to 16 projects being selected the following year, with the vast majority (14) being small-scale hydropower; there was also one landfill gas and one wind facility.[42]

Debate in the province continued, with the Premier's Alternative Energy and Power Technology Task Force (its report entitled 'A Vision and Implementation Plan for Growing a Sustainable Energy

Cluster', was released in 2006[43]) helping to set the agenda. The Government brought out its 'BC Energy Plan: A Vision for Clean Leadership' on 27 February 2007. Amongst the goals in this was the following: 'Ensure clean or renewable electricity generation continues to account for at least 90 per cent of total generation. These include sources of energy that are constantly renewed by natural processes, such as large and small hydroelectric, solar, wind, tidal, geothermal, wood residue and energy from organic municipal waste.'[44] This has led to another request for proposals. Issued in June 2008, it is intended to achieve 5,000 GWh per year of energy. The definition of 'clean' was yet to be determined; additionally, although cost effectiveness would certainly be a key criterion for assessment, a number of other factors could eventually also be part of the calculation.[45]

Moving east, in 2003 the Saskatchewan Government announced that it would be implementing a new 'Green Power Portfolio' of initiatives. Central to this would be both large-scale and small-scale renewable electricity. With respect to the former, it also announced at this time that a partnership had been reached with ATCO Power to develop 150 MW of wind farms in the province. With respect to the latter, it noted that SaskPower, the province's main utility, would be issuing a call for proposals for small-scale renewable energy projects that 'could include flare gas, wind, low-impact hydro, biomass, biogas, heat recovery from an existing waste heat source and solar'.[46] Each of these two strategies continued to be pursued during the subsequent five years.

Considering the larger-scale renewable electricity facilities, the Government announced in 2007 that it planned to expand wind generation in Saskatchewan, with 'a goal of an additional 100 MW by 2012'.[47] And depending upon how the scale issue is divided, it is also relevant to include here the 50 MW target for waste heat recovery projects and the 20 MW target for biomass forestry projects, which were pledged in the same communication.[48]

Turning to the smaller scale, in 2004 SaskPower issued its first call for proposals for 'environmentally preferred power'.[49] Three projects, representing 13 MW of capacity, were selected (two wind power and one heat-recovery).[50] A second phase was launched in May 2005, with a target of 45 MW.[51] One year later, four project proposals were selected; three involve heat-recovery technology and the other involves wind power.[52] In September 2007, plans for a third phase of the program were announced.[53] Together, these strategies involving both larger-scale and smaller-scale renewable electricity production facilities form the cornerstone of what has been called the province's '30% renewable portfolio standard by 2020'.[54]

Continuing our travels eastward, we now move on to the Maritimes. In 1998, the Province of New Brunswick issued a discussion paper initiating exploration of the future of the province's electricity strategy.[55] In that, a renewable portfolio standard (RPS) was explicitly mooted, prompted by the following question: Should public policy require that a certain portion of power supplied be 'green'? A task force, at arm's length from Government, was immediately established in order to begin to gauge public reaction to the issues raised therein. Members of this task force found that virtually 'everybody who made a presentation to the task force spoke to the importance of the environment both in general terms and as it relates to energy.'[56] When, however, asked whether it had plans to develop 'green power resources within its system', NB Power, the province's main utility, told the Legislative Assembly of the province that it did not.[57] Moreover, when the options were summarized, the section on 'environment' focused primarily on demand side management issues; the supply side, particularly renewables, was given little attention.[58]

Nevertheless, this report helped to set the agenda for the Government's Select Committee on Energy to consider. In its report, members encouraged the province to consider increased use of green power, but stopped short of recommending mandatory requirements.[59] Instead, believing that it was 'difficult for New Brunswick to provide such [green] power by itself', the Committee argued that the province should 'become a strong advocate of "green power" and, through its membership in the Canadian Council of Ministers of the Environment, take the lead in urging that a national program of research and development of "green power" sources and standards be initiated'.[60] Two years later, the Government released a White Paper on the issue. In this, the importance of environmental issues was again highlighted; however, again, no explicit instructions about RPS were given to the soon-to-be-formed Electricity Market Design Committee. Instead, it was noted that '[a]ccordingly, the Province will monitor the development of Renewable Portfolio Standard programs in other jurisdictions and assess the benefits for New Brunswick.'[61]

Nevertheless, the RPS concept was endorsed by the Electricity Market Design Committee in its final report, released in 2002. It called for an RPS, focusing upon 'additional' renewable electricity, rising over time. It also recognized that the renewable electricity could be sourced from outside of New Brunswick.[62] The government accepted this recommendation, which had developed out of regulations following from the new Electricity Act (which received Royal Assent on 11 April 2003). More specifically, the 'Electricity from Renewable Resources Regulation—Electricity Act', which was filed on 27 July 2006, obliged 'standard service suppliers' to ensure that, in 2007, at least one per cent of their electricity was sourced from 'new' (post-2001) renewable electricity generators. These generators had to have the Environmental Choice certification, but did not necessarily have to be located in New Brunswick. This obligation would ramp up by one per cent a year until it reached 10 per cent in 2016 (and beyond).[63]

Turning to Nova Scotia, in 2001 the Government published an Energy Strategy, which was intended to lay out both short-term and longer-term priorities for the province's development of a 'successful energy industry' that would 'provide people with enduring social and economic benefits'.[64] As part of that, the Government indicated that it would create a short-term, voluntary 'renewable energy target for new [independent power producers] renewable generation totaling 2.5 per cent of [Nova Scotia Power, the province's main utility]'s current generation capacity, or approximately 50 MW'. It was also agreed that after monitoring this voluntary commitment for a period of three years, a 'longer-term mandatory renewable energy portfolio standard (RPS)' would be established.[65] This strategy, however, indicated government priorities, rather than immediately becoming government policy.

To determine how to implement the recommendations contained in the Energy Strategy, the Government established the Electricity Marketplace Governance Committee (EMGC) the following year (2002). Composed of a range of stakeholders from across the province, the Committee, in its final report submitted in 2003, recommended that a mandatory RPS be adopted, and that it take effect in 2006. Particularly noteworthy elements of their recommendations included the fact that the renewable electricity level should be additional to what was already present in Nova Scotia—to achieve that, they suggested that the level should be five per cent above what was present in 2001 (the identified base year) by 2010. And second, it was noted that the renewable energy must be generated within Nova Scotia.[66]

Following this report, the Government passed a new Electricity Act, which received Royal Assent on 18 October 2004.[67] This embodied, in law, the RPS (now referred to as a 'renewable energy standard') and set the stage for the details to be laid out in subsequent regulations. Those regulations were forthcoming in early 2007. They followed many of the recommendations of the EMGC, though they also introduced a second target for the renewable energy standard. That second target was 2013, and it was noted that the target would then be 10 per cent (again, above the 2001 baseline).[68] It was also noted, however, that Nova Scotia Power would be able to contribute to that target, whereas for the 2010 target Nova Scotia Power had to source the renewable electricity from independent power producers.

In June 2003, the PEI Energy Corporation released a Draft PEI Renewable Energy Strategy. In that document, it was proposed that the province implement an RPS with a target of 10 per cent by 2010.[69] Public consultations held after that time suggested that Islanders wanted a higher value; it was reported that most respondents 'agreed that setting an electricity RPS of 10 to 15 per cent by 2010 was a worthwhile and an attainable goal'.[70] As a result, in its Strategy document one year later, the Government committed to 'an RPS for electricity of at least 15 per cent by 2010. Over the longer term, the Province will evaluate opportunities for having 100 per cent of its electrical capacity acquired by renewable energy by 2015.'[71]

The Renewable Energy Act was passed during the fall 2004 session of the Legislative Assembly. Regulations were approved by the Government in December 2005, which thus allowed the Act to be proclaimed. Central to the Act is the requirement that at least 15 per cent of electricity be sourced from renewable resources by 2010. A proposed part of the Act that would then oblige the equivalent of 100 per cent of electricity to be sourced from renewable resources by 2015 was withdrawn; the Minister noted that 'there has been some concern that the current wording in the act does not accurately reflect [the intent to] . . . have at least 200 MW of renewable energy.'[72] Noteworthy in the Act is that renewable resources are rather broadly defined, and that their location (that is, inside or outside of the province) is not particularly important.

Consumer Demand for 'Green Power'

An alternative way of encouraging renewable electricity is to leave it to the market, that is, leave it to customers (be they industrial, commercial/institutional, agricultural, and/or residential) to demand green power, and then permit suppliers to 'arise' to meet this demand. Clearly, to facilitate this, particular institutional structures—at its most basic, the presence of a competitive marketplace and the ability to enter into contracts with particular suppliers—must be in place. Alberta has relied primarily upon this strategy to promote the increased use of renewable electricity.

Soon after the electricity market in Alberta opened to competition on 1 January 2001, the province established a renewable energy target. More specifically, in its 2002 climate change plan, the Government said that it expected the 'renewable and alternative energy portion of the province's total electricity capacity to grow by 3.5 per cent by 2008'.[73] This was interpreted by some as moving the province's electricity system from one in which there was approximately two per cent renewable (in 2002) to 5.5 per cent by 2008. This was largely achieved, with the province having experienced considerable growth in wind power capacity during this period, rising more than three-fold to 524 MW in early 2008.[74] Much of that growth has been stimulated through the emergence of green power markets in Alberta. Indeed, the utilities serving Calgary and Edmonton—ENMAX and EPCOR, respectively—were amongst the pioneers of green power marketing in Canada.[75] Newer entrants, such as Bullfrog Power, are now very active in Alberta.

Broader debate in Alberta continues, specifically with respect to whether there should be a more explicit role for government in the promotion of renewable electricity. Central to these discussions has been the Renewable and Alternative Energy Project Team, established in 2004 by the Clean Air Strategic Alliance (which is, itself, a non-profit association comprised of stakeholders from government, industry, and nongovernmental organizations, working to make consensus recommendations to the provincial government). While they could not reach unanimity on all issues explored during their deliberations, at least some of their recommendations suggest that a formal policy—perhaps a variation on a RPS (entitled, in this case, the 'retailer-based method')—could be forthcoming.[76]

Feed-In Tariffs

Finally, we conclude our examination of the Canadian provinces with Ontario. As already noted, Ontario has pursued a variety of strategies to promote renewable electricity. Indeed, the publication of a report by an Advisory Committee on Competition in Ontario's Electricity System in 1996 marked the beginning of a period of specialized discussion on the issue.[77] The focus here, alternatively, is upon the development of feed-in tariffs—that is, guaranteed payments for quantities of renewable electricity.

In the evolving debate in Ontario, we jump to the year 2004. Spurred by the level of attention being given to a new debate about feed-in tariffs (catalyzed, in significant part, by the Ontario Sustainable Energy Association, a provincial nongovernmental organization), the Ontario Government commissioned a report on the issue towards the end of that year.[78] This report was received in May 2005, and the government made it public in August 2005. At that time, the Ontario Minister of Energy indicated his commitment to feed-in tariffs (which were now being called, in proposed government action, 'standard offer contracts') and instructed the Ontario Power Authority—a governmental body designed to advance planning in the province's electricity sector—to develop further details regarding price and potential generator access to the grid. Stakeholders were consulted during this process. On 21 March 2006, the Government announced the following policy: the government would develop legislation which meant that generators of small-scale renewable electricity generators (in this case, defined as less than 10 MW and powered by wind, solar photovoltaic, thermal electric solar, renewable biomass, biogas, biofuel, landfill gas, or waterpower and must be located in Ontario) would be able to enter into 20-year contracts with the Ontario Power Authority, selling the electricity they generated back to the Authority at guaranteed prices. These prices were C$0.11 per kWh for most technologies, though C$0.42 per kWh for solar electricity; a C$0.0352 per kWh premium was also offered to projects that demonstrate that they can operate reliably during peak demand periods.[79]

Amendments to electricity rules in the province to facilitate the execution of standard offer contracts were made by the Ontario Energy Board later in 2006, and the program was launched on 22 November 2006. By November 2008, the Ontario Power Authority had on its books 1,413 MW of capacity under contract. This was divided amongst wind (90 contracts accounting for 53 per cent of capacity), solar-photovoltaics (279 contracts with 37 per cent of capacity), bio-energy (21 contracts with 5 per cent of capacity), and water power (20 contracts with 5 per cent of capacity). Another 22 applications were, at that time, in process.[80]

It is widely accepted that the program has exceeded all expectations. As noted by the Ontario Power Authority (OPA) itself: 'The program achieved more than 1,300 MW of contracted projects in a little more than a year. When the Renewable Energy SOP was launched in 2006, it was expected to develop 1,000 MW over 10 years.'[81] This encouraged a series of changes in May 2008. First, notwithstanding the comments above about uptake, there was still a significant misfit between the number of contracts signed and the number of 'shovels in the ground' (i.e., projects actually reaching operation). Of the 410 contracts agreed to, less than one-half (147) had reached operation by November 2008. The uptake in the solar-photovoltaics area was particularly slow: more than one-third of contracts agreed were in operation, but together they represented less than two per cent of committed capacity. While this indicates that small-scale systems (often in the neighbourhood of 3 kW) were being encouraged—thus being quite true to the intention of many feed-in tariff systems—there was a concern that the unfulfilled contracts were in fact 'filling up' the available transmission capacity for such projects. Therefore, the OPA introduced a new requirement that projects must meet certain interim project deadlines. The OPA argued that this 'will enable other project developers to move ahead in the standard offer program in order to get new renewable generation online more quickly'.[82]

Conclusions

The purpose of this chapter has been to review the means whereby provinces have attempted to promote the use of renewable resources in their respective electricity supply systems. Our review has revealed that a number of different strategies are in operation across Canada. In a number of provinces, particularly those dominated by large-scale hydropower resources and with modest experience of electricity industry restructuring, governments have produced targets (often resource-specific, with a focus upon wind power) that have then been implemented by utilities through request for proposals procedures. This has sometimes been under the auspices of a renewable portfolio standard banner, though the presence of a dominant utility nevertheless meant that the actual strategy was still quite similar to what has often been called a request for proposal approach. Others have focused attention away from supply to the grid, and instead turned to consumer demand, with green power marketing and/or feed-in tariffs playing a role in some Canadian provinces.

How does this activity across Canada compare to global standards and benchmarks, both in terms of levels of renewable electricity activity on the ground and innovation with respect to renewable electricity policies? Regarding the former, let us consider two of the most popular 'new' renewables: wind and solar-photovoltaics. With respect to wind, at the end of 2007 the World Wind Energy Association reported that Canada had 1,846 MW of capacity installed. This represented just under two per cent of global capacity, and ranked Canada eleventh in the world.[83] As a point of reference, note that, in terms of total electricity production, the 628 TWh we generated in 2005 represented 3.4 per cent of global generation, and ranked us sixth.[84] Turning to solar-photovoltaics, the International Energy Agency reported that installed capacity in Canada was 20.5 MW in 2006. This represented less than 0.4 per cent of the installed capacity reported by 20 IEA countries; the country ranked eleventh of these 20 countries.[85] These two figures suggest, therefore, that we are lagging behind with respect to the deployment of renewable electricity.

Turning to policies, although they were somewhat 'slow starting', Canadian provinces have, collectively (as this review has revealed), begun to experiment with the range of renewable electricity policies currently being pursued worldwide. Reference to global reviews suggest the same.[86] Moreover, recalling the importance of 'integration' identified at the outset of this chapter, there are instances of innovation that are particularly noteworthy. Efforts to integrate multiple goals in policy (for example, economic development and electricity performance, as evidenced in the hydropower jurisdictions' efforts with requests for proposals), while difficult, are certainly laudable. These efforts have the potential to invigorate public debate and to integrate goals across traditional sectors, as desires to advance sustainability would seem to require. The introduction of a feed-in tariff in Ontario, moreover, was practically 'revolutionary' in a North American context, breaking, as it did, the grip on policy discourse that the renewable portfolio standard appeared to hold on the continent until approximately 2006. Moreover, experiments to develop, concurrently, different kinds of policy strategies—Ontario's multiple-track approach was highlighted earlier in this chapter; Prince Edward Island's consideration of a renewable portfolio standard and a feed-in tariff simultaneously is another example—are also to be welcomed. Indeed, one of the conclusions of a major review by the International Energy Agency in 2004 was that 'significant market growth has always resulted from combinations of policies, rather than single policies.'[87] But these have been the exception rather than the rule. For the most part, policies are still relatively new and relatively basic. Of course, with time comes experience, and the ability to reflect upon the pros and cons of past activity, and the preferences for the way forward, will hopefully follow.

Questions for Review

1. What kinds of environmental/sustainability problems have traditionally been associated with electricity systems?
2. What policy strategies show the most promise for encouraging the use of renewables in electricity systems?
3. Why have the provinces varied in their commitments to renewables, as well as in their strategies for encouraging renewables?
4. To what degree can we consider Canadian jurisdictions to be truly innovative in this policy area?

Notes

1. See, for example, José Goldemberg and Thomas B. Johansson, eds, *World Energy Assessment: Overview, 2004 Update* (New York, NY: United Nations, 2004).
2. Ibid.
3. International Energy Agency, 'Electricity/Heat in Canada in 2005', available at http://www.iea.org/Textbase/stats/electricity data.asp?COUNTRY_CODE=CA.
4. Mary Jane Patterson and Ian H. Rowlands, 'Beauty in the Eye of the Beholder: A Comparison of "Green Power" Certification Programs in Australia, Canada, the United Kingdom and the United States', *Energy & Environment* 13, 1 (2002): 1–25.
5. TerraChoice Environmental Marketing, 'CCD-003: Electricity—Renewable Low-impact', available at http://www.ecologo.org/en/seeourcriteria/details.asp?ccd_id=228.
6. International Energy Agency, 'Electricity/Heat in Canada in 2005'.
7. See, for example, Volkmar Lauber, 'REFIT and RPS: Options for a Harmonised Community Framework', *Energy Policy* 32 (2004): 1405–14; David Toke, 'Renewable Financial Support Systems and Cost-Effectiveness', *Journal of Cleaner Production* 15 (2007): 280–87; Wilson Rickerson and Robert C. Grove, 'The Debate over Fixed Price Incentives for Renewable Electricity in Europe and the United States: Fallout and Future Directions' (Washington, DC: The Heinrich Böll Foundation, February 2007).
8. Ian H. Rowlands, 'Envisaging Feed-in Tariffs for Photovoltaic Electricity: European Lessons for Canada', *Renewable & Sustainable Energy Reviews* 9, 1 (2005): 51–68.
9. Ole Langniss and Ryan Wiser, 'The Renewables Portfolio Standard in Texas: An Early Assessment', *Energy Policy* 31, 6 (2003): 527–35.
10. Catherine Mitchell, 'The Renewables NFFO: A Review', *Energy Policy* 23, 12 (1995): 1077–91.
11. See, for example, Reinhard Haas, *Review Report on Promotion Strategies for Electricity Renewable Energy Sources in EU Countries* (Vienna: Institute of Energy Economics, Vienna University of Technology, 2001); International Energy Agency,

'Global Renewable Energy Policies and Measures Database', available at http://www.iea.org/textbase/pm/grindex.aspx; N.H. van der Linden et al, *Review of International Experience with Renewable Energy Obligation Support Mechanisms* (Petten, The Netherlands: ECN Netherlands, ECN-C-05-025, May 2005).

12. David G. Duff and Andrew J. Green, 'A Comparative Evaluation of Different Policies to Promote the Generation of Electricity from Renewable Sources', in Steven Bernstein, Jutta Brunnée, David G. Duff, and Andrew J. Green, eds, *A Globally Integrated Climate Policy for Canada* (Toronto, ON: University of Toronto Press, 2008), 223–8.

13. Judith Lipp, 'Renewable Energy Policies and the Provinces', in G. Bruce Doern, ed., *Innovation, Science, Environment: Canadian Policies and Performance, 2007–2008* (Montreal, QC: McGill-Queen's University Press, 2007), 179–83.

14. For a broader consideration of the federal level, see, for example, Mark S. Winfield with Clare Demerse and Johanne Whitmore, 'Climate Change and Canadian Energy Policy', in Steven Bernstein, Jutta Brunnée, David G. Duff, and Andrew J. Green, eds, *A Globally Integrated Climate Policy for Canada* (Toronto, ON: University of Toronto Press, 2008), 261–63. While with respect to municipal policies, note that while two Canadian cities (Toronto and Vancouver) were listed in a global review of 33 'selected cities with renewable energy goals and/or policies', neither had a 'renewable energy goal', or a 'policy for solar PV' (REN21, *Renewables 2007: Global Status Report* (Paris: Renewable Energy Policy Network for the 21st Century [Secretariat], 2008), 30.

15. Ian H. Rowlands, 'The Development of Renewable Electricity Policy in the Province of Ontario: The Influence of Ideas and Timing', *Review of Policy Research* 24, 3 (2007): 185–207.

16. Government of Manitoba, 'Winds of Opportunity—Clean Power for Manitoba's Future', available at http://www.gov.mb.ca/stem/energy/wind/files/winds_of_opportunity.pdf, p.2.

17. Government of Manitoba, 'Energy Minister Announces New Step in Plan to Further Harvest Manitoba's Wind-Power Potential', available at http://www.gov.mb.ca/chc/press/top/2005/11/2005-11-21-01.html; 'Green and Growing: Building a Green and Prosperous Future for Manitoba Families', available at http://www.gov.mb.ca/greenandgrowing/.

18. Government of Manitoba, 'Energy Minister Announces Next Step in Plan to Further Harvest Manitoba's Wind-Power Potential', available at http://www.gov.mb.ca/chc/press/top/2005/11/2005-11-21-01.html.

19. Government of Manitoba, 'Next Phase of Manitoba Wind Strategy to Power 100,000 Homes: Chomiak', available at http://www.gov.mb.ca/chc/press/top/2006/09/2006-09-07-02.html.

20. Government of Manitoba, 'Provinces Calls for New Projects to Advance Manitoba's Wind Development Strategy', available at http://www.gov.mb.ca/chc/press/top/2007/03/2007-03-30-130500-1395.html.

21. Manitoba Hydro, 'Manitoba Hydro Receives Wind Proposals', available at http://www.hydro.mb.ca/news/releases/news_07_07_30.shtml.

22. Manitoba Hydro, 'Potential Purchase of Output from Manitoba Wind Powered Electrical Generation Facilities', available at http://www.hydro.mb.ca/regulatory_affairs/pdf/electric/information_requests/round2/Appendix_59-RFP025089_(2007_03_31)_Final.pdf.

23. Manitoba Hydro, 'Wind Request Moves to Next Stage', available at http://www.hydro.mb.ca/news/releases/news_07_12_14.1.shtml.

24. Manitoba Hydro, 'Manitoba Hydro Progresses in Evaluation of Wind Energy Proposals', available at https://www.hydro.mb.ca/news/releases/news_08_03_31.shtml.

25. Government of Manitoba, 'Province Calls for New Projects to Advance Manitoba's Wind Development Strategy', available at http://news.gov.mb.ca/news/index.html?archive=&item=1395.

26. *Global Power Report*, 'Hydro Québec Distribution Issues RFP for 1,000 MW of Wind Energy from 2006', 15 May 2003, 16.

27. *Global Power Report*, 'Cartier Wind Joint Venture, Northland Power Win in Solicitation to Supply 1,000 MW to HQD', 7 October 2004, 19.

28. *Platts Electric Utility Week*, 'Hydro-Québec Picks Winners for 740 MW of Wind Power, Seeks Additional Capacity', 11 October 2004.

29. *Platts Commodity News*, 'PLATTS – Hydro-Québec Issues RFP for 2,000 MW of Wind Power in Province', 31 October 2005.

30. Hydro-Québec, 'Second Call for Tenders', available at http://www.hydroQuébec.com/learning/eolienne/pop_appel_2.html.

31. Reuters, 'Hydro-Québec Gets Rush of Wind-Power Proposals', 20 September 2007.

32. Hydro-Québec, 'Tender Call for 2,000 MW of Wind Power: Hydro-Québec Accepts 15 Bids', available at http://www.hydroQuébec.com/4d_includes/of_interest/PcAN2008-053.htm.

33. Government of Québec, *Using Energy to Build the Québec of Tomorrow: Québec Energy Strategy 2006–2015* (Québec City, 2006).

34. Government of Newfoundland and Labrador, 'Electricity Policy Review', available at http://www.nr.gov.nl.ca/mines&en/industry/policyreview.

35. Newfoundland and Labrador Hydro, 'Newfoundland and Labrador Hydro Announces 25 MW Wind Generation RFP', available at http://www.nlh.nl.ca/hydroweb/newsarchive.nsf/NewsArchive/26D934E246CBC063A325710100682085.

36. Government of Newfoundland and Labrador , 'Newfoundland and Labrador Hydro Announces Outcome of Wind Generation Request for Proposals', available at http://www.releases.gov.nl.ca/releases/2006/nr/1002n07.htm.

37. Newfoundland and Labrador Hydro, 'Hydro Announces it will Issue a Second RFP for Additional Wind Power', available at http://www.nlh.nl.ca/hydroweb/newsarchive.nsf/NewsArchive/0E6E4FA8CA29C68EA32571FB005AEB01.

38. Newfoundland and Labrador Hydro, 'Hydro Signs Power Purchase Agreement for Fermeuse Wind Project', available at http://www.nlh.nl.ca/hydroweb/newsarchive.nsf/NewsArchive/A7D7D61C15A64B09A32573AF00572DD6.

39. Government of Newfoundland and Labrador, *Focusing our Energy: Newfoundland and Labrador Energy Plan* (St. John's, NL, 2007).

40. *Strategic Considerations for a New British Columbia Energy Policy: Final Report of the Task Force on Energy Policy*, 15 March 2002, 26.

41. *Energy for our Future: A Plan for BC* (Victoria, BC: Government of British Columbia, 2002), 36.

42. BC Hydro, '2002/03 Green Power Generation', available at http://www.bchydro.com/info/ipp/ipp958.html.

43. Government of British Columbia, 'Report Released on Sustainable Energy Opportunities', http://www.em.gov.bc.ca/AlternativeEnergy/AEPT_report.pdf.

44. Government of British Columbia, *The BC Energy Plan*, available at http://www.energyplan.gov.bc.ca.

45. BC Hydro, 'Clean Power Call', available at https://www.bchydro.com/rx_files/info/info57130.pdf.

46. Government of Saskatchewan, 'SaskPower Media Fact Sheet', available at http://www.gov.sk.ca/news-archive/2003/10/02-740-attachment.pdf.

47. Government of Saskatchewan, 'Sustainable and Renewable Electricity Sources Will Power Saskatchewan's Future', available at http://www.gov.sk.ca/news?newsId=4b28f4d5-a6ba-4c6f-81c9-94058f3990e7.

48. Ibid.

49. SaskPower, 'SaskPower Issues Request for Proposal for Environmentally Preferred Power Generation', available at http://www.saskpower.com/aboutus/news/?p=163#more-163.

50. SaskPower, 'First Year Projects Selected For Environmentally Preferred Power Generation', available at http://www.saskpower.com/aboutus/news/?p=126#more-126.

51. SaskPower, 'Call for Request for Proposals for Environmentally Preferred Power', available at http://www.saskpower.com/aboutus/news/?p=91#more-91.

52. SaskPower, 'Second Phase Projects Selected for Environmentally Preferred Power Program', available at http://www.saskpower.com/aboutus/news/?p=40#more-40.

53. Government of Saskatchewan, 'Sustainable and Renewable Electricity Sources'.

54. *Renewable Energy Report*, 'Saskatchewan Sketches Plan to Secure 30% Renewable Power Generation by '20', Issue 139, 1 October 2007.

55. *Electricity in New Brunswick Beyond 2000, Discussion Paper* (Fredericton, NB: Government of New Brunswick, February 1998), 12.

56. *Electricity in New Brunswick and Options for its Future, Special Task Force* (Fredericton, NB: Government of New Brunswick, July 1998), 6.

57. Legislative Assembly of New Brunswick, 'Change Issues', available at http://www.gnb.ca/legis/business/committees/previous/reports-e/electricityfuture/change-e.asp.

58. Legislative Assembly of New Brunswick, 'Summary of Options', available at http://www.gnb.ca/legis/business/committees/previous/reports-e/electricityfuture/summary-e.asp.

59. *Report of the Select Committee on Energy: Electricity Restructuring in New Brunswick*, Fourth Session, 53rd Legislative Assembly of the Province of New Brunswick, May 1999, 24.

60. Ibid., 24.

61. *White Paper: New Brunswick Energy Policy* (Fredericton, NB: Government of New Brunswick, 2001), 59.

62. New Brunswick Market Design Committee, *Final Report* (Fredericton, NB: Government of New Brunswick, April 2002), 64.

63. Government of New Brunswick, 'Electricity from Renewable Resources Regulation—Electricity Act', available at http://www.gnb.ca/0062/PDF-regs/2006-58.pdf.

64. *Seizing the Opportunity: Nova Scotia's Energy Strategy, Volume 1* (Halifax, NS: Government of Nova Scotia, 2001), 6.

65. Ibid., 29.

66. *Electricity Marketplace Governance Committee, Final Report* (Halifax, NS: Government of Nova Scotia, 2003), 62–71.

67. Government of Nova Scotia, 'Electricity Act', available at http://www.gov.ns.ca/legislature/legc/bills/59th_1st/3rd_read/b087.htm.

68. Government of Nova Scotia, 'Reneawble Energy Standard Regulations', available at http://www.gov.ns.ca/just/regulations/regs/erenew.htm.

69. *Prince Edward Island, Renewable Energy Strategy, Public Discussion Document* (Charlottetown: PEI Energy Corporation, June 2003), 15.

70. *Energy Framework and Renewable Energy Strategy* (Charlottetown: Government of Prince Edward Island, Department of Environment and Energy, June 2004), 9.

71. Ibid., 15.

72. Government of Prince Edward Island, 'Renewable Energy Act Proclaimed and Regulations Passed', available at http://www.gov.pe.ca/news/getrelease.php3?number=4419.

73. *Albertans & Climate Change: Taking Action* (Edmonton, AB: Government of Alberta, Alberta Environment, 2002), 3.

74. Alberta Electricity System Operator, 'Guide to Wind Power in Alberta', available at http://www.aeso.ca/downloads/Wind(5LR).pdf.

75. Johanne Whitmore and Matthew Bramley, *Green Power Programs in Canada—2003* (Drayton Valley: Pembina Institute, 2004).

76. Renewable and Alternative Energy Project Team, *Recommendations for a Renewable and Alternative Electrical Energy Framework for Alberta* (Edmonton, AB: Government of Alberta, March 2007).

77. Rowlands, 'The Development of Renewable Electricity Policy in the Province of Ontario'.

78. Material in this paragraph is taken from *ibid*.

79. For more on this development, see Rowlands, 'The Development of Renewable Electricity Policy in the Province of Ontario'.

80. Ontario Power Authority, *A Progress Report on Renewable Energy Standard Offer Program* (Toronto, ON, November 2008).

81. Ontario Power Authority, 'Celebrating Success and Forging Ahead on Renewable Energy', available at http://powerauthority.on.ca/SOP/Page.asp?PageID=924&ContentID=6538.

82. Ibid.

83. World Wind Energy Association, 'Wind Turbines Generate More Than 1% of the Global Electricity' (Bonn: World Wind Energy Association, Press Release, 21 February 2008).

84. IEA, *Key World Energy Statistics* (Paris: International Energy Agency, 2007), 27.

85. IEA, *Trends in Photovoltaic Applications, Survey Report of Selected IEA Countries between 1992 and 2006* (Paris: International Energy Agency, Report IEA-PVPS T1-16:2007, 2007), 4.

86. See, for example, REN21, *Renewables 2007*.

87. IEA, Renewable Energy Market and Policy Trends in IEA Countries, quoted in REN21, *Renewables 2007*, 21.

13

From Old to New Dynamics in Canadian Forest Policy: Dynamics Without Change?

Michael Howlett, Jeremy Rayner, and Chris Tollefson[1]

Throughout much of the last two decades, forest policy discourse across Canada was dominated by a noisy clash between the defenders of traditional 'command-and-control' regulation and proponents of a new approach to governance more reliant on voluntary, community, and market instruments to secure the goals of sustainable forest management.[2] This struggle took place in the context of a range of challenges to the Canadian forest sector. Some of the challenges were very familiar ones—modernization of plants, job loss, global competition, and boom and bust conditions linked to the rise and fall of the US housing market—but others were decidedly novel, such as climate change, the mountain pine beetle epidemic, and uncertainty surrounding the implications of Aboriginal rights and title decisions.

In the wake of these challenges came some significant changes in forest policy discourse, associated especially with the rise of new community-based actors challenging existing professional experts employed by industry and government. The arrival of new actors has helped open up what had once been a rather closed forest policy community, dominated by the state and its corporate licensees joined by a shared discourse of professional forest management for timber production.[3] Prominent among the newcomers were First Nations, buoyed by a series of legal victories affirming their aboriginal rights and title over public or Crown forest in BC and the Maritimes. But there was also a broad coalition of other new actors involved in forest certification programs, including members of the scientific community concerned with issues such as global warming and the potential role of forests in climate change mitigation and adaptation strategies.[4]

The incorporation of these new actors necessarily brought with it a more widespread acceptance of new values and approaches in forest policy discourse, as the sustainable forest management (SFM) planning paradigm, long dominant within international negotiations on resources and the environment,[5] was increasingly integrated into existing Canadian federal and provincial forest policy regimes. This integration process occurred through a variety of vehicles—including the National Forest Strategy (NFS), Corporate Social Responsibility (CSR) and the forest certification movements—thereby consolidating the idea that the central goal of SFM is a more holistic approach to managing forests in order to produce a wide range of values beyond wood fiber, underpinned by a commitment to maintaining ecosystem integrity.

It soon became clear that SFM discourse carried with it a powerful impetus towards new forest governance arrangements, to be achieved through a variety of state and non-state means including new policy mixes and new institutional configurations.[6] However, while political, administrative, and policy discourses are significant elements of governance arrangements and of transitions in governance modes, new discourses will constantly 'bump-up' against the existence of old institutional orders and political power arrangements present in existing governance arrangements, limiting their impact and influence on governance change. Thus, the last decade has seen a series of experiments in the provinces with new on-the-ground mixes of policy tools and instruments used to formulate and implement forest policy. In many jurisdictions, traditional prescriptive regulation and direct subsidies came to be accompanied by experiments involving performance standards, incentives, codes of conduct, certificates, and various kinds of procedural instruments, including intensive local and regional planning efforts and consultative and participatory policy-making efforts.[7] By no means were all of these experiments considered successful and, to add to the confusion, many of them were subsequently reversed and a renewed emphasis on market and economic instruments (re)emerged.[8]

Even so, several features of forest policy development are suggestive of an often mooted wider shift from a 'government' to 'governance' orientation in resource and environmental policy-making in general,[9] and forest policy, specifically.[10] However, exactly what is meant by a new governance orientation, whether the shift towards a governance orientation has actually taken place, and if it has contributed or not to the achievement of environmental goals in forestry are all open questions that form the subject of this chapter.

From Government to Governance: Defining Governance and Governance Change

Governments govern, that is, they control the allocation of resources between social actors; provide a set of rules and operate a set of institutions setting out 'who gets what, where, when, and how' in society; and manage the symbolic resources that are the basis of legitimacy. Governing thus involves the establishment of a basic set of relationships between governments and their citizens which can vary from highly structured and controlled to arrangements that are monitored only loosely and informally, if at all. Thus, in its broadest sense, 'governance' is a term used to describe the *mode* of government coordination exercised by state actors in their effort to solve familiar problems of collective action and legitimation inherent to government and governing.[11] Governance is about establishing, promoting, and supporting a specific type of relationship between governmental and non-governmental actors in the governing process.

However, part of the problem of conceptualizing any possible shift from government to governance in any particular sector of government activity is the multi-dimensional character of governance itself. The general idea of a move from a state that directs social actors by means of hierarchical, imperative coordination to one that is engaged in steering loose networks of state and non-state actors through reflexive self-organization ('plurilateralism') is basic to the shift from governing to governance.[12] Nonetheless, comparative studies of governance shifts around the world have revealed that a whole variety of institutional arrangements, coordination mechanisms, and modes of regulation have emerged in response to local conditions. In general, we would, first, expect institutional arrangements to move from relatively formal, top-down coordination rules towards more informal and ambiguous arrangements subject to continuous renegotiation. Second, explanations of how such arrangements operate in practice have often appealed to the relative policy capacities of public and private actors who now have to work together in the absence of hierarchy. In the forest policy context, it is important to bear in mind that this balance has often been decisively shifted in favour of private actors—both corporate and NGO—by the internationalization of policy domains that were once treated as a matter of purely domestic policy-making. Finally, without hierarchy, 'hard' legal arrangements that depend on a recognition of the state's right to legislate and regulate within its sphere of competence are likely to be replaced by 'soft law' arrangements where actors enforce their own codes of conduct based on trust and reputation.

So much for the theory. In the real world, a great deal of the complexity and 'messiness' of observable governance shifts stems from the fact that developments appear not to take place in lock-step along these three dimensions of governance. Institutional arrangements may be pushed quite far towards informality by governments themselves in the expectation that non-state policy-making capacity will emerge in due course and without complete reliance on soft law. The result is a fairly common set of arrangements identified as 'governance in the shadow of hierarchy'. On the other hand, governments may fight the development of emergent non-state capacity, hanging on to formal institutions that are increasingly 'hollowed out' by the actual practice of policy-making and implementation that now takes place in networks that are not given any official recognition. The outcome of such battles often depends on whether the state can create new alliances with non-state actors who are prepared to support state direction of policy networks.

Conceptualizing Modes of Governance

To assess whether a shift from government to governance has occurred in forest policy and with what effect, it is necessary to reduce the complexity described in the previous section. While many permutations and combinations of possible governance arrangements exist,[13] recent studies have focused on four basic, or 'ideal', types found in many jurisdictions and sectors in liberal democratic states. These are the legal, corporatist, market, and network governance forms.[14] Each mode (see Figure 13.1 below) has a different focus, form of control, aim, and preferred service delivery mechanism and procedural policy orientation.

In terms of the discussion of governance shifts in the previous section, legal and market governance will tend towards the 'hard' and 'formal' kinds of arrangements. While this is obvious for legal governance it may seem counterintuitive for market governance, but only if we overlook the considerable formal underpinning of property rights, the enforcement of contracts, and regulatory standard-setting that markets require to operate successfully. Markets, however, clearly involve more pluralateralism than legal governance, a feature that they share with networks and which distinguishes them from corporate governance with its focus on planning and predictability. These relationships are summarized in Figure 13.2.

In this simplified model, the 'new' governance represents a shift towards network governance and away from both the legal forms associated with classic nineteenth-century government and the corporatist and market models familiar to many countries and sectors in the twentieth century, including Canadian forest policy.

Many authors have suggested that network governance emerged from a distinct historical trajectory that began with the 'crisis of command and control' in its mid-twentieth century form of the public provision of goods and services and the detailed, prescriptive regulation of markets, and ends with network steering.[15] However, as Box 13.3 suggests, there are other possible trajectories,

Mode of Governance	Central Focus of Governance Activity	Form of State Control of Governance Relationships	Overall Governance Aim	Prime Service Delivery Mechanism	Key Procedural Tool for Policy Implementation
Legal Governance	Legality: Promotion of law and order in social relationships	Legislation, Law and Rules	Legitimacy: Voluntary Compliance	Rights: Property, Civil, and Human	Courts and Litigation
Corporatist Governance	Management of Major Organized Social Actors	Plans	Controlled and Balanced Rates of Socio-economic Development	Targets: Operational Objectives	Specialized and Privileged Advisory Committees
Market Governance	Competition: Promotion of Small- and Medium-sized Enterprises	Contracts and Regulations	Resource/Cost Efficiency and Control	Prices: Controlling for Externalities, Supply, and Demand	Regulatory Boards, Tribunals, and Commissions
Network Governance	Relationships: Promotion of Inter-actor Organizational Activity	Collaboration	Co-Optation of Dissent and Self-Organization of Social Actors	Networks of Governmental, and Non-Governmental Organizations	Subsides and Expenditures on Network Brokerage Activities

Figure 13.1 Modes of Governance

Source: Modified from Considine, M. 2001. *Enterprising States: The Public Management of Welfare-to-Work.* Cambridge: Cambridge University Press; English, L.M., Skellern, M. 2005. 'Public-Private Partnerships and Public Sector Management Reform; A Comparative Analysis', *International Journal of Public Policy* 1(1/2): 1–21.

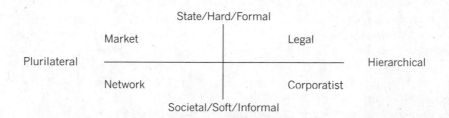

Figure 13.2 Governance Space and Mode

including arriving at network governance via experiments with market or corporatist arrangements or failing to shift out of the other quadrant at all. Many of these trajectories have been clearly visible in environmental and natural resource policy over the past two decades, including the initial promotion of market governance in the waves of privatization and de-regulation, contracting out and other activities associated with the 'new public management' (NPM) ethos of the late twentieth century,[16] and, after negative experiences with privatization, a move to re-regulation relying on old legal and planning policy instruments.[17]

A shift to a new mode of governance, in the sense of network governance, thus represents only one alternative to the other possible forms of coordination. Whether such a shift has actually taken place in Canadian forest policy and exactly what it would look like, however, remain open, empirical questions. Our aim in the remainder of the chapter is to examine these questions more closely by looking at the specific kinds of new forest governance experiments that have taken place at both the federal and provincial levels under the impetus of SFM discourse and their outcomes. Predictably, the record will show that the governance shift is not a simple movement from law to networks. Instead, an altogether more complex and tentative series of movements and counter-movements can be observed.

From Government to Governance in Canadian Forest Policy?

What are we looking for? Neil Gunningham has defined 'new governance' in the resource and environmental areas succinctly as:

> . . . involving a cluster of characteristics: participatory dialogue and deliberation, devolved decision-making, flexibility rather than uniformity, inclusiveness, transparency, institutionalized consensus-building practices, and a shift from hierarchy to heterarchy. Not all these characteristics need to be present for a particular experiment to be regarded as involving new environmental governance, but the more characteristics that are present, the greater is the claim as falling within this category.[18]

In what follows, we examine the record of policy initiatives at both the federal and provincial levels in Canada for evidence of the appearance of this cluster of characteristics in the area of forest policy. In addition, on the basis of our analysis in the preceding sections, we will carefully distinguish between the claim that a particular cluster is a network governance initiative and evidence that it is better characterized as market or corporatist governance instead.

Constitutionally, the federal government has only a limited ability to influence Canadian forest policy-making and the pattern of federal government involvement has generally been one of episodic interest followed by swift retrenchment in the face of provincial hostility.[19] Consequently, forest policy-making in Canada has occurred largely at the provincial level. Although left to their own devices when it came to forest policy and legislation, the major forest-owning provinces exhibited substantial policy convergence in the second half of the twentieth century. The existence of this sphere of activity within a multi-level governance setting makes the situation more complex than is often the case, but also provides more examples and cases to be gleaned for evidence of transitions in governance.[20]

The Federal Government

The favoured policy instrument used to implement forest policy in all Canadian provincial jurisdictions has been the 'evergreen' tenure, essentially a lease over a large area of public forest for 15–25 years, often with the construction and operation of a manufacturing facility ('appurtenances') as a condition of tenure, and carrying with it various management requirements which are assessed when monitoring and renewing the licence. For much of the 1970s and 1980s, the Canadian forest policy community would have described the gradual extension of this kind of tenure and management arrangement as a strategy of sustainable forest management, pointing out both the incentives for licencees to take a long-term view of their responsibilities for reforestation and the increasingly strict management requirements to protect other forest values.[21] In fact, the main strategic direction was one of managing forests for sustained commercial timber production. The controversies that this policy generated were largely technical ones, concerned with how to plan and manage forests and the forest industry to ensure a smooth transition from cutting the old forest to cutting second- and third-growth stands with different volume and value characteristics. Discussions were carried on within a relatively closed policy community, where participants recognized and respected each other's technical expertise to address the specific problems at hand.[22] This was classic corporatist governance.

However, while these technical discussions preoccupied provincial governments and their licencees, there were significant changes in public awareness of the ecological, social, and cultural values of forests taking place outside the forest policy community. In retrospect, it is easy to see that such changes posed a major challenge to the closed, expert forest policy regime.[23] With public forests already substantially committed to timber production for the decades ahead and investment decisions already made on this basis, demands to change forestry practices in ways that reduced timber volumes or, worse, set aside substantially more protected areas were essentially redistributive in their impact. Whatever happened, there would be winners and losers.

At the time, however, the closed policy communities in the major timber producing provinces were blindsided by the intensity of opposition to business-as-usual. The standard response—a paternalistic statement that opponents were arguing from a position of scientific ignorance and would quickly come around once they were educated to the realities of modern commercial forest management—got nowhere. At the outset, both sides dug in their heels and there were some dramatic confrontations in forests across Canada. Because Canada is particularly vulnerable to changes in international public opinion about forest practices—especially in the crucial US market on which Canadian companies are so dependent—these confrontations quickly spilled over into the international arena. The first international boycotts organized by environmentalists and aimed at Canadian forest products were a most unpleasant reminder of the industry's exposed position.[24]

As a result, by the early 1990s the Canadian forest policy community had begun to embrace the emerging ideas of sustainable development and recognized Sustainable Forest Management (SFM) as an idea whose time had come. These ideas promised a comprehensive reframing of forest policy debates, a new policy paradigm capable of breaking out of the impasse that pitted management against preservation in a zero sum game. Implementing the new paradigm demanded a much more participatory style of planning and management, a substantial shift from the closed, expert networks that had only recently been organized at the provincial level around the issues of timber supply and industry modernization. It also required addressing the perception that Canada was trading unfairly in international forest products markets on a foundation of unsustainable forest management arrangements.

Both requirements revealed the drawbacks of the existing legal and institutional arrangements for forest policy in Canada. International affairs, for example, lay squarely within federal jurisdiction, while public consultation over licensing fell clearly into exclusive provincial legal territory. The glare of international publicity raised issues of Canadian practice that demanded a coordinated response from both levels of government, but these operated within the confines of a closed and fragmented forest policy community.

As a result, the federal government sought a role for itself as the 'coordinator' of provincial policies in order to comply with international forest and sustainable development initiatives. In this process, the National Forest Strategy documents, periodically negotiated between federal and provincial governments since 1906, were to become critical components of this joint effort at mutual reinvention (see Figure 13.3 below).[25]

As this figure shows, the federal government has moved some distance from 'old' to 'new' governance over this close to 22-year time period. Moreover, at each iteration of the NFS, the process became more participatory and, until NGOs became disenchanted with the Strategies, inclusive. Towards the end of the series, there were also serious efforts at tracking progress and imposing accountability.

However, it must be recalled that the efforts of the federal government in this sector do not translate immediately into on-the-ground changes in forest policy or outcomes because of the virtually exclusive provincial jurisdiction over this area.[26] While the federal government did at least try to address the implementation deficits that rapidly became apparent, improving reporting and

1981	1987	1992	1998	2003
Wood Supply	Forest management	Forest ecosystems Forest management	Forest ecosystems Forest management	Ecosystem-based management
Markets and Market Opportunities	Trade and investment	Forest industry Global forests	Forest industry Global view	Forest products benefits
Human Resources	Employment	Forest communities	Forest communities	Sustainable forest communities
Research and Development	Research and development	Forest science	Forest science	Knowledge and innovation
	Public awareness	Public participation	Public participation	The urban forest and public engagement
		Aboriginal peoples	Aboriginal peoples	Rights and participation of Aboriginal peoples
		Private woodlots	Private woodlots	Private woodlots
				Reporting and accountability

Figure 2.1 Partisan Origins of the 2006 Green Party Vote

Sources: Canada, *A Forest Sector Strategy for Canada* (Ottawa: Ministry of the Environment, 1981); Canadian Council of Forest Ministers, *Sustainable Forests: A Canadian Commitment: National Forest Strategy 1998–2003—National Forest Congress Version* (Ottawa: Canadian Council of Forest Ministers, 1998); Canadian Council of Forest Ministers, *Sustainable Forests: A Canadian Commitment* (Ottawa: Canadian Council of Forest Ministers 1992); Canadian Council of Forest Ministers, (1987) *A National Forest Sector Strategy for Canada* (Ottawa: Ministry of Supply and Services); National Forest Strategy Coalition, *A Sustainable Forest: The Canadian Commitment: National Forest Sector Strategy, 2003–2008*, Final Version, online at http://nfsc.forest.ca/nfs5.pdf, accessed 23 August 2003.

accountability and shifting responsibility for the NFS from the signatories of the Forest Accords that accompanied each Strategy to an inter-governmental forum, the Canadian Council of Forest Ministers, implementation remains weak. The draft NFS for 2008 attempts to make a virtue out of this particular necessity by positioning itself as a 'vision' document, focusing on only two themes: climate change and the transformation of the forest sector. In stressing its role as the articulator of a vision to enable debate, it is in line with the contemporary 'transition management' approach to network governance[27] but it is very unclear what capacity, if any, the federal government retains to steer the networks that it seeks to create.

The Provinces

The record of the provinces in this area, on the other hand, is quite mixed. The overall situation with 'new governance' initiatives conforming to the cluster characteristics identified by Gunningham is summarized in Box 13.1.[28]

As this record shows, the provinces have had very different histories in this area, ranging from no new governance-type initiatives in Manitoba and Saskatchewan, to crisis-inspired ones in Alberta and BC. In BC licencees, First Nations, and NGOs created a parallel planning process under international pressure which forced a reluctant government to accept the outcome. This is one of the very few examples of a significant shift on all the dimensions of new governance arrangements. Only New Brunswick and Québec seem to have fully engaged with the new spirit of consultation and participation in forest management. The Québec experiment with decentralization is especially significant.

This does not exhaust the types of initiatives undertaken by Canada's 10 provincial governments over this time period, however. Several other initiatives can be classified as 'new–old'—involving new actors but aimed at essentially the same goals as were old governance arrangements. The record of these initiatives is set out in Box 13.2.

Box 13.1 Provincial New Governance Initiatives Post 2000

- More participatory opportunities and capacity building
  - Outcomes of New Brunswick Action Plan (2005)
    - 12 Public Advisory Committees at three levels
    - Enhanced licensee stakeholder committees
  - Quebec – outcomes of Coulombe Commission
    - More decentralization
  - Ontario and Nova Scotia – provincial stakeholder 'Forest Alliances'
  - Alberta – SREM and the Land Use Framework process
- More benchmarking and accountability
  - Provincial involvement in State of the Forest reporting
  - Use of the Montreal Process criteria and indicators (C & I)
- Some tolerance of institutional ambiguity
  - BC Central Coast Land Use Decision
  - New Relationship co-management initiative

Box 13.2 Provincial New–Old Governance Initiatives Post 2000

- Agreements with First Nations on wood supply and production
  - BC agreements with 127 First Nations, including 47 direct tenures
  - Manitoba Treaty Land Entitlement (TLE) process and the Eastside Planning Initiative
  - Nova Scotia and New Brunswick formalize agreements with Mi'kmaq
- Certification
  - NB makes adherence to some certification standard a requirement for all licensees
  - Other provinces provide varying levels of support for licensees to certify their forest management operations
- Use of market instruments to promote sustainability goals
  - Alberta's voluntary ILM agreements
  - Sustainability covenants

As this box shows, most of these initiatives deal with aboriginal forestry and could easily be misconstrued as new governance arrangements because they involve consultations and other types of participation by actors hitherto excluded from forest governance. However, most of these initiatives are predominantly economic development measures aimed at integrating First Nations into a corporatist relationship with government and other licencees and, as such, do not feature the participatory or deliberative characteristics associated with the plurilateral side of the governance space. The continuing influence of the forest certification movement is also evident here. This is particularly true with respect to the growing success of the NGO-sponsored Forest Stewardship Council (FSC) standards in several provinces. In this context, it is important to distinguish between competing certification schemes. For its part, the FSC aspires to and has invested heavily in the development of an ambitiously novel mode of forest governance that departs significantly from prevailing state-centric models. The FSC approach, characterized by some as a pioneering iteration of 'global democratic corporatism',[29] is thus strongly suggestive of a move to network governance. Other schemes (CSA, SFI, etc.), while likewise representing illustrations of what Cashore et al. have termed 'non-state, market driven' governance, are much more closely nested within and aligned with existing governance forms.[30] And, finally, the drive for market-oriented reforms that began in the 1990s continues with efforts to value ecosystem services and allow various kinds of contractual side arrangements between stakeholders, such as Alberta's experiment with voluntary agreements between forest companies and oil and gas companies, which is aimed at improving access management and reducing the footprint of the two industries.

While these by no means exhaust the policy initiatives carried out during this period, most of the rest can be characterized as simply 'business-as-usual' arrangements with private companies, completely congruent with and characteristic of 'old governance' in the forest sector. Though often presented in SFM language, they conform to the mix of legal and corporatist approaches that have characterized provincial forest policy for the last half century. Examples from the provinces are set out in Box 13.3.

As predicted, the record is a very mixed one, with old governance initiatives just as common as new ones during the period under investigation. A significant number of cases where new actors, often First Nations, pursue older objectives of forest management primarily for commodity production add further complexity to the picture.

> **Box 13.3 Provincial Old Governance Initiatives Post 2000**
>
> - Modernize the old timber harvesting regimes
>   - Renewed focus on timber supply and industry competitiveness
>   - Changes to the 'settings' of key instruments (e.g., Annual Allowable Cut)
>   - Further efforts to tighten up audit and oversight of licensees
> - New discourses absorbed into old policy frameworks
>   - Ecosystem based management (EBM)
> - Experiments with new instrument mixes
>   - BC's outcomes-based management and commitment to further deregulation
>   - Continued downsizing and 'restructuring' of ministries and agencies in many provinces

Conclusion

In this chapter, we introduced a two-dimensional framework designed to capture the complexity of the changes involved in shifts among modes of governance. Within this framework, movement along the *horizontal* 'hierarchy' to 'pluralateralism' dimension is also associated with changes along a composite vertical dimension involving the relative formality of institutional arrangements, the balance of power between state and social actors, as well as hard and soft modes of regulation.[31] The quadrants identify unique clusters of governance arrangements that belong to one of four ideal types: legal, corporatist, market, or network governance.

We argued that while, in theory, we might expect developments along one dimension to map neatly onto the other in a simple 'government to governance' transition, in practice, much of the messiness of contemporary forest policy in Canada can be explained by the failure of policy development to move at the same speed, or even in the same direction, along both dimensions. The resulting tensions and incongruencies can sometimes be managed or mitigated but may also eventually set off unpredictable new rounds of policy change.[32] As our inventory of policy changes in the provinces shows, the outcome in most cases was a great deal of policy activity. However, in forest policy, as in so many other policy sectors, there was no smooth transition 'from government to governance'; instead, traditional governing arrangements of top-down regulation co-existed with innovative, untested efforts at shared decision-making, participatory standard-setting, results-based regulation, bottom-up steering, and other kinds of interactive policy processes.[33]

What has been the outcome of all this frenetic activity? In the provinces, particularly those with significant forest industries, the trend has been more towards market rather than network governance. Even if we count certification as a network rather than a market instrument, the tendency towards incentive-based instruments is clear everywhere except New Brunswick, where the growing importance of private forest holdings may provide an explanation. As we have noted, much of what has been taken to be 'new governance' is actually the belated recognition of Aboriginal rights and title and the hasty improvisation of a new level of government to government policy coordination to add to the complex mix of vertical and horizontal coordination that already characterizes the forest policy sector.

At the federal level, there have been attempts to compensate for a lack of both legislative jurisdiction and the ability to provide meaningful incentives by genuine experiments with network governance. The various iterations of the NFS and the Forest Accords that accompany them have certainly provided an important forum for the diffusion of Sustainable Forest Management discourse and for efforts at 'open coordination' through information gathering and dissemination. However, their inability to achieve much in the way of coordination and steering capacity merely casts doubt on whether network governance is really suitable to achieve environmental goals without support from the other modes of governance. .

The overall outcome, then, is a plurality of governance arrangements in which elements of network governance are layered on top of new experiments in market governance, themselves coexisting uneasily with legacies from the era of corporatist planning and legalistic regulation. Thus, while the sector itself has been in almost constant crisis, buffeted by competition and protectionism in its traditional markets and almost always on the defensive with its environmental critics, very little has actually changed on the ground. The situation resembles the health policy case described by Robert Alford more than 30 years ago: dynamics without change.[34] The explanation of this paradoxical outcome is very similar to the one Alford gave for health policy. As has been noted in other policy sectors, the plurality of governance arrangements results in a diffusion of political power that often benefits private actors (both old and new) at the expense of public ones.[35] Many of the key features of the old regulation and subsidy approach to forest policy (for example, centralized control over such important elements of forest production as allowable cuts and land tenure by hierarchical government departments and specialized forest agencies) benefit well-organized interests and are, as a result, deeply entrenched in traditionally closed policy subsectors that have proven highly resistant to change despite developments in other, less critical subsectors.[36] Network governance is unlikely to prove powerful enough to overcome the inertia that such arrangements have generated.

Moreover, on a larger plane, a growing body of empirical research (both in other sectors and other jurisdictions) reflects a well-founded skepticism about the validity of the 'government to governance' hypothesis[37] and its 'new environmental governance' variant. This skepticism has been fueled by the multiplicity of approaches to defining and operationalizing the concept of 'new governance' that have increasingly provoked questions about whether the 'government to governance' hypothesis and the literature on 'new governance' is capable of offering a coherent way of understanding and managing policy change.[38] While we have attempted to provide an operational version of the larger thesis in this chapter, doubts about whether there is anything especially new about new environmental governance and whether it can deliver sustainability in forestry or in any other natural resource and environmental policy sector remain unresolved.[39]

Questions for Review

1. What has been the significance of the new community actors in forest policy discourses and processes?
2. What is meant by the shift from 'government' to 'governance' in Canadian forest policy?
3. What policy instruments have traditionally been used in Canadian forest policy? What are the main alternatives?
4. Of the initiatives taken by provincial governments, which show signs of truly moving toward sustainable forest management?

Notes

1. The authors acknowledge research support from the Sustainable Forest Management Network of Centres of Excellence, and research assistance from Andrea Balogh, Airi Schroff, and Tim Thielmann.

2. C. Tollefson, ed., *The Wealth of Forests: Markets, Regulation and Sustainable Forestry* (Vancouver: UBC Press, 1998); B. Cashore, et al., *In Search of Sustainability: British Columbia Forest Policy in the 1990s* (Vancouver: UBC Press, 2001).

3. J. Wilson, *Talk and Log: Wilderness Politics in British Columbia* (Vancouver: UBC Press, 1998).

4. S. Kamieniecki, 'Testing Alternative Theories of Agenda-Setting: Forest Policy Change in British Columbia', *Policy Studies Journal* 28, 1 (2000): 176–89; M. Howlett, 'Policy Venues, Policy Spillovers and Policy Change: The Courts, Aboriginal Rights and British Columbia Forest Policy', in B. Cashore, G. Hoberg, M. Howlett, J. Rayner, and J. Wilson, eds, *In Search of Sustainability: British Columbia Forest Policy in the 1990s* (Vancouver: UBC Press, 2001), 120–40; B. Cashore, G. Auld, and D. Newsom, 'Forest Certification (Eco-Labeling) Programs and their Policy-Making Authority: Explaining Divergence among North American and European Case Studies', *Forest Policy and Economics* 5 (2003): 225–47.

5. D. Liefferink, 'The Dynamics of Policy Arrangements: Turning Round the Tetrahedron', in B. Arts, and P. Leroy, eds, *Institutional Dynamics in Environmental Governance* (Dordrecht: Springer, 2006), 45–68; D. Humphreys, 'Forest Negotiations at the United Nations: Explaining Cooperation and Discord', *Forest Policy and Economics* 3 (2001): 125–35.

6. M. Howlett and J. Rayner, 'Do Ideas Matter? Policy Subsystem Configurations and the Continuing Conflict Over Canadian Forest Policy', *Canadian Public Administration* 38, 3 (1995): 382–410; M. Howlett and J. Rayner, 'Globalization and Governance Capacity: Explaining Divergence in National Forest Programmes as Instances Of "Next-Generation" Regulation in Canada and Europe', *Governance* 19, 2 (2006): 251–75; T. Michaelson, L. Ljungmann, M.H. El-Lakany, P. Hyttinen, K. Giesen, M. Kaiser, and E. von Zitzewitz, 'Hot Spot in the Field: National Forest Programmes—A New Instrument within Old Conflicts of the Forestry Sector', *Forest Policy and Economics* 1, 1 (2000): 95–106.

7. M. Purdon, 'The Nature of Ecosystem Management: Postmodernism and Plurality in the Sustainable Management of the Boreal Forest', *Environmental Science and Policy* 6 (2003): 377–88; K. Hogl, 'Patterns of Multi-Level Co-Ordination for NFP-Processes: Learning from Problems and Success Stories of European Policy-Making', *Forest Policy and Economics* 4 (2002): 301–12; M. Howlett and J. Rayner, 'Globalization and Governance Capacity: Explaining Divergence in National Forest Programmes as Instances Of "Next-Generation" Regulation in Canada and Europe', *Governance* 19, 2 (2006): 251–75.

8. C. Tollefson, ed., *The Wealth of Forests: Markets, Regulation and Sustainable Forestry* (Vancouver: UBC Press, 1998); B. Cashore, et al., *In Search of Sustainability: British Columbia Forest Policy in the 1990s* (Vancouver: UBC Press, 2001); N. Castree, 'Neoliberalising Nature: The Logics of Deregulation and Reregulation', *Environment and Planning A* 40 (2008): 131–52.

9. A. Jordan, R. Wurzel, and A. Zito, 'New Instruments of Environmental Governance', *Environmental Politics* 12, 3 (2003): 1–24.

10. P. Gluck, J. Rayner, and B. Cashore, 'Change in the Governance of Forest Resources', in G. Mery, R. Alfaro, M. Kanninen, and Labovikov, eds, *Forests in the Global Balance—Changing Paradigms* (Helsinki: IUFRO, 2005), 51–74.

11. R.A.W. Rhodes, 'The New Governance: Governing without Government', *Political Studies* 44 (1996): 652–67; J.A. de Bruijn and E.F.T. Heuvelhof, 'Policy Networks and Governance', in D.L. Weimer, ed., *Institutional Design* (Boston: Kluwer, 1995); J. Kooiman, 'Governance and Governability: Using Complexity, Dynamics and Diversity', in J. Kooiman, ed., *Modern Governance* (London: Sage, 1993), 35–50; J. Kooiman, 'Societal Governance: Levels, Models, and Orders of Social-Political Interaction', in J. Pierre, ed., *Debating Governance* (Oxford: Oxford University Press, 2000), 138–66; E. Klijn, and J. Koppenjan, 'Interactive Decision Making and Representative Democracy: Institutional Collisions and Solutions', in O. van Heffen, W. Kickert, and J. Thomassen, eds, *Governance in Modern Society: Effects, Change and Formation of Government Institutions* (Dordrecht: Kluwer, 2000), 109–34.

12. J. Zielonka, 'Plurilateral Governance in the Enlarged European Union', *Journal of Common Market Studies* 45, 1 (2007): 187–209; P.G. Cerny, 'Plurilateralism: Structural Differentiation and Functional Conflict in the Post-Cold War World Order', *Millenium* 22, 1 (1993): 27–51.

13. K. Van Kersbergen and F. Van Waarden, '"Governance" as a Bridge between Disciplines: Cross-Disciplinary Inspiration Regarding Shifts in Governance and Problems of Governability, Accountability and Legitimacy', *European Journal of Political Research* 43, 2 (2004): 143–72.

14. M. Considine, *Enterprising States: The Public Management of Welfare-to-Work* (Cambridge: Cambridge University Press, 2001); M. Considine and J.M. Lewis, 'Bureaucracy, Network, Or Enterprise? Comparing Models of Governance in Australia, Britain, the Netherlands, and New Zealand', *Public Administration Review* 63, 2 (2003): 131–40.

15. J. Kooiman, 'Governance and Governability: Using Complexity, Dynamics and Diversity', in J. Kooiman, ed., *Modern Governance* (London: Sage, 1993), 35–50; J. Kooiman, 'Societal Governance: Levels, Models, and Orders of Social-Political Interaction', in J. Pierre, ed., *Debating Governance* (Oxford: Oxford University Press, 2000), 138–66; E. Klijn and J. Koppenjan, 'Interactive Decision Making and Representative Democracy: Institutional Collisions and Solutions', in van O. Heffen, W. Kickert, and J. Thomassen, eds, *Governance in Modern Society: Effects, Change and Formation of Government Institutions* (Dordrecht: Kluwer, 2000), 109–34.

16. J. Jordana and D. Levi-Faur, 'The Politics of Regulation in the Age of Governance', in J. Jordana and D. Levi-Faur, eds, *The Politics of Regulation: Institutions and Regulatory Reforms for the Age of Governance* (Cheltenham: Edward Elgar, 2004), 1–28.

17. M. Ramesh and M. Howlett, *Deregulation and its Discontents: Rewriting the Rules in Asia* (Aldershot: Edward Elgar, 2006); A. Hira, D. Huxtable, and A. Leger, 'Deregulation and Participation: An International Survey of Participation in Electricity Regulation', *Governance* 18, 1 (2005): 53–88.

18. N. Gunningham, *The New Collaborative Environmental Governance. International Meeting on Law and Society in the 21st Century* (Berlin: Humboldt University, 2007), 2.

19. M. Howlett, 'The Federal Role in Canadian Forest Policy: From Territorial Landowner to International and Intergovernmental Coordinating Agent', in M. Howlett, ed., *Canadian Forest Policy: Adapting to Change* (Toronto: University of Toronto Press, 2001), 378–418; J.M. Beyers and L. Anders Sandberg, 'Canadian Federal Forest Policy: Present Initiatives and Historical Constraints', in L. Anders Sandberg and S. Sorlin, eds, *Sustainability—The Challenge: People, Power and the Environment* (Montreal: Black Rose Books, 1998), 99–107.

20. M. Lodge and K. Wegrich, 'Governing Multi-Level Governance: Comparing Domain Dynamics in German Land–Local Relationships and Prisons', *Public Administration* 83, 2 (2005): 417–42.

21. B. Cashore, et al., *In Search of Sustainability: British Columbia Forest Policy in the 1990s* (Vancouver: UBC Press, 2001).

22. M. Howlett and J. Rayner, 'The Business and Government Nexus: Principal Elements and Dynamics of the Canadian Forest Policy Regime', in M. Howlett, ed., *Canadian Forest Policy: Adapting to Change* (Toronto: University of Toronto Press, 2001), 23–64.

23. M. Howlett and J. Rayner, 'Do Ideas Matter? Policy Subsystem Configurations and the Continuing Conflict Over Canadian Forest Policy', *Canadian Public Administration* 38, 3 (1995): 382–410.

24. S. Bernstein and B. Cashore, 'Globalization, Four Paths of Internationalization and Domestic Policy Change: The Case of Eco-forestry in British Columbia, Canada', *Canadian Journal of Political Science* 33, 1 (2000): 67–99.

25. J. Simmons, 'Patterns of Process: Understanding the Role of Non-Governmental Actors in the Development of the Canada Forest Accord and the National Forest Sector Strategy 1998–2003'. Paper delivered at the Annual Meetings of the Canadian Political Science Association, Laval University, 2001; M. Howlett, 'The 1987 National Forest Sector Strategy and the Search for a Federal Role in Canadian Forest Policy', *Canadian Public Administration* 32, 4 (1989): 545–63.

26. M. von Mirbach, L. Ellis, and M. Purdon, *Walking the Talk: A Priority Analysis of Canadian Actions in Implementing Intergovernmental Panel on Forests and Intergovernmental Forum on Forests Proposals for Action, with Strategic Priorities for Further Work*. Report prepared for the Canadian Environmental Network Caucus, available at http://www.cen-rce.org/eng/caucuses/forest/docs/unff_1.htm, 2002, retrieved 29 March 2007.

27. R. Kemp and D. Loorbach, 'Transition Management: A Reflexive Governance Approach', in Jan-Peter Voss, Dierk Bauknecht, and Rene Kempeds, *Reflexive Governance for Sustainable Development* (Cheltenham: Edward Elgar, 2006), 103–30; J. Rotmans, Rene Kemp, and Marjolein van Asselt, 'More Evolution Then Revolution: Transition Management in Public Policy', *Foresight* 3, 1 (2001): 15–31.

28. These figures are derived from http://canadaforests.nrcan.gc.ca/news/qc, retrieved 10 March 2008; http://www.fnmr.gov.sk.ca/lands/tle/, retrieved 10 March 2008; http://www.forestindustry.poyry.com/en/index.html; http://www.gnb.ca/0399/provincial_advisory_committee-e.asp; http://www.gnb.ca/0399/scientific_advisory_committee-e.asp; http://www.landuse.gov.ab.ca, retrieved 8 March 2008; http://www.novaforestalliance.com/inside.asp?cmPageID=95; http://www.tlec.ca/, retrieved 8 March 2008; 'Alberta should continue aggressive approach towards mountain pine beetles, committee advises', Government of Alberta News Release, 1 September 2006; *Annual Accountability Report for the Fiscal Year 2000–2001*, Nova Scotia Department of Natural Resources, 11; *Annual Accountability Report for the Fiscal Year 2001–2002*, Nova Scotia Department of Natural Resources, 2; *Annual Accountability Report for the Fiscal Year 2004–2005*, Nova Scotia Department of Natural Resources, 12; *Annual Accountability Report for the Fiscal Year 2006–2007*, Nova Scotia Department of Natural Resources, December 2007, 3; *Annual Report 2000–2001*, Environment, Energy, and Forestry, http://www.gov.pe.ca/af/agweb/index.php3?number=70200; *Annual Report 2003–2004, Manitoba Conservation*, 15; *Annual Report 2005–2006*, Manitoba Conservation, 9; *Annual Report 2006–2007*, Manitoba Conservation, 91; *Annual Report 2006–2007*, Mi'kmaq-Nova Scotia-Canada Tripartite Forum, 1; *Annual Report 2006–2007*, NB DNR, 64; *Bill 71*

(2005, Ch.3)—An Act to Amend the Forest Act and Other Legislative Provisions Applicable to Forest Management Activities, National Assembly, Quebec Official Publisher, 22 March 2005; Five-year Report on the Status of Forestry, April 2001–March 2006, Conservation Ministry Manitoba; Forest Resource Protection and Development Objectives-General Forest Management Plans 2007–2012, Implementation Document, MRNFP, Quebec 2005; Forests—Building a Future for Quebec, Executive Summary, 2008, 3; Forests—Building a Future for Quebec, Quebec Natural Resources, 2008, 60; Mi'Kmaq and Maliseet-New Brunswick Relationship Building/Bilateral Agreement, 8; Minister's Council on Forest Sector Competitiveness Report, May 2005, 1; New Brunswick Crown Forests: Assessment of Stewardship and Management, Jaakko Poyry Consulting, November 2002; Nova Scotia's Code of Forest Practice—A Framework for the Implementation of Sustainable Forest Management, Nova Scotia Natural Resources, 2004; Provincial Sustainable Forest Management Strategy 2003, Department of Forest Resources and Agrifoods, Forest Service of Newfoundland and Labrador, 2, 10; Public Forests: A Valuable Island Resource, Public Forest Council, http://www.gov.pe.ca/envengfor/index.php3?number=71976&lang=E, retrieved 29 February 2008; Rapport de la Commission d'étude sur la gestion de la forêt publique québécoise, online at http://www.mrnfp.gouv.qc.ca/commission-foret/, accessed 30 March 2007; Room to Grow: Final Report of the Ontario Forest Accord Advisory Board on Implementation of the Accord, March 2002, 5; The State of British Columbia's Forests 2006, Ministry of Forests and Range, 94.

29. C. Tollefson, F. Gale, and D. Haley, Setting the Standard: Certification, Governance and the Forest Stewardship Council (Vancouver: UBC Press, 2008).

30. B. Cashore, G. Auld, and D. Newsom, Governing Through Markets. Forest Certification and the Emergence of Non-State Authority (New Haven: Yale University Press, 2004).

31. C. Tollefson, F. Gale, and D. Haley, Setting the Standard: Certification, Governance and the Forest Stewardship Council (Vancouver: UBC Press, 2008).

32. M. Howlett, 'Analyzing Multi-Actor, Multi-Round Public Policy Decision-Making Processes in Government: Findings from Five Canadian Cases', Canadian Journal of Political Science 40, 3 (2007): 659–84; G.R. Teisman, 'Models for Research into Decision-Making Processes: On Phases, Streams and Decision-Making Rounds', Public Administration 78, 4 (2000): 937–56.

33. D. Russell and A. Jordan, 'Gearing-up Governance for Sustainable Development: Patterns of Policy Appraisal in UK Central Government', Journal of Environmental Planning and Management 50, 1 (2007): 1–21.

34. R. Alford, 'The Political Economy of Health Care: Dynamics Without Change', Politics and Society 2 (1972): 127–164.

35. B. Arts, Pieter Leroy, and Jan van Tatenhove, 'Political Modernisation and Policy Arrangements: A Framework for Understanding Environmental Policy Change', Public Organization Review 6, 2 (2006): 93–106; A. Heritier and S. Eckert, 'New Modes of Governance in the Shadow of Hierarchy: Self-Regulation by Industry in Europe', Journal of Public Policy 28, 1 (2008): 113–38.

36. J. Rayner, M. Howlett, J. Wilson, B. Cashore, and J. Hoberg, 'Privileging the Sub-Sector: Critical Sub-Sectors and Sectoral Relationships in Forest Policy-Making', Forest Policy and Economics 2, 3–4 (2001): 319–32.

37. I. Bode, 'Disorganized Welfare Mixes: Voluntary Agencies and New Governance Regimes in Western Europe', Journal of European Social Policy 16, 4 (2006): 346–59; W. Walters, 'Some Critical Notes on "Governance"', Studies in Political Economy 73 (2004): 27–46; L. Hooghe and G. Marks, 'Unraveling the Central State, but How? Types of Multi-Level Governance', American Political Science Review 97, 2 (2003): 233–43.

38. T. Tenbensel, 'Multiple Modes of Governance: Disentangling the Alternatives to Hierarchies and Markets', Public Management Review 7, 2 (2005): 267–88; C.J. Hill, and L.E. Lynn, 'Is Hierarchical Governance in Decline? Evidence from Empirical Research', Journal of Public Administration Research and Theory 15, 2 (2004): 173–95; J. Greenaway, B. Salter, and S. Hart, 'How Policy Networks Can Damage Democratic Health: A Case Study in the Government of Governance', Public Administration 85, 3 (2007): 717–38; E.-H. Klijn and Chris Skelcher, 'Democracy and Governance Networks: Compatible of Not?', Public Administration 85, 3 (2007): 587–608.

39. A. Jordan, 'The Governance of Sustainable Development: Taking Stock and Looking Forwards', Environment and Planning C: Government and Policy 26 (2008): 17–33; P. Berke, J. Crawford, J. Dixon, and N. Ericksen, 'Do Cooperative Environmental Planning Mandates Produce Good Plans? Empirical Results from the New Zealand Experience', Environment and Planning B: Planning and Design 26 (1999): 643–64.

14

The Politics of Extinction: The Birth of Canada's Species At Risk Act

Stewart Elgie[1]

On 11 June 1992, at the Rio Earth Summit, Canada became the first western nation to sign the Convention on Biological Diversity[2]—a landmark treaty meant to protect the Earth's diversity of wild species. At the time, though, Canada had no domestic law to protect endangered species, and no intention of passing such a law. This chapter traces the tumultuous events of the subsequent decade, which resulted in the passage of the federal Species At Risk Act[3] (SARA) in 2002.

The chapter explores these events using two lenses. First, it examines the developmental stages in the policy cycle: agenda-setting, the formulation and introduction of legislation (twice), the Bill's transformation in Parliament (twice), and its eventual passage. Second, the chapter analyzes the main policy drivers that influenced SARA's creation using the three-part analytical framework developed by Cashore et al.,[4] which focuses on the explanatory value of institutions, actors, and ideas in the policy-making process. To this I have added a fourth factor: timing.

The main *institutions* examined are federalism, in terms of the constitutional and political limits it imposes on federal power, and our executive-driven, Westminster-style government. Both were major factors in SARA's development, although their influence was tempered by the unusually strong role played by backbench MPs. The principal *actors* driving the SARA initiative were environmental nongovernmental organizations (ENGOs), with one group, the Sierra Legal Defence Fund, playing a particularly entrepreneurial role. Industry and landowner groups generally played an oppositional role, although some took a surprisingly collaborative approach with ENGOs. Scientists, not normally a political force, also played a critical role.

Of the many *ideas* which influenced SARA, cross-national learning was particularly important; the US experience provided both positive and negative lessons. One of the most interesting aspects of the SARA story is that, in many ways, the timing was bad for a federal environmental law reform initiative: the environment was low in the opinion polls and a low priority for government, the federal–provincial pendulum was swinging in the direction of deference to provinces, and the federal focus on deficit fighting impeded its appetite for any significant new measures. Nevertheless, new endangered species legislation was passed.

Weaving these events and drivers together, the author argues that SARA's history demonstrates the importance of two dominant institutional factors in Canadian environmental policy-making: federalism and executive-driven government. The analysis also shows that actors, through concerted entrepreneurial efforts, can expand the normal policy space provided by these institutions to achieve more ambitious legislative results. It is not easy, however.

The Endangered Species Problem

The extinction of animal and plant species is not a new problem. What is new is the *rate* of extinction in modern times; it is estimated that two to three species every hour become extinct worldwide—at least 1,000 times the 'natural' rate.[5] The bulk of modern extinctions are occurring in the tropics, where most of the Earth's estimated 5–30 million species are found.[6]

Species loss is also an issue in Canada, although the problem is less advanced than in most other parts of the world. Canada's official list of species at risk numbers 565, including 235 that are 'endangered'—the highest category of risk.[7] These numbers understate the problem, however, because less than one per cent of Canada's estimated 280,000 species has been assessed.[8] Preserving species is widely seen as an important policy goal for a number of reasons:

1. *Ecosystem health*: Wild species play a vital role in maintaining the planet's ecological functions—clean air and water, and healthy soils and food chains—which humans depend on for their survival.[9]
2. *Medicine*: Nearly half of the medicine prescribed in North America comes from wild species, yet only a small percentage of the earth's species have been screened to determine their medicinal value.[10]
3. *Recreation and inspiration*: Wildlife viewing is very popular: 1 in 5 Canadians enjoy watching wildlife.[11] It can provide a sense of awe, and remind us of our 'wild' roots.
4. *Identity*: Wild species also play an important role in Canada's national identity; they adorn our currency, artwork, and flags.
5. *Economics*: In 1991, Canadians spent an estimated $8.3 billion on wildlife-related activities, which generated 5.4 billion in government tax revenues and 188,000 jobs.[12]
6. *Ethics*: Many people believe that all species have an inherent right to exist, and that it is immoral for human beings to wipe out other species simply to meet our own desires.[13]

Almost all modern extinctions are caused by human activity, and four factors play particularly important roles.[14] The single greatest cause of species extinction is destruction of habitat. As the prairies are plowed, wetlands are drained, and forests are cut, many resident species are displaced. Habitat loss is a major threat for over 80 per cent of Canada's species at risk.[15] Over-hunting, historically, was the main cause of extinction, leading to the demise of species such as the passenger pigeon. It is still a problem today for some Canadian species at risk, such as the grizzly bear, which is hunted both legally and illegally. Air and water pollution threaten numerous species. For example, toxic contamination of the St Lawrence River poisons beluga whales—in some cases so severely that they must be disposed of as hazardous waste when they die.[16] Another threat already imperiling the polar bear and other Arctic species is climate change. Finally, once introduced into a new ecosystem, foreign species can prey on or out-compete native species. A prime example of this growing problem is the sea lamprey, which has caused the decline of several Great Lakes species.

Policy History, Institutions, and Actors

The history of endangered species legislation (ESL) begins in the United States, where the world's first ESL law was passed in 1968 during the early years of the first 'wave' of environmental concern.[17] The US Endangered Species Act[18] (ESA) was significantly strengthened in 1973 in order to provide mandatory protection for all endangered species and their habitat.

North of the border, Canada's endangered species protection efforts had a slower start. Provinces had the lead role in wildlife management, but only two passed ESL in the 1970s: Ontario (in 1971) and New Brunswick (in 1973). At the federal level, the Canadian Wildlife Service (CWS) was actively involved in endangered species research but played only a limited role in wildlife regulation; it focused mainly on migratory birds (because of a 1916 treaty with the US) and federal protected areas. The federal government showed little interest in following the legislative path of its southern neighbour.[19]

However, the growing public and scientific concern over species loss inspired two major ENGOs to hold a national conference in 1976 on protecting endangered species.[20] The conference led to the 1977 creation of the Committee on the Status of Endangered Wildlife in Canada (COSEWIC), a body made up of wildlife experts from federal and provincial governments and three ENGOs. Its mandate is to identify and list Canada's threatened species.[21] By 1988, COSEWIC had listed over 100 species, and federal and provincial governments decided a new body was needed to develop recovery plans for those species. To this end they created the Recovery of Nationally Endangered Wildlife program (ReNEW).[22] Like COSEWIC, ReNEW had no legal status or power, and its plans were voluntary. Hampered by limited funds and mandate, ReNEW had completed only 18 recovery plans by 2000.[23]

ReNEW was created at the beginning of the second 'wave' of public environmental concern.[24] This period also saw the passage of ESL in two more provinces, Manitoba and Québec, both in 1989. Like the early laws in Ontario and New Brunswick, these statutes were not as extensive or stringent as those in the US. In the two decades since the passage of the US Act, then, Canada had taken a very different policy direction on endangered species, emphasizing two voluntary, nation-wide bodies coordinated by the CWS, buttressed by four provincial laws.

The Birthing of SARA

The Conception

The origin of the push for federal ESL in Canada can be traced to the signing of the Convention on Biological Diversity (CBD) at the Rio Earth Summit in June 1992. That fall, Parliament's Environment Committee held hearings into what steps Canada should take to implement the treaty. The Sierra Legal Defence Fund (SLDF) pulled together a group of nature organizations and secured a spot on the agenda. The ENGOs took the position that the CBD required Canada to pass ESL, especially Article 8(k), which reads: 'Each nation shall, as far as possible and as appropriate . . . develop necessary legislation . . . for the protection of threatened species.'[25] Environment Canada (EC) took the opposite view, testifying that 'it is not necessary . . . to enact new law to enable the convention to be implemented by Canada.'[26]

Surprisingly, the committee sided with the ENGOs. Its final report in April 1993 recommended that the federal and provincial governments 'take immediate steps to develop an integrated legislative approach to the protection of endangered species. . .'.[27] It is unusual for a Parliamentary committee to disagree with its parent Minister in a time of majority government. However, it was not the only time this would happen in SARA's journey.

In the summer and fall of 1993, ENGOs held meetings with senior officials in EC. These meetings confirmed that there was little federal appetite for proceeding with ESL at that time.[28] Recognizing that the initiative for ESL would not come from EC, and buoyed by the election of a new Liberal government in late 1993, SLDF decided to bring ENGOs together in a public campaign for ESL. It convened a meeting at the World Wildlife Fund (WWF) offices in Toronto in March 1994, to which it invited a number of major ENGOs, including WWF, Canadian Nature Federation, Sierra Club, and the Canadian Parks and Wilderness Society.

After two days of discussions, the groups made several important strategic decisions. First, they decided to form a coalition to push for ESL. This would help to overcome one of the major weaknesses of Canada's environmental movement—its fragmentation.[29] Second, the groups decided to focus their efforts at the federal level. Lacking resources to campaign in every jurisdiction, they hoped that pushing federally would also induce provinces to act. Third, they knew that protecting ecosystems and habitat was the key to conserving wildlife, but chose to push for species-focused legislation for several reasons: the federal government had broader constitutional authority over species than over habitat (lands); species would have greater resonance as an issue with the public and politicians; and a species law could be used as a gateway for conserving habitat. Fourth, after debating the strengths and weaknesses of the US ESA, particularly its reactive 'critical care' focus (which had spurred significant conflict), they decided to push for a law that took a more preventive approach, but still required action. Finally, given the federal bureaucracy's resistance to ESL, the groups decided they had to focus their efforts mainly at the political level.[30] To achieve these aims, they formed the Canadian Endangered Species Coalition (CESC), which would be funded by a multi-year grant from the Richard Ivey Foundation. Without this core support, and later grants from other foundations, the campaign for ESL would not have been possible.

To help ramp up public awareness of the issue, SLDF contacted The Body Shop, which soon agreed to run a campaign in its 100+ stores across Canada. The campaign ran in October 1994, using the slogan 'Their Otter Be A Law'. It was highly successful. Over 60,000 people signed a petition calling for strong federal ESL. More importantly, The Body Shop teamed up with *OWL Magazine*, which ran a simultaneous nation-wide contest inviting young Canadians to write a letter to the Environment Minister explaining why she should protect endangered species. Over 2,000 children wrote in.[31]

The challenge for the CESC was how to turn this wave of public support into a government commitment. The Environment Minister, Sheila Copps, was early in her mandate and had not yet fully developed her policy agenda; indeed, the timing in the policy cycle is an important consideration for any new issue. Based on several meetings with Copps and her staff, the CESC believed that the Minister might be ready to move on ESL. They were right. Recognizing that Copps was a populist, the CESC decided to hold an event on Parliament Hill to present the petitions and children's letters to the Minister. At the event, held on 17 November 1994, Minister Copps announced that she was committed to passing ESL and would introduce a draft Bill within a year.[32]

Less than one year after its formation, the CESC had succeeded in securing a political commitment for federal ESL. Little did they know that it would take eight more years to turn this commitment into legislation.

The First Trimester (1994–1996)

In developing a campaign strategy, the CESC faced three major challenges. First, in order to secure the political support for a strong law it needed to generate and maintain significant public support and media attention, despite the poor timing. Second, it could not rely on the traditional executive-driven process for drafting legislation because it was clear that the coalition wanted a very different kind of law than the EC did—which wanted something narrower in scope and more discretion-laden. And, third, the CESC wanted to avoid the backlash that the American ESA had generated with industry and landowners.

To start, the CESC decided that the simplest, fastest way to ramp up public support was to begin by activating its organizations' members. Through action alerts, newsletters, and magazine articles the ENGOs managed to generate more than 50,000 letters to EC in 1995–96, indicating a remarkably broad base of public concern for endangered species.[33] The second strategy was to build a broad base of support across sectors and regions. By the end of 1995, the coalition's list of supporters numbered more than 100 organizations and included physicians, labour unions, farmers, churches, green businesses, scientists, and others.

Ensuring that the drafting of the Bill, or at least its core elements, was not left solely up to EC was more difficult. To do this, the CESC decided to push for the creation of a multi-stakeholder task force to develop recommendations for legislation. The coalition believed it had a better chance of finding common ground with major industries than with federal departments. In addition, ENGOs wanted to avoid the type of polarization and conflict spawned by the US Act. They saw the task force as an opportunity to build an agreed-upon approach to a Canadian law; Minister Copps agreed. In March 1995 she appointed a multi-stakeholder body, including representatives from forestry, mining, oil and gas, agriculture, fisheries, environmental law, wildlife groups, and scientists. The mandate of the new Endangered Species Task Force was to develop recommendations for federal ESL.

In August 1995, the dynamics of the campaign changed markedly when the federal government released its draft proposal for ESL. The proposed law reflected the stark difference of views between EC and ENGOs; it would apply only on federal lands (excluding those in the north), and leave protection of endangered species and their habitat completely up to ministerial discretion.[34] ENGOs were livid, and they worked swiftly to brief media on the shortcomings of the proposal. The result was a front page story in the next day's *Globe and Mail* with a headline reading, '[l]egislation does not protect habitat, applies only to federal lands'.[35] The issue of federal ESL was now on the media's radar screen, and the battle lines were beginning to be drawn.

Media coverage of the legislative proposal helped the CESC increase public support for strong ESL. There was now a tangible threat around which to rally supporters. It also served to galvanize the scientific community. A few days after the proposal's release, a McGill scientist, Dr John Schoen, wrote an editorial in the *Globe and Mail* condemning the proposal for its failure to protect habitat.[36] This editorial caught the attention of several other scientists, and together they worked with the CESC to organize a sign-on letter by Canada's scientists calling for key improvements to the federal proposal, particularly having it apply on all lands and making habitat protection mandatory.[37] In November they released the letter, signed by over 200 Canadian scientists, including a Nobel prize-winner. It made headline news.[38]

The narrow scope of the legislative proposal also raised a warning flag about the federal government's limited view of its role in species protection. SLDF soon confirmed that the Department of

Justice had advised EC that Parliament had very limited constitutional authority to protect species outside federal lands and waters.[39] Seeing this as an exceedingly narrow interpretation of the constitution, SLDF approached one of Canada's top constitutional law experts, professor Dale Gibson, to write a legal opinion on the issue. Gibson's opinion concluded that the federal government had solid constitutional powers to protect all endangered species[40]—a view shared by the Canadian Bar Association.[41] Subsequent meetings with senior Justice lawyers led to a modest revision of Justice's opinion, recognizing that Parliament likely had authority over species that migrate across a national or provincial border ('cross-border species').[42] But Justice still did not agree that Parliament had authority to protect all endangered species.

Recognizing that the federal government would not support legislation covering all endangered species, the CESC focused its attention on shoring up support for protecting cross-border species. The most natural ally in this cause was the US government, which was spending millions annually under its ESA to protect these species in the US part of their range. Through its connections with American NGOs, the CESC worked to try to have the White House encourage Canada to protect shared species at risk—efforts that eventually would bear fruit.

During this time, the Task Force was meeting regularly. Initially, the industry and environmental groups were far apart in their views on both the content of and the need for federal ESL. Over time, however, they began to move closer together as each came to understand the other side's legitimate concerns and as they identified alternative legislative approaches to accommodate those concerns. By May 1996—to the surprise of most Task Force members—the group reached agreement on almost all aspects of federal ESL.[43] The key points of agreement were that species listing decisions should be made by COSEWIC, not government; the protection of critical habitat should be required, but through a recovery plan rather than at the time of listing (as in the US) in order to allow stakeholders to be involved in crafting habitat protection measures (this was a key point of compromise); and, the law should apply to the full extent of federal jurisdiction, including to cross-border species. The one major area of disagreement was on the need for 'citizen suits', to allow private enforcement of the Act.

Following the release of the Task Force's report, the next stage was drafting the Bill. Here, several tensions came into play. On the one hand, federal resource and industry departments (such as Fisheries and Oceans, Natural Resources, and Northern Affairs), generally wanted to avoid legislation that imposed new mandates on their management of lands and resources, or that gave the Environment Minister new power over those lands and resources. At the same time, the provinces did not want to see new federal legislation that affected the management of their lands and resources, or that intruded into their traditional authority over wildlife.[44]

On the other hand, the Environment Minister's office wanted legislation as close as possible to the Task Force recommendations.[45] However, it had only limited success in achieving this wish because of two major institutional factors in the law-making process. First, the details of legislative drafting are controlled mainly by the lead department, working with Justice lawyers, within the parameters of the Cabinet-approved drafting orders. Ministers' offices normally have limited capacity to get involved in the drafting details. Second, other affected federal departments must sign off on draft legislation before it is introduced in Parliament, giving them significant ability to influence its content.[46] These two factors meant that the drafting of ESL largely reflected the wishes of federal departments and provinces, whose views were fed into the drafting process via EC.

The issue of protecting cross-border species was an exception. The CESC had highlighted this as an area where federal leadership was needed, and they were supported by the Task Force report and (eventually) by Justice's constitutional advice. On the other hand, the provinces and most federal departments were opposed to such an extension of federal authority.[47] The US also weighed in. In October 1996, in the final stages of drafting, US Secretary of Interior Bruce Babbit wrote to Minister Marchi (Copps' successor) to encourage 'the establishment of national authority for the protection of endangered cross-border species. . .'.[48] This US intervention helped tip the balance in favour of including cross-border species, and they were included in the Bill.[49]

Before proceeding with ESL, the federal government also needed to lay the federal–provincial groundwork for it to act. EC wanted to move into the endangered species field in a way that did not jeopardize federal–provincial cooperation on wildlife and other environmental issues.[50] In a larger sense, ESL was going forward at a time when EC was pursuing a strategy of reconciliation (some would say retreat) with the provinces in the aftermath of the failed constitutional reform efforts under Mulroney and the 1995 Québec Referendum. The embodiment of these efforts at environmental peacemaking was the proposed Canada-Wide Accord on Environmental Harmonization, which sought to define federal and provincial roles in environmental regulation in order to 'prevent overlap'.[51] Critics—of which there many—saw it as a transparent attempt to weaken the federal environmental role.[52] In October 1996, EC was in the home stretch of securing federal–provincial agreement for the Harmonization Agreement; it could ill afford to have federal ESL disrupt the delicate détente it was building with provinces.

To navigate these treacherous federal–provincial waters, Minister Marchi decided to propose a National Accord for the Protection of Species at Risk. The Accord would require each jurisdiction to put in place endangered species legislation within its sphere of responsibility, and identified 13 key elements that such laws must address. Marchi proposed the Accord at the annual federal–provincial wildlife ministers' meeting on 2 October 1996. Spurred on by strong media coverage of the event, the provinces all agreed to it, in principle.[53] The Accord was a remarkable policy instrument. For provinces, it created a sense of security that Ottawa would not take over the whole area of endangered species protection. For the federal government, it served as recognition that it had a legitimate role in species protection. For ENGOs, it validated their strategy that pushing at the federal level would generate provincial results as well.

The Second Trimester: The Introduction of Federal ESL (Round One)

The Accord paved the way for Marchi to move forward with federal ESL, and he did so on 31 October 1996. The Canadian Endangered Species Protection Act (CESPA) was a great disappointment to ENGOs; it left species listing up to the federal cabinet's discretion; habitat protection was optional, even on federal lands; and the scope of the Bill was limited to federal lands and waters. The one positive feature of the Bill, for ENGOs, was that it included cross-border species, although it gave the federal government a residual role and only covered direct harm to species, not habitat.[54]

The CESC was sharply critical of the Bill, as reflected in the national media coverage.[55] Within a week, several newspaper editorial boards had come out criticizing the Bill as too weak.[56] Industry and landowner groups generally appeared to be content with the Bill;[57] however, there was criticism from some quarters, particularly western cattle producers and British Columbia loggers.[58]

After the first reading in Parliament, the Bill was referred to the Standing Committee on Environment, which heard from a wide array of witnesses from different sectors. Virtually all ENGOs took the position that the Bill was far too weak to be effective, particularly in the areas of listing, habitat protection, and narrow application (just federal lands).[59] Scientists took a similar view, both before committee and in a new letter to the Prime Minister signed by over 300 scientists.[60] Industry and landowner groups' reaction to the Bill was mixed; most supported the idea of legislation but expressed concerns about several issues, including the lack of consideration of socio-economic factors, the lack of compensation for affected land owners, the application to cross-border species, and the power for citizen enforcement actions.[61] Several industry and landowner groups warned against following down what they saw as the US path of litigation and conflict.[62]

The CESC's aim was to convince the Committee to make significant improvements to the Bill. Such changes are almost unheard of in the Canadian law-making system because, in a majority government, the party in power holds most of the seats on committees and its members typically vote as directed by the Minister. In addition, MPs on committees, even if they wanted to make changes to a Bill, have very limited staff capacity to analyze legislation and draft amendments. But the CESC had strategies for overcoming these obstacles. First, SLDF prepared a 100-page, detailed, clause-by-clause analysis of the Bill with specific wording recommendations for each section it wanted to amend. This helped to overcome MPs' lack of staff capacity to do such an analysis. Second, CESC representatives attended the committee's clause-by-clause deliberations and were available for advice and drafting support as needed. This unconventional strategy was premised on the realization that MPs on a committee have tremendous power to amend a Bill, if only they can be convinced and enabled to use it. The Environment Committee, which included several independent-minded members with strong pro-environment views,[63] seemed a good candidate for such MP activism.

The hearings had made a real impression on the Committee and convinced most members that the Bill needed strengthening.[64] But there was still the challenge of turning this motivation into specific legislative revisions. Here, SLDF's strategy of providing detailed recommended wording changes worked; most of the changes it recommended were introduced as proposed amendments by committee members,[65] who eventually voted to make over 130 amendments to the Bill. The Committee's key amendments included making habitat protection mandatory on federal lands and waters; expanding the definition of a species' 'residence'; and strengthening protection for cross-border species by making federal protection mandatory where a province did not have equivalent protection. The CESC did not achieve all its goals (for example, it was unsuccessful in getting listing decisions made by scientists, or having the Bill apply to all lands and species) but it had helped to secure significant changes.

Those changes sparked a strong backlash from some quarters. A number of industry and landowner groups believed the revised Bill was too legalistic. They took out media ads warning it would produce the kinds of 'litigation and socio-economic hardship' seen in the US.[66] The provinces were also outraged, but for a different reason; they objected to the federal assertion of authority over cross-border species, which they saw as inconsistent with the [National] Accord. A strongly worded letter to Minister Marchi, signed by the wildlife ministers from every province and territory, insisted that this section 'must be deleted'.[67] At the same time, other federal departments, particularly Fisheries and Oceans, worked within government circles to oppose the changes, which they saw as unjustifiably changing and intruding on their responsibilities.[68] The CESC, on the other hand, generally saw the changes as going just far enough to make the Bill worth supporting, a view echoed by the *Globe and Mail* editorial board.[69]

The Prime Minister's office stepped in to try to resolve the conflict. After hearing from all sides, it crafted a package of compromise amendments, which weakened many of the Committee's changes but generally left their key elements intact.[70] These amendments were introduced in Parliament in late March 1997,[71] at which time it appeared likely the Bill would eventually pass (albeit opposed by the Reform Party). However, before the debate was concluded, Prime Minister Chrétien called an unexpectedly early election on 28 April 1997, just 3.5 years into his mandate. The CESPA was dead . . . for now.

The Third Trimester: The Introduction of Federal ESL (Round Two)

In the subsequent election campaign, the Liberals, who were eventually re-elected, reiterated their commitment to ESL.[72] However, the perception in government was that the CESPA had become a 'no win' issue; all constituencies were angry about it, albeit for different reasons.[73] Therefore, the new Environment Minister, Christine Stewart, opted to go back to the drawing board for a new round of consultations, hoping to identify new approaches to build support. Little overt progress was made over the next two years.

During this lull period, a number of forces were at work. First of all, a small band of three ENGOs (CNF, Sierra Club, and Canadian Wildlife Federation), two industry groups (the forestry and mining industry associations) and the National Agriculture-Environment Committee, decided they would try to revive and build on the common ground that had been identified by the Task Force. They formed the Species At Risk Working Group (SARWG), which began meeting regularly to try to forge a consensus position on acceptable elements for ESL. The group would eventually agree on a package that called for science-based listing, mandatory habitat protection, compensation rights for affected landowners, and no citizen suit powers. It also agreed that a stewardship program must accompany any legislation. However, the group could not reach clear agreement on the constitutional scope of federal legislation.[74]

Canada's scientists were also active, building support for a third common letter on ESL. This time they secured over 600 signatories, emphasizing the importance of science-based listing and habitat protection, and securing front-page coverage in the national media.[75]

In addition, SLDF was working to shore up the constitutional basis for broad federal legislation. In September 1997 it had helped secure a landmark legal victory in the *Hydro Québec* case,[76] establishing that the federal government had broad authority to address environmental problems under its 'criminal law' power in the Constitution. In an effort to convince a still-reluctant Justice Department to exercise these new powers, SLDF retained Gerard LaForest, a recently retired Supreme Court judge who had authored the judgment in Hydro Québec. He wrote an opinion concluding that the federal government had the power to pass broad legislation protecting all endangered species and their habitats.[77] Following meetings with Justice, this opinion was released publicly and made front page news.[78]

The CESC also was active on a number of fronts during this period. It commissioned a major poll and released the results. Not surprisingly, the poll showed very high support (94 per cent) for federal ESL, including mandatory habitat protection (79 per cent) and a science-based listing process (65 per cent), even if it meant sacrificing economic development (86 per cent).[79] At the same time, though, other polls showed that the environment was still a low priority for voters, and endangered species was not an important overall public concern.[80]

Also during this time, the CESC began to publish an annual report card ranking each jurisdiction in Canada on its progress toward meeting its commitments under the National Accord. These reports, and the resulting media coverage, highlighted the fact that most provinces were meeting less than half of the Accord's required elements.[81] Provinces soon began to fill this gap. In the three-year period following CESPA's demise, from 1997–2000, four provinces brought in new ESL.[82]

In March 1999, matters came to a head. EC released a draft proposal for a new federal ESL. Echoing back to 1996, the proposal would make habitat protection optional, and leave listing decisions to Cabinet, not scientists.[83] ENGOs and the media pounced on the proposal. Newspaper headlines read 'Toothless proposals will not help wildlife'[84] and 'Chainsaw Jean'.[85]

These events set the stage for the next iteration of federal ESL. The triggering event was a cabinet shuffle; in July 1999, Christine Stewart was replaced by David Anderson, a self-proclaimed environmentalist. One of Minister Anderson's first acts was to announce that new federal legislation would provide protection for all endangered species and their habitats (apparently Justice had finally agreed that Parliament had such power).[86]

In December 1999, Anderson released his proposal for new legislation. True to his word, the proposed law would cover all species, although the federal role would be residual outside its own lands and waters; Ottawa could apply its law only if a province was not providing effective protection, using a so-called 'safety net' power. Another new feature was that the law would allow for compensation to affected landowners, and be accompanied by a stewardship program and significant new federal funding. But in other areas the proposal was similar to the one from March; habitat protection was optional (even on federal lands), there was no citizen enforcement power, and listing decisions would be left to cabinet.[87] Because of these weaknesses, ENGOs were sharply critical of the proposal.[88] On the other hand, Anderson's emphasis on stewardship and compensation found welcome ears with industry and landowners, who were generally positive in their media comments—a major change from the CESPA experience.[89]

On 11 April 2000, the long-awaited Species At Risk Act (SARA) was introduced in Parliament. Its key features followed closely the federal proposal from a few months earlier, as did the response of ENGO, industry, and landowner groups.[90] Somewhat surprisingly, most provinces appeared to be comfortable with the Bill, including the federal safety net powers. Anderson had assured them it would only be used as a last resort, and it left provinces with primary responsibility for most species and habitat.[91] Alberta, however, saw the safety net as an invasion of provincial powers, and threatened a constitutional challenge—which never emerged.[92]

The Bill went through second reading in Parliament, and was referred to committee for review. But soon after the hearings started, Jean Chrétien again called an unexpectedly early election on 22 October 2000. Like CESPA, SARA died on the order paper. However, the Bill was reintroduced by Minister Anderson and the re-elected Liberals early in 2001. It was referred to committee, which heard from a wide range of witnesses. Virtually all ENGOs and scientists called for the Bill to be significantly strengthened in the areas of habitat, listing, and scope of coverage,[93] while industry and landowner groups were generally supportive of the Bill, with most seeking only modest changes.[94]

One noteworthy development was that SARWG held its ground. Even though Anderson's proposal addressed more of industries' concerns (compensation and citizen suits) than those of the ENGOs, the forestry and mining industry associations stuck to the agreement they had reached and joined environmentalists in calling for SARA to be significantly stronger in key areas, especially habitat and listing.[95]

Again, the CESC was left in the difficult position of having to try to secure significant changes to the Bill at committee stage. This time around, though, they did not have the benefit of surprise: their strategy was expected. Minister Anderson was determined not to repeat the CESPA experience. When he appeared before the committee he warned that the Bill strikes a delicate balance between competing interests and could not survive any major amendments.[96]

The CESC used the same basic strategy as in 1997. SLDF prepared a lengthy brief that set out detailed recommendations for wording revisions.[97] And CESC representatives worked closely with

MPs from all sides, hoping to cobble together a multi-party base to vote for its desired changes. With the Liberals whipping their members heavily, the CESC realized it would be lucky to secure one or two Liberals to vote its way; it would need to secure almost all the opposition votes, including those of the Alliance Party (which generally opposed strong environmental measures) and the Bloc Québécois (which opposed expansions of federal jurisdiction). However, the hearings had convinced most of the MPs that the Bill needed significant improvements.[98]

As the Committee's clause-by-clause voting proceeded, the votes on key amendments were very close. But in most cases it voted in favour of amendments put forward by the CESC (with some changes), often by a one vote margin. In the end, the Committee made over 100 changes, including making habitat protection mandatory in areas of federal responsibility; adopting a compromise approach on listing, one that required Cabinet to respond to scientists' listing recommendations within a fixed time and give reasons if it did not follow them (the 'negative option' approach); making the application of the safety net mandatory (so SARA would apply whenever a province was not providing 'effective protection'); and requiring regulations on compensation for affected landowners.[99]

Despite multi-party support for these changes, and support from some major industry and environmental groups, the Minister and the PMO saw them as going too far—particularly the changes to the safety net, which would upset the provinces.[100] As a result, after the Committee reported its revised Bill back to Parliament on 3 December 2001, the Minister proposed amendments that would claw back most (but not all) of its key changes to the Bill.[101]

Birthing Pains: The Passage of SARA

Normally, in a majority Parliament, this would have been the end of the matter. The government would have used its majority to push through its changes over the objections of the opposition. But three things made this situation unusual. First, federal ESL had been before Parliament for over five years. During that time, a number of Liberal MPs had been through the Environment Committee, or had been briefed by the CESC, and therefore understood the issue well enough to know that that the changes proposed by the committee were anything but radical (as Minister Anderson claimed). Second, a growing number of Liberal MPs were frustrated by the government's poor environmental record. Third, Chrétien's hold over his backbench MPs was weakening, largely due to increasing pressure on him to step aside in favour of Paul Martin.[102]

In early May 2002, as the date for a final vote on the government's changes to the Bill approached, the Liberal whip encountered unprecedented pushback from MPs about voting as directed by the government. As many as 37 MPs were reportedly threatening to vote against the government, and in favour of restoring the committee's changes.[103] In its eight years in power, the Chrétien government had not lost a significant vote in Parliament, but now faced the prospect of doing so over SARA. This led to a standoff. Anderson threatened to let the Bill die if the renegade MPs did not back down. They called his bluff, believing the government could not abandon ESL after seven years of public commitments.[104] So the Bill sat in limbo for weeks, with neither side willing to budge.

During this period, backroom discussions began between the Prime Minister's Office (PMO) and several of the holdout MPs. The MPs identified four key areas for change: listing, habitat protection, migratory birds, and the safety net. It soon became clear that the PMO would not agree to any changes to strengthen the safety net, so that was off the table. After some back and forth, changes to the listing process were agreed to, restoring the negative option approach adopted by the committee.

Habitat and migratory birds proved more difficult; Anderson resisted mandatory habitat protection in areas of federal authority, wanting to preserve ministerial discretion. On migratory birds, everyone agreed that the birds themselves were within federal responsibility but the PMO was unwilling to protect their habitat because this could involve significant entanglement with provincial and private lands.[105] The stalemate continued.

Then, circumstances conspired to break the impasse. On 31 May, Paul Martin suddenly announced he was considering leaving Cabinet, precipitating a power showdown with Chrétien. The Prime Minister wanted to take control of the agenda. He needed a popular issue, and one that would show he was listening to MPs. SARA offered a perfect opportunity to do both. Hours after Martin's announcement, Karen Kraft Sloan, the unofficial leader of the holdout MPs, received a call from the PMO seeking to reach agreement to move forward on SARA. They were willing to agree to make habitat protection mandatory for species on federal lands, but not for migratory birds' habitat generally. The CESC and SLDF argued for holding firm on migratory birds (so the law would apply outside federal lands), but Kraft Sloan was concerned that the coalition of MPs could not be held together for a fight on that issue, since the government had moved significantly on listing and habitat. With some reluctance, she agreed to support the Bill if the listing and habitat changes were made.[106]

On 11 June 2002—exactly 10 years after Canada had signed the CBD at Rio—the House of Commons voted to pass the Species At Risk Act. The Bill was subsequently approved by the Senate (albeit with a strong report urging future improvements to the safety net), and became law on 12 December 2002.

Conclusions

The eight-year history of SARA's creation evokes many of the most powerful themes in Canadian environmental policy-making. However, it also involves several unusual factors, which resulted in SARA becoming one of the most far-reaching pieces of federal environmental legislation ever seen in Canada.

In particular, SARA's process and outcome exemplified the importance of two major institutional realities in Canada. The decentralized federalism that has characterized Canada since its birth limited the reach of SARA; the federal government was very reluctant to encroach on traditional areas of provincial jurisdiction and, when it did so, it crept forward gingerly.[107] The constitutional division of powers—and Justice's narrow interpretation of it—also limited the federal government's reach, although those limits were expanded somewhat by the Supreme Court while the Act was in formation. And Canada's Westminster-style of government meant that the executive branch was the main driver in shaping the law, and it preferred a law that was much more discretion-laden than what most Parliamentarians wanted.[108]

Moreover, the major actors that traditionally influence Canadian environmental policy-making played strong roles in shaping SARA. The tension between environmental groups, on the one hand, and industry and landowners groups on the other, reverberated throughout the Act's creation and helps to explain the final product in large part.

Also, ideas played an important role in the SARA debate, particularly cross-national learning from the US.[109] The positive lessons from the US ESA motivated ENGOs to push for ESL, and the negative lessons motivated industry and landowner groups (and even ENGOs) to push for a different style of law than the US had. In addition, the importance of the idea of endangered species should not be overlooked. Protecting animals threatened with extinction was a powerful motivator for the public, media and politicians. SARA's creation shows how these different forces—institutions, actors, and ideas—interacted in shaping Canadian environmental law and policy.

In addition, several important timing and context factors exerted a significant influence on the formation of SARA. The traditional academic wisdom is that environmental policy moves during periods of peak public environmental concern, yet SARA was developed during a 'trough' in public concern, when the environment was consistently low in the polls.[110] The federal priority on deficit fighting further lessened the government's willingness to take on costly new mandates, although this began to change after the books were balanced in 1998, allowing for a large funding package that was a big factor in SARA's success.[111] SARA also came at a time when the federal government was pursuing a strategy of provincial appeasement on the environment, in the aftermath of the Québec separation referendum and Mulroney's failed constitutional reform efforts. Each of these factors worked against the development of any significant new federal environmental initiative.

Given these hostile contextual factors, and the traditional institutional constraints on federal environmental power, it is remarkable that SARA got on the policy agenda at all, let alone ended up becoming a fairly potent law. The explanation for this surprising outcome lies in the fact that a number of other unusual factors came into play in shaping SARA.

First, the ESL campaign marked the first time that Canada's environmental groups had come together and worked so proactively to set the national legislative agenda, something that happens more frequently in the US.[112] Their concerted efforts to galvanize public and media support helps to explain why SARA came about in a period of low public environmental concern. This push was led by SLDF, although many organizations played key roles in the campaign. Without SLDF's entrepreneurial efforts, it is quite possible that the campaign for federal ESL would not have happened, at least in such an organized and proactive way.[113] The same can be said for the Richard Ivey Foundation, which provided the core funding for the campaign (later buttressed by other funders), demonstrating the important role that the philanthropic community can play in policy change—something that is much more common in the US, which has far greater foundation wealth.

A second unusual factor was the emergence of cooperation between ENGOs and major industry. This cooperation began with the Task Force, and strengthened with the emergence of SARWG. ENGOs and industry typically had played conflicting roles in the development of environmental legislation or policy. The ESL campaign occurred at a time when these traditional conflictual roles were starting to change. In particular, the forest industry, having been through the 'war in the woods' in BC and elsewhere, was changing its approach and trying to make environmental leadership a core part of its business strategy ('if you can't beat 'em, join 'em').[114] The mining industry was beginning to move in a similar direction.[115] On the other side, some ENGOs, such as WWF, were increasingly pursuing a strategy of industry collaboration. Such collaboration, unusual at that time, has become more common over the subsequent decade.[116]

A third unusual factor was the high degree of influence that backbench MPs had in the development of SARA. This influence, remarkable in Canada's executive-driven system of government, arose because the CESC made a deliberate (and heretical) strategy choice to focus on MPs to strengthen SARA and a handful of Liberal MPs were willing to defy the Environment Minister's directions in order to strengthen the bill, at the risk of marginalizing themselves within the party. These remarkable MPs (particularly Karen Kraft Sloan, Charles Caccia, Clifford Lincoln, Gar Knutson, and Joe Jordan) showed that backbench MPs can have real power in Canada's law making system—more than is traditionally assumed—if they choose to exercise it.

Finally, two unusual actors played an important role in the ESL initiative. Scientists are normally a fairly apolitical group and not prone to collective action, yet they came together in large numbers to push for effective ESL. The presence of these respected, impartial voices had a real influence on MPs and the larger public.[117] Also, the legal community played an important role in pushing a reluctant federal government to use the full scope of its constitutional powers. The Canadian Bar Association, and two of Canada's top constitutional law experts, weighed in to counter the narrow legal advice being given by the Department of Justice.

Together, these four unusual factors help to explain why one of the most far-reaching pieces of federal environmental legislation emerged in the face of institutional constraints and difficult political timing. It is also important to note the impact that the SARA initiative had on provinces. Over the eight-year course of the federal campaign, six provinces passed their own laws (the other four already had a law)—despite the fact that there was little direct pressure from ENGOs in most of those provinces.[118] One might debate whether the provinces' actions were driven more by a desire to pre-empt federal intrusion into the endangered species field or to meet their commitments under the National Accord (which was a product of the federal ESL initiative)—likely both factors came into play to varying degrees.[119] However, the end result appears to validate the CESC's strategy: pushing for action at the federal level was an effective way to spur provincial action as well.

In sum, the SARA process and outcome exemplified the importance of two major institutional realities of Canadian policy-making: decentralized federalism and executive driven government. The entrepreneurial efforts of ENGOs (particularly SLDF), combined with activist MPs and scientists, helped to stretch the normal federal policy space provided by these two institutions, and did so in a difficult time in the environmental policy-making cycle. The interplay between these two institutional constraints and the ENGOs' entrepreneurial efforts resulted in a law that was more discretion-laden and decentralist than NGOs and their allies wanted, but more mandatory and far reaching than the federal government (or provinces) wanted.

In essence, two main policy lessons emerge from the SARA experience: first, institutions and timing matter a lot—they shape the policy playing field to a large extent; and second, individuals and organizations, through creative strategies and entrepreneurial efforts, can overcome some of the limits imposed by institutions and timing. To put it simply, institutions and timing are the political hand that is dealt, but how the actors—particularly policy entrepreneurs—play that hand can have a real influence on the policy outcome.

Addendum

SARA came into force on 5 June 2003. In the subsequent 5.5 years (as of the time of writing), the government's performance in implementing Act has been underwhelming, to say the least. A review of the statistics for the Act's three key steps—listing of species, preparation of recovery strategies, and identification and protection of critical habitat—tells the story.

The government's track record is respectable when it comes to listing. Of the species recommended for listing by COSEWIC, 77 per cent have been legally listed under SARA by the federal Cabinet.[120] Thus, nearly one-fourth of species at risk have been left unprotected, including the Atlantic Cod, Wood Bison, and Polar Bear. By comparison, provinces have listed only 37 per cent of COSEWIC-recommended species under provincial endangered species laws.[121] The explanation for this difference can be found mainly in the structure of the laws. Under SARA's 'negative option' approach, a COSEWIC-recommended species automatically becomes listed unless Cabinet elects not to do so within nine months, in which case it must publicly provide written reasons (SARA, s. 27). Most provincial laws have no such time limits or accountability requirements. The one province that does have such requirements, Newfoundland, has listing levels similar to the federal ones (88 per cent of COSEWIC-recommended species).[122]

The federal track record for completing recovery strategies is less impressive. Once a species is listed, SARA requires that a recovery strategy be prepared within a fixed time—one year for endangered species and two for threatened. (SARA allowed an additional two years for species 'rolled over' as part of the initial list under the Act.) These strategies are the key documents that lay the blueprint for protection and recovery efforts for species. Of the 307 species listed as endangered and threatened under SARA (as of December 2007) only 98 have had a recovery strategy prepared within the prescribed time limit.[123] More than two-thirds are still without a strategy—and for most of them the strategy is over 18 months late.

The experience with identifying and protecting habitat is particularly poor. Habitat destruction is the main threat facing over 80 per cent of Canada's species at risk.[124] SARA requires that, 'to the extent possible', a recovery strategy must identify a species' critical habitat (i.e., the habitat it needs to survive (SARA, s. 41(1)(b)). Of the 98 species for which recovery strategies have been completed to date, only six fully identify critical habitat (and four of those are in parks or protected areas). Another 12 'partially' identify it.[125] That leaves 82 per cent of species with no critical habitat identified—and thus no possibility of habitat *protection* under SARA.

When one takes into account all the species that have been 'left out' at each stage (listing, recovery strategy, and habitat identification), less than 5 per cent of the species identified by COSEWIC as endangered or threatened have made it through to the point of having their critical habitat identified (even partly) under SARA, which is the most important step under the Act, since it is the foundation for habitat protection.

While a full explanation for the limited implementation of SARA in its first five years is beyond the scope of this paper, a few observations can be made. To some extent it can be traced to initial growing pains, as EC and DFO put in place the policies, procedures and personnel to implement this sizeable new statutory mandate. Part of the explanation also lies in Parliament's failure to allocate sufficient funding for departments to fully carry out SARA's requirements. At least some of the explanation, though, can be found in the same forces that were at play during the creation of the Act. The federal bureaucracy was opposed to the inclusion of so many mandatory requirements and time limits in SARA, particularly for listing and habitat protection. Those provisions were ultimately included in the Act at the insistence of elected MPs. However, the responsibility for implementing those provisions now rests with federal departments, the same ones that resisted their inclusion in the Act. It is very likely that the departments' lack of enthusiasm for SARA's mandatory requirements is one of the factors contributing to the limited implementation to date.

In particular, it is evident that departments are often resistant to the idea of identifying critical habitat (for a variety of reasons). For example, there have been two lawsuits brought by ENGOs against departmental determinations that it was 'not possible' to identify a species' critical habitat (involving the Piping Plover and Nooksack River Dace). In each case, after the lawsuit was filed, the department reversed its initial decision and decided that it *could* in fact identify the species' critical habitat—in effect admitting its violation of the Act.[126]

Thus, to some extent, the tensions that existed between ENGOs and federal departments during the development of SARA still continue during the Act's implementation. The forum has just shifted from Parliamentary committee-rooms to courtrooms. That being said, there is no doubt that protection of endangered species in Canada has advanced dramatically as a result of the passage of SARA and its provincial cousins. Even with SARA's implementation shortcomings, the current protection and recovery efforts for species at risk are an order of magnitude greater than they were just a decade ago. And as federal departments gain experience, they are beginning to do a better job of preparing recovery strategies and identifying critical habitat.[127]

The passage of SARA represented a landmark change in endangered species management in Canada. The Act did not eliminate the underlying tensions and diverging interest in the broader endangered species debate. However, it did create a major new institution: one that generates ongoing momentum for the protection of endangered species, with its regular deadlines and action-forcing requirements. In effect, while SARA does not guarantee a particular outcome for endangered species, it tilts the scales in favour of their protection. Thus it serves as a prime illustration of the important role that institutions can play in environmental policy.

Questions for Review

1. What are the main factors threatening wildlife species?
2. Which institutions and actors have been major influences on the approach and provisions of the Species At Risk Act (SARA) in Canada?
3. To what extent and in what ways is SARA an example of environmental policy leadership in Canada?
4. What factors are most likely to shape the implementation phase of SARA?

Notes

1. The author discloses that he played a lead role in the Canadian campaign for endangered species legislation, as managing lawyer of Sierra Legal Defence Fund. This article seeks to present an objective assessment of the Act's creation, but no doubt reflects the author's perspectives and biases in places. The author thanks Marta Keller for her excellent research assistance on this article.
2. *Convention on Biological Diversity*, 5 June 1992, 1760 U.N.T.S., (1992) 31 I.L.M. 818.
3. *Species at Risk Act,* S.C. 2002, c. 29.
4. Benjamin Cashore et al., *In Search of Sustainability: British Columbia Forest Policy in the 1990s* (Vancouver: UBC Press, 2001), 10–13.
5. Edward O. Wilson, *The Diversity of Life* (Cambridge: The Belknap Press of Harvard University Press, 1992), 280.
6. Robert M. May, 'How many species inhabit the earth?', *Scientific American* 267, 4 (1992): 42–48.
7. See Committee on the Status of Endangered Wildlife in Canada, available at http://www.cosewic.gc.ca/eng/ sct5/index_e.cfm.
8. Bill Freedman et al., 'Species at Risk in Canada', in K. Beazley and R. Boardman, eds, *Politics of the Wild: Canada and Endangered Species* (Oxford: Oxford University Press, 2001), 30–31.
9. Karen Beazley, 'Why Should We Protect Endangered Species?', in *Politics of the Wild*, Beazley and Boardman (2001).
10. Wilson, *Diversity of Life*, 285.
11. Environment Canada, *The Importance of Nature to Canadians: Survey Highlights*, 1996.
12. Environment Canada, *The Importance of Nature to Canadians: Executive Summary*, 1991.
13. Beazley, 'Why Should We Protect', 15–18.
14. Beazley, 'Why Should We Protect', 21.
15. Freedman et al., 'Species at Risk', 26.

16. Dianne Draper and Maureen G. Reed, 'Fresh Water', in *Our Environment: A Canadian Perspective* (Toronto: Nelson, 2005), 250.

17. Kathryn Harrison, *Passing the Buck: Federalism and Canadian Environmental Policy* (Vancouver: UBC Press, 1996), 56–62.

18. *Endangered Species Act*, 16 USC. § 1531 (1973).

19. Stephen Bocking, 'The Politics of Endangered Species: A Historical Perspective', in *Politics of the Wild*, Beazley and Boardman.

20. Ibid., 127.

21. Freedman et al., 'Species at Risk', 27–35.

22. Bocking, 'Politics of Endangered Species', 128.

23. Freedman et al., 'Species at Risk', 35–36.

24. Harrison, *Passing the Buck*, 116–120.

25. *Convention on Biological Diversity*.

26. Canada, Parliament, *Minutes of Proceedings and Evidence of the Standing Committee on Environment*, 34th Parl., No. 47 (23 November 1992), 15.

27. Canada, Parliament, Report of the Standing Committee on Environment, *A Global Partnership*, April 1993, 30.

28. Robert Slater (former Deputy Minister of EC), interview by Stewart Elgie, 3 July 2008.

29. William Amos, Kathryn Harrison, and George Hoberg, 'In Search of a Minimum Winning Coalition', in *Politics of the Wild*, Beazley and Boardman, 148.

30. The author was present at the event.

31. Ian Yolles (Director of Social Inventions, The Body Shop), in discussion with Stewart Elgie, October 1996.

32. Tom Spears, 'Law to Protect Endangered Species', *Ottawa Citizen*, 18 November 1994.

33. Cathy Wilkinson (former advisor to the Minister of the Environment), interview by Stewart Elgie, 11 July 2008.

34. Environment Canada, *The Canadian Endangered Species Protection Act: A Legislative Proposal* (August 1996).

35. Robert Matas, 'Ottawa Unveils Endangered Species Law', *Globe and Mail*, 18 August 1995.

36. 'If Ottawa Wants to Protect Species, it Should Save Their Habitats', *Globe and Mail*, 24 August 1995.

37. Scientists for Species, available at http://www.scientists-4-species.org.

38. Robert Matas, 'Ottawa Failing Endangered Species, Scientists Say', *Globe and Mail*, 23 November 1995.

39. Canada, Department of Justice, 'Endangered Species, Legislative Options' (legal opinion provided to author on 16 November 1995).

40. Dale Gibson, *Endangered Species Protection and the Parliament of Canada*. Sierra Legal Defence Fund, 1995.

41. Gordon Proudfoot (President of the CBA), letter to Sergio Marchi, 4 June 1996 (in the author's possession).

42. Dale Gibson, letter to George Thomson (Deputy Minister of Justice), 15 December 1995 (in the author's possession).

43. Task Force on Endangered Species Conservation, *Report on Federal Endangered Species Legislation* (Environment Canada, May 1996).

44. Slater, interview.

45. Wilkinson, interview.

46. Slater, interview.

47. Ibid.

48. Bruce Babbit, letter to Sergio Marchi, undated (in the author's possession).

49. Wilkinson, interview.

50. Slater, interview.

51. Canada-Wide Accord on Environmental Harmonization, 29 January 1998, available at http://www.ccme.ca/assets/pdf/accord_harmonization_e.pdf.

52. Stewart Elgie, 'The Harmonization Accord: A Solution In Search Of A Problem', *Canada Watch*, March 1998.

53. Anne McIlroy, 'Tentative Endangered Species Accord Reached', *Globe and Mail*, 3 October 1996.

54. Bill C-65, *Canadian Endangered Species Protection Act*, 2d Sess., 35th Parl., 1996.

55. Anne McIlroy, 'Wildlife Bill Too Loose, Critics Say', *Globe and Mail*, 1 November 1996.

56. 'Endangered and Spaced Out', *Globe and Mail*, 5 November 1996; 'Endangered Species Law Needs More Teeth', *Vancouver Sun*, 4 November 1996.

57. Barry Wilson, 'New Endangered Species Rules "acceptable" for Farmers', *The Western Producer*, 7 November 1996.

58. Jack Munro (Chair of BC Forest Alliance), 'It's Time to Start Asking Questions About Bill C-65', *Vancouver Sun*, 10 December 1996; Joanne Paulson, 'Cattle Farmers Averse to Endangered Species Bill', *Saskatoon Star Phoenix*, 15 November 1996.

59. Canadian Endangered Species Coalition, 'Analysis of Bill C-65' (November 1996; in the author's possession).

60. Scientists for Species.
61. Canadian Association of Petroleum Producers, Canadian Pulp and Paper Association, Mining Association of Canada, National Agriculture Environment Committee, 'Proposed Revisions to Bill C-65' (December 1996). (Paper provided to the author.)
62. BC Hydro, 'Comments on Bill C-65', January 1997. (Paper provided to the author.)
63. In particular the Chair, Charles Caccia, and Liberal MPs Karen Kraft Sloan and Clifford Lincoln.
64. Confidential interview by Stewart Elgie, July 2008.
65. Gar Knutson, MP, introduced most of the amendments proposed by SLDF.
66. 'Litigation or Cooperation', *The Hill Times*, 17 February 1997; 'Dear Mr Prime Minister: Don't put B.C. Business, Workers and Communities on the Endangered Species List'.
67. Provincial and territorial wildlife ministers to Sergio Marchi, 24 January 1997 (in the author's possession).
68. Slater, interview.
69. 'Space for Species', *Globe and Mail*, 19 March 1997.
70. Wilkinson interview.
71. Anne McIllroy, 'Noxious Changes Weaken Species Bill', *Globe and Mail*, 31 March 1997.
72. *Securing Our Future Together*. Ottawa: Liberal Party of Canada, April 1997, 52.
73. Slater, interview.
74. Species At Risk Working Group, *Conserving Species At Risk Cooperatively* (September 2000), available at http://www.sierraclub.ca/national/programs/biodiversity/wilderness/sarwg-comments-sara-09-00.pdf.
75. 'Tough Endangered Species Law Demanded', *Globe and Mail*, 24 February 1999.
76. *R. v. Hydro-Québec*, [1997] 3 S.C.R. 213.
77. Gerard LaForest and Dale Gibson, 'Federal Protection of Endangered Species and the Constitution', November 1999 (in the author's possession).
78. Donna Jacobs, 'Wildlife Law is Far Too Weak: report', *Ottawa Citizen*, 16 March 2000.
79. Pollara, 'Canadian Attitudes and Opinions Towards Protection of Endangered Species', February 2001, (Survey provided to author.)
80. Amos et al., 'Minimum Winning Coalition', 145–6.
81. Norm Ovenden, 'Ottawa, Provinces, Fail to Protect Species, Groups Say', *Edmonton Journal*, 30 September 1997.
82. *Endangered Species Act*, S.N.S. 1998, c. 11 (N.S.); *Wildlife Conservation Act*, R.S.P.E.I. 1998, c. W-4.1 (PEI); *Wildlife Act, 1998*, S.S. 1998, c. W-13.12 (Sask); *Wildlife Act*, R.S.A. 2000, c. W-10 (Alb).
83. Environment Canada, *Protecting Species At Risk–Update* (March 1999) (in the author's possession).
84. *Vancouver Sun*, 9 April 1999.
85. *Ottawa Citizen*, 7 April 1999.
86. 'Bill Would Outlaw Destruction of Endangered Species' Habitat', *Globe and Mail*, 25 August 1999.
87. Environment Canada, 'Canada's Plan for Protecting Species at Risk' (Dec. 1999), available at http://dsp-psd.pwgsc.gc.ca/Collection/En21-203-1999-1E.pdf.
88. Anne McIllroy, 'Ottawa's Endangered Species Plan Called Inadequate', *Globe and Mail*, 18 December 1999.
89. Connie Watson, 'A Fine Balance', CBC Radio News, 17 December 1999.
90. Canadian Press, 'Farm Group Hails Endangered Species Law', 13 April 2000; Anne McIlroy, 'Law No Species Saver, Environmentalists Say', *Globe and Mail*, 12 April 2000.
91. Slater, interview.
92. Ed Struzik, 'Alta. May Challenge Feds' New Wildlife Bill', *Edmonton Journal*, 12 April 2000.
93. SLDF, 'Summary Brief on Bill C-5', 27 March 2001 (in the author's possession).
94. Council of Forest Industries of BC, 'SARA: Finding the Balance', 10 August 2000. (Paper provided to the author.)
95. SARWG, 'Conserving Species'.
96. Andrew Duffy, 'Wildlife Bill Strikes Balance, Minister Says: Species at Risk Act "a titanic failure", Environmentalists Argue', *Ottawa Citizen*, 12 April 2000.
97. SLDF, 'Recommended Revisions to Bill C-5', 13 May 2001 (in the author's possession).
98. Confidential interview, July 2008.
99. Bill C-5, *Species at Risk Act*, 1st sess., 37th Parliament, 2001 (as amended by the Standing Committee on Environment and Sustainable Development).
100. Confidential interview, with former staffperson in Minister Anderson's office, July 2008.
101. The government's key revisions are summarized by Kate Smallwood, available at http://www.scientists-4-species.org (under 'Letter Campaign').

102. Kate Jaimet, 'Liberals Demanded Favours to Pass Bill', *Ottawa Citizen*, 27 December 2002.
103. Confidential interview, July 2008.
104. Ibid.
105. Ibid.
106. Karen Kraft Sloan, in discussion with Stewart Elgie, 31 May 2002 and 1 June 2002.
107. Harrison, *Passing the Buck*, discusses the importance federalism in environmental policy.
108. Richard J. Schultz, 'Introduction', in *Federalism, Bureaucracy, and Public Policy* (Montreal: McGill-Queen's University Press, 1980), 2–10, discusses the importance of executive-driven government in Canadian policy-making.
109. Mary Illical and Kathryn Harrison, 'Protecting Endangered Species in the US and Canada: The Role of Negative Lesson Drawing', *Canadian Journal of Political Science* 40, 2 (2007): 367–94.
110. Amos et al., 'Minimum Winning Coalition', 144–5.
111. Slater, interview.
112. ENGOs had set the national agenda before on *non*-legislative issues before, such as protected areas.
113. The theory of 'policy entrepeneurs' comes largely from J.W. Kingdon, *Bridging Research and Policy: Agendas, Alternatives, and Public Policies* (New York: HarperCollins, 1995).
114. Christopher Eliott, *Forest Certification: A Policy Network Perspective* (Jakarta: Centre for International Forestry Research, 2000), 125–68; Benjamin Cashore, Graeme Auld, and Deanna Newsom, *Governing Through Markets* (New Haven: Yale University Press, 2004), 59–87.
115. See, for example, the Whitehorse Mining Initiative, available at http://www.mining.ca/www/Links/Initiative_White horse.php.
116. See, for example, Canadian Boreal Initiative, available at http://www.borealcanada.ca.
117. Kraft Sloan, interview.
118. For a summary of provincial endangered species laws see http://www.environmentaldefence.ca/reports/Endangered%20 Species_Final_ebook.pdf.
119. Catherine Hoffman, 'Keeping up with the Feds: The Provincial Response to Canada's Species at Risk Act', LLM thesis, University of Ottawa, 2008.
120. Stewart Elgie, 'Statutory Structure and Species Survival: How Constraints on Cabinet Discretion Affect Endangered Species Listing Outcomes', *Journal of Environmental Law and Practice* 19 (2008): 1–32.
121. Ibid.
122. Ibid.
123. Stewart Elgie, Scott Findlay, and Linda Burr, *SARA implementation database*, information in author's possession.
124. Freedman et al., 'Species at Risk', 26
125. Elgie et al., *SARA implementation database*.
126. 'Feds Change Direction After Endangered Species Lawsuit', *EcoJustice Newsletter*, 9 February 2007; 'Feds Work to Protect Endangered Species Only When Sued', *EcoJustice Newsletter*, 19 March 2008.
127. Elgie et al., *SARA implementation database*.

15

Water Pollution Policy in Canada: Cases from the Past and Lessons for the Future

Carolyn Johns and Mark Sproule-Jones

Nearly 50 years after the introduction of water pollution legislation in Canada, 30 years after a concerted effort in the Great Lakes to address water quality, and almost 10 years after the shocking drinking water pollution tragedy in Walkerton, Ontario, drinkable, swimmable, and fishable waters remain elusive policy goals in many coasts, lakes, and rivers. Despite some progress, water pollution remains an important environmental problem. Policy debates about the quantity and quality of water resources in Canada are increasingly on the agendas of all levels of government in both urban and rural communities across the country.

Water is essential to life. It is a vital resource that is essential for all environmental and societal processes.[1] A person can live without food for more than a month but can live for only a few days without water.[2] Canada boasts nine per cent of the world's available freshwater supply (surface water and groundwater) and 24 per cent of the world's wetlands.[3] Approximately eight per cent of Canada is covered by freshwater in lakes and rivers; however, 68 per cent of all Canada's freshwater is in the form of ice, and once groundwater is added, over 99 per cent of freshwater supplies are accounted for. The amount of remaining fresh water—including all lakes, rivers, and streams—accounts for less than one per cent of the total supply![4] Despite Canada's comparative water wealth, uses of water have increased and intensified, many communities face shortages, and poor water quality is an issue in many watersheds. Recent reports indicate these problems will likely become worse as a result of climate change.[5]

In the 1970s governments and communities began to take action to address water pollution. 'First Generation' policy efforts focused on obvious point sources or 'end-of-pipe' sources of water pollution such as industrial effluent and municipal sewage outfalls. Governments and communities identified and tried to control the wide range of users who primarily were using waterways for dumping treated and untreated wastes. By the late 1980s, Next Generation efforts began to focus on a much wider range of water stakeholders and the connection between water pollution and ecosystems was increasingly apparent. Scientists highlighted that toxic chemicals were having significant environmental impacts and, in jurisdictions like the United States, 'non-point sources' such as runoff from agriculture, urban areas, and golf courses were significant sources which required different policy approaches.[6] In addition, Next Generation approaches began to move beyond the command-and-control type instruments described in Chapter 4 by Mark Winfield to a wider range and mix of policy instruments. However, by the mid-1990s progress began to slow as the environment and water quality issues were trumped by economic issues on the political agendas of Canadian governments.

In this chapter, we review water pollution policy efforts in Canada, both in general and in two cases, to highlight how policy has evolved over time and what challenges remain. The first section of the chapter outlines the multiple uses and users of water that have resulted in degradation of water quality. This section outlines how an increase in the number of uses and the institutionalized hierarchy of uses sets the stage for political conflict. The second section provides a brief overview of policy efforts by governments and water stakeholders. This section is followed by two case studies. Both cases are situated in the Great Lakes and are illustrative of policy goals, processes, instruments and actors in watersheds across Canada. The cases illustrate that Canada has come some way since First Generation efforts, but the move to Next Generation water pollution policies in the past decade has been slow and variable. This, in turn, has an impact on Canada's ability to move toward approaches which integrate water quantity and quality; address the cumulative impacts of climate, air, and land use in cross-medium approaches;[7] and link natural and social systems at the watershed scale[8] in what has broadly been labelled as 'integrated water resource management'.[9]

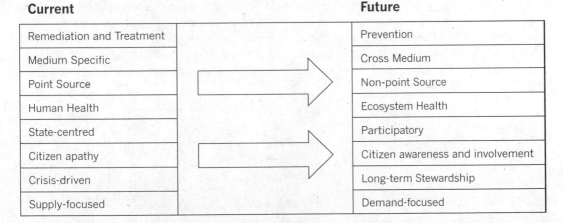

Current	Future
Remediation and Treatment	Prevention
Medium Specific	Cross Medium
Point Source	Non-point Source
Human Health	Ecosystem Health
State-centred	Participatory
Citizen apathy	Citizen awareness and involvement
Crisis-driven	Long-term Stewardship
Supply-focused	Demand-focused

Figure 15.1 Next Generation Water Policy

This chapter outlines the challenges Canada faces in moving to Next Generation approaches despite the significance of water to the economy, environment, society, and the cultural identity of the country. In keeping with the themes of this book, the themes of leadership and policy innovation are central to the analysis.

Multiple-uses and the Water Pollution Challenge

Given the vastness of Canada's water resources, it is not surprising that the human uses of water are numerous and varied. Consider for a moment your own local watershed. Water as a resource can simultaneously serve in any or all of the following purposes: a source of drinking water, a habitat, a transportation route, a waste disposal outlet, a source of energy, an input into many manufacturing and commercial processes, a recreational and tourism attraction, a resource needed for food production, a climatic component, and a source of spirituality. In many Canadian watersheds, users include not only local actors but also those along the Canada–US border and international users. Economic uses have been central to the evolution of water policy. From the earliest uses of water for shipping, fishing, agriculture, forestry, and human settlements to the more recent for industry, electricity, recreation, and bottling, there has been a gradual increase in the number of uses of water. Primary industries which utilize water in production account for nearly six per cent of the GDP in 2000, accounting for over $45 billion and employing more than 650,000 people[10] and some 45 per cent of Canadian industries.[11]

These demands in many watersheds are increasing. The potential for competition and conflict between these multiple uses is self-evident. Policies related to water management are also complicated by the fact that people sharing a single water resource may be separated by vast geographic, cultural, and political spaces, thus making it difficult for users to even recognize their hydrological interdependence and the implications of their use for others. For example, a farmer upstream may be using water for his crops and livestock production and, knowingly or unknowingly, be a source of polluted runoff for those users downstream.

Water is thus a deceptively complex resource to govern and is often characterized as a common pool resource. Common pools are distinctive because they are inherently shared and 'subtractible' in that, if one person removes or degrades part of a common pool, there is less available and reduced quality for the others who share it. Resources of this type are vulnerable to destruction through over-use, over-consumption, and over-pollution because sustainable management of common pools

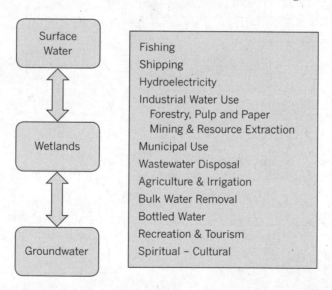

Figure 15.2 Water Uses in Canada

Source: Adapted from Sproule-Jones, et al. 2008. *Canadian Water Politics: Conflicts and Institutions* (Montreal and Kingston: McGill-Queen's University Press).

usually requires cooperation and trust among those who use and share the resource, and this can be very difficult to achieve. In the absence of cooperation, unrestrained competition among resource users can result in accelerated resource use and, eventually, a 'tragedy of the commons' in which the resource is completely depleted or degraded to the detriment of all.[12] These factors all set the stage for a number of different, concurrent, and enduring water pollution problems.

A Brief History of Water Pollution Policies

As water historians will attest, the impact of water on human settlement patterns and economic development uses of Canada's vast water resources were well established by the mid-to-late nineteenth century and continue to define many of the rules and policies related to water resource management that endure today. Water policy for both water quantity and quality has evolved separately[13] over two broad historical periods—the common law period and the public law period.[14] Across the country, early conflicts related to water quality were based on common law and private litigation adjudicated by the courts. Over time, common law has been supplemented and replaced by statutory law under the authority of the Canadian Constitution and legal challenges related to private litigation, jurisdictional conflicts and Aboriginal treaty rights. The Canadian constitution does not explicitly allocate responsibility for water resource management to the federal or provincial governments. Over time, a complex layering of legislation, authorities, and agreements have evolved to manage water resources and address water pollution in Canada.[15]

The federal government derives its powers related to water pollution and resource management from some legal sources which pre-date Confederation and various statutes passed under its constitutional powers (see Table 15.1). The current federal policy regime relies especially on regulations under the Fisheries Act, Canadian Environmental Protection Act, Canadian Environmental Assessment Act, Navigable Waters Protection Act; programs under the International Boundary Waters Treaty; the Great Lakes Water Quality Agreement (GLWQA); and the auspices of the International Joint Commission (IJC), as well as through spending programs and negotiated agreements with the provinces under the Canada Water Act (which remains the first and only piece of federal legislation explicitly related to water resource management) and the Federal Water Policy (which was developed in 1987 following the Pearse Inquiry on Federal Water Policy).[16]

In practice, water resource management is primarily governed by provincial regulations within the context of Canadian federalism.[18] Section 92 outlines provincial constitutional powers (the territories fall under federal jurisdiction) under which provinces have legislated in a variety of areas related to water quality including public health, drinking water, municipal treatment and sewage systems, agricultural and industrial uses, and water takings. Provinces have also delegated large areas of responsibility over local matters such as water supply, sewage collection, land-use planning, and water quality regulations to a variety of different municipal and regional authorities. In Ontario, and more recently in other provinces, water pollution is also the responsibility of watershed authorities. Local governments and agencies are the primary policy actors involved in water and sewage treatment, domestic water supply, and general water infrastructure. Ontario's experience is used here as a reasonably typical example of provincial laws and regulations (see Table 15.2).

In addition to independent legislative actions by federal, provincial, and local governments, 'the most-effective problem solving is often accomplished through intergovernmental agreement rather

Table 15.1 Federal Water Pollution-related Legislation and Agencies

Federal Water-Related Legislation

Fisheries Act (1868, 1970, 1985)

Navigable Waters Act (1882); Navigable Waters Protection Act (1985)

Canada Shipping Act (1985, 2001)

Arctic Waters Pollution Prevention Act (1985)

Canada Water Act (1970)

International River Improvements Act (1970)

Department of Environment Act (1978, 1985)

Canadian Wildlife Act (1985, 1994)

Canadian Environmental Protection Act[17] (1988, 1999)

Canadian Environmental Assessment Act (1992)

International Boundary Waters Treaty Act (1909)

Great Lakes Water Quality Agreement (1972, 1978, 1987)

Great Lakes Charter (1985), Annex 2001

Federal Water-related Policies

Federal Water Policy 1987

Federal Wetlands Policy 1991

Agricultural Policy Framework 2002; 2006

Canadian Drinking Water Guidelines (1968, 1972, 1978, 1986, 2996, 2006)

Other Policy Related Inquiries

Inquiry on Federal Water Policy (1984–85)

Green Plan (1990–93)

Policy Research Initiative

Clean Water Network

Federal Departments and Agencies with Water Policy-Related Mandates

Environment Canada

Canada Centre for Inland Waters

National Water Research Institute

Fisheries and Oceans

Health Canada

Natural Resources Canada

Transport Canada

Agriculture and Agri-food Canada

Foreign Affairs and International Trade

Indian Affairs and Northern Development

Parks Canada

Others

Industry Canada

Office of the Auditor General, Coimmissioner of Environment and Sustainable Development

Public Works and Government Services

Infrastructure Canada

National Defence Canada

Policy Research Initiative

National Roundtable of Environment and Economy

Intergovernmental

Canadian Council of Ministers of the Environment, Water Agenda Development Committee

Transboundary

Internationmal Joint Commission and related boards

than legislative dictates'[19] and watershed level efforts across the country. The Canadian Council of Ministers of the Environment (CCME) brings environment ministers and officials together to discuss water quality issues. The Canada Wide Accord on Environmental Harmonization, which was signed by all provinces (except Québec) in 1998, is the most comprehensive multilateral agreement related to the environment. However, sub-agreements on water quality management have not been negotiated or formalized.[20] For many years, the governments have cooperated to develop water quality guidelines, drinking water quality guidelines, and, more recently, the CCME has been involved in water quality monitoring and municipal effluent issues,[21] a national freshwater water quality index tool,[22] and groundwater as a priority issue.[23] In addition, the federal government and Ontario have

Table 15.2 Ontario's Water Pollution-Related Legislation and Agencies

Ontario's Water-Related Legislation	Ontario's Ministries and Agencies with Water-Related Mandates	Areas of Responsibility
Ontario Water Resources Act	Environment	Water takings and industrial and municipal discharges to surface source water protection.
Conservation Authorities Act	Natural Resources	Dams and other 'improvements' to lakes and rivers (e.g., canals); forestry, approval of gravel pits and quarries, construction of oil, gas and brine wells.
Environmental Protection Act	Agriculture, Food and Rural Affairs	Farms and intensive livestock operations
Canada–Ontario Agreement on the Great Lakes	Conservation Authorities	Flood plain management; watershed management; conservation; source protection
Municipal–Industrial Strategy for Abatement 1986	Northern Development and Mines	Mineral exploration, mine operation, closure, and remediation
Nutrient Management Act 2002	Transportation	Road and highway construction and maintenance
Safe Drinking Water Act 2002	Municipal Affairs	Land-use planning; financing of municipal infrastructure
Clean Water Act 2006	Consumer and Business Services Technical Standards and Safety Authority	Underground storage tanks for fuels and other materials.

Source: Adapted and expanded from Winfield, M. 2002. *IDRC Policy Workshop on Local Water Management* (Ottawa: IRDC).

had several bilateral agreements related to the GLWQA. Many of these efforts have been targeted at the watershed level and involve non-government organizations and local actors.

Paralleling the growth of the environmental movement outlined by Paehlke in Chapter 1 of this volume, since the 1970s the number of interest groups and community groups involved in partnership arrangements to manage water resources and address water use conflicts has increased dramatically. Many different groups have been very active in water quality policy over the past few decades. In terms of non-governmental stakeholders virtually all industries and agricultural operations use water and are important stakeholders in water management. There are national organizations such as the Canadian Water Resources Association and Canadian Water and Wastewater Association who represent private and public sector water resource professionals. There are also a number of regional industry associations such as the Council of Great Lakes Industries Association, and industry-specific groups related to shipping ports, fishing, and other commercial and industrial uses. In addition, there are recreation groups and hunting and fishing groups like Ducks Unlimited with water agendas.

In Canada, water protection agendas are primarily represented by broader environmental groups at the national and provincial levels. The Canadian Environmental Law Association, Eco-justice, Environmental Defence Canada, the Council of Canadians, Pollution Probe, the Canadian Institute of Environmental Law and Policy, the Nature Conservancy of Canada and the Canadian Environmental Network all have water programs. Some are also networked with US and international organizations. In addition, there are numerous local groups with water agendas and many of these are networked on specific issues at the watershed level. There are even virtual water stakeholders and watchdogs like water.ca and listservs, like H2Oinfo. Finally, there are various research and academic networks with water research agendas such as the Canadian Water Network.

As an increasing number of these water policy stakeholders and scientists highlighted the problems of water pollution, First Generation approaches evolved primarily as a 'command-and-control' system of regulation over industries, municipalities, and other point sources. In this period, governmental agencies (primarily at the provincial level) developed standards for water effluent from the 'end-of-the-pipe' based on available scientific evidence about water pollution, available technologies of control and the available knowledge of the assimilative capacities of the ambient environment. Government agencies then issued regulations and enforce compliance over waste dischargers.[24] However, some 30 years after federal and provincial legislative actions and the development of regulatory regimes in many industrialized jurisdictions, the traditional point source framework of pollution control began to be criticized for failing to curtail the degradation of water resources.[25]

By the late 1980s, a different perspective was emerging whereby the dominant model of water pollution control which was the product of negotiations and bargaining between regulators and dischargers based on debatable scientific information[26] was increasingly contested. A shift was occurring that involved consultation with other users and interests, including environmentalists. By the 1990s, policy-makers increasingly recognized uncertainties in science, limitations of engineering and technological approaches, and the complexity of water pollution from an ecosystem perspective. Governments also began shifting to a broader range of more market-based instruments such as voluntary guidelines and financial incentives.[27] Combined with a political shift away from environmental priorities and a focus on the economy by governments at all levels, the shift to Next Generation water pollution policy efforts slowed.

To assess the evolution and current state of water policy in Canada, we now turn to two real-world water pollution cases both of which are in Ontario in the Great Lakes basin (see Figure 15.3). The Great Lakes themselves support 35 million inhabitants, some 10 million Canadians, and eight of Canada's 20 largest cities.[28] The basin occupies a half a billion square kilometres and contains 18 per cent of the world's fresh surface water.[29] Despite some indicators of environmental progress in the basin,[30] increasing and multiple uses contribute to pollution in many watersheds.[31] By the late 1980s, an estimated 57 million tonnes of liquid waste were being dumped into the Great Lakes annually.[32] More recent estimates by environmental groups indicate hundreds of thousands of chemicals, some 625 million kilograms of pollutants and over 90 billion litres of untreated sewage are released annually into the basin. [33] Both cases in the basin reflect policies, processes, and actors common to water pollution issues in other parts of the country.

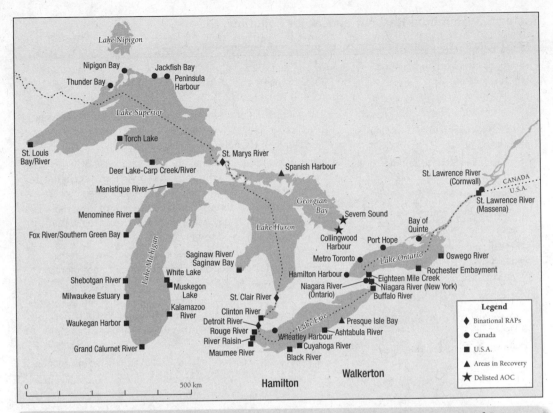

Figure 15.3 Areas of Concern in the Great Lakes, Identified by the International Joint Commission and the Sites of Hamilton and Walkerton, Ontario

The Case of Hamilton Harbour, Randle's Reef, and Point Source Remediation

Our first case is set in Hamilton Harbour which lies at the western edge of Lake Ontario, the deepest and most populated lake on the Canadian side of the Great Lakes Basin and Ontario's largest commercial port. The Harbour measures some 40 km² and is accessible by a human-made ship canal, completed in 1830. Some half a million people live in the watershed, with 56 per cent of the employment in heavy manufacturing.[34] The multiple uses of Hamilton Harbour, including shipping and heavy industry and municipal uses have contributed to water pollution. In 1987, the IJC identified 43 polluted bays, harbours, and river mouths on the Great Lakes (see Figure 15.3). These polluted areas are called 'Areas of Concern' (AOCs) and mandated governments in the US and Canada, under the GLWQA, to cooperate in addressing water pollution through multi-stakeholder efforts and Remedial Action Plans (RAPs). Hamilton Harbour was designated as an AOC because it suffers from many of the 'impaired uses' listed in Table 15.3.

Table 15.3 Hamilton Harbour and Water Pollution

AOC Use Impairments due to water pollution	Additional Indicators
Variety of impaired human, and ecosystem uses: • Restrictions on fish and wildlife consumption • Degradation of fish and wildlife populations • Fish tumours and other deformities • Bird and animal deformities or reproductive problems • Degradation of benthic populations • Restrictions on dredging • Undesirable algae/eutrophication • Taste and odour in drinking water • Beach closings • Degradation of aesthetics • Added costs for agriculture or industry • Degraded phytoplankton and zooplankton • Degraded fish and wildlife habitat.	• 25 per cent of the habour is reclaimed land for industrial and port purposes; only 25 per cent of the wetlands that existed in 1800 still remain. • Seven industrial and four municipal point sources discharge 27 billion gallons of liquid waste annually or 40 per cent of the volume of Harbour waters (Sproule-Jones, 1993). • Water quality conditions include elevated levels of phosphorus, ammonia, heavy metals (like iron), polyaromatic hydrocarbons (toxic coal tar), and polychlorinated biphenols (toxic 'engine' lubricants). Some 50 percent of toxic materials (by weight) are still discharged into the Great Lakes. Current pollution controls require only partial reductions. • Dissolved oxygen levels vary by season and levels in the water and anoxic conditions can occur in summer months. • Pathogens come largely from three munucipal sewage treatment plants and storm drains (many of which take sewer overflows on rainy days). As a result, water contact sports are banned and beaches were often closed from 1930 to 1998 and frequently since then. • Sport fishers and citizens are advised to limit fish consumptions. • Accumulated toxic wastes reside in Hamilton Harbour and many other Areas of Concern.

Source: International Joint Commission, Areas of Concern and Remedial Action Plans; Environment Canada and US, EPA, State of the Lakes Ecosystem Reports.

Although the environmental and water pollution problems identified are specific to Hamilton Harbour, the impaired uses are typical of water pollution problems in other AOCs and watersheds across the country. The clean-up and remedial process, although touted at the time as innovative and unique, is also illustrative of the politics of clean-up efforts across the country. The RAP process itself was an experiment involving the creation of institutions designed to increase stakeholder involvement. The RAP process involved two stages: first, the identification of problems that needed to be remediated; and, second, an implementation plan to be 'de-listed' as an AOC. It was successful in Stage 1 and had some success in Stage 2 but, like many other RAPs on the Great Lakes, was less successful in implementation.[35] Indeed, progress slowed considerably in implementing the GLWQA in the late 1990s[36] with only three AOCs delisted by 2008 (see Figure 15.3).[37] The politics related to the primary 'hotspot' in Hamilton Harbour illustrates some reasons why.

Randle's Reef

Randle's Reef is a natural rocky reef some 5–8 metres underwater near a shipping pier used for the offloading of coal and which is owned by Stelco (now US Steel). The reef and surrounding harbour bed form a water lot owned by the Hamilton Port Authority (HPA), an authority with powers that pre-date Confederation. An outfall from the steel company discharges into the area. The sediments at Randle's were contaminated largely by coal tar compounds and metals. In 1984 a spill from the company was certified and appropriately dredged and removed by the Ontario Ministry of Environment (MOE). However, since that time scientific studies revealed many metals (especially iron) exceeded MOE 'Severe Effect Levels' and detectable levels of other toxic chemicals such as PCBs (polychlorinated biphenyls), dioxins, furans, and organochlorines are present. PAH levels (polycyclic aromatic hydrocarbons which are coal tar contaminants, known carcinogens and extremely toxic to humans and other species) exceeded 800 parts per million in some sediment cores, levels which are only exceeded in Canada at the infamous Sydney Tar Ponds in Nova Scotia. The problem is compounded by wave action from ships berthing nearby, which redistribute the sediments across the harbour bed. By 1994, Environment Canada (EC) had devised, in consultation with MOE, a plan to remove some 30,000 m^3, or approximately the volume of sediments at Randles that exceeded 800ppm.

In terms of strategies, early in the process EC determined it did not want to risk losing a court case against Stelco for violating the Fisheries Act. EC had authority to use this Act as a major piece of 'in site' water pollution control. However, it had no unambiguous proof that the contaminated sediments may not have originated from another point or accumulated from non-point sources. Stelco naturally argued for their innocence. EC also wanted to demonstrate that it could engage in productive partnerships with industries like Stelco and provincial agencies like the MOE. EC thus proposed a three-way split of the clean-up costs. Interestingly, this was purely an Ontario Region policy and EC, at its headquarters in Ottawa, was silent on the issue. Stelco refused to endorse any plan.

In 1995, the Canadian Minister of Environment committed to pay $5 million of the estimated total cost to dredge, treat, and dispose of the sediments. The province initially promised to match this sum, but with an intervening election of the Harris government in Ontario, the sum was reduced to $1 million. EC conducted a Comprehensive Environmental Assessment Study of technical options to remove the sediments. Stelco persuaded EC to freeze the release of the study, replace their negotiators, and examine an option to incinerate the sediments in Stelco's scrap metal furnace. Stelco even proposed that the parties use untendered outsourcing to Stelco client organizations to do the necessary clean-up work to limit everyone's costs. It took almost six years to meet, discuss, and ultimately reject these options.

By 2001, EC began again due in part to pressures from the local stakeholders group. The incineration option had threatened the EC plan to reduce air pollution. This time, they persuaded the Port to remove objections to infilling in navigable waters and they offered instead to 'confine, fill, and cap' the Reef based on a model used in Thunder Bay. This meant dumping more, potentially contaminated, sediments from other sites on top of the Reef and then covering it with clay soil and a hard asphalt surface cap. The Port was enthusiastic since they were going to get a new shipping pier—initially of nine acres and now 50 acres—paid for by government environmental funds. They could issue the navigable waters permit and EC could proceed with its environmental assessment of this option. Stelco would be absolved of all liabilities under the Fisheries Act and the evidence would be literally buried under contaminated fill. It was a win–win–win solution for EC, the Port, and for Stelco especially, but not for the environment. The new 50-acre port facility will cost $90 million and the federal and provincial governments have recently pledged one-third each. The remainder will have to be raised locally from the Port Authority, the municipalities, and other stakeholders—an unlikely prospect. Furthermore, given the historical and continuing environmental impacts of industry and municipal effluent, Hamilton Harbour is no closer to being de-listed as an AOC.

The Case of Walkerton, Non-point Source Water Pollution, and Drinking Water

Nearly 10 years ago Canadians were shocked by the event known as the 'Walkerton Tragedy' in which seven residents of a small town in Ontario died and over 2,000 more became ill after drinking water polluted with E.coli bacteria that had come from animal waste that leached into the ground water.[38] This tragedy pushed issues regarding water quality and environmental contamination by traditional water users to the very top of the political agenda in Ontario and garnered national media coverage.

Although all provinces, including Ontario, had regulations to control point sources of water pollution for some point sources, many sources were required only to meet water quality and drinking water quality objectives and only British Columbia had a five-year program to deal specifically with non-point source (NPS) water pollution prior to Walkerton.[39] Most other provinces, including Ontario, had only indirect policy instruments to deal with polluted runoff: voluntary best management practices (BMPs) supported by cost-shared subsidies, some land-use regulation under provincial planning legislation, and indirect water protection through tax incentives and conservation easements.[40] Agricultural waste and the negative ecological implications of farming practices were not covered directly by Ontario's EPA and governed by the Ministry of Environment (MOE) but rather left to the discretion of the Ontario Ministry of Agriculture Food and Rural Affairs (OMAFRA) under the Farm Practices Protection Act[41] and other voluntary agro-environmental policies and programs based on BMPs and Environmental Farm Plans.[42]

In the late 1990s, the MOE, as the lead agency in point-source water pollution management was enduring significant funding and staff cuts under the Harris government's Common Sense Revolution, which emphasized de-regulation and downsizing of the environmental bureaucracy.[43] The Ministry's operating budget declined from a high in 1989–90 of $454 million to $164.8 million in 1999–00. Staffing levels at MOE dropped from a high of 2,450 in 1990 to 1,460 in 1999.[44] The Ministry of Natural Resources (MNR), which also has an important policy role in protecting wetlands, forests, fish habitat streams, and other aspects of water resource management in Ontario including non-agricultural, rural land, also faced significant budget reductions. Conservation Authorities (Ontario's long standing watershed agencies) and Ontario's Great Lakes efforts also faced serious declines during this period. Overall, the main thrust of Ontario water policy and focus of the provincial bureaucracy, prior to Walkerton, was to regulate some industrial and municipal point sources and focus on drinking water quality objectives through point source permitting, not non-point sources.[45]

During this same period, the federal government was not actively involved in defining the problem of NPS pollution beyond Environment Canada's role in some basic research on selected watercourses[46] and funding some agro-environmental initiatives. Federal legislation and implementation efforts pre-Walkerton reflected the federal government's role in research and its emphasis on providing some infrastructure funding to indirectly support point source efforts.[47] As outlined in the previous case, federal engagement in water pollution policy in the Great Lakes also declined during this period. In summary, prior to Walkerton the state of water policy in Canada and Ontario was in decline and narrowly focused on point-sources. No federal or provincial policy instrument strategies had been initiated to address NPS water pollution problems and only some indirect provincial and municipal policy instruments addressed this type of water pollution.

Post Walkerton Policy Changes

In response to the water pollution tragedy in Walkerton and the outpouring of public concern and demands for accountability from the opposition, the Harris government appointed Justice Dennis O'Connor to head the Walkerton Inquiry, an independent commission under the Public Inquiries Act in Ontario. In his Part I report released in 2002, Justice O'Connor argued that 'the primary, if not the only, source of the contamination was manure that had been spread on a farm near Well 5. The owner of this farm followed proper practices [in place at the time] and should not be faulted in any way.'[48] He used what were widely accepted as BMPs in spreading the manure. Justice O'Connor also outlined that the existing Ontario Drinking Water Objectives (ODWO) in 2000 failed and stated that: 'I am satisfied that matters as important to water safety and public health as those set out in these guidelines should instead have been covered by regulations—which, unlike guidelines, are legally binding.'[49] In addition, Justice O'Connor found that for years, the Public Utilities Commission (PUC) operators (Stan and Frank Koebel) engaged in a number of improper operating practices, including failing to monitor, false reporting, and ignoring MOE guidelines and directives.

Despite the capacity issues of the MOE before the Walkerton tragedy, in his Part II report Justice O'Connor recommended that the MOE be the lead provincial agency with regard to all aspects of providing safe drinking water, including watershed-based source protection. He recommended that existing institutional arrangements be used to develop and implement several new pieces of legislation. The successive Eves (Conservative) and McGuinty (Liberal) governments committed to implementing all of the recommendations from the O'Connor reports and passed three major new pieces of legislation.

The *Safe Drinking Water Act* (SDWA) passed by the Eves government in 2002 was based on a multi-barrier approach to protect water 'from source to tap'. It designated and funded MOE as the lead agency in developing and implementing regulations related to the treatment and distribution of drinking water.[50] In the same year The *Nutrient Management Act* (NMA) was also passed to replace the voluntary system that existed prior to Walkerton and gave some BMPs the force of law. The NMA provides a comprehensive nutrient management framework for Ontario's agricultural industry, municipalities, and other generators of materials containing nutrients through the review and approval of nutrient management plans, certification of land applicators, and a new registry system for all land applications of waste under MOE.[51] In addition, after significant expert and public consultation, the government passed the *Clean Water Act* (CWA) in December 2006. This legislation required the establishment of Source Water Protection Committees (SWPCs) consisting of local actors to develop Source Water Protection Plans (SWPPs) for watersheds in Ontario and designated MOE and conservation authorities as the lead agencies.[52] Although this legislation has been criticized because sources, such as some wells on private property, are excluded from protection plans, it is a post-Walkerton policy improvement and has more recently made explicit linkages to water quality efforts in the Great Lakes.[53]

There have been very few policy studies which focus on the impact of the Walkerton tragedy and inquiry on water policy in Ontario and Canada. Clearly there is evidence that this tragedy stimulated a legislative response in Ontario. There is anecdotal evidence that drinking water is 'safer' in Ontario post-Walkerton as a result of the reinvestment in water policy institutions, restructuring of the MOE, renewed faith in regulatory approaches, and a new policy instrument mix to address both point and non-point sources of water pollution in the province.[54] There is no evidence, however, that water quality has improved. When compared with the Hamilton Harbour case in this chapter, and the broader themes of the volume on leadership and innovation, there are some common policy lessons.

Policy Lessons from the Cases

In comparing these cases, it is evident that water pollution policy in Canada has evolved during the past 30 years but that significant water pollution challenges remain. The cases highlight the goals, process, instruments, actors and outcomes which are evident in watersheds throughout the country. Both cases reveal the endemic conflict between the various users of rivers, coasts, lakes, and aquifers, particularly between waste disposers and those other users that rely on unpolluted waters for drinking, swimming, and fishing. What is notable in both these cases is how the historic shipping, waste disposal and industry group of users remain dominant, despite challenges from new users and environmental interests. In both cases, industries have enjoyed major powers to dump partially treated wastes into adjacent waters and farmers enjoyed the freedoms to use their lands and waters without major regulations, forcing other users to challenge these established uses. This pattern is evident in other water policy cases where similar winners and losers can be found on the west coast, the east coast, the Prairie rivers, and the St Lawrence.[55] In many ways, this is due to the 'rig of the political game' or the way our institutions and policy processes are structured and how they respond to conflicts among users.

The Walkerton tragedy revealed the weaknesses of water pollution policy and the need to re-align historical water rights, interests, and institutional arrangements. Despite the nerve that the Walkerton tragedy hit with policy-makers and the public, and despite the resulting policy efforts and resources in the aftermath of the Walkerton Inquiry, agricultural interests have a firm economic stake in ensuring that these institutions are not altered significantly and that regulatory point source instruments are not applied to non-point source problems. Similarly, in the Randle's Reef case, the established interests of the polluting industry (in this case US Steel, formerly Stelco) and the regulator (Environment Canada) and the power of the Hamilton Port Authority to issue cleanup permits on its navigable waters trumped other interests. The game was rigged to limit the influence of other stakeholders through judicious selection of participants in decision-making committees. Both cases highlight how existing uses are entrenched and how challenging it is to move water quality goals to the front and centre in terms of water uses. Both cases also highlight the need to re-balance water uses.

Another general lesson is that governments are typically at the centre of water resource disputes as regulators. Notably, they are often government departments or ministries, like Environment Canada or provincial environmental ministries. These bureaucratic institutions have broad discretionary powers granted by legislation and report to ministers, cabinets, and legislatures with varying degrees of frequency and detail. These substantial discretionary powers allow them (in many provinces and situations) to act like owners and proprietors to manage, lease, include, and exclude users. Provincial departments enjoy this kind of status related to water takings and permissible pollution and in general still treat water as a 'free' good, useable for some wastes (for industrial, municipal and agriculture uses), some with partial regulations (like wastes from municipal sewage treatment plants), and some even with no regulations (like pharmaceuticals in waste waters). The cases, however, raise serious questions about governments as environmental leaders related to water policy.

Both cases also highlight the intergovernmental and inter-agency challenges inherent in water pollution policy. In the Randle's Reef and Hamilton Harbour case the federal government was the lead agency coordinating a policy process with involvement of DFO and the Ontario Ministry of the Environment under the auspices of fisheries regulations and Great Lakes clean-up efforts. However, after almost 20 years of study and policy debate, the configuration of interests remained stable, with government agencies and industry together against many local stakeholders and environmentalists.

In the Walkerton case, despite similar drinking water pollution events in North Battleford, Saskatchewan in 2001 and the Kashechewan First Nation in 2005,[56] the federal government was noticeably absent and the drinking water focus put the provincial government at the centre of this water pollution case. Walkerton became an intra-governmental dispute process between agriculture interests on the one hand and public health and environmental interests on the other. It took a public inquiry, nongovernmental stakeholders, new legislation, new financing for provincial agencies, and long-term political commitment to reconfigure the interests related to drinking water pollution. Both cases thus highlight the challenge of institutional and environmental policy innovation when certain uses and interests are entrenched.

The other lesson evident in both cases is that, increasingly, government agencies and polluters find their powers are contested. In both cases, public and stakeholder involvement increased over time. The Hamilton Harbour case is an example of community involvement designed along the lines of participatory democracy. Institutional innovation in the Great Lakes AOCs was designed to increase stakeholder involvement in RAPs. However, in the Randle's Reef case it was clear that, although provision has been made for community stakeholders to be involved in the remediation processes, their influence as an 'add on' to the traditional managerial approach in these processes was slight, and governmental and industry actors felt little compunction about manipulating these processes to serve their own ends. Efforts made by EcoJustice and Environment Hamilton to persuade ministers to question the decisions of their bureaucrats proved ineffective. Ministers are told that these are technical issues and regulators and regulatees have objective, unassailable technical knowledge. This was another way to keep stakeholders at the margins. Scientific uncertainty and lack of public knowledge of the state of water quality in many watersheds makes this a common theme in Canadian water policy.

The Walkerton tragedy mobilized public interest. A public inquiry created policy space for the mobilization of environmental groups, altered the status quo among users and state managers, and resulted in some policy change. The inquiry presented a temporary government institution and policy window for environment and public health interests to focus on drinking water policies and make some significant policy changes in the decade that followed. As a result, drinking water was brought to the top of the policy agenda in Ontario.

Both cases also highlight the costs of water pollution and the impact of declining environmental policy capacity in the 1990s that reinforced a narrow focus on point source water pollution. Although other jurisdictions, such as the US, had passed federal and state legislation to address non-point sources and had realized that water quality objectives would not be met without this important part of a water policy framework, Canadian jurisdictions lagged in recognizing the significance of non-point source pollution and source protection[57] and integrating efforts in the Great Lakes.[58] The focus on source protection as part of the drinking water policy framework also helped bring the significance of NPS water pollution problems to the attention of policy-makers. However, the connections between human health and ecosystem health are not clearly integrated in the post-Walkerton policy framework and a broad integration of drinking water policies and non-point source water policies remains to be seen as the province implements source water protection under the CWA. Declining capacity in Environment Canada and related to GLWQA efforts in the 1990s are reflected in the Randle's Reef case, where EC was anxious to strike a deal with industry in order to show that collaboration could be a prudent economic and environmental strategy.

Finally, both cases also highlight the evolution of policy responses and the attempts to move beyond First Generation approaches as a result of scientific findings, stakeholder demands, and community awareness of water pollution problems. However, the cases highlight the centrality of the point source policy regime and First Generation water pollution goals. The Hamilton Harbour case illustrates that many water pollution problems are historical and pose a unique challenge as time distances past point-source polluters from clean-up responsibilities. The Walkerton tragedy highlights the significance of non-point source water pollution which, until Walkerton, was not part of the water pollution policy regime in Ontario or other parts of Canada. Related to this, how water pollution issues are framed and perceived by the public and policy-makers is critical to the approaches used to address them. In the Hamilton Harbour case, bargaining and negotiation characterized the typical way water pollution clean-up problems were defined and how solutions were devised. In the Walkerton case, by framing drinking water contamination as a public health issue rather than as a pollution and environmental issue, some substantive policy change did occur. In contrast to the pre-Walkerton period, the instrument choice has shifted back from voluntary, moral suasion to a more regulatory approach based on watershed protection efforts.

Current approaches to water pollution suggest the enduring impact of institutions and rights of users even in the aftermath of significant water pollution events. Our cases also illustrate the slow pace of policy and institutional changes. In some cases, it may be due to perceived improvements in water quality, as in the Great Lakes. In other instances, there may be limited knowledge, such as with groundwater and provincial water extraction regimes. The cases also illustrate that crisis, particularly human health crisis, may be the most significant stimulus of policy and institutional change. They also highlight that sometimes policy and institutional change comes from within the state itself, from public inquiries, the Supreme Court, or intergovernmental sources. However, parliaments and legislatures also seem to lack the interest and capacity to reform government arrangements and proactively protect water resources without the spur of a severe crisis like Walkerton. Challenges to the system from environmentalists or Aboriginal groups have had some impact, but change only seems extensive when unanticipated crises, like the Walkerton disaster, occur. In other cases existing institutional arrangements are challenged by new water users, international actors, or organized environmental groups. But on the whole, policy responses remain reactive and remedial rather than proactive and preventative.

Conclusion: Enduring Issues and Outstanding Challenges

Many challenges remain if Canada is going to move toward Next Generation approaches to water pollution policy. Some, such as the need for leadership, are not unique to water pollution as an environmental problem. However, others specifically relate to the state of water science and knowledge, how water pollution problems are defined, and the rigid institutional constraints based on a hierarchy of water uses which prevent institutional and policy innovation designed to meet future water challenges.

First, there is the fight for a new distribution of rights to use waters. Currently, those individuals and groups of users with recognized water rights enjoy a privileged legal position in relation to those without similar rights and they can use this advantage to fend off challenges or encroachments to their water use. This conflict between rights holders and non-rights holders is the essence of many of the water use controversies, particularly those conflicts between economic users with entrenched water rights and environmentalists, Aboriginal peoples, and citizens without entrenched rights. In other words, those user groups that lay claim early on and have their rights recognized in the early stages of resource exploitation put themselves in a strong position long into the future, and fight any challenges to their rights from the legal high ground. Thus, the main power dynamic of many water use conflicts is defined by the fortuitous circumstance of which water users were first to have their water rights claims recognized in law.

Yet, in Canada's current constitutional context, it cannot be taken for granted that economic users are always the earliest recognized claimant of Canada's water resources. Increasingly, Canada's Aboriginal peoples are making recognized claims that are prior to *any* economic use in Canada, and this has considerably altered the power dynamics of some water use conflicts. The Aboriginal claims for water and fishing rights are distinct because they are being recognized retroactively, often in the courts, as a result of the enforcement of neglected treaties from the past and the affirmation of Aboriginal resource rights stemming from section 35 of the *Constitution Act, 1982*. The retroactive nature of these Aboriginal rights means that existing economic uses that were allowed to develop in the absence of recognized Aboriginal rights are significantly threatened; this creates serious potential conflict, and even violence.

Second, the continuing fights between different levels of government and between different management agencies within a level of government will become more pronounced as water policy becomes more cross-medium and transboundary in character. Canadian politics have regularly included disputes between one or more provincial governments and the federal government. These 'vertical' disputes are often over jurisdiction and, in the Great Lakes situation, include the US federal and state governments. There are also frequently 'horizontal' disputes between government agencies at the same level. Whether vertical or horizontal in nature, the disputes are usually rooted in support of different users in different regions of the country.

Third, there is a fight for community and stakeholder participation in order to change government and industry dominated policy processes. Traditionally, a strong state managerialism has dominated water resource policy. The government (particularly provincial governments) are seen as the only actors able to regulate and settle rivalries between multiple users. In contrast, significant community involvement is a more recent development in Canadian governance, having arrived since the advent of the environmental movement. Advocates of community-based governance on both the left and right of the political spectrum object to paternalistic state managerialism on a number of grounds. First, they argue that bureaucracies are inherently political, and politicians champion policies that help them secure votes and protect vested interests, not policies that are necessarily in the broader public interest. Second, those communities that live with and depend on a resource often have the most intimate knowledge of the resource and are more capable of defining the public interest, devising rules to restrain resource rivalries, and ensure accountability than remote bureaucracies. Third, Canada's past use of state managerialism has been far from impressive. Although state managerialism has a long history, this approach to natural resource management has not resulted in environmental protection and balanced water policies. In addition, the trend in Canada is toward a more participatory model of governance as many community groups demand to be directly involved in pressing water governance issues. Our cases highlight the need for innovative institutional change that can effectively integrate and balance state managerialism with the participatory model so that community participation is no longer regarded as just a mere afterthought.

Finally, we must address the challenge of moving from First Generation to Next Generation policies. Fundamentally, this is a shift from remediation and reactive policies to preventative policies. This fight is not one in which many politicians, bureaucrats, or users want to engage. It requires recognition of long-term policy goals and integration of point and non-point source regimes; drinking water policies (focusing on human health) and water quality policies (focusing on ecosystem health); water, land, air, climate policies; and water quantity and quality policies. It also requires increasing recognition of transboundary and international dimensions of water policy. This shift will also require a significant collective investment in water resource science and policy infrastructure at the watershed level. The governance system with government agencies acting as regulators, managers, and advocates of particular uses needs to evolve, arguably more quickly, to deal with Next Generation agendas like: climate change and water scarcity; transboundary challenges including those along the 3,000 plus kilometre boundary between Canada and the United States; declines in wild fish stocks; loss of wetlands; contamination of groundwater; and the growing use of chemicals and their unknown potential impacts on human and ecosystem health. There are signs that this is beginning in Ontario and other provinces, but there have been repeated calls for, and debates about, the federal government's role in this policy area.[59] The current minority Conservative government has continued the policies of the previous Liberal government and ignored calls to update the Federal Water Policy which has not be renewed in over 20 years. Even in the midst of the 2008 election campaign, when environmental issues were central to the platforms of opposition parties, water policy was not on the agenda. It was instead eclipsed by climate change as the environmental issue deserving of federal policy attention and, shortly thereafter, by the downturn in the economy. Much to the despair of environmental groups, there seems to be an entrenched perception in Ottawa that water is foremost a provincial responsibility and that provincial governments are managing multiple uses of water and the sources of water pollution in their watersheds quite well. The case studies in this chapter highlight the shortcomings of this assumption.

In order to collectively manage and protect Canada's water quality, people turn to governments or to the courts, or they take their own collective actions to find solutions. It is evident that uses of water will only increase in the future, water pollution will continue, and the policy capacity to confront Next Generation water pollution challenges will remain elusive without significant policy and institutional changes. The challenge for policy-makers is to anticipate the changes that will be forthcoming and move toward Next Generation approaches if Canada is to prevent water pollution in the future and protect its most valuable natural resource.

Questions for Review

1. Who are the main stakeholders in relation to Canada's water policy regime and are there any signs that this is changing?
2. What do the Randle's Reef and Walkerton water pollution cases have in common in terms of the policy process? How are they different?
3. Why did the Walkerton crisis occur? How effective have been the measures put in place to prevent another such crisis?
4. What is the difference between 'First Generation' and 'Next Generation' water pollution policy and are there signs that we moving toward the latter?

Notes

1. P.H. Gleick, *Water Crisis: A Guide to the World's Fresh Water Resources* (New York: Oxford University Press, 1993).
2. Canada, Environment Canada, *Freshwater Website. Freshwater Facts for Canada and the World*. 2005. Available at http://www.ec.gc.ca/water/en/info/facts (cited 26 January 2006).
3. Canada, Environment Canada, *Freshwater Website: The Nature of Water*. 2003. Available at http://www.ec.gc.ca/water/en/nature/e_nature.htm (cited 29 July 2005).
4. Canadian Atlas Online, 'This Water Rich Land'. 2006. Available at http://www.canadiangeographic.ca/atlas (cited 19 January 2006).
5. Canada, Environment Canada, *National Overview: Summary of 2002 Data* (Ottawa: Environment Canada, 2004); Canada, Environment Canada, *Water and Climate*. 2008. Available at http://www.ec.gc.ca/water/en/nature/clim/e_clim.htm.
6. United States, Environmental Protection Agency, *EPA Progress Report* (Washington, DC: Environmental Protection Agency. See also Clean Water Act Amendments 1987, Sec. 319.
7. Donald F. Kettl, ed., *Environmental Governance: A Report on the Next Generation of Environmental Policy* (Washington, DC: Brookings Institution Press, 2002).
8. F. Berkes and C. Folkes, ed. *Linking Social and Ecological Systems* (New York: Cambridge University Press, 1998).
9. There is a growing literature on integrated water resource management. For a summary see Canada, Policy Research Initiative, *Integrated Water Resource Management Briefing Note*. 2006. Available at http://www.policyresearch.gc.ca/doclib/BN_SD_IntWater_200406_e.pdf.
10. Canada, Environment Canada, *Freshwater Website. Freshwater Facts for Canada and the World*. 2005. Available at http://www.ec.gc.ca/water/en/info/facts (cited 27 January 2006).
11. Environment Canada, *Highlights of Accomplishments in the Great Lakes*. Available at http://www.on.ec.gc.ca/greatlakes/default.asp?lang=En&n=7CB9D131-1.
12. G. Hardin, 'Tragedy of the Commons', *Science* 162, 1 (1968): 1243–49.
13. David R. Boyd, *Unnatural Law: Rethinking Canadian Environmental Law and Policy* (Vancouver: UBC Press, 2003).
14. Stephen Brooks, 'Water Policy', in Stephen Brooks and Lydia Miljan, eds, *Public Policy in Canada: An Introduction*, 4th ed. (Toronto, ON: Oxford University Press, 2003).
15. C. Johns and K. Rassmussen, 'Institutions for Water Resource Management in Canada', in M. Sproule-Jones, C. Johns, and B.T. Heinmiller, eds, *Water Politics in Canada: Conflicts and Institutions* (Montreal and Kingston: McGill-Queen's University Press, 2008).
16. See Environment Canada, *Federal Water Policy*. Available at http://www.ec.gc.ca/Water/en/info/pubs/fedpol/e_fedpol.pdf. See also Canada, Inquiry on Federal Water Policy, *Currents of Change: Final Report of the Inquiry on Federal Water Policy* (Ottawa: Environment Canada, 1985); International Joint Commission, *The Great Lakes Water Quality Agreement*. Available at http://www.ijc.org/rel/agree/quality.html.
17. The Canadian Environmental Protection Act superseded the Clean Air Act, the Environmental Contaminants Act, the Ocean Dumping Control Act, and Part III of the Clean Water Act.
18. Mark H. Sproule-Jones, *Governments at Work: Canadian Parliamentary Federalism and Its Public Policy Effects* (Toronto: University of Toronto Press, 1993).
19. M. Hessing, M. Howlett, and T. Summerville, *Canadian Natural Resource and Environmental Policy: Political Economy and Public Policy*, 2nd ed. (Vancouver: University of British Columbia Press, 2005), 64.
20. Canadian Council of Ministers of the Environment, *Water Accord Backgrounder*. 1999. Available at http://www.ccme.ca/about/communiques/1999.html?item=13 (cited 29 July 2005).
21. Canadian Council of Ministers of the Environment, Municipal Wastewater Effluent Development Committee, *Municipal Wastewater Effluent in Canada*. 2006. Available at http://www.ccme.ca/assets/pdf/mwwe_general_backgrounder_e.pdf (accessed May 2008).
22. Canadian Council of Ministers of the Environment, *A Canada-wide Framework for Water Quality Monitoring*. 2006. Available at http://www.ccme.ca/assets/pdf/wqm_framework_1.0_e_web.pdf (accessed May 2008).
23. Canadian Council of Ministers of the Environment, Water Agenda Development Committee 'Request for Proposals: Review and Assessment of Canadian Groundwater Resources, Management and Current Research Mechanisms and Priorities', July 2008.
24. J. Dryzek, *The Politics of the Earth* (Toronto: Oxford University Press, 1997), 63–83.
25. Organisation for Economic Co-operation and Development, *Environmental Performance Reviews: Progress in the 1990s* (Paris: OECD, 1996).

26. A.H. Dorcey and C.L. Riek, 'Negotiation-based Approaches to the Settlement of Environmental Disputes in Canada', in *The Place of Negotiation in Environmental Assessment* (Ottawa: Canadian Environment Research Council, 1987).

27. Edward A. Parson, ed., *Governing the Environment: Persistent Challenge, Uncertain Innovations* (Toronto: University of Toronto Press, 2001).

28. Environment Canada, *Highlights of Accomplishments in the Great Lakes*. Available at http://www.on.ec.gc.ca/greatlakes/default.asp?lang=En&n=7CB9D131-1.

29. State of the Lakes Ecosystem Conference (SOLEC), *Reports 2007: Ontario*. Environment Canada. Available at http://www.epa.gov/greatlakes/solec/sogl2007/index.html.

30. Environment Canada, *Highlights of Accomplishments in the Great Lakes*. Available at http://www.on.ec.gc.ca/greatlakes/default.asp?lang=En&n=7CB9D131-1.

31. See Great Lakes Information Network, Water Pollution in the Great Lakes. 2006. Available at http://www.greatlakes.net/teach/pollution; Environmental Defence, Stats Can Population Figures Show Great Lakes Under Threat: Region's growth far higher than national average. 2007. Available at http://www.environmentaldefence.ca/pressroom/viewnews.php?id=271.

32. T. Colborn, et al. *Great Lakes, Great Legacy?* (Washington, DC: Conservation Foundation and Ottawa: Institute for Research on Public Policy, 1990), 64.

33. Great Lakes Information Network, *Water Pollution in the Great Lakes*. 2006. Available at http://www.great-lakes.net/teach/pollution; Pollution Watch 2006, *Partners in Pollution: An Assessment of Continuing Canada and US Contributions to Great Lakes Pollution*. Available at http://www.pollutionwatch.org; Sierra Legal 2006. *The Great Lakes Sewage Report Card*. Available at http://www.sierralegal.org.

34. Mark H. Sproule-Jones, *Governments at Work: Canadian Parliamentary Federalism and Its Public Policy Effects* (Toronto: University of Toronto Press, 1993).

35. Mark H. Sproule-Jones, *Restoration of the Great Lakes: Promises, Practices, Performance* (Vancouver: University of British Columbia Press, 2002).

36. Lee Botts and Paul Muldoon, *Evolution of the Great Lakes Water Quality Agreement* (East Lansing, Michigan: Michigan State University Press, 2005).

37. In 2008 the Oswego River was the third AOC, and first US AOC, to be delisted.

38. Ontario, Commission of the Walkerton Inquiry, *Part One Report of the Walkerton Inquiry* (Toronto, ON: Ontario Ministry of the Attorney General, 2002).

39. British Columbia, *Tackling Non-point Source Water Pollution in British Columbia: An Action Plan* (Victoria, BC: Ministry of Environment, Lands and Parks, Water Management Branch, 1999); C. Johns, *Non-point Source Water Pollution Management in Canada and the United States: A Comparative Analysis of Institutional Arrangements and Policy Instruments* [PhD dissertation] (Hamilton: McMaster University, 2000).

40. Ian C. Attridge, *Conservation Easement Valuation and Taxation in Canada*. Report No. 97–01, prepared for the North American Wetlands Conservation Council and Environment Canada, Canadian Wildlife Service, Habitat Conservation Division (Ottawa: Environment Canada, 1997); Ontario, Ministry of Natural Resources, *Guide to Conservation Land Tax Incentive Program* (Toronto: Ministry of Natural Resources, 1999); C. Johns, *Policy Instruments to Manage Non-point Source Water Pollution: Comparison of US States and Ontario*. Paper commissioned for the Walkerton Inquiry (Toronto: Ministry of the Attorney General, Queen's Printer for Ontario, 2002).

41. E. Montpetit and W. Coleman, 'Policy Communities and Policy Divergence in Canada: Agro-environmental Policy Development in Quebec and Ontario', *Canadian Journal of Political Science* 32 (1999): 4, 701; E. Montpetit, 'Sound Science and Moral Suasion, Not Regulation: Facing Difficult Decisions on Agricultural Non-point Source Pollution', in D. VanNijnatten and R. Boardman, eds, *Canadian Environmental Policy: Context and Cases*, 2nd ed. (Toronto: Oxford University Press, 2002), 274–85.

42. Op.cit. Johns, 2000, 2002.

43. See Judith McKenzie, 'Walkerton: Requiem for the New Public Management in Ontario?', *International Journal of Environment and Pollution* 21, 4 (2004): 309–24; Scott Prudham, 'Poisoning the Well: Neoliberalism and the Contamination of Municipal Water in Walkerton, Ontario', *Geoforum* 35 (2004): 343–59.

44. Ontario, Ministry of Environment, *Business Plan, 1999* [Previously available at: http://www.gov.on.ca/MBS/english/press/plans99/env.html#allocations] (accessed 14 December 2000); Anita Krajnc, 'Wither Ontario's Environment? Neo-conservatism and the Decline of the Environment Ministry', *Canadian Public Policy* March (2004): 111–27; James Merritt and Christopher Gore, *Drinking Water Services: A Functional Review of the Ontario Ministry of the Environment*, Walkerton Inquiry Commissioned Paper # 5 (Ontario: Ministry of the Attorney General, 2002); D.R. O'Connor, *Part Two Report of the Walkerton Inquiry: A Strategy for Safe Drinking Water* (Toronto, ON: Ontario Ministry of the Attorney General, 2002).

45. Op.Cit. Johns, 2000, 2002.

46. Canada, National Water Research Institute, Aquatic Ecosystem Protection Branch, *Non-point Sources of Pollution Project*. 1998. [Previously available at: www.cciw.ca/nwri-e/aepb/nonpoint] (accessed 5 December 1998].

47. Op.Cit. Johns, 2000.

48. Ontario, Commission of the Walkerton Inquiry, *Part One Report of the Walkerton Inquiry* (Toronto, ON: Ontario Ministry of the Attorney General, 2002), 2.

49. Ibid.

50. Ontario, Ministry of Environment, *The Safe Drinking Water Act*. 2005. Available at http://www.ene.gov.on.ca/envision/water/sdwa/index.htm.

51. Ontario, Ministry of Environment, *The Nutrient Management Act*. 2005. Available at: www.ene.gov.on.ca/envision/land/nutrient_management.htm (cited 29 July 2005).

52. Ontario, Ministry of Environment, *Clean Water Act*. 2007. Available at http://www.ene.gov.on.ca/en/water/cleanwater/index.php.

53. Ontario. Ministry of Environment. 2007. *The Great Lakes and the Clean Water Act, 2006*. http://www.ene.gov.on.ca/en/water/greatlakes.

54. Carolyn Johns, 'Non-point Source Water Policy Institutions in Ontario Before and After Walkerton', in M. Sproule-Jones, C. Johns, and B.T. Heinmiller, eds, *Water Politics in Canada: Conflicts and Institutions* (Montreal and Kingston: McGill-Queen's University Press, 2008) 203–39.

55. M. Sproule-Jones, C. Johns, and B.T. Heinmiller, eds, *Water Politics in Canada: Conflicts and Institutions* (Montreal and Kingston: McGill-Queen's University Press, 2008).

56. Saskatchewan, Environment and Resource Management, *The North Battleford Water Inquiry*. 2002. Available at http://www.northbattlefordwaterinquiry.ca/pdf/finalsubmission-governmentofsask.pdf. (cited 29 July 2005). In 2005 high levels of E.coli were found in Kashechewan and the community had to be evacuated. Nearly 100 of Canada's 600 Aboriginal reserves had boil water advisories in 2006. See http://www.cbc.ca/news/background/Aboriginals/kashechewan.html.

57. Op.Cit. Johns, 2000.

58. Barry Rabe and J.B. Zimmerman, 'Beyond Environmental Regulatory Fragmentation: Signs of Integration in the Case of the Great Lakes Basin', *Governance* 8, 1(1995): 58–77.

59. Peter H. Pearce, *Water Management in Canada: The Continuing Search for a Federal Role*. Keynote address at the 51st Annual Conference of the Canadian Water Resources Association, 1998, Vancouver, BC; Peter H. Pearce and Frank Quinn, 'Recent Developments in Federal Water Policy: One Step Forward, Two Steps Back', *Canadian Water Resources Journal* 21, 4 (1996): 329–40; Canada, Policy Research Initiative, *Freshwater for the Future: Policies for Sustainable Water Management in Canada*. 2006. Available at http://www.policyresearch.gc.ca; K. Bakker, ed., *Eau Canada: The Future of Canada's Water* (Vancouver: University of British Columbia Press, 2007); J. Churchill, et al., *Navigating the Shoals: Assessing Water Governance and Management in Canada* (Toronto: Conference Board of Canada, 2007); Great Lakes United, *The Great Lakes Blueprint 2007*. Available at http://www.glu.org.

16

Mercury Science–Policy Debates: A Case Study of Natural versus Anthropogenic Mercury in Canada

Bruce Lourie

> And when the woods and groves are felled, then are exterminated the beasts and birds, very many of which furnish a pleasant and agreeable food for man. Further, when the ores are washed, the water which has been used poisons the brooks and streams, and either destroys the fish or drives them away. Therefore the inhabitants of these regions . . . find great difficulty in procuring the necessities of life . . .[1]

Georgius Agricola, quoted above, was the founding father of modern mining and yet over 400 years ago he recognized the ecological and human health impacts of resource extraction. His comments are both prophetic and a sad testament to the history of resource extraction—an activity that did not begin in Canada until nearly 300 years after Agricola's death. Quoting an historical figure from the world of mineral extraction may seem counterintuitive in an introduction to a case study of environmental policy and toxic substances; however, this quotation seems appropriate to the case at hand.

This chapter is not only an examination of the challenges Canada faces with respect to the regulation of toxic substances; it is also a story of competing science, intergovernmental conflict, federal policy inconsistency, the inappropriateness of science funding in the context of 'client-focused' government priorities, and Canada's role as global purveyor of toxic metals and minerals. The chapter provides corollary insight into toxic pollution policy discourse in Canada and over a decade of mismanagement of the environmental science–policy interface in Canada. Finally, it is a story of 'bureaucratic inertia' as described by Toner and Meadowcroft in Chapter 6 of this volume, where the single-minded efforts of industry-aligned bureaucrats put Canada's economic and international trade priorities well ahead of domestic environmental protection.

Mercury is a substance that illustrates well the considerable lag between science consensus and policy action in Canada. In particular, the 'natural versus anthropogenic mercury' debate discussed herein highlights the strategic use of science, which has led to a perverse application of public policy—designed to favour the interests of industry over those of the public.[2]

Context

Mercury has been selected as the focus of this investigation largely because of the extensive body of research that exists on the subject of the ecological and human health effects of mercury. It is possible that mercury has been studied as much as, and for as long as, any other toxic element, although lead has also been examined extensively through the centuries. Mercury was known and used in Roman times, with well-documented cases of toxic effects dating back 2,000 years. The affliction of the British 'mad hatters', made famous by Lewis Carroll in the nineteenth century, was caused by overexposure to mercury. Mercury was used as a preservative in the fur felt hat manufacturing process and many of the 'hatters' suffered from mercury poisoning. More recent poisoning events have occurred in Minamata, Japan, in the 1950s; Grassy Narrows, Ontario, in the 1960s; and Iraq in the 1970s. The Japanese poisonings were caused by effluent from chemical companies polluting ocean life upon which the locals depended. In Grassy Narrows the cause of the mercury pollution was a chlorine production plant (chlor-alkali plant) where the chlorine was used to manufacture paper. In Iraq, the mercury poisoning occurred after the local population ate grain that was treated with a mercury-based preservative. The grain was meant to be planted, not eaten. These events have provided the basis for our modern understanding of acute mercury toxicity. In Minamata, Japan, despite the strong evidence gathered by local physicians, conclusive evidence of the source of the contamination was demanded by government officials, and this led to the continued poisoning of hundreds of thousands of citizens.

Berkes documents problems related to scientific uncertainty and mercury pollution in Canada in the 1970s.[3] At that time, the primary scientific uncertainty centred on the supposed lack of 'evidence' of Minamata disease in the Grassy Narrows population. Massive amounts of mercury were entering numerous watercourses in Ontario (thousands of kilograms per year in some cases) and populations were dependent on fish in these watercourses for protein and livelihood. There was evidence that fish in these areas had been contaminated by mercury. However, industry was unprepared to act without documented evidence of human poisoning.[4] Governments of the day demonstrated behaviour consistent with chronic downplaying of environmental concerns and did little 'to dispel these uncertainties and to educate the public'.[5]

Through the late 1980s and early 1990s, the debate began to shift away from acute poisoning events toward the neurobehavioural effects of chronic, low-level exposure *in utero* and in early childhood. The results of longitudinal research into low-level chronic exposure in children now guide contemporary mercury health and environmental standard setting. Table 16.1 illustrates three phases of the environmental science–policy interface for mercury, reflecting changes in mercury use, in exposure, and in understanding of the environmental and health risk characteristics of mercury. The table shows predominant trends within each phase; they are not definitive or exclusive descriptions.

Mercury may be seen as a bellwether for how governments address toxic substances management and control. The evidence of human harm is indisputable. If mercury use and exposure cannot be managed under Canada's toxic pollution policy framework, it is difficult to imagine whether any toxic substance can be adequately controlled to minimize human and environmental harm.

Table 16.1 Three Phases of the Mercury Science–Policy Interface

Timeframe	Phase 1 Pre-1960 Direct Elemental Exposure Phase	Phase 2 1960–1990 Modern Industrial Phase	Phase 3 1990 to present Postmodern Global Pervasive Phase
Science	Mercury metal a well-known neurotoxin	Mercury methylation and bioaccumulation discovered	Chronic low-level health effects detected related to foetal and child development
Mercury Form of Exposure	Metallic vapour and direct ingestion	Methylmercury in fish and as preservative in grain	Methylmercury in fish and marine mammals
Mercury Release	Direct use or extraction of metallic mercury volatilizing in air	Direct release or use of methylmercury or inorganic compounds	Pervasive global mercury concentrations from multiple historical and present releases
Exposure Point	Occupational hazard, beaver felt hats, mercury miners, product manufacturing	Ingestion of fish and seafood or accidental consumption of preserved food (grain) in specific contaminated areas	Ingestion of fish and marine mammals with elevated mercury due to global mercury uptake. Specific populations and/or consumption patterns (First Nations, inland fisherman, tuna)
Concentration	High metallic vapour concentrations in air	Elevated methylmercury concentrations of up to 100,000 times higher than background	Very low, measured in ppm or ppb
Evidence of Hazard	Serious neurological and behavioural damage and disease leading to death	Modest to severe neurological damage with death in serious cases	Subtle developmental impairment in children
Temporal Exposure Profile	Acute and chronic exposure	Acute exposure	Chronic exposure
Spatial Profile	Site-specific occupational setting	Facility-based or local ecosystem pollution event	Pervasive presence with weather-based global concentration anomalies
Uncertainty Profile	Little uncertainty regarding gross cause-effect relationship but lack of scientific research	Initial uncertainty regarding cause-effect and source contributions. No uncertainty remains regarding acute toxicity	Medical consensus regarding evidence of problem, considerable uncertainty regarding extent of harm and benefits of action
Policy Response	Restrict worker hours, improve working conditions	Regulate chlor-alkali plant emissions and major sectoral uses (paint, batteries, etc.)	Regulate incidental emitters (incineration, smelters, coal) and expand global research efforts

Mercury Policy Framework

The Canadian Environmental Protection Act, 1999 (CEPA), entitled 'An Act respecting pollution prevention and the protection of the environment and human health in order to contribute to sustainable development', came into force on 31 March 2000, following an extensive parliamentary review of the 'original' CEPA 1988. CEPA is Canada's primary environmental protection legislation focusing on the management of toxic substances, although it is limited to substances 'not otherwise regulated by law'.[6] CEPA is the legislation that authorizes federal action to control mercury use and release, and it gives the federal government authority to

- protect human health and the environment, including its biological diversity;
- promote pollution prevention;
- apply the precautionary principle;
- effectively manage toxic substances within strict timeframes;
- virtually eliminate releases of man-made substances determined to be persistent, bioaccumulative and toxic;
- achieve the highest level of environmental quality while taking into consideration social, economic, and technical concerns.

Substances are deemed 'CEPA-toxic' if they have or may have an immediate or long-term harmful effect on the environment or its biological diversity; constitute or may constitute a danger to the environment on which life depends; or constitute or may constitute a danger in Canada to human life or health. CEPA is jointly administered by the federal Ministers of the Environment and Health. Human health issues related to toxic substances are administered by the Minister of Health, while all other aspects of the Act are administered by the Minister of the Environment.

Mercury is a designated CEPA-toxic substance, although with the exception of the 2007 program to remove mercury switches from vehicles, CEPA has never been used to regulate mercury in Canada.[7] Instead, the federal government relies on other mechanisms, notably the Canada-Wide Standards process under the Canadian Council of Ministers of the Environment (CCME). The Canada-Wide Accord on Environmental Harmonization, was signed in January 1998 by the CCME members (all provinces with the exception of Quebec). A sub-agreement to the Accord, the Canada-Wide Standards (CWS) is a framework to set priorities, develop non-regulatory standards in consultation with stakeholders, and implement work plans to address potentially toxic substances. The CCME endorses the principles of sustainable development, pollution prevention, and the precautionary principle as means of managing toxic substances.

The CCME does not have the authority of the federal government to set national requirements for action, but rather provides for 'regional flexibility' and allows jurisdictions to use a 'variety of regulatory and voluntary measures' to meet goals set by the parties to the Harmonization Accord.[8] In practice, each of the signatory provinces participates in consensus-building processes with stakeholders aimed at achieving consensus on common Canada-wide targets,[9] which are then to be implemented by the provinces.

The Science–Policy Debate

One of the most contentious issues at the science–policy interface regarding mercury has been the debate concerning the relative contributions of anthropogenic and natural mercury to the global cycle. There is uncertainty about the total amounts, and more importantly, the relative amounts, of natural versus anthropogenic mercury released into the atmosphere, and this has led to considerable debate within science and policy circles in Canada and abroad. The debate in Canada was largely between the federal departments of Natural Resources Canada (NRCan) and Environment Canada. NRCan and its agents promoted the idea that mercury in the environment came largely from natural sources, whereas Environment Canada, along with the global mercury research community, took their cue from evidence that suggested human sources contributed to more than half of the global mercury pool.

Natural sources of mercury include volcanoes, forest fires, evaporation from soil, and water.[10] Anthropogenic sources include coal-fired electric power plants (the largest source globally), metal smelters (the largest in Canada), incinerators, landfill sites, and the re-emission of historical anthropogenic releases from water and soil. Figure 16.1 illustrates the primary anthropogenic sources of mercury in Canada. It should be noted that four of the top five sources are related directly or indirectly to mining and mineral processing and/or coal combustion.

Scientists have undertaken considerable research on global mercury cycling with attempts to estimate the relative anthropogenic contributions of mercury. This research includes measuring natural mercury flux, deposition rates, global transport, and anthropogenic emission sources. Understanding the mercury cycle is fundamental to understanding mercury behaviour in the environment, including regional and global aspects of mercury pollution.[11]

At the core of this issue is an important policy consideration. The relative amount of anthropogenic mercury entering the global cycle has a bearing on the effectiveness of efforts to reduce mercury emissions. The greater the natural contribution, the less effective will be efforts to control anthropogenic sources. For example, if natural mercury sources are thought to exceed anthropogenic sources by a considerable margin, the argument used by mercury emitters is that any effort to control their emissions sources will offer negligible benefit to the environment due to the large natural component that continues to 'pollute' the environment. At mercury science symposia such as the biennial 'Mercury as a Global Pollutant' conference, discussion often revolves around natural

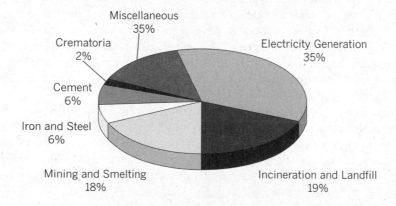

Figure 16.1 Canadian Mercury Emissions (Per cent by Sector, 2003)

Source: Adapted from Environment Canada. (2007). 'Mercury and the Environment', available at http://www.ec.gc.ca/MERCURY/SM/EN/sm-cr.cfm?SELECT=SM.

versus anthropogenic contributions to the total estimated mercury pool. However, over time the uncertainty regarding mercury contributions from natural sources has been a less common point of discussion, given the convergence of research that 'points unequivocally' to the important contribution of anthropogenic mercury.[12]

Early estimates of the total and relative quantities of mercury in the global pool contained wide margins of error, and that led to uncertainty about the data.[13] Weiss et al. estimated natural mercury emissions at between 25,000 and 150,000 tonnes/year and anthropogenic contributions at 6,700 tonnes/year.[14] In 1979, Lantzy and MacKenzie estimated natural emissions at 29,300 and anthropogenic at 11,500 tonnes/year.[15] By 1991, Lindqvist et al. had reduced the natural estimate to 3,000 tonnes/year and the anthropogenic to 4,500 tonnes per year.[16] Notably, the relative anthropogenic emissions shift dramatically from averages of well below 30 per cent in the early estimates to 60 per cent in the Lindqvist et al. estimate. Subsequent work by Mason and his colleagues in 1994 narrowed the estimates to natural emissions of 2,200 tonnes and anthropogenic emissions of 2,700 tonnes.[17] With these revised estimates, the contribution of anthropogenic mercury (including anthropogenic mercury re-emitted from oceans) is estimated to be between 55 and 68 per cent of total mercury emitted to the atmosphere.

The debate regarding natural versus anthropogenic mercury was most prominent in the mid-to-late 1990s, and Canada played an important role in this debate. In 1994, a Canadian government researcher working with the Geological Survey of Canada (GSC), an agency of Natural Resources Canada, wrote a critical review of anthropogenic mercury flux research in the journal *Environmental Science & Technology*.[18] This paper, by Rasmussen, helped focus much of the global controversy at the time. The author noted that when studies suggest that a significant portion of the mercury found in remote regions is of anthropogenic origin, 'their validity needs careful examination.'[19] One interpretation of this statement may be that it implies that studies identifying anthropogenic mercury as a major issue are somehow invalid. Given the active debate underway at the time on the origins of mercury, combined with the relevance of the issue to environmental policy, the paper became somewhat of a lightning rod. The nature and style of the research findings and conclusions in this GSC paper illustrate well the emerging trend of scientific research being used to promote a vested interest. The research paper reveals what is perhaps the primary intent of the work, which relates more to policy than science, by suggesting that the 'conclusions hold serious implications to both government and industry.' If the findings were of purely academic interest than presumably there would not be 'serious implications'.

This 1994 paper was cited in an Ecological Monitoring and Assessment Network (EMAN) paper.[20] EMAN is a creation of Environment Canada, and Coker, the EMAN paper's author, was also employed by the Geological Survey of Canada. Coker supports one of Rasmussen's primary arguments—namely, that inaccuracies arise from using vertical core samples to estimate anthropogenic deposition because of surface enrichment (*diagenesis*) following deposition. Coker states that due to surface enrichment, core samples do not identify anthropogenic mercury nor do they indicate atmospheric deposition. Coker cautions that 'knowledge of the processes by which a metal is mobilized, transported, precipitated, and possibly remobilized, is of prime concern in order to comprehend possible controls on that metal's dispersion . . . .' Although ostensibly a scientific paper, Coker enters the realm of policy by describing potential emission controls on industrial facilities as a 'prime concern'.

In 1995, R.G. Garrett (Rasmussen's supervisor at the GSC) presented to the Canadian Mercury Network Workshop, making the point that natural mercury emissions from geological faults and deep sea hydrothermal sources were significant and that certain rock types are 'natural hazards' due to the high levels of mercury they contain. Garrett's presentation referenced Rasmussen's 1994 research paper a number of times. In addition to pointing out these natural emissions, Garrett cites studies suggesting that the long-range transport of mercury from major smelting point sources in Canada cannot be detected and that within a relatively short distance (120 km) of major smelting point sources, mercury levels are no higher than natural background levels. This seemed to contradict the work of Lucotte et al., researchers at the Université du Québec a Montréal involved in the Community Mercury Research Network (COMERN), which found anthropogenic mercury to be 'ubiquitous' at sites up to 1,400 km from industrial sources.[21]

Garrett concludes that 'the distribution of Hg [mercury] in the Canadian environment is regionally controlled by geological factors,' and he notes that 'clearly future research must be focused on this issue in order to assess the relative contribution of natural and anthropogenic processes in affecting the environment, and to assist in selecting appropriate effective risk management options.[22] Reference to risk management options introduces the policy interface into this scientific paper and the emphasis on naturally existing mercury provides an early indication of the direction of subsequent NRCan research efforts. The focus on the significance of geological mercury, together with references to the modest regional impacts of smelters fits well with the mission of Natural Resources Canada, 'the government lead in promoting the responsible development and use of Canada's mineral and metal resources'.[23]

In 1997, Togwell Jackson, a research scientist with Environment Canada, produced a paper entitled 'Long-range atmospheric transport of mercury to ecosystems, and the importance of anthropogenic emissions—a critical review and evaluation of the published evidence.'[24] Jackson notes that the purpose of his review is 'to resolve the controversy regarding the role of natural emissions' and specifically the GSC research, in order to determine the extent of anthropogenic atmospheric mercury releases in remote ecosystems and to consider how lake sediment cores should be interpreted.

This particular scientific debate is worth expanding upon, since it was one of the most contentious elements of the GSC research and is a featured argument in much of the Natural Resources Canada literature on natural mercury. Lake sediment core samples provide an historical record of atmospheric deposition. Substances that fall from the sky into lakes deposit themselves on the lake bottom where they become part of sediment layers that are buried with successive years of detritus and lake sediment. After hundreds of years of this process, sediment layers provide an historical record of atmospheric deposition.

Lake sediment cores of a metre or more are commonly extracted to identify mercury concentrations at various depth intervals, which are correlated to specific time horizons.[25] A large body of literature produced over the past several decades shows that mercury in the upper portion of the sediment cores (i.e., the most recent deposition layers) contain the greatest mercury concentrations, declining with depth until they level off in the portions deposited during pre-industrial times.[26] Typical mercury deposition profiles are shown as bar or line graphs that equate mercury concentration with depth and/or date. Engstrom and Swain used this method to evaluate mercury deposition in Minnesota and Alaska.[27] Their data show gradual increases in mercury measured in the environment from the mid-1800s until the 1940s, sharp increases in deposition beginning in the 1940s, up to the peak period in the 1960s and 1970s, and slight declines in mercury deposition after 1980 to the present. Prior to 1850, mercury deposition rates are relatively constant. Sediment cores have been used to determine deposition rates in remote lakes around the world, and the findings are strikingly similar globally. It is this method of scientific research that helps support the commonly cited figure that post-industrial mercury deposition rates are 1.5–3 times higher than pre-industrial deposition rates in remote regions and 2–10 times higher in industrial areas.[28]

The original 1994 Rasmussen paper argued that 'post-depositional diagenetic processes' explained the higher mercury concentrations in the upper (more recent) portions of lake sediment cores. *Diagenesis* is a geological term that refers to chemical and physical changes in sediments that take place prior to, or as part of, the transformation from sediment to sedimentary rock. Rasmussen's postulate that these specific processes exist is based on the supposition that chemical reactions lead to physical processes whereby mercury migrates to the top of the sediment following deposition. These processes, according to Rasmussen, resulted in the higher concentrations seen in the upper levels of the core samples. In other words, the higher concentrations in the upper levels are the result of a natural process, not an anthropogenic one.

In his paper, Jackson noted that 'Rasmussen (1994) has questioned the quantitative significance of emissions due to human activities in the long-range atmospheric distribution of Hg, claiming that insufficient attention has been paid to the assessment of natural sources of Hg in the Earth's crust.' He also notes Rasmussen's challenge to the evidence of mercury enrichment in the upper portion of core samples of lake sediments from remote regions but refers to the diagenetic processes in sediment cores as 'only negligible' in their effect. Further, Engstrom and Swain's paper on atmospheric deposition using sediment cores provides important evidence of mercury levels following industrial emissions and use patterns, including a decrease in Hg concentrations after 1980, matching the proportionate decline in industrial mercury emissions during the same period.[29] This evidence calls into question the postulate that mercury enrichment is caused primarily by the migration of mercury to the uppermost levels of sediments. More specifically, Engstrom and Swain reference Rasmussen's work on diagenesis, stating that 'such mechanisms cannot explain' their findings.[30]

In 1998, four of the world's leading mercury researchers responded directly to the 1994 Rasmussen paper. This collaboration—authored by Fitzgerald, Engstrom, Mason, and Nater—was supported by an additional 17 mercury scientists from around the world, including several Canadian government researchers, all of whom contributed materially and critically to the paper. The authors' contention is that not only are the GSC researcher's 1994 conclusions unsupportable, but the case for atmospheric mercury contamination was 'stronger than ever'. Fitzgerald et al. point to erroneous and/or outdated information as the source of the GSC assumptions. They specifically address 'the weaknesses in interpretation and the choices of information used to support the contention that geological sources of mercury are the principal contributors of mercury in remote locations.' They also affirm the validity of lake sediment core sample data that show post-industrial anthropogenic enrichment, thereby dismissing Rasmussen's diagenetic process arguments.

The scientists involved in the Fitzgerald paper felt the need to provide a collective global critique to end the controversy, a controversy that in many ways was created and promoted largely by Canadian government researchers, with Canadian government and resource industry funding. Some of the scientists involved in the Fitzgerald paper appear to have recognized the critical link between science and policy. Clarifying the science to help resolve the policy controversy was an explicit motivation behind the publication, according to one government official involved in the process. Demonstrating the science community's collective voice in support of globally accepted mercury measurement methodologies was another.

The seminal US Mercury Report to Congress was completed in the same year as the Fitzgerald et al. paper.[31] At eight volumes and 2,000 pages, it is almost certainly the most comprehensive report on mercury in the environment ever produced. In the report, the US Environmental Protection Agency (EPA) identifies anthropogenic mercury emissions at between 50 and 75 per cent of the total annual atmospheric emissions, which is consistent with the summary of the literature prepared by Jackson.[32]

With a global science consensus having emerged and with Canadian researchers (both inside and outside the federal government) playing an important role in the research and the consensus process, it seems surprising that this issue became a renewed research priority for the Canadian government. Indeed, in 1999, the Canadian government embarked on a three-year, $600,000 study 'to obtain better estimates of natural mercury emissions from major Canadian natural sources/geological features, such as soils, water surfaces, vegetation, and fault zones.' Rasmussen was one of the researchers involved in this study, although at that time under the employ of Health Canada.

The Metals in the Environment Research Network (MITE-RN) was established with federal government funding in 1998, including a $3.5 million National Science and Engineering Research Council (NSERC) grant, to match $1.95 million from the Mining Association of Canada and Ontario Power Generation. Unspecified in-kind contributions were made by Environment Canada, Natural Resources Canada, and the Department of Fisheries and Oceans Canada. Moreover, participation in the MITE-RN mercury research by University of Guelph, the MITE-RN host, was made possible in part by funding from the Canada Foundation for Innovation, another federal government funding source.[33] The NSERC award was provided to 'help answer critical research questions being asked by scientists and policy makers.'[34]

Meanwhile, mercury scientists were no longer asking these questions and the only policy makers asking them seemed to be those responsible for mineral and metals development policy in Canada. The NSERC announcement, for example, notes that the outcome of this research is 'to implement polices that support the sustainable use of metals in Canada'.[35] This language is consistent with 'sustainability discourse' used throughout NRCan literature which tends to support the continued exploitation and use of mercury and other metals and minerals, including lead and asbestos.

The NSERC grant for MITE-RN appears to be related to the federal government's competitiveness and innovation strategies. According to Lopreite, NSERC's funding emphasis shifted to include a focus on partnerships between universities and industry (specifically research networks), and one of the objectives of the shift was to help Canada's resource economy become more globally competitive.[36]

MITE-RN was a joint government, industry, and academic research venture and fell under the auspices of the Canadian Network of Toxicology Centres (supported by, among others, the Mining Association of Canada and the Canadian Chemical Producers Association) located at the University of Guelph. MITE-RN was established to provide policy advice to the government on the issue of metals in the environment. The focus of MITE-RN and the sponsors involved was therefore less on scientific research and more on the risk management aspects of metals in the environment as they relate to metals control policy in Canada. It is through this lens that one better understands how the research priorities and research findings of MITE-RN appear disconnected from, and inconsistent with, the research priorities and findings of the global mercury research community.

MITE-RN's Board of Directors included representatives of several of the largest metal (including mercury) emitters in Canada (Inco, Noranda, and Ontario Power Generation), along with government officials and academics involved in the research.[37] In March 2001, MITE-RN organized a 'science–policy workshop' with three plenary presentations: one from a senior Environment Canada official, one from the Mining Association of Canada, and one from an Ontario Power Generation (OPG) employee (who was also a MITE-RN Board member).[38] The focus of the OPG presentation was on the question of natural versus anthropogenic emissions, and the conclusion was that 'natural sources are believed to be large but are poorly understood.'[39] In one of the presentation slides, emissions from coal plants were compared to releases from natural sources in Canada. The figure used for natural sources was from a 20-year-old Environment Canada reference that suggested an extremely high level of natural emissions in Canada, and this prompted discussion demonstrating considerable concern among Environment Canada participants present in the room. Interestingly, the MITE-RN summary notes of the workshop refer to some gaps in knowledge about natural sinks evident in Ontario Power Generation's presentation but exclude any reference to the Environment Canada participants' concerns about the presentation of obsolete data.[40] After MITE-RN was terminated in 2004, MITE entered its Phase II, the Metals in the Human Environment Research Network, in 2005.

In December 2002, the United Nations Environment Program published the Global Mercury Assessment.[41] This 250-page report documents all major aspects of mercury in the environment, including a chapter on sources and cycling of mercury to the global environment. Both the 1998 Fitzgerald et al. and the 1997 Jackson papers are referenced in the global cycling chapter. No papers by Rasmussen, Garrett, MITE-RN, or any NRCan researchers are referenced. The UNEP study concludes that 'natural sources account for less than 50 per cent of the total releases.'

In June 2004, MITE-RN prepared a 'Science Brief' (as part of their final round of publications) entitled 'Separating Natural from Human-Related Metals in the Environment.'[42] The brief highlights the significance of natural sources of metals in the environment, noting that 'elevated concentrations are not always the result of human activities.' The brief also states that 'unnecessarily stringent environmental regulation of the industrial sector, based on incomplete knowledge of natural sources, may result in severe economic consequences with no measurable benefit to Canadians or the environment.' Despite the designation as a 'Science Brief' the strongest statements relate to policy, not science. Yet even the policy warning seems over stated since regulations specific to the use of, or emissions from, mercury are rare in Canada.

The brief goes on to say that 'surprisingly, research on natural sources of metals and their impact and contribution to elevated concentrations at remote and background sites has been relatively scarce.' This statement ignores the decades of extensive global effort dedicated to precisely that type of research. For example, Jackson based his 1997 paper on the 'wide range of relevant published information' on sources of mercury in the environment, as opposed to indicating that the research on natural versus anthropogenic mercury has been 'scarce'. Jackson asserts that 'an impressive amount of evidence comprising many different kinds of information supports the conclusion that the anthropogenic contribution to the long-range atmospheric flux of mercury rivals or exceeds the natural contribution in quantitative importance.'[43] Eight years earlier, Miller (1989) had noted that 'levels of mercury sufficient to justify governmental warnings are now found in fish taken from waters far from any known sources, and our new understanding of the atmospheric dynamics of the metal makes it perfectly understandable that this should be so.'[44] Further, Fitzgerald et al. concluded their paper with this statement: '[I]n summary, there is much published literature on the mercury cycle' and 'much recent research on mercury.'

Finally, the MITE-RN brief ends with a section entitled 'Additional Information,' where four references are provided. Three of these four references are to papers written by either Garrett or Rasmussen, including Rasmussen's 1994 paper (which was discredited by Jackson and Fitzgerald et al.). None of the broadly accepted, peer-reviewed research from acknowledged mercury researchers is cited in the MITE-RN materials.

With the natural versus anthropogenic debate settled within the scientific community (although still actively disputed within NRCan), Environment Canada launched the Canada-Wide Standards process to set mercury content and emission control guidelines for a number of products and sectors. The standards apply to waste incinerators, base metal smelting, dental amalgam, and fluorescent lamps. Progress has been made by each of these sectors in limiting the release of mercury to the environment.[45] The mercury content in fluorescent lamps sold in Canada was reduced by over 70 per cent between 1990 and 2003, consistent with global efforts of the manufacturers. The dental amalgam capture standard appears to be less successful. Over 1,000 kg of mercury dental waste was estimated to have entered Canadian wastewater in 2003 but had the standards been applied to all dental offices in Canada that number may have been 16 kg.[46] An important difference between the two standards is that the fluorescent lamp standard is a pollution prevention effort consistent with Environment Canada's priorities. This means that less mercury is being used in the product. By contrast, the dental amalgam standard is based on pollution capture and control, an older model of environmental policy that tends to be far less effective.

The mercury standards developed under the CWS process are typically generated by the mercury-using and mercury-emitting proponents in the process and represent the codification of business-as-usual practices. It is also worth noting that CEPA, the federal government's primary toxic substance regulatory tool was not used to create the Canada-Wide Standards, and this is consistent with the policy interests of NRCan to avoid the application of CEPA to metals. No regulatory requirements are involved in the CWS process, and the voluntary guidelines are administered and monitored at the provincial level.

Policy Analysis

The case of the Geological Survey's research raises a number of important questions regarding the purpose, use, understanding, independence, rigour, and funding of scientific research in Canada. The issue is not the expertise or integrity of the individual researchers. They are working within their mandate honestly and effectively. The issue is the government's mandate. For example: What are the standards for independent scientific research in Canada? To what extent are government-funded organizations accountable for their understanding and representation of accepted, peer-reviewed scientific research? Are federal funding agencies mandated to support the vested interests of federal departments and their 'clients' (in this case the natural resource sector) even when research they accept as valid is not supported by global academic consensus? What are the economic and political implications of scientific research in Canada, and what bodies, if any, consider these? And what motives may explain Canada's departure from the prevailing world view regarding anthropogenic metal emissions?

Related to some of these questions, the federal government initiated a government-wide exercise in 1998 to investigate the science-policy interface. This effort led to the 1999 Science Advice for Government Effectiveness (SAGE) report. SAGE was the first initiative of the Council of Science and Technology Advisors, established by the federal government in 1998 (the year MITE-RN was formed) to provide external advice to Cabinet concerning the management of the federal science and technology enterprise. The SAGE report describes these six principles for effective science advice: early issue identification, inclusiveness, sound science and science advice, uncertainty and risk, transparency and openness, and review. The SAGE principles were developed because of a recognition that the federal government 'requires an effective science advisory process that leads to better government decisions, minimizes crises and unnecessary controversies, and capitalizes on opportunities'.[47]

It does not appear, however, that the SAGE principles have been applied to the natural versus anthropogenic mercury research activities of the federal government; in fact, most of the SAGE principles appear to have been violated in this research. Had SAGE not already existed, one conclusion of this case study would be for the establishment of federal guidelines to help ensure the procurement of priority, peer-reviewed science. It is interesting (though not encouraging) to note that much of the mercury research described above was funded and carried out by federal agencies *after* the completion of the SAGE report. Despite considerable effort to improve guidance on science advice to government through the SAGE process, federal government departments and funding agencies supported unnecessary scientific research; introduced confusion and uncertainty into otherwise well-established scientific understanding; were highly aligned to the interests of industrial 'clients' of government departments; and did not conform to basic standards of academic research.

The anthropogenic versus natural mercury debate highlights one of the fundamental problems endemic to the science–policy interface in Canada as it relates to environmental policy decision-making—namely, the manufacturing of scientific uncertainty in cases where the scientific research points to the need for regulation. This issue is not unique to Canada or to environmental issues: '[M]anufacturing uncertainty and creating doubt about scientific evidence is ubiquitous in the organized opposition to the government's attempts regulate health hazards.'[48]

Two possibilities may have led to the federal government's continued support for, and promotion of, inaccurate and arguably unnecessary research. It is possible that the research scientists and funding bodies involved were unaware of the global literature on mercury and the critical assessments of the GSC work. This seems highly unlikely, however, given the tightly knit mercury research community and the numerous global events such as 'Mercury as a Global Pollutant' conferences that provide opportunities for mercury researchers from all disciplines to convene. In fact, representatives from NRCan and the GSC attend these events regularly. The second possibility is that the ongoing research and research-funding decisions were influenced by some who had an interest in promoting a particular set of policy outcomes, regardless of the scientific credibility of the research.

There are at least two factors that together may support the second explanation. First, NRCan and the GSC are 'client-focused' agencies and their clients are primarily the extractive resource industries. This phenomenon is part of the federal government's shift to a market-based mandate. Similar issues, for example, have been raised in connection with drug approvals at Health Canada, where scientists have been instructed to relax procedures in order to accommodate 'corporate clients' in the pharmaceutical sector.[49] Leiss describes in detail many cases where political and corporate interests have interfered in environmental, health, and resource science, resulting in decisions that favour the interests of departmental clients over public interest.[50] For instance, in a Science and Technology Management Framework developed for NRCan in 1995, one of the objectives listed was 'to enhance client focus'. In a 1999 evaluation report, the evaluators concluded that 'NRCan remained responsive to client needs.'

The second factor that may explain the MITE-RN research program is that government research funding has shifted from independent government research to jointly funded research, whereby federal research dollars require matched funding. In many cases, government funding is matched with industry funds in cases where the research is driven by an economic imperative related to industrial interests. A number of researchers have commented that this approach can lead to a situation where the research agenda is set by the industry funding partners even though federal funding is also part of the equation. Stephen Bocking, in his analysis of the science-policy interface in Chapter 5, expresses a similar concern. An evaluation of NRCan's Science and Technology Management

Framework noted: 'There is a feeling that the "commercial" approach has resulted in less emphasis on conducting scientific research aimed at the public good which may or may not generate income for NRCan in the future and a greater emphasis on working with large paying businesses.'[51] The MITE-RN initiative is a good example of this approach. According to some scientists, this is a serious impediment to independent research in Canada and can lead to questionable public spending when corporate interests have a governance role in scientific research findings.[52]

It is not difficult to imagine how a government department that sees the mining industry as its client base and is instructed to be more 'client focused' (working within a framework that requires matched research funding from industry) might fund and promote research that is consistent with industrial interests. In some cases this may be a useful mechanism for leveraging resources. The departments are following the government's explicit mandate. The government, however, seems to be directing departments to place private interests of clients ahead of the public interest. Departmental and agency staff have done an excellent job in fulfilling this mandate. To be clear it is not the integrity of the government staff or individual researchers receiving funding that is in question, but the political shift to a client-focused mandate. The fact that a quasi-independent research body such as MITE-RN would choose to highlight only those scientific papers and ideas that support a one-sided perspective, and moreover, studies that have been dismissed by the global scientific community, raises different questions surrounding the general assumption of objectivity and credibility of academic institutions.

If the case of the mercury policy debates were unique, it might be excused as the work of zealous government employees eager to fulfill the directives and mandate of their department. Sadly, similar scenarios surround the regulation of lead, asbestos, and greenhouse gases in Canada. This country is increasingly criticized at international *fora* for its continued extraction of asbestos, its export of the substance to impoverished countries, and its lack of effort to discover and use alternatives. In fact, NRCan continues to support research suggesting that Canada's asbestos is safe. Climate change research has been dealt with in a similar way, although on a much more significant global scale, with well-publicized cases of industry-sponsored organizations, more notably in the United States, established with the sole purpose of casting scientific doubt on the cause, severity, or even existence of global warming as a phenomenon.

Conclusions

The science–policy debate on natural versus anthropogenic mercury in the environment casts a pall over Canada's reputation for credible, independent scientific research. It also provides insight into the shifting science-policy interface in environmental policy making and the increasing role of government-funded, 'client-based' policy research designed to meet the objectives of corporations as clients. Public interest and environmental protection become secondary in this model of public policy.

There is a fundamental flaw in Canada's procurement, oversight, and use of scientific research as it relates to environmental policy making. The mercury science debates mimic, although in a much less public way, the scientific and internecine battles between Environment Canada and Natural Resources Canada, notably on climate change policy, that characterize the failed environmental policies of the Chrétien years.

This chapter has revealed a number of serious failures in the federal policy system that contravene any efforts to demonstrate leadership in environmental policy making. The first failure relates to the inappropriateness of the federal government giving Natural Resources Canada the responsibility of leading the mercury research, given the department's mandate to promote 'the responsible development and use of Canada's mineral and metal resources' and to 'enhance client focus'.[53] This arrangement amounts to a direct conflict of interest on the part of NRCan. As with much mission-driven research, or 'mandated science', as described by Salter,[54] the ideal policy outcome for NRCan would be for the research to reveal that anthropogenic sources were minimal and specifically that atmospheric deposition (e.g., from smelters) was minimal while asserting the need for 'more careful examination' prior to introducing any restrictions. The second failure relates to the power imbalance within the federal policy system and Environment Canada's subordinate and largely ineffective role in regulating toxic substances. The third failure lies in the sub-contracting of government research to third-party quasi-academic institutions, which poses inherent risks. In this particular case, the governance and funding model of MITE-RN, for example, seem antithetical to the independence of the matter under investigation. This approach raises questions about the government's adherence to even the most rudimentary rules regarding scientific independence. The fourth failure consists of the federal government's efforts to enhance policy-relevant science advice (i.e., SAGE), which have failed to have any bearing on the actual procurement and use of science as a basis for sound decision making in the area of environmental policy.

Finally, the mercury debate reveals that Canada is a global environmental policy laggard. Not only has this country demonstrated a lack of policy leadership, but Canadian officials are also taking an active role in undermining global policy efforts to control the use of toxic metals. This is, to a great extent, an outgrowth of Canada's environmental policy stance: one of client-focused science and the deliberate fomenting of scientific uncertainty to cast doubt on the utility of regulating toxic substances.

Concluding on one of the few positive notes in this analysis, the efforts of independent scientists globally and government scientists at Environment Canada, such as those that led and contributed to the paper by Fitzgerald et al., resulted in critical contributions to the betterment of science and policy. Although millions of taxpayer dollars were devoted to unnecessary efforts, and years of obfuscation and delay were endured, peer-reviewed science won the day despite, not thanks to, the federal government's management and use of scientific and policy research efforts.

Questions for Review

1. Why is mercury an important case when reflecting on the prospects for Canadian environmental policy activism?
2. What were the main developments that led to recognition of the importance of anthropogenic sources of mercury in the environment?
3. What does the mercury case tell us about the role of government-supported science? How independent can such science be? How independent should it be?
4. How might we relate Bocking's discussion of basic science, regulatory science, advocacy science, and innovation science in Chapter 5 to the mercury case?

Notes

1. Georgius Agricola, *De Re Metallica*, Book I (1556), in H.C. Hoover and L.H. Hoover, trans. (New York: Dover, 1950).
2. Anthropogenic in this case refers to mercury generated or released into the environment from human activity.
3. Fikret Berkes, 'The Mercury Problem: An Examination of the Scientific Basis for Policy-making', in *Resources and the Environment*, O.P. Dwivedi, ed., (McClelland and Stewart, Toronto, 1980), 269–87.
4. Ibid.
5. Ibid.
6. Supreme Court Decision *Canada v. Hydro-Québec*.
7. Mercury regulation exists under the Hazardous Products Act banning mercury in coatings on toys and through a regulation grand fathered into CEPA restricting mercury emissions from chlor-alkali plants. These followed mercury concerns that arose in the 1960s and 1970s.
8. Canadian Council of Ministers of the Environment, *Policy Statement for the Management of Toxic Substances*. Available at http://www.ccme.ca/3e_priorities/3ec_toxic/3ec1_toxic/3ec1a.html#statement.
9. The term 'Canada-wide' is used, as opposed to either 'federal', which implies federal government authority, or 'national', which implies the participation of all provinces.
10. UNEP (2002) *Global Mercury Assessment*, United Nations Environment Programme (Geneva: UNEP Chemicals 2002).
11. Paul F. Schuster, D.P. Krabbenhoft, D.L. Naftz, L.D. Cecil, M.L. Olson, J.F. Dewild, D.D. Susong, J.R. Green, and M.L. Abbott, 'Atmospheric Mercury Deposition during the Last 270 Years: A Glacial Ice Core Record of Natural and Anthropogenic Sources,' *Environ. Sci. Technology* 36 (2002): 2303–10.
12. W.F. Fizgerald, D.R. Engstrom, R.P. Mason, and E.A. Nater, 'The Case for Atmospheric Mercury Concentration in Remote Regions', *Environ. Sci. Technology* 32 (1998): 1–7.
13. T.A. Jackson, 'Long-range Atmospheric Transport of Mercury to Ecosystems, and the Importance of Anthropogenic Emissions—A Critical Review and Evaluation of the Published Evidence', *Environ. Review* 5 (1997): 99–120.
14. H. Weiss, V.M. Koide, and E.D. Goldberg, 'Mercury in a Greenland Ice Sheet: Evidence of Recent Input by Man', *Science* 174 (1971): 692–4.
15. R.J. Lantzy and F.T. Mackenzie, 'Atmospheric Trace Metals: Global Cycles and Assessment of Man's Impact,' *Geochim. Cosmochim. Acta* 43 (1979): 511–25.
16. O.K. Lindqvist, M. Johansson, A. Astruo, L. Anderson, G. Bringmark, L. Hovsenius, A. Hakanson, M. Iverfeldt, M. Mieli, and B. Timm, 'Mercury in the Swedish Environment', *Water, Air and Soil Pollution* 55 (1991): 30.
17. R.P. Mason, W.F. Fitzgerald, and F.M.M. Morel, 'The Biogeochemical Cycling of Elemental Mercury: Anthropogenic Influences', *Geochim. Cosmochim. Acta* 58 (1994): 3191–8.
18. P.E. Rasmussen, 'Current Methods of Estimating Atmospheric Mercury Fluxes in Remote Areas', *Environ. Sci. Technology* 28 (1994): 2233–41.
19. Ibid.
20. W.B. Coker, 'Processes Effecting Mercury and Associated Metals In LakeSediment Columns', *Ecological Monitoring and Assessment Network*, (Environment Canada, 1995). Available at http://www.eman-rese.ca/eman/reports/publications/mercury95/part15.html.
21. M.A. Lucotte, A. Mucci, C. Hillaire-Marcel, P. Pichet, and A. Grondin, 'Anthropogenic Mercury Enrichment in Remote Lakes of Northern Québec (Canada)', *Water Air Soil Pollution* 80 (1995): 467–76.
22. R.G. Garrett, 'Regional and Large Scale Patterns of Mercury Distribution: Influential Factors'. Proceedings, Mercury Research Network, 1995.
23. NRCan, 2006. Available at http://www.nrcan.gc.ca/ms/au_e.htm.
24. Jackson, 1997.
25. D.R. Engstrom and E.B. Swain, 'Recent Declines in Atmospheric Mercury Deposition in the Upper Midwest', *Environ. Sci. Technology* 31 (1997): 960–7.
26. Jackson, 1997.
27. Engstrom and Swain, 1997.
28. UNEP, 'Global Mercury Assessment', United Nations Environment Programme (Geneva: UNEP Chemicals, 2002).
29. Engstrom and Swain, 1997.
30. Ibid.
31. EPA (US Environmental Protection Agency) 'Mercury Study Report to Congress', December 1997.
32. Ibid.

33. Innovation.ca, 2000. Available at http://www.innovation.ca/evaluation/Guelph.pdf.
34. University of Guelph News Release, 'Metals Research Network Receives $3.5 million from NSERC', 7 June 1999.
35. NSERC, 'Announcement of Funding to MITE-RN', 6 June 2005. Available at http://74.125.95.132/search?q=cache: lLQWuqpJZ3YJ:www.nserc.gc.ca/programs/resnet/mite+rn_e.htm+nserc+mite+rn&hl=en&ct=clnk&cd=1&gl=ca.
36. D.C. Lopriete, 'The Natural Science and Engineering Research Council as a Granting and Competitiveness Granting Body', in B. Doern, ed., *Innovation, Science, Environment*, (Kingston: McGill-Queen's University Press, 2006).
37. NSERC, 'Announcement of Funding to MITE-RN', 6 June 2005.
38. The author attended this 'science–policy workshop'.
39. MITE-RN Science Policy Workshop Report, May 2001.
40. Ibid.
41. UNEP, 'Global Mercury Assessment,' United Nations Environment Programme (Geneva: UNEP Chemicals, 2002).
42. MITE-RN 'Separating Natural From Human-related Metals in the Environment', *Science Brief*, June 2004.
43. Jackson, 1997.
44. D.R. Miller, 'Mercury in Canadian Rivers', in P. Bourdeau, J.A. Haines, W. Klein, and C.R. Krishna Murti, eds, *Ecotoxicology and Climate* (Toronto: John Wiley & Sons Ltd., 1989).
45. CCME, 'Canada Wide Standards for Mercury: A Report on Progress', *Canadian Council of Ministers for the Environment*. June 2005. Available at http://www.ccme.ca/assets/pdf/joint_hg_progress_rpt_e.pdf.
46. Ibid.
47. SAGE Report.
48. D. Micheals and C. Monforton, *American Journal of Public Health*, Supplement 95, 1 (2005): Supplement.
49. Steven Turner, 'Of Milk and Mandarins: rSBT, Mandated Science and the Canadian Regulatory Style', *Journal of Canadian Studies* 36, 3 (2001).
50. William Leiss, *In the Chamber of Risks: Understanding Risk Controversies* (Kingston: McGill-Queen's University Press, 2001); William Leiss, 'Between Expertise and Bureaucracy: Risk Management Trapped at the Science/Policy Interface'. Available at http://www.leiss.ca/articles/62.
51. NRCan, Evaluation of NRCan's Science and Technology Management Framework, 2000. Available at http://www.nrcan.gc.ca/evaluation/reprap/2000/stmf-cgst-eng.php.
52. Joseph Zayed, personal interview by author, August 2005.
53. Canada, 'Natural Resources Canada 1997–1998 Estimates', *A Report on Plans and Priorities Pilot Document* (Ottawa: Natural Resources Canada, 1997).
54. Liora Salter, *Mandated Science: Science and Scientists in the Making of Standards* (Dordrecht: Kluwer Academic Press, 1998).

17

Reform, Not Revolution: Pesticides Regulation in Canada

Sarah B. Pralle

On 12 December 2002, a 30-year hiatus in pesticides reform in Canada ended when the new Pest Control Products Act (PCPA) received Royal Assent. The legislation was the result of over 10 years of effort on the part of government officials, industry representatives, and public interest organizations to revamp the outdated 1969 federal pesticides[1] law requiring pre-market testing and registration of pest control products. The government hailed the law as a significant step forward, and environmental groups were cautiously optimistic that Canada was finally moving toward a tougher, more protective pesticide regulatory regime. Meanwhile, municipalities around the country were banning non-essential uses of lawn and garden pesticides on public and private property. Even the Supreme Court of Canada was involved in the reform battle; in a 2001 decision granting municipalities the right to regulate lawn pesticides, it endorsed the precautionary principle, which asserts that governments should take action to protect human health and the environment even in the face of scientific uncertainty if the potential damage is severe and/or irreversible, as a legitimate basis for regulatory decision-making on pesticides.

Progress around pesticides in the late 1990s and early 2000s is surprising. In general, these were not good times for environmentalists in Canada, as numerous chapters in this volume demonstrate. The government's increasing embrace of neo-liberal ideologies signalled a waning enthusiasm for strong environmental regulation. Indeed, budget cuts to environmental agencies and programs in the 1990s indicated a lack of commitment on the part of the federal government to prioritize environmental issues.[2] Enforcement and implementation suffered, and a 1999 audit by Canada's Commissioner of the Environment and Sustainable Development lamented the gap between the government's words and its actions. Meanwhile, environmental regulatory responsibilities were further devolved to provincial governments, a move that worried environmentalists who believed that it would encourage provincial 'races-to-the-bottom'.[3] And, opportunities for meaningful citizen involvement in environmental decision-making fell short of public expectations; as David Boyd put it in 2003, 'the public's role is still largely restricted to being notified of government decisions and provided with an opportunity to comment upon proposed decisions.'[4]

Canadian pesticide politics, however, has bucked each of these trends. The new Pest Control Products Act signifies a more aggressive federal role in regulating pesticides to protect human health and the environment. The legislation embraces a command-and-control regulatory regime, a marked departure from the voluntary initiatives that were popular alternatives to strict legislative standards and mandates in the 1990s.[5] Moreover, jurisdictional competition among local, provincial, and federal institutions has facilitated, rather than hampered, innovative policy reforms. This is particularly the case in the campaign to ban cosmetic pesticides, as anti-pesticide activists have successfully targeted local city councils when blocked in federal and provincial venues. Local action, in turn, has put pressure on higher levels of government to address weaknesses in provincial and federal regulation of lawn care chemicals. Finally, citizens have participated in the reform process, most notably at the local level but also in the federal arena. Indeed, the reform of the Pest Control Products Act involved consultations with key stakeholders, including environmental and health organizations; this was a significant departure from the more closed policy-making processes of the past.

Pesticide policy reform in Canada, however, is not an unqualified success. Reform was long overdue and some environmentalists worry that the new law, while impressive on paper, may not be fully implemented and enforced.[6] Implementation, after all, is a much less visible process, and one in which industry groups often participate vigorously in an attempt to ease the regulatory burden of legislation. Even if implemented, the law largely aims at preventing the worst chemicals from being used or abused, rather than replacing them with non-chemical alternatives. The Canadian agricultural industry is still heavily reliant on pesticides, and serious efforts to decrease pesticide use through alternatives like Integrated Pest Management (IPM) and organic agriculture are lacking.[7] Indeed, Canada falls short when compared with many European countries, which have been more aggressive in banning suspect pesticides, and where residue limits for pesticides on foods are significantly lower and experimentation with new and innovative policy tools suggests a path toward more sustainable agricultural practices.

This chapter examines the path to pesticides policy reform in Canada with an eye toward identifying and explaining the factors driving the changes. Pesticides reform at the federal level was driven by both internal and external factors. Within Canada, the public became increasingly concerned about the negative health impacts of pesticides, prompted in part by several studies authored by the US government. A public opinion poll in 2000 indicated that large majorities of Canadians disapproved of the high levels of pesticide use in Canadian agriculture, suggesting that pesticide reduction had become something of a 'valence' issue.[8] However, increasing public awareness and concern cannot, on their own, explain the reform process. Policy entrepreneurs in government played a key role by authoring reports that forcefully and publicly called for an overhaul of the PCPA. These reports not only helped raise public concern, but legitimized and reinforced the claims of environmentalists and health activists who found powerful, reform-minded allies in the federal government.

A complete explanation of why the federal government modernized its pesticide law, however, requires that we look beyond Canada's borders. In the mid-1990s, the United States passed the Food Quality Protection Act, the most comprehensive and significant overhaul of its pesticide and food safety laws in decades. The Canadian government, quite simply, was forced to consider tougher regulations in order to maintain access to US markets and to fulfill the goal of harmonizing its regulations with the United States and Mexico under the auspices of the North American Free Trade Agreement (NAFTA). The pesticides and agricultural industries, while not supportive of every change in the law, realized the need for updating the Pest Control Products Act to facilitate free trade. Importantly, these industries also saw an opportunity to streamline the registration process so that Canadian farmers had access to the latest and least toxic products on the market.

A somewhat different set of factors explains the successful campaigns to ban and restrict cosmetic pesticides on lawns and gardens. Unlike the reform of the Pest Control Products Act, which had many features of a top-down process, the movement against cosmetic pesticides was bottom-up. Activists in towns and cities around the country urged adoption of pesticides bylaws, and found a receptive audience at the local level. The pesticide industry was initially caught off guard, having focused most of its energy on the federal reform process. Indeed, the pesticides and landscaping industries were late to launch an effective counter campaign in the conflict over cosmetic pesticides, allowing momentum to build around municipal pesticides restrictions. The popularity and spread of local pesticide bylaws eventually led the provinces of Québec and Ontario to issue province-wide bans on the cosmetic use of pesticides, an example of 'trickle-up' policy diffusion and an indication of the success of the anti-pesticides movement.[9]

Federal Pesticide Regulation: The Path to Reform

Prior to the 1960s, Canada did little to regulate pesticides beyond implementing labelling laws to ensure product effectiveness and to discourage fraud. As in the United States, pesticide use in Canada grew in the post-World War II era as chemical research during the war led to a new class of relatively inexpensive, highly effective pesticides. Widespread concern about their potential environmental and health effects was rare until Rachel Carson sounded the alarm about pesticides in her 1962 book *Silent Spring*. Due in part to a growing public awareness about pesticides and other toxins, Canada assumed more regulatory control over the sale and use of pesticides in 1969 with the passage of the Pest Control Products Act. The law required the pre-market clearance, registration, and labelling of all pesticides products manufactured, imported, and sold in the country. Canada also regulates pesticides via the Food and Drug Act, which sets limits, or 'tolerances' for pesticide residues on various food items. This chapter focuses on the Pest Control Products Act because it has been the primary target for policy reform. Registration by Agriculture Canada was supposed to ensure that the benefits of the product outweighed any risks it might pose to both humans and the environment, and the process allegedly removed the most harmful products from the market. Provincial laws added another layer of regulation, as provinces retained authority over post-registration pesticide sales, distribution, and use. Provinces were also involved in the certification and training of applicators and vendors, they issued permits for some restricted use pesticides, and several provinces required notification of pesticide applications by pest control operators. (Until the 1990s, municipal governments played little role in pesticide regulation.)

Sales of pesticides in Canada—90 per cent of which are used in agriculture—increased markedly after the passage of the 1969 pesticides law even as public unease about them intensified. Spending on agricultural pesticides increased over 400 per cent from 1970–1995, for example, and the industry estimated sales to be about $1.4 billion in 1997.[10] Currently, over 7,000 products containing 500 active ingredients are registered in Canada; many were registered in the decade prior to and immediately after passage of the 1969 PCPA, when scientific knowledge about their adverse impacts was rather limited and regulatory standards were lower.[11] Under the 1969 PCPA re-evaluation of existing pesticides was discretionary, even though many pesticides previously thought to be harmless have been proven otherwise. In addition, Agriculture Canada's process of evaluation and re-evaluation of pesticides was clouded in secrecy; the agency relied on industry data concerning a product's toxicity and effectiveness and kept even this information from the public.[12] Critics suspected, not unreasonably, that Agriculture Canada privileged its primary clients—farmers—over the public interest by allowing many suspect pesticides to enter and remain on the market. The public had little reason to trust the agency, particularly as a series of reports and reviews highlighted the weaknesses of Canada's regulatory regime and raised alarm about the potential dangers of pesticides to human health.

Reports and Reviews

Notably, some of the earliest and most critical assessments of Canada's pesticide law originated within the government beginning in the 1980s. A 1987 study by the Law Reform Commission confirmed a number of problems with the legislation and its implementation, including the frustratingly slow process of safety re-evaluation of existing pesticides.[13] Not surprisingly, the government gave no indication that it would adopt the Commission's 23 recommended improvements to the PCPA. Rather, it formed a multi-stakeholder advisory group—the Pesticide Registration Review Team—to investigate needed reforms, hold public hearings, and negotiate for possible legislative changes. In 1990, the Review Team released its recommendations for policy reform in what became known as the 'Blue Book'[14]; again, no immediate action followed. But Jean Chrétien, then leader of the opposition Liberal Party, endorsed the Blue Book recommendations and promised to reform the PCPA if elected. When the Liberal Party won the election in 1993, Chrétien's government issued a plan for implementing the Review Team's proposals (the 'Purple Book').

An important component of the implementation plan involved moving responsibility for pesticides registration and review from Agriculture Canada to Health Canada. In 1995, the Pest Management Regulatory Agency (PMRA) was created within Health Canada without amending the law itself. Some anti-pesticide activists dismissed the move as 'an effort to pacify Canadians worried about the health effects of chemical pesticides . . . The Act itself was hardly changed.'[15] But shifting regulatory responsibility to the health ministry was perhaps more significant than environmentalists recognized. While Agriculture Canada was largely beholden to farmers and industry, Health Canada had a mandate to put public health first. If policy change did not immediately follow, the move opened up an opportunity for policy to favour health and environmental concerns over commercial and agricultural ones.[16]

In the early 1990s, scientific reports about the negative impacts of pesticides on human health surfaced in the United States and attracted attention in both the US and Canada.[17] A 1993 study by the US-based National Academy of Sciences (NAS), 'Pesticides in the Diets of Infants and Children', highlighted the special vulnerability of children to pesticides, followed by a 1996 Environmental Protection Agency study titled simply 'Environmental Health Threats to Children'. Anti-pesticide activists in Canada seized on these studies to frame pesticides policy reform as a health and safety issue, a frame that appeared to resonate with the Canadian public. As Kathleen Cooper of the Canadian Environmental Law Association (CELA) noted, her organization relied on the NAS report and began to work with physicians to focus the debate on the health impacts of pesticides (particularly on children).[18] An activist with the Sierra Club claimed simply that 'health arguments won out.'[19]

The end of the decade ushered in another set of government reports about the inadequacies of the federal government's approach to pesticides regulation. This time, the criticisms were aimed at the new Pest Management Regulatory Agency, and the reports exposed the agency's lack of progress in implementing the Blue Book recommendations and emphasized the on-going weaknesses of the PCPA. The House of Commons Standing Committee on Environment and Sustainable Development did not mince words in its 2000 report. Among other things, it urged the government to give 'absolute precedence' to the protection of human health, recommended an increased safety factor in determining food tolerance levels to take account of the vulnerability of children, called for the re-evaluation of all pesticides registered before 1995, and urged the government to use the precautionary principle 'when there is mounting scientific evidence of the adverse effects of certain pesticides'.[20] Cooper of CELA called it a 'scathing review' and part of a five- to six-year saga of reform efforts and 'non-stop criticism'.[21]

The long road to reform finally produced results in 2002, when Health Minister Anne McLellen introduced amendments to the Pest Control Products Act. The bill addressed many of the weaknesses in the old law: it put a priority on health and environmental concerns,[22] allowed for more public involvement in the regulatory process, and strengthened the 'post-registration' control of pesticides by requiring regular re-evaluations of older pesticides and increasing penalties for non-compliance, for example. However, it did not accomplish everything laid out in earlier reports nor did it meet all the demands of environmental activists. David Boyd, an environmental lawyer and author of critical reports for the David Suzuki Foundation, noted several problems:

> Unfortunately, the new law fails to require the substitution of safer products for more harmful products, emphasize pollution prevention, establish specific targets or timelines for reducing pesticide use, ban cosmetic and nonessential uses of pesticides, make the precautionary approach govern all decisions, or emphasize IPM.[23]

As discussed below, activists had to look to other policy venues for progress on the issue of cosmetic pesticides, and there are continuing their efforts to strengthen Canada's pesticides laws and policies.

Access and Participation

Of the several notable improvements to the PCPA, one was an opening up of the pesticides registration process. As mentioned, transparency was low under the old pesticides regulatory regime; interested citizens or organizations had no way of knowing how the government evaluated pesticides or what information the agency used to make registration decisions. Information was kept from other government agencies as well; as Boyd said about the old regulatory regime, '[t]he veil of secrecy around pesticide information has been so tight that the PMRA refused to share information even with other federal agencies such as Environment Canada and the Department of Fisheries and Oceans.'[24] The new law attempts to daylight the process by giving the public access to evaluation reports on registered pesticides and allowing them to view the test data on which these evaluations are based. Such information is vital if environmental and health organizations want to effectively challenge the PMRA's decisions.

Significantly, the reform process itself marked a positive step toward greater public participation in pesticides policymaking. The Pest Management Advisory Council (PMAC) was established in 1998 to promote dialogue between stakeholders and the Pest Management Regulatory Agency, and to provide advice to the Ministry of Health on pesticide regulatory issues. Council members represented a variety of interest groups, including industry, health, and environmentalists. For example, the 17 members on the 2000 council included representatives from the Crop Protection Institute, the Canola Council of Canada, the Canadian Association of Physicians for the Environment, and the Sierra Club. Cooper, of the Canadian Environmental Law Association, admitted that it was unusual for environmentalists to be in such a position; it was also 'very useful to be on the council. . . We asked questions of the agency and had access to information we wouldn't get otherwise.'[25] A Sierra Club representative agreed that they had 'lots of access' and went further by claiming that the text of the new PCPA 'had a lot to do with NGOs [nongovern-mental organizations]'.26 The PMAC continues to meet and includes a relatively balanced represen-tation of interest groups. According to one environmental activist, environmental groups are now regular players and are 'seen as stakeholders'.27

Incentives and the Elephant Next Door

If the government praised the new Pest Control Products Act as an overhaul of Canada's pesticide regulatory regime, it also claimed that several provisions in the new law simply formalized what Health Canada was already practicing. Indeed, in an 'information note' published in June 2006 when the new law went into force, the PMRA noted that, '[i]n 1998, as a matter of policy, the PMRA established policies that required additional protection for children and pregnant women and took into account pesticide exposure from all sources, including food and water.'28 Why would the agen-cy assume a more protective regulatory stance if it was not required by law to do so? The answer provides further insight into the pesticides reform process.

Canada had a strong incentive to strengthen its regulatory regime to be more in line with the American laws. The regulatory gap between the two countries grew dangerously wide in 1996 when the United States passed the Food Quality Protection Act, significantly updating its approach to pesticides regulation. The FQPA recognized the special vulnerability of children to pesticides, and it required the EPA to consider the 'aggregate risk' of exposure to multiple pesticides when deciding tolerance levels. It also mandated screening pesticides for potential 'endocrine disruptors', among other things.29 Because the United States is Canada's most important trading partner, Canada can-not afford to have widely divergent standards that might threaten the free movement of agricultural products between the two countries. Moreover, harmonization agreements under the North Ameri-can Free Trade Agreement (NAFTA) have provided continued pressure on Canada to bring its regula-tions in line with those in the United States.30 One indication that Canada was following the lead of the United States is the remarkable similarities between the US FQPA and the PCPA (as amended).31

Importantly, the Food Quality Protection Act compelled the EPA to expedite the review and regis-tration of so-called 'reduced risk' pesticides. Reduced risk pesticides are determined to pose a lesser risk to humans, non-target species, and the environment. Ideally, such pesticides could replace older, more toxic chemicals on the market; an expedited review process would bring them to mar-ket sooner and therefore prevent unnecessary risks to the public and the environment. However, expedited reviews in the United States put farmers and pesticide companies in Canada at a competi-tive disadvantage. Without the same access to newer and more effective pesticides, the agricultural industry in Canada suffered. Indeed, the industry had long complained about the lengthy review process for pesticides and urged the government to streamline the process.

In short, the agricultural and pesticides industries, which in the past had stood as significant barriers to policy reform, also called for changes to the nation's pesticide law. With industry, environ-mentalists, and health groups all advocating for policy change, the odds of reform significantly increased. Naturally, these groups did not always agree on the nature and extent of reforms; as Cooper admitted, '[r]arely do we [environmentalists and industry] agree. But we agreed on the need for new legislation.'32 Industry was not only concerned about harmonizing its standards to those in the US and facilitating the registration process; as public attention to and concern about the potentially negative health impacts of pesticides grew, the pesticide industry sought for ways to reassure the public that its products were safe. A strengthened Pest Control Products Act might appease some critics. When the new PCPA went into effect, Lorne Hepworth, President of CropLife Canada, claimed that 'we have supported the new PCPA from introduction through Royal Assent.'[33] But if industry was relatively cooperative in forwarding reforms of the pesticide testing and registration process, it remained steadfastly opposed to banning and severely restricting lawn and garden pesticides. On this issue, it clashed head-first with environmental and health organizations.

Bans and Bylaws: Cosmetic Pesticides and Local Politics[34]

Meryl Hammond was a founding member of the group Citizens for Alternatives to Pesticides (CAP), a grassroots organization committed to ending the non-essential uses of pesticides on lawns and gardens. Just two years after its founding in 1992, representatives from CAP met with Minister of Health Canada, 'sure that she would do the right thing and pass a federal law to ban the cosmetic use of pesticides'.[35] But Hammond, as well as other anti-pesticide activists, soon learned otherwise. Their efforts to enact a nation-wide ban on cosmetic pesticide use gained little traction even when the issue of pesticide reform was on the federal agenda and negotiations for amending the Pest Control Products Act were in full force. According to Hammond, activists got the 'complete runaround'; federal officials told them to seek out provincial officials, while provincial ministers passed the buck back to the federal level.[36] 'No one wanted to touch it,' Hammond added.[37]

The campaign to ban the non-essential use of lawn and garden pesticides thus reverted to the local level. Anti-pesticide activists adopted a town-by-town, city-by-city approach, and it worked; about 140 communities have now banned or severely restricted the cosmetic use of pesticides on public and private property.[38] And evidence suggests the bylaws are more than an exercise in symbolic politics. In a study prepared by the Canadian Centre for Pollution Prevention and Cullbridge Marketing and Communication, communities with municipal bylaws (combined with education programs) achieved a 50 to 90 per cent reduction in pesticide use after the laws went into effect.[39]

Canada has gone further than the United States and many European countries in regulating lawn care chemicals, a somewhat unexpected development given its laggard status in the area of agricultural pesticides regulation. What explains the considerable success of the movement to restrict cosmetic pesticides? Several factors can be identified. As in the case of federal pesticides reform, a focus on human (and especially children's) health raised public concern about lawn care chemicals and put considerable pressure on officials to take measures to reassure the public. Unlike the federal case, the courts played a central role in the reform of lawn care pesticide use. The Supreme Court not only granted municipalities the right to regulate in this area but legitimized environmentalists' calls for a precautionary approach to regulation. The final explanation for the success of the campaign is that anti-pesticide activists simply outmaneuvered their opponents. The pesticides industry in Canada was late to launch an effective campaign against the bylaws movement, thus allowing momentum to build around municipal pesticides restrictions and leading to further regulatory diffusion.

Policy Innovation and Diffusion

While the vast majority of pesticides in Canada are used in agriculture, non-agricultural uses have increased as suburbanization has expanded lawn coverage and ushered in an era of intensive chemical management of the suburban landscape. Globally, the sale of nonagricultural pesticides is growing at a rate of four per cent a year, and this increase is fuelled, in part, by increased lawn cov-erage.[40] Anti-pesticide activists started paying attention to urban pesticide use in the 1980s, noting that homeowners applied pesticides in greater concentration than farmers even if their aggregate use was less. When studies indicated that some of the most popular lawn pesticides were poten-tially toxic to humans—for example, the herbicide 2, 4-D—public concern about their safety grew. Kathleen Cooper received numerous calls in the late 1980s and early 1990s from people alarmed about pesticide use in municipal parks and at schools.[41] The first campaigns against the cosmetic use of pesticides were thus aimed at restricting use on public property, mainly in recreational park areas, on school property, and around daycare centres. These efforts reflected a concern for chil-dren's health, a main theme in the cosmetic pesticides campaign.

In 1991, the small town of Hudson, Québec went beyond the public (and often voluntary) restric-tions being considered elsewhere. In April, it issued a ban on cosmetic pesticides used on public and private property.[42] Hudson's bold policy initiative caught the attention of environmental and health advocates, aided by a series of lawsuits by the lawn and garden care industry that raised the visibil-ity of the town's bylaw even further. As outlined further in Marcia Valiante's chapter in this volume, two landscaping companies charged with violating the Hudson bylaw challenged the legislation in a series of court cases lasting 10 years. In June 2001, the legal battle ended when the Supreme Court of Canada gave municipalities the green light to enact pesticide bylaws, citing provincial legislation that gave towns and cities the authority to regulate in the interest of a community's health and wel-fare. The Supreme Court victory was the 'mouse that roared', a focal event that galvanized the public and policymakers to take action.[43] After the Hudson decision, municipalities throughout Canada gained confidence in their right to enact bylaws restricting the use of cosmetic pesticides, and the bylaws spread.[44]

The bylaw movement was fuelled by national networks of activists and policymakers. In 1996, Toronto Environmental Alliance, Sierra Club of Canada, World Wildlife Fund, Citizens for Alterna-tives to Pesticides, and the Canadian Labour Congress launched the Campaign for Pesticides Reduc-tion (CPR). The original coalition of regional and national environmental/labour groups expanded to a network of 75 organizations within a year. Physician and health organizations performed a critical role in this network by providing expertise and adding legitimacy to the anti-pesticides campaigns. Local anti-pesticide groups were joined by organizations like the Canadian Cancer Society, the Lung Association, the Family College of Physicians, nurses associations, and other health organizations which provided important testimony before city councils about the risks of pesticides to children.[45] As Cooper noted, bylaw supporters appeared 'calm' and 'reasonable' during public hearings: 'We had doctors beside us . . . and we did not come off as wild-eyed and crazy' in front of often very conservative city councilors.[46]

Meryl Hammond of CAP thought the national alliance would help them 'get their foot in the federal door'.[47] But when prospects for a national ban looked bleak, the coalition focused on sup-porting local efforts where activists were more successful. According to one activist, the grassroots approach was a 'way to get people across the country working on it and bring people together.'[48] In short, these networks were an important factor in the diffusion and success of the municipal bylaws campaign. Anti-pesticide activists suggested that without them, the movement would have remained fragmented, with small towns pursuing bylaws in isolation without the benefit of broader knowledge, experience, and expertise.[49] Networks also developed among municipal officials, foster-ing sub-national communication and policy innovation among city councilors and bureaucrats. The 'limited engagement of ideas and innovations' across political boundaries that Barry Rabe described in reference to Canadian environmental politics in the late 1990s was clearly challenged by the municipal pesticides campaigns.[50] Indeed, the anti-pesticides bylaw movement appears to fit more optimistic accounts of the possibilities for local policy innovation. Rather than engaging in 'races to the bottom', in this case sub-national jurisdictions faced 'upward' pressures to strengthen environmental regulation as constituents demanded action from their city councils.

Unequal Mobilization and Organization

The rapid mobilization of anti-pesticide groups stands out against the pesticide industry's relative lack of organization and coordination around the cosmetic pesticides issue. While the lawn care and pesticide industries became better organized over time, they were late to get started. As Debra Conlon of CropLife Canada said, 'Industry did not take the Hudson issue seriously enough. We didn't ask how to isolate it and stop it from growing versus just reacting to it. . . Our industry did not see the trend.'[51] Another industry analyst admitted that, 'there is a tinge of regret from some LCOs [lawn care operators] who realize that had the industry been organized in the first place, they might be winning the battle.'[52] Chris Lemcke of Weed Man (a lawn care chain) agreed: 'If the Green Industry had started lobbying and getting involved in the local politics years ago, it would not likely be in this position today.'[53]

With the growth of strict anti-pesticide ordinances at the local level, industry was forced to battle each pesticide proposal at the grassroots. According to Conlon, pesticide trade organizations like CropLife Canada were ill-prepared to fight battles in hundreds of city councils around the country. The industry was organized and active at the federal level, as discussed above, and played a large role in the reform of the Pest Control Products Act. According to both environmental activists and industry spokespeople, industry was 'way more sophisticated at the federal level' than at the local level.[54] Conlon of CropLife Canada admitted, 'We were not organized at the local level and we are still not organized there. You have to be interacting with them [local communities] on a daily basis.'[55] Local venues, according to Conlon, were not particularly receptive: 'We had zero clout, zero energy [at the local level]. We would fly in where there was a problem, expect to give our say and that is because traditionally this level was not regulated.'[56]

Because the lawn care pesticides sector in Canada was relatively small (and therefore lacked the resources to fight the bylaw movement on its own), it needed to form alliances with other affected industries such as the agricultural pesticides sector and landscaping companies. However, the various affected industries failed to form strong, working alliances at the start of the campaign. The relative absence of coalitions can be attributed in part to anti-pesticide activists, who found ways to divide the opposition. Hudson's bylaw (which became a model for many other municipalities) excluded agricultural uses of pesticides and exempted golf courses for five years. According to one industry analyst, this left the lawn care industry 'to fight on its own'.[57] Over time, the pesticides and lawn care industry joined together and waged more sophisticated grassroots opposition campaigns. In 2001, for example, lawn care professionals, golf course superintendents, and pesticide manufacturers formed a coalition to fight Toronto's proposed bylaw. However, in the face of a probable ban by the Toronto city council the coalition faltered; lawn care companies broke with their allies and made a deal with the city council for a partial ban.[58] The coalition, which had plans to raise one million dollars a year to fight the bylaws movement, disintegrated.

In sum, Canadian environmental groups successfully exploited opportunities at the local level to advance the regulation of lawn care pesticides. Efforts by the pesticides industry to arrest the movement have largely failed. The courts, rather than prohibiting local regulation, endorsed it and the underlying regulatory rationale. As the movement has spread and gained in popularity, provincial governments have considered, and in two cases have passed, province-wide ordinances against cosmetic pesticide use. And while the federal government has not acted to ban cosmetic pesticides, it has created a 'Healthy Lawns' initiative intended to decrease reliance on chemical lawn management.

The campaign against cosmetic lawn and garden pesticides represents a significant threat to the agricultural and pesticides industries. The goal of the campaign is to severely restrict or completely ban the non-essential uses of pesticides on lawns and gardens—pesticides that have been deemed 'safe' by the Pest Management Regulatory Agency. The implicit message is that there is no safe level of exposure to pesticides or, at the very least, that the benefits of some pesticides are not worth the risks of exposure. This message threatens some key tenets of the pesticide industry: first, that when used responsibly, pesticides are safe for humans and the environment; and, second, that the benefits of pesticides largely outweigh their costs. As Lorne Hepworth of the Crop Protection Institute of Canada said in response to calls for pesticides bans:

> While it's important to ensure public health and environment are safeguarded, the benefits to farmers must be part of the risk-benefit equation. To do otherwise is wrong-headed and would put Canada's agriculture out of business.[59]

Industry, not surprisingly, continues to tout the benefits of pesticides in hopes of averting more calls for bans on their products.

The Possibilities and Limits of Reform

Canada's decades-long experience with pesticides policy is encouraging in many ways. It suggests that major environmental policy reform is possible, even in eras characterized by regulatory retrenchment and retreat. While long overdue, the new Pest Control Products Act represents a significant step forward in Canada's approach to pest management. And the numerous municipal (and now provincial) bylaws to restrict and ban cosmetic pesticides distinguish Canada as a leader and innovator in this area. Indeed, Canada has gone much further than the United States and Europe when it comes to regulating lawn care chemicals, a somewhat unexpected development given its laggard status in other areas of environmental regulation and protection.[60]

The invocation of the precautionary principle in the campaigns to amend Canada's pesticides laws may prove to be one of the most significant aspects of these reform efforts. Advocates of a precautionary approach to environmental policymaking accept that uncertainty is inherent in regulating toxic substances. They argue, however, that this uncertainty should not prevent action: in fact, in the face of potentially significant harm, the burden of proof should be on those advocating the use of the chemicals rather than on those advising restraint and protection. While Canada has signed several international agreements citing the precautionary principle, 'Canadian environmental law is generally based on the opposite of the precautionary principle, in that conclusive scientific evidence of harm is necessary before steps will be taken to limit an activity or restrict the use of a particular substance.'[61] This makes the new PCPA and the campaigns to ban cosmetic pesticides especially significant.[62] Environmental and health advocates hope that legislative references to the precautionary principle, combined with the Supreme Court's noteworthy endorsement of it in its 2001 decision, will spill over to other areas of environmental regulation.

Whether the precautionary principle actually guides the decisions of bureaucrats in the Pest Management Regulatory Agency, however, remains to be seen. Some environmentalists remain skeptical about whether the agency will implement and enforce the new PCPA with sufficient vigor. Problems with lax enforcement of environmental regulations in the past may be fuelling this skepticism, and some environmentalists are wasting no time in serving as watchdogs to Health Canada. Just a year after the new PCPA went into effect, for example, the David Suzuki Foundation sent a letter to the Minister of Health requesting that the agency initiate a special review of 60 active ingredients used in pesticides in Canada, on the grounds that the ingredients had been banned by one or more OECD (Organisation for Economic Development) countries. The organization has also pointed to the limitations of Canada's laws concerning pesticide residue levels on foods, claiming that Canada has some of the weakest standards among industrialized nations.[63]

The Suzuki Foundation's most recent criticisms point to a disadvantage in Canada's pesticide reform process. Canada, in reforming its federal pesticides law and setting standards for residue levels, has looked to the United States as a model and point of reference. On the one hand, emulating the US has strengthened Canada's main pesticide law, as detailed in this chapter. But in other respects, it serves as a barrier: when compared to the European Union, the United States has weaker protections for pesticide residues in food products, for example. Environmentalists are arguing that Canada should be using the European Union as its benchmark, not the United States. As the Suzuki Foundation says in its report, *The Food We Eat*, 'One of the main problems with North American harmonization . . . is that both Canada and the U.S. fare poorly in protecting public health from pesticide risks in comparison to the European Union and Australia . . . Canada clearly needs to emulate the world's leaders, rather than taking a narrow North American approach.'[64] Environmentalists are now looking to Europe, not the United States, as a model for Canada.

Commercial concerns and trade agreements may drive decisions about specific pesticides and pesticide residue levels in the near future. The volume of trade in agricultural products between Canada and the United States continues to shape Canada's policies, along with trade agreements like NAFTA. For example, when the Canadian government banned the pesticide lindane for use on canola crops in 2001, a US-based chemical corporation sued the government under NAFTA, claiming the government's action had cost them upwards of $100 million. The lindane case reveals how US-Canadian trade agreements can serve to both strengthen and weaken Canadian pesticides policy. It was well-known that the Canadian government did not ban lindane because of its environmental and health effects. Rather, the pesticide became the object of a trade dispute between the two countries after the US banned the pesticide. Farmers in the United States complained they were at a competitive disadvantage because lindane substitutes were expensive, thereby increasing the price of US canola crops.[65] Canada responded by announcing a federal ban, only to be sued by the US-based corporation that produced the pesticide.

In the end, the pesticide-by-pesticide regulatory approach adopted by both the United States and Canada may prove inadequate in responding to the concerns of the public, environmentalists, and health activists. The real challenge in the pesticides policy arena is finding alternatives to pesticides and transitioning away from the large-scale use of chemicals in agriculture. From this perspective, Canada has a long way to go. It ranks high in per capita use of pesticides when compared to other OECD nations; about three-quarters of Canada's crop lands are sprayed with pesticides; only two per cent of farmers use biological controls; and while organic agriculture is growing at an impressive rate in Canada (around 20 per cent per year), it is negligible in terms of total agricultural production.[66] Efforts to decrease the use of pesticides by supporting organic agriculture and using strategies like

Integrated Pest Management suffer from lack of funds and the difficulties involved in training farmers to use less chemically intensive methods of pest control.[67]

However, some signs of hope come from two very different sources: local communities and international institutions. The grassroots campaigns to ban cosmetic pesticides in Canada suggest a level of public concern, involvement, and willingness to sacrifice that suggests continued public pressure to find alternatives to pesticides. Much of the public supports the bans on cosmetic pesticide use and, in doing so, are implicitly accepting that weeds and other unwanted pests may be the price for a healthier environment. To the extent that pesticide use is driven in part by consumer imperatives for blemish-free and bug-free produce, the public's growing awareness about the health impacts of pesticides might increase their tolerance for less-than-perfect fruits and vegetables.[68] This, in turn, would decrease the pressure on farmers to spray for purely aesthetic reasons.

Another positive sign can be found in the United Nation's recent call for what anti-pesticide activists hail as a 'real revolution in agriculture'. In a report released in April 2008, the UN's International Assessment of Agriculture Science and Technology for Development emphasized the need for ecologically sustainable agriculture and called for a radical change in the way that the world grows its food.[69] Such a change will require significant government involvement and intergovernmental cooperation. Canada would do well to look to Europe for positive examples of how to pursue a truly innovative and precautionary approach to pesticides regulation—one designed to prevent risk by decreasing our dependence on chemical pesticides. Several European countries, such as Sweden, Denmark, and the Netherlands, have achieved a 50 per cent pesticide reduction without any significant drop in agricultural productivity.[70] They have done this through innovative policies such as pesticide taxes, and have supported organic agriculture and research into alternatives at levels that suggest they are interested in more than just symbolic policies. If Canada is serious about pesticides reform, these countries can serve as positive models and suggest a path to a less pesticide-ridden future.

Questions for Review

1. What environmental issues are generated by the use of pesticides?
2. To what extent have developments in the US influenced Canadian law and politics on pesticides?
3. Why did many of Canada's local governments become key players on pesticides issues?
4. What does this case tell us about the pathways of environmental policy diffusion in Canada?

Notes

1. I use the term 'pesticides' generically to refer to chemical compounds used to kill unwanted plants and animals. Pesticides include herbicides, insecticides, rodenticides, and fungicides.
2. For example, Environment Canada's budget fell 30 per cent from 1988–1998; the budgets of the Department of Fisheries and Oceans, Parks Canada, and the Canadian Forest Service also suffered. See David R. Boyd, *Unnatural Law: Rethinking Canadian Environmental Law and Policy* (Vancouver: UBC Press, 2003), 239–241.
3. See Robert Paehlke, 'Environmentalism in One Country: Canadian Environmental Policy in an Era of Globalization', *Policy Studies Journal* 28, 1 (2000): 160–175.

4. Boyd, 2003, 245; see also Debora L. VanNijnatten, 'Participation and Environmental Policy in Canada and the United States: Trends Over Time', *Policy Studies Journal* 27, 2 (1999): 267–87.

5. For a discussion of voluntary policy instruments, see the chapter by Mark Winfield in this volume. Canada's embrace of so-called 'smart regulation' in 2002 was supposed to signal a departure from the minimalist and deregulatory approaches of the 1990s. However, Winfield notes that in practice, 'smart regulation seems to incorporate much of the substantive directions of the minimalist model, while adding a more insidious element of establishing the promotion of economic interests of regulated entities as explicit goals of regulatory activity.' Mark S. Winfield, 'Governance and the Environment in Canada: From Regulatory Renaissance to "Smart Regulation"', *Journal of Environmental Law and Practice* 17, 2 (2007): 69–83.

6. David R. Boyd, 'The Food We Eat: An International Comparison of Pesticides Regulations'. Report prepared for the David Suzuki Foundation (Vancouver: David Suzuki Foundation, 2006).

7. Integrated Pest Management attempts to decrease the use of chemical pesticides by taking a holistic approach to pest management. It employs multiple pest management strategies, including biological controls, crop rotation, and careful timing of interventions and applications. The goal is not to eradicate pests but to 'apply a minimal level of control that will maintain a pest below an economic damage threshold'. See Mark L. Winston, *Nature Wars: People v. Pests* (Cambridge, MA: Harvard University Press, 1997), 163. IPM has its skeptics, however, who dub it 'Integrated Pesticide Management' because practitioners often rely on traditional chemical pesticides while giving lip service to the approach.

8. A valence issue elicits consensus among the electorate, as opposed to position issues which divide the public (typically, although not exclusively along partisan lines). The 2000 public opinion poll referred to found that 97 per cent of Canadians believe it is important to reduce the amount of pesticides in food, water, and soil; 89 per cent supported cutting pesticide use in half; and 70 per cent believed pesticides in food pose high or moderate risk to their health. Boyd, 2003, 114.

9. Murray Campbell, 'Ontario Bans Lawn and Garden Chemicals', *Globe and Mail*, 22 April 2008. Available at http://www.theglobeandmail.com/servlet/story/RTGAM.20080422.wpesticides0422/EmailBNStory/National/Ontario (accessed 22 April 2008). When the Ontario pesticide law goes into effect in 2009, municipalities will be banned from enacting tougher pesticide regulations. Consequently, not all environmentalists are happy about the provincial law.

10. Mark Abley, 'Pesticide Peril Growing Steadily', *The Gazette* [Montreal], 3 July 1991: A1; Boyd, 2003, 115. These sales numbers are estimates, as Canada has not generated national data on pesticides sales and use as is the norm in other western countries. The 2002 revisions to the PCPA establish a public registry to track this type of data and two new regulations to Canada's Chemicals Management Plan announced in 2006 require the government to collect data on adverse effects and sales. 'Croplife Canada Supports New Pest Control Regulations', *Canada NewsWire*, 12 December 2006.

11. As one government official noted in a 1998 report, 'many pesticides used in Canada today were evaluated against previous and less stringent . . . standards.' Quoted in Abley, 1999.

12. Environmentalists also criticized the government for not requiring pesticide manufacturers to disclose the full list of ingredients in a product. Under the PCPA, they were only required to list the active ingredients. See Abley, 1999.

13. J.F. Castrilli and Toby Vigod, *Pesticides in Canada: An Examination of Federal Law and Policy* (Ottawa: Law Reform Commission of Canada, 1987).

14. Pesticide Registration Review Team, *Final Report, Recommendations for a Revised Federal Pest Management Regulatory System* (Ottawa: Supply & Services, 1990).

15. Angela Rickman, 'Canadian Activists Win Pesticide Bylaws', *Pesticide Campaigner* 14, 2 (2004): 8.

16. Bureaucratic responsibility for pesticides regulation in the United States was shifted from the Department of Agriculture to the Environmental Protection Agency (EPA) in 1972 with the passage of the Federal Insecticide, Fungicide, and Rodenticide Act. Christopher Bosso argues that this marked an important turning point in the history of US pesticides politics given that the EPA had a mandate to protect human health and the environment. While the Office of Pesticides Programs (OPP) within the EPA was not immune to pressure from industry and agricultural groups, it was certainly less biased toward these groups at the outset. Christopher Bosso, *Pesticides and Politics: The Life-Cycle of a Public Issue* (Pittsburgh, PA: University of Pittsburgh Press, 1987).

17. George Hoberg notes how negative media attention to pesticides in the US can spill over to the Canadian media market and thus raise public concern in Canada. He uses the cases of EDB (ethylene dibromide) and Alar in the 1980s to illustrate his point. See George Hoberg, 'Sleeping with the Elephant: The American Influence on Canadian Environmental Regulation', *Journal of Public Policy* 11, 1 (1991): 107–31.

18. Phone interview with author, 21 June 2005.

19. Phone interview with author, 23 June 2005. The interviewee requested anonymity.

20. Standing Committee on Environment and Sustainable Development, 'The House of Commons Environment Committee calls on Canadians to Reduce Pesticide Use to Protect Human Health and the Environment', News Release, 16 May 2000. Katherine Boothe and Kathryn Harrison note that the work of the committee was 'something of an exception to the rule that strong party discipline limits policy entrepreneurship in the Canadian parliament, as the committee's outspoken and independent chair, Charles Caccia, was a thorn in his own government's side throughout the 1990s.' Katherine Boothe and Kathryn Harrison, 'The Influence of Institutions on Issue Framing: Children's Environmental Health Policy in the United States and Canada'. Paper presented at the Annual Meeting of the American Political Science Association, Washington, DC, 2–5 September 2005.

21. Phone interview with the author, 21 June 2005.

22. The new law clarifies that the Minister of Health's primary objective is to protect humans and the environment from unacceptable risks from pesticides. Such a clarification is necessary when government agencies are charged with both regulating and promoting certain behaviors and products. For decades, the US Department of Agriculture was responsible for regulating pesticides for the public interest *and* for ensuring that farmers had access to effective pest control products. Serving 'two masters' is a difficult situation for any government agency, but was especially problematic in this case because the agency's natural constituency was farmers, not the public. See Bosso, 1987.

23. Boyd, 2003, 123.

24. Boyd, 2003, 121.

25. Phone interview with author, 21 June 2005.

26. Phone interview with author, 23 June 2005.

27. Representative from the Sierra Club, phone interview with the author, 23 June 2005. For a list of current PMAC members, see Pest Management Advisory Council, 'Current Members', March 2008. Available at http://www.pmra-arla.gc.ca/english/advbod/membership-ef.pdf.

28. Pest Management Regulatory Agency, 'The New Pest Control Products Act', Information Note, 28 June 2006.

29. Endocrine disruptors mimic the body's hormones and can alter the body's chemistry and produce adverse developmental, neurological, reproductive, and immune effects in humans and wildlife. See National Institute of Environmental Health Sciences, 'Endocrine Disruptors', June 2006. Available at http://www.niehs.nih.gov/health/topics/agents/endocrine/docs/endocrine.pdf.

30. In responding to the 1999 report by the Commissioner of the Environment and Sustainable Development, the 'Official Opposition' said, 'Given that fully 50% of Canada's agricultural production is exported to the United States, priority effort must be made to align reevaluation activities with those of the U.S. The PMRA should step up work . . . to harmonize data requirements with NAFTA partners and those of other OECD countries.' Official Opposition Report on Pesticides, 'Pesticides: Making the Right Choice for the Protection of Health and the Environment', May 2000.

31. For a comparison of the texts of the two statutes, see Boothe and Harrison, 2005.

32. Phone interview with author, 21 June 2005.

33. Quoted in 'CropLife Canada Applauds Government for Bring the New Pest Control Products Act into Force', *Canada NewsWire*, 28 June 2006.

34. For a thorough analysis of the movement against cosmetic pesticides, see Sarah Pralle, 'The Mouse that Roared: Agenda-Setting in Canadian Pesticides Politics', *Policy Studies Journal* 34, 2 (2006): 171–94 and 'Timing and Sequence in Agenda Setting and Policy Change: A Comparative Study of Lawn Care Pesticide Politics in Canada and the U.S.', *Journal of European Public Policy* 13, 7 (2006): 987–1005.

35. Meryl Hammond, phone interview with author, 17 November 2005.

36. For an analysis of how Canada's federal system can encourage the shifting of responsibility to other levels of government, see Kathryn Harrison, *Passing the Buck: Federalism and Canadian Environmental Policy* (Vancouver: UBC Press, 1996).

37. Hammond, phone interview with author, 17 November 2005.

38. Murray Campbell, 'Ontario Bans Lawn and Garden Pesticides', 22 April 2008.

39. See Canadian Centre for Pollution Prevention and Cullbridge Marketing and Communication, 'The Impact of By-Laws and Public Education Programs on Reducing the Cosmetic/ Non-Essential, Residential Use of Pesticides: A Best Practices Review', 24 March 2004. The David Suzuki Foundation estimated in 2006 that the municipal laws apply to over eleven million Canadians, or about 37 per cent of the population. See Boyd, 2006, 26.

40. See Paul Robbins and Julie Sharp, 'The Lawn-Chemical Economy and Its Discontents', *Antipode* 25, 5 (2003): 956–79.

41. Phone interview with author, 21 June 2005.

42. Technically, the law did not completely ban cosmetic pesticides. It exempted golf courses for five years and allowed the use of pesticides under some conditions (e.g., pest outbreaks) with proper permits.

43. For more on the policy impact of focusing events, see Thomas Birkland, *After Disaster: Agenda Setting, Public Policy, and Focusing Events* (Washington, DC: Georgetown University Press, 1997).

44. Prior to the Supreme Court's decision, only one municipality outside Quebec had passed a bylaw; after the decision, municipalities in Nova Scotia, New Brunswick, Ontario, and British Columbia enacted pesticide restrictions. Katrina Miller, a toxics campaigner for the Toronto Environmental Alliance, said that the Hudson decision was critical in getting larger cities like Toronto to consider bylaws. Phone interview with author, 15 June 2005. Kathleen Cooper of CELA claims they were 'bombarded' by phone calls in the spring of 2001 after the Supreme Court decision: 'Everybody was waiting for that decision . . . People all over the country were pushing [for bylaws] but were waiting because they were afraid of being sued.' Phone interview with author, 21 June 2005.

45. Bob Diamond (of Humber Environment Action Group), phone interview with author, 20 June 2005; Christine Brown (of Citizens for Alternatives to Pesticides), phone interview with author, 16 June 2005.

46. Phone interview with author, 21 June 2005.

47. Phone interview with author, 17 November 2005.

48. Phone interview with author, 23 June 2005. The activist requested her name not be used.

49. Angela Rickman, 'Canadian Activists Win Pesticide Bylaws', *Global Pesticide Campaigner* 14, 2 (2004): 1.

50. Barry Rabe, 'Federalism and Entrepreneurship: Explaining American and Canadian Innovation in Pollution Prevention and Regulatory Integration', *Policy Studies Journal* 27, 2 (1999): 288–306.

51. Phone interview with author, 16 June 2005.

52. Jason Stahl, 'Under Attack', *Landscape Management* 43, 2 (2004): 28.

53. Quoted in Stahl, 2004, 28.

54. Kathleen Cooper, phone interview with author, 21 June 2005.

55. Phone interview with author, 16 June 2005.

56. Ibid.

57. Stahl, 2004, 23.

58. Stahl, 2004.

59. Quoted in Charlie Anderson, 'Feds Told to Bug Off: Pesticides Worth the Risk to Farmers, Say Producers', *The Vancouver Province* [British Columbia], 17 May 2000: A4.

60. For a comprehensive analysis of Canada's environmental policies and practices, including how they compare to those in the US and Europe, see Boyd, 2003.

61. Boyd, 2003, 234.

62. Section 17 of the PCPA requires Health Canada to use the precautionary approach when conducting 'special reviews' of pesticides during the re-evaluation process, reviews designed to 'verify continued acceptability of registered pesticides'. Karen Dodds, Executive Director, Pest Management Regulatory Agency. Letter to Ann Rowan of the David Suzuki Foundation, 26 June 2007. Available at http://www.davidsuzuki.org/files/SWAG/Health/PMRA_response_June_2007.pdf. Many of the bans on cosmetic pesticides also reference the precautionary principle; the Hamilton (Ontario) City Council, for example, endorsed the precautionary principle in 2005 while Quebec's pest management code (Quebec was the first province to ban on certain cosmetic pesticides) has a 'strong basis' in the precautionary principle. David Suzuki Foundation, 'Pesticide Free? Oui!: An Analysis of Quebec's Pesticide Management Code and Recommendations for Effective Provincial Policy', April 2008: 5.

63. In a comparison of maximum residue limits (MRLs; the amount of pesticide residues legally allowed on food) on forty pesticide/ food combinations among Canada, the European Union, the United States, and Australia, Canada has a weaker MRL in thirty cases. See Boyd, 2006.

64. Boyd, 2006, 22.

65. 'NAFTA Commission May Ban Lindane in North America', *Environmental News Service*, 26 September 2003. Available at http://www.ens-newswire.com/ens/sep2003/2003-09-26-04.asp (accessed May 14, 2008).

66. Boyd, 2003, Chapter 4.1.

67. As Mark Winston points out, the complexity of IPM 'has been its downfall . . . farmers require simple solutions. IPM is not simple' (Winston, 1997, 163–4). See also Robin Cowan and Philip Gunby, 'Sprayed to Death: Path Dependence, Lock-In, and Pest Control Strategies', *The Economic Journal* 106 (May 2008): 521–42.

68. Winston (1997: 172) claims that '60 to 80 per cent of pesticides on oranges, 40 to 60 per cent on tomatoes, and 10 to 20 per cent on most other fruits and vegetables is strictly for cosmetic reasons.'

69. '55 Countries Endorse Real Revolution in Agriculture', *Pesticides Action Network North America*, Press Release, 15 April 2008.

70. Winston, 1997; see also Boyd, 2003.

Appendix[1]

Select Bibliographies for Environmental Issues

Urban Environment

Alternatives Journal 26, 3 (Summer 2000). (Issue devoted to 'The End of Sprawl: Ways to Redesign Cities for Better Living'.)

Alternatives Journal 29, 3 (Summer 2003). (Issue devoted to 'Urban Community Planning and Development'.)

Bundale, Avril. 'Greening Together: The Ecovillage Movement Grows from Grassroots to Mainstream', *Alternatives Journal* 30, 5 (2004): 16–17.

Canada Mortgage and Housing Corporation. 'The Hockerton Housing Project', *The Sustainable Community: A Practical Guide*. Ottawa: CMHC, 2001.

———. 'Profile for Community Action Series', *Green Cities: A Guide for Sustainable Community Development*. Victoria, BC: Harmony Foundation of Canada, 2005.

Canadian Urban Institute and the Urban Environment Centre. *Sustainable Building: Canada on the Move*. Melbourne: World Sustainable Building Conference, International Initiative for Sustainable Built Environment, 2008.

Canadian Urban Transit Association. *Green Transit: Environmental Innovation Benefiting all Canadians*. Toronto: CUTA, 2001.

Carnevale, R., and E.A. Crawford. 'Battling Gridlock', *Alternatives Journal* 34, 5/6 (2008): 20–1.

Draper, D. *Our Environment: A Canadian Perspective*. Toronto: ITP Nelson, 2009. (Fourth edition, Ch. 13: 'Sustainability and the City'.)

Ferguson, K., A. Perl, M. Holden, and M. Roseland. 'Supporting global sustainability by rethinking the city', *Journal of Urban Technology* 14, 2 (2007): 3–13.

———. 'Seeking Urban Sustainability on the World Stage', *Habitat International* 32, 3 (2008): 305–17.

Li, Y., S.C.W. Yeung, and W. Seabrooke. 'Urban Planning and Sustainable Development Under Transitional Economy: A Case Study of Guangzhou', *International Journal of Sustainable Development and World Ecology* 12, 3 (2005): 300–13.

[1] The editors would like to thank Eric Stein, of the Master's of International Public Policy program, Wilfrid Laurier University, for his assistance in updating this Appendix.

Paehlke, Robert. 'Greenville: Applying Green Principles to Buildings and Urban Planning is a Sound Long-term Investment of Public Dollars', *Alternatives Journal* 30, 5 (2004): 12–15, 17.

Polèse, M., and R. Stren. *The Social Sustainability of Cities*. Toronto: University of Toronto Press, 2000.

Senecal, G., and P.J. Hamel. 'Compact City and Quality of Life: Discussions of the Canadian Approach to Sustainability Indicators', *Canadian Geographer* 45, 2 (2001): 306–18.

Wakefield, S.E.L, S.J. Elliot, and D.C. Cole. 'Social Capital, Environmental Health and Collective Action: A Hamilton, Ontario Case Study', *Canadian Geographer* 51, 4 (2007): 428–43.

Internet Sources

Canadian Journal of Urban Research
http://ius.uwinnipeg.ca/cjur_overview.html

Canadian Urban Institute
http://www.canurb.com

City of Toronto Sustainability Strategy
http://www.toronto.ca/sustainability/

Intergovernmental Committee on Urban and Regional Research
http://www.muniscope.ca

National Air Pollution Surveillance Network (monitors and assesses the quality of the ambient air in Canadian urban centres)
http://www.etc-cte.ec.gc.ca/NAPS/index_e.html

Toronto Environmental Alliance
http://www.torontoenvironment.org/

Toronto Green Standard
http://www.toronto.ca/planning/greendevelopment.htm

Toronto Regional Sustainability Program
http://www.oceta.on.ca/TORSUS/

Arctic/Northern Environment

Fitzpatrick, P., A.J. Sinclair, and B. Mitchell. 'Environmental Impact Assessment under the Mackenzie Valley Resource Management Act: Deliberative Democracy in Canada's North?' *Environmental Management* 42, 1 (2008): 1–18.

Ford, J.D., B. Smit, and J. Wandel. 'Vulnerability to Climate Change in the Arctic: A Case Study from Arctic Bay, Canada', *Global Environmental Change—Human and Policy Dimensions* 16, 2 (2006): 145–60.

Ford, J.D., and B. Smit. 'A Framework for Assessing the Vulnerability of Communities in the Canadian Arctic to Risks Associated with Climate Change', *Arctic* 57, 4 (2004): 389–400.

Government of the Northwest Territories. *Northern Voices, Northern Waters: Towards a Water Resource Management Strategy for the Northwest Territories*. Yellowknife: Environment and Natural Resources, June 2008.

Government of Nunavut. *Energy for our Future: Approaching Ikummatiit—Developing a Nunavut Energy Strategy*. Iqaluit: Energy Secretariat, December 2006.

Indian and Northern Affairs Canada. *Indigenous Peoples and Sustainable Development in the Canadian Arctic—A Canadian Contribution to the Land Use Dialogue at the Eighth Session of the United Nations Commission on Sustainable Development.* 24 April–5 May. Ottawa: INAC, 2000.

———. *Report on Adaptation to Climate Change Activities in Arctic Canada.* Ottawa: Northern Affairs Program, 2007.

Mallory, Mark L., et, al. 'A Review of the Northern Ecosystem Initiative in Arctic Canada: Facilitating Arctic Ecosystem Research Through Traditional and Novel Approaches', *Environmental Monitoring and Assessment* 113 1–3 (2006): 19–29.

Northern Perspectives, published by the Canadian Arctic Resources Committee. Full text available at: http://www.carc.org/northern_perspectives.php. See, for example, issues devoted to: 'Persistent Organic Pollutants: Are We Close to a Solution?', 26, 1 (Fall/Winter 2000).

'Impact and Benefit Agreements: Tools for Sustainable Development?', 25, 4 (Fall/Winter 2000).

'On Thinning Ice', 27, 2 (Spring 2002).

'Pipeline Perspectives', 29, 1–2 (Summer 2004).

Yukon Government. *Climate Change Action Plan.* Whitehorse: Environment Yukon, 2009.

Internet Sources

Canadian Arctic Resources Committee
http://www.carc.org

Environment Canada, The Arctic Ecosystem
http://www.mb.ec.gc.ca/nature/ecosystems/da00s04.en.html

Environment Canada, The Green Lane (Media Advisory)
http://www.ec.gc.ca/press/arctoz_m_e.htm

Environment Yukon
http://www.environmentyukon.gov.yk.ca

Government of the Northwest Territories—Land and Environment
http://www.gov.nt.ca/agendas/land/index.html

Health Canada, Northern and Arctic Environment 1996–7
http://www.hc-sc.gc.ca/msb/fnihp/artic_e96.htm

International Arctic Environment Data Directory
http://www.grida.no/add/add-data.htm

Nunavut Planning Commission
http://npc.nunavut.ca/eng/index.html

Nunavut Environmental Database
http://ned.nunavut.ca

Northwest Territories Environment and Natural Resources
http://www.enr.gov.nt.ca/main/subject_environ.htm

University of Waterloo on the Arctic environment
http://www.arts.uwaterloo.ca/ANTHRO/rwpark/ArcticArchStuff/Environment.html

Wilfrid Laurier University Cold Regions Research Centre
http://info.wlu.ca/~wwwgeog/ColdRegions4/index.htm

Yukon Department of Renewable Resources
http://www.renres.gov.yk.ca

Energy and Fuels

Oil and Gas

Alberta Energy Resources Conservation Board. *Alberta's Reserves 2007 and Supply/Demand Outlook 2008–2017*. Calgary: Alberta Energy Resources Conservation Board, 2008.

Cuddihy, J., et al. 'Energy use in Canada: Environmental Impacts and Opportunities in Relationship to Infrastructure Systems', *Canadian Journal of Civil Engineering* 32, 1 (2005): 1–15.

Davis, Jerome D. 'North American Oil and Natural Gas: Current Trends, Future Problems?', *International Journal* 60, 2 (2005): 429–36.

Holroyd, P., and T. Simieritsch. *The Waters That Bind Us: Transboundary Implications of Oil Sands Development*. Toronto: Pembina Institute, 2009.

Jeremy Moorhouse, et al. *Under-Mining the Environment: The Oil Sands Report Card*. Toronto: Pembina Institute, 2008.

Lax, A. *Political Risk in the International Oil and Gas Industry*. Scarborough, Ont.: Prentice-Hall Canada, 2000.

Natural Resources Canada. *Canadian Natural Gas Review of 2007/08 & Outlook to 2020*. Ottawa: Energy Sector, Petroleum Resources Branch, Natural Gas Division, 2008.

———. *Energy Efficiency Trends in Canada, 1990 to 2005*. Ottawa: Office of Energy Efficiency, 2005.

———. *Energy Use Data Handbook, 1990 to 2006*. Ottawa: Office of Energy Efficiency, 2006.

———. *The Fuel Focus Report: Canadian Oil Market Review of 2006 & Outlook to 2020*. Ottawa: Energy Sector, Petroleum Resources Branch, Oil Division, 2007.

Nikiforuk, A. *Tar Sands: Dirty Oil and the Future of a Continent*. Vancouver: Greystone Books, 2008.

Ross, Nicola. 'Time for an Oil Change: Emissions Reduction in Alberta', *Alternatives Journal* 31, 4/5 (2005): 13.

Story, K. 'Managing the Impacts of Hibernia: A Mid-Term Report', in Bruce Mitchell, ed., *Resource and Environmental Management in Canada*. Don Mills: Oxford University Press, 2004.

Torrie, R., and R. Parfett. 'Mind the Gap: The Crucial Gap in Canada is Not the One between Our Actions and Our Kyoto Commitments, But between What We are Doing and What We Need to Do', *Alternatives Journal* 26, 2 (2000): 22.

Vine, E. 'Strategies and Policies for Improving Energy Efficiency Programs: Closing the Loop between Evaluation and Implementation', *Energy Policy* 36, 10 (2008): 3872–81.

Vitello, C. 'Trouble in the Oil Patch: Sabotage Renews Interest in Potential Sour-Gas Flaring Hazards', *Hazardous Materials Management Magazine* 11, 2 (Apr.-May 1999): 10–14.

Woynillowicz, Dan., et al. *Oil Sands Fever: The Environmental Implications of Canada's Oil Sands Rush*. Toronto: Pembina Institute, 2005.

Internet Sources

Canadian Gas Association
http://www.cga.ca
Canadian Petroleum Products Institute
http://www.icpp.ca/cppi.html

Natural Resources Canada, Oil Division
http://www.nrcan.gc.ca/es/erb/od/
Natural Resources Canada, Natural Gas Division
http://www.nrcan.gc.ca/es/erb/ngd/
Pembina Institute for Appropriate Development
http://www.pembina.org

Hydroelectricity

BC Hydro. *The BC Energy Plan: A Vision for Clean Energy Leadership*. Victoria: BC Hydro, 2007.

Chamberland, A., C. Belanger, and L. Gagnon. 'Atmospheric Emissions: Hydro-electricity versus Other Options', *Ecodecision* 19 (Winter 1996): 56–60.

Clugston, M. 'Power Struggle: Plans for a $12b Hydro Project Straddling the Labrador–Quebec Border Heal Old Wounds and Re-open Others', *Canadian Geographic* 118, 7 (Nov.–Dec. 1998): 58–76.

Frey, G.W., and D.M. Linke. 'Hydropower as a Renewable and Sustainable Energy Resource Meeting Global Energy Challenges in a Reasonable Way', *Energy Policy* 30, 14 (2002): 1261–5.

Froschauer, K., and A. van den Hoven. 'Limiting Regional Electricity Sector Integration and Market Reform: The Cases of France in the EU and Canada in the NAFTA Region', *Comparative Political Studies* 37, 9 (2004): 1079–103.

Hydro-Québec. *Sustainability Report 2007: Sustainable Energy*. Montreal: Hydro- Québec, 2007.

Hydro One. *Environmental Policy*. Toronto: Hydro One, 2008.

Jing, Ma., and K.W. Hipel. 'Strategic Analysis of the James Bay Hydroelectric Dispute in Canada', *Canadian Journal of Civil Engineering* 32, 5 (2005): 868–80.

McCutcheon, S. *Electric Rivers: The Story of the James Bay Project*. Montreal: Black Rose Books, 1991.

Manore, J.L. *Cross-Currents: Hydroelectricity and the Engineering of Northern Ontario*. Waterloo, Ont.: Wilfrid Laurier University Press, 1999.

Whittington, R. 'Hydro and the CDM: The Role of Hydroelectricity in Meeting Kyoto Obligations', *Refocus* 8, 1 (2007): 54–6.

Internet Sources
BC Hydro
http://eww.bchydro.bc.ca
Canadian Hydropower Association
http://www.canhydropower.org
Canadian Hydro Developers Inc.
http://www.canhydro.com
Hydro-Québec
http://www.hydro.qc.ca
Manitoba Hydro
http://www.hydro.mb.ca
Newfoundland & Labrador Hydro
http://www.nlh.nf.ca

Nuclear Power

Canada, Atomic Energy Control Board. *Radioactive Emission Data from Canadian Nuclear Generating Stations, 1986 to 1995*. Hull, Que.: Atomic Energy Control Board, July 1997.

———. *Canadian National Report for the Convention on Nuclear Safety*. Ottawa: Government of Canada, 1998.

———. *Policy on Protection of the Environment: Proposed Regulatory Policy*. Ottawa: Government of Canada, 1998.

Canada, Department of Finance. *1999–2000 Estimates, Part III, Report on Plans and Priorities: Atomic Energy Control Board*. Ottawa: Public Works and Government Services Canada, 1999.

Carbon, M. *Nuclear Power: Villain or Victim? Our Most Misunderstood Source of Energy*. Madison, Wis.: Pebble Beach Publishers, 1997.

Duffey, R.B. *Canadian Solutions to Global Energy and Environment Challenges: Green Atoms*. 2006 IEEE EIC Climate Change Conference, Piscataway, NJ, 2006.

Gordon, S. 'The Greening of the Atom: Atomic Energy of Canada Wants to Shift the Long-running Battle over Nuclear Energy to its Critics' Environmental Turf', *Financial Post Magazine* (Nov. 1998): 14–20.

Lermer, G. 'The Dismal Economics of Candu', *Policy Options* 17, 3 (1996): 16–20.

Nuclear InfoRing. 'Nuclear Power: Energy for Today and Tomorrow'.

Ontario Power Generation. *2007 Results of Radiological Environmental Monitoring Programs*. Toronto: Environment Programs Department, 2007.

Ronald E. Hagen. 'Prospects for Nuclear Energy in Canada, the USA and Mexico', *International Journal of Global Energy Issue* 30, 1–4 (2008): 324–41.

Ryland, D.K., H. Li, and R.R. Sadhankar. 'Electrolytic Hydrogen Generation using CANDU Nuclear Reactors', *International Journal of Energy Research* 31, 12 (2007): 1142–55.

Internet Sources

Canadian Nuclear Association
http://www.cna.ca

Canadian Nuclear Safety Commission
http://www.cnsc-ccsn.gc.ca/eng/

Canadian Nuclear Society
http://www.cns-snc.ca

Energy Probe
http://energy.probeinternational.org

Natural Resources Canada, Nuclear Energy Division
http://nuclear.nrcan.gc.ca

Nuclear Information and Resource Service
http://www.nirs.org

Nuclear InfoRing
http://www.radwaste.org/radring/rad_member.html

Nuclear-Related WWW Sites
http://www.nci.org/nci-hot.htm

32000

Alternative Fuels

AhYou, K., and G. Leng. *Renewable Energy in Canada's Remote Communities*. Ottawa: Natural Resources Canada, 1999.

Bell, J., and T. Wies. *Greening the Grid: Powering Alberta's Future with Renewable Energy*. Toronto: Pembina Institute, 2009.

Champagne, P. 'Feasibility of Producing Bio-ethanol from Waste Residues: A Canadian Perspective', *Resources, Conservation and Recycling* 50, 3 (2007): 211–30.

Climate Change Solutions. *Canada Biomass-Bioenergy Report*. Ottawa: IEA Bioenergy Task 40-Biotrade, 2006.

Domac, J., et al. 'Socio-economic Drivers in Implementing Bioenergy Projects', *Biomass & Bioenergy* 28, 2 (2005): 97–106.

Guha, S., H.M. Soloumah, and N.C. Kar. 'Status of and Prospect for Wind Power Generation in Canada', *Wind Engineering* 29, 3 (2005): 253–70.

Harmin, J., H. Hummel, and R. Canapa. *Review of the Role of Renewable Energy in Global Energy Scenarios*. Ottawa: Implementing Agreement on Renewable Energy Technology Deployment, 2007.

Karimi, S. 'Thirteen Years after Rio: The State of Energy Efficiency and Renewable Energy in Canada', *Bulletin of Science, Technology and Society* 25, 6 (2005): 497–506.

Khan, Faisal I., et al. 'Life Cycle Analysis of Wind–Fuel Cell Integrated System', *Renewable Energy* 30, 2 (2005): 157–77.

Li, M., and Li Xianguo. 'Investigation of Wind Characteristics and Assessment of Wind Energy Potential for the Waterloo Region, Canada', *Energy Conversion and Management* 46, 18–19 (2005): 3014–33.

McKenney, D.W., et al. 'Spatial Insolation Models for Photovoltaic Energy in Canada', *Solar Energy* 82, 11 (2008): 1049–61.

Main, M., et al. 'Assessing the Energy Potential of Agricultural Bioenergy Pathways for Canada', *Canadian Journal of Plant Science* 87, 4 (2007): 781–92.

Pearce, N., 'Worldwide Tidal Current Energy Developments and Opportunities for Canada's Pacific Coast', *International Journal of Green Energy* 2, 4 (2005): 365–86.

Prescott, R., G.C. van Kooten, H. Zhu. 'The Potential for Wind Energy Meeting Electricity Needs on Vancouver Island', *Energy & Environment* 18, 6 (2007): 723–46.

Rowlands, Ian. 'Solar PV Electricity and Market Characteristics: Two Canadian Case Studies', *Renewable Energy* 30, 6 (2005): 815–34.

———. 'The Development of Renewable Electricity Policy in the Province of Ontario: The Influence of Ideas and Timing', *Review of Policy Research* 24, 3 (2007): 185–207.

Steenblik, R. 'Liberalisation of Trade in Renewable Energy and Associated Technologies: Biodiesel, Solar Thermal and Geothermal Energy', *OECD Trade and Environment Working Papers* 1 (2006).

Syed, Ali M., et al. 'Environmental and Economic Impacts of Integrating Photovoltaic and Wind-Turbine Energy Systems in the Canadian Residential Sector', *Bulletin of Science, Technology & Society* 28, 3 (2008): 210–18.

Weis, T.M. and A. Ilinca. 'The Utility of Energy Storage to Improve the Economics of Wind–Diesel Power Plants in Canada', *Renewable Energy* 33, 7 (2008): 1544–57.

Yemshanov, D., and D. McKenney. 'Fast-growing Poplar Plantations as a Bioenergy Supply Source for Canada', *Biomass & Bioenergy* 32, 3 (2008): 185–97.

Internet Sources

Association of Power Producers of Ontario
   http://www.appro.org
Blue Energy Tidal Power
   http://www.bluenergy.com
Canadian Renewable Fuels Association
   http://www.greenfuels.org
Canadian Wind Energy Association
   http://www.canwea.ca
Energy and Environment: Links and Resources
   http://www.zebu.uoregon.edu/energy.html
Natural Resources Canada, Renewable and Electrical Energy Division
   http://www.reed.nrcan.gc.ca

Waste Management

Solid Waste

Bharadwaj, L., S. Nilson, and I. Judd-Henrey. 'Waste Disposal in First-Nations Communities: The Issues and Steps toward the Future', *Journal of Environmental Health* 68, 7 (2006): 35–9.

Carter-Whitney, M. and C. Webb. *Waste Bytes! Diverting Waste Electrical and Electronic Equipment in Ontario*. Toronto: Canadian Institute for Environmental Law and Policy, 2008.

Chang, E., D. Macdonald, and J. Wolfson. 'Who killed CIPSI?', *Alternatives Journal* 24, 2 (1998): 21–5.

Crittenden, G. 'The Blue Box Conspiracy', *The Next City* 9, 3 (1997): 34.

Ferrara, I., and P. Missios. 'Recycling and Waste Diversion Effectiveness: Evidence from Canada', *Environmental & Resource Economics* 30, 2 (2005): 221–38.

Maclaren, V.W. 'Waste Management: Integrated Approaches', in B. Mitchell, ed., *Resource and Environmental Management in Canada: Addressing Conflict and Uncertainty*. Don Mills, Ont.: Oxford University Press, 2004.

Sinclair, A.J. 'Assuming Responsibility for Packaging and Packaging Waste', *Electronic Green Journal* 12 (2000). Available at: http://egj.lib.uidaho.edu/index.php/egj/article/view/2773.

Solid Waste Management Services. *New and Emerging Policies, Practices and Advisory Group: Final Report*. Submitted to the City of Toronto Works Committee, 2004.

———. *Solid Waste Management Business Plan—A Made in Toronto Solution*. City of Toronto, 2005.

Thorpe, B. 'Industry's Environmental Responsibility beyond the Point of Sale: True Waste Reduction Through Extended Producer Responsibility: A Challenge for Quebec'. Brief Submitted to the BAPE (Bureau d'Audiences Publiques sur l'Environnement) Commission of Enquiry on Solid Waste Management. Montreal: Greenpeace Quebec, Aug. 1997.

Ungar, S. 'Recycling and the Dampening of Concern: Comparing the Roles of Large and Small Actors in Shaping the Environmental Discourse', *Canadian Review of Sociology and Anthropology* 35, 2 (May 1998): 253–76.

Wagner, T., and P. Arnold. 'A New Model for Solid Waste Management: An Analysis of the Nova Scotia MSW Strategy', *Journal of Cleaner Production* 16, 4 (2008): 410–21.

Yeomans, Julian Scott. 'Improved Policies for Solid Waste Management in the Municipality of Hamilton-Wentworth, Ontario', *Canadian Journal of Administrative Sciences* 21, 4 (2004): 376–93.

Internet Sources

Ontario, Ministry of the Environment
   http://www.ene.gov.on.ca
BC Solid Waste Management
   http://www.env.gov.bc.ca/epd/epdpa/mpp/solid_waste_index.html
Alberta Environment Waste Program
   http://www3.gov.ab.ca/env/Waste/
Quebec Ministère du Développement durable, de l'Environnement et des Parcs
   http://www.mddep.gouv.qc.ca/matieres/inter_en.htm
Solid Waste and Recycling
   http://www.solidwastemag.com
Solid Waste Association of North America
   http://www.swana.org

Hazardous Waste

Baxter, Jamie. 'From Love Canal to Environmental Justice: The Politics of Hazardous Waste on the Canada-US Border', *Canadian Public Policy* 30, 2 (2004): 235–6.

Canadian Institute for Environmental Law and Policy. *Ontario: Open for Toxics*. Toronto: Canadian Institute for Environmental Law and Policy, June 2000. Available at: http://www.cielap.org/pdf/opentoxicsweb.pdf.

Carter-Whitney, Maureen. *Hazardous Waste in Ontario: Progress and Challenges*. Toronto: Canadian Institute for Environmental Law and Policy, 2007.

Hazardous Materials Management Magazine. Available at: http://www.hazmatmag.com.

Johnson, Genevieve Fuji. 'The Discourse of Democracy in Canadian Nuclear Waste Management Policy', *Policy Sciences* 40, 2 (2007): 79–99.

Leiss, W. 'Nuclear Waste Management at the Interface of Science and Policy: The Canadian Experience', *Energy & Environment* 19, 3/4 (2008): 413–26.

McFarlane, D. 'Beyond NIMBY: Hazardous Waste Siting in Canada and the United States', *Journal of Politics* 58, 1 (Feb. 1996): 258–61.

O'Neill, K. 'Out of the Backyard: The Problems of Hazardous Waste Management at a Global Level', *Journal of Environment and Development* 7, 2 (1998): 138–63.

Rabe, B. *Beyond NIMBY: Hazardous Waste Siting in Canada and the United States*. Washington: Brookings Institution Press, 1994.

Stanley, A. 'Citizenship and the Production of Landscape and Knowledge in Contemporary Canadian Nuclear Fuel Waste Management', *Canadian Geographer* 52, 1 (2008): 64–82.

Winfield, M. *Hazardous Waste and Toxic Substances*. Toronto: Canadian Institute for Environmental Law and Policy, n.d.

Internet Sources

Environment Canada, Hazardous Waste
http://www.ns.ec.gc.ca/pollution/hazardouswaste.html

Fisheries Management

Atlantic Fisheries

Alcock, Frank. 'Bargaining, Uncertainty and Property Rights in North Atlantic fisheries', *Dissertation Abstracts International* 64-12A (2003): 4612.

Barry, D. 'The Canada-European Union Turbot War: Internal Politics and Transatlantic Bargaining', *International Journal* 53, 2 (Spring 1998): 253–84.

Blades, K. *Net Destruction: The Death of Atlantic Canada's Fishery*. Halifax: Nimbus Publishing, 1995.

Canada, Fisheries and Ocean Canada. *Atlantic Fisheries Policy Review—A Policy Framework for the Management of Fisheries on Canada's Atlantic Coast*. Ottawa: Minister of Fisheries and Oceans, 2004. Available at http://www.dfo-mpo.gc.ca/fm-gp/policies-politiques/afpr-rppa/framework-cadre-eng.htm.

———. *National Plan of Action on Illegal, Unreported and Unregulated Fishing*. Ottawa: Minister of Fisheries and Oceans, 2005. Available at http://www.dfo-mpo.gc.ca/npoa-pan/npoa-iuu-eng.htm.

Coward, H., R. Ommer, and T. Pitcher, eds. *Just Fish: Ethics and Canadian Marine Fisheries*. St John's: ISER Books, 2000.

Dianne Draper. 'Marine and Freshwater Fisheries, in B. Mitchell, ed., *Resource and Environmental Management in Canada: Addressing Conflict and Uncertainty*. Don Mills, Ont.: Oxford University Press, 2009.

Food and Agriculture Organization, United Nations. Code of Conduct for Responsible Fisheries. Available at http://www.fao.org/fishery/ccrf/en.

Fu, Caihong, R. Mohn, and L.P. Fanning. 'Why the Atlantic Cod (Gadus morhua) Stock Off Eastern Nova Scotia has not Recovered', *Canadian Journal of Fisheries and Aquatic Sciences* 58, 8 (2001): 1613–23.

Kearney, John F. 'Extreme Makeover: The Restructuring of the Atlantic Fisheries', *Archives of Ophthalmology* 123, 4 (2005): 156.

Mathews, D.R, and L. Felt, eds. *Finding Our Sea Legs: Linking Fishery People and Their Knowledge with Science and Management*. St John's: ISER Books, 2000.

Northern Cod Review Panel. *Independent Review of the State of the Northern Cod Stock: Final Report* (The Harris Report). Ottawa: Department of Fisheries and Oceans, 1990.

Payne, Dexter C. 'Overcoming Ineffective Institutions: Alternative Approaches to International Fisheries Conservation', *Dissertation: Humanities and Social Sciences* 66, 5 (Nov. 2005): 1948.

Richards, L., and J. Maguire. 'Recent International Agreements and the Precautionary Approach: New Directions for Fisheries Management Science', *Canadian Journal of Fisheries and Aquatic Sciences* 55, 6 (June 1998): 1545–52.

Shelton, P.A. 'The Weakening Role of Science in the Management of Groundfish Off the East Coast of Canada', *ICES Journal of Marine Science* 64, 4 (2007): 723–29.

Soboil, M.L., and J.G. Suitnen. 'Empirical Analysis and Transboundary Management for Georges Bank Multispecies Fishery', *Canadian Journal of Fisheries and Aquatic Sciences* 63, 4 (2006): 903–17.

Thompson, A. 'Canadian Foreign Policy and Straddling Stocks: Sustainability in an Interdependent World', *Policy Studies Journal* 28, 1 (2000): 219–35.

Internet Sources

Fisheries and Oceans Canada
http://www.maritimes.dfo.ca
Fisheries and Oceans Canada, Fisheries Management, Atlantic Region
http://www.pac.dfo-mpo.gc.ca/ops/fm/fishmgmt_e.htm
Fisheries Resources Conservation Council
http://www.frcc-ccrh.ca
Government of Newfoundland and Labrador, Department of Fisheries and Aquaculture
http://www.fishaq.gov.nl.ca

Pacific Fisheries

'Canada, U.S. Sign Salmon Pact', *Toronto Star*, 1 July 1999.

DeCloet, D. 'The Apartheid Fishery is Scuttled: The Provincial Court Rules Ottawa's Aboriginal Fishing Strategy Illegal', *British Columbia Report* 9, 23 (9 Feb. 1998): 11.

Glavin, T. 'Sea of Change: As West Coast Fisheries Collapse, Human Activity is Blamed', *Canadian Geographic* 119, 4 (May–June 1999): 38–48.

Grafton, R. Quentin. 'Incentive-based Approaches to Sustainable Fisheries', *Canadian Journal of Fisheries and Aquatic Sciences* 63, 3 (2006): 699–711.

Griffin. S. 'Something Fishy's Going On: An Insider's Look at the Salmon Fishing Industry in BC', *Briarpatch* 28, 5 (June 1999): 9–12.

Munro, G., T. McDorman, and R. McKelvey. 'Transboundary Fishery Resources and the Canada–United States Pacific Salmon Treaty', *Canadian–American Public Policy* 33 (Fall 1998): 1–48.

Pauly, Daniel. 'The Sea Around Us Project: Documenting and Communicating Global Fisheries Impacts on Marine Ecosystems', *A Journal of the Human Environment* 36, 4 (June 2007): 290–95.

Springer, A.L. 'The Pacific Salmon Controversy: Law, Diplomacy, Equity, and Fish', *American Review of Canadian Studies* 27 (1997): 385–409.

Stewart, C., and R. Rogers. 'Prisoners of Their Histories: Canada–US Conflicts in the Pacific Salmon Fishery', *American Review of Canadian Studies* 27 (1997): 253–69.

Taylor, E. 'Fishing for Control: Former Enemies Join Forces as BC Coastal Communities Seek to Manage Their Own Fisheries', *Alternatives* 24, 2 (Spring 1998): 7–8.

Vasarhelyi, C., and V.G. Thomas. 'Reflecting Ecological Criteria in Laws Supporting the Baja to Bering Sea Marine Protected Areas Network Case Study', *Environmental Science & Policy* 1, 5 (2008): 394–407.

Internet Sources

Fisheries and Oceans Canada
  http://www.maritimes.dfo.ca
Fisheries and Oceans Canada (Pacific Region): Fisheries management
  http://www.pac.dfo-mpo.gc.ca/ops/fm/fishmgmt.htm

Great Lakes Water Quality

Annin, Peter. *The Great Lakes Water Wars*. Chicago: University of Chicago Press, 2006.

Barlow, M. 'Our Water's Not For Sale', *Canadian Perspectives* (Winter 1999): 6.

Botts, Lee, and Paul Muldoon. *Evolution of the Great Lakes Water Quality Agreement*. Toronto: Canadian Environmental Law Association, 2008.

Caldwell, L. 'Disharmony in the Great Lakes Basin: Institutional Jurisdictions Frustrate the Ecosystem Approach', *Alternatives Journal* 20, 3 (July–Aug. 1994): 26–33.

Canada, Department of Foreign Affairs and International Trade. 'Amendments to International Boundary Waters Treaty to Protect Great Lakes from Bulk Water Removals'. News release No. 250, 22 Nov. 1999.

Canada, Environment Canada. Great Lakes Charter Annex Implementing Agreements. Available at http://www.on.ec.gc.ca/greatlakes/default.asp?lang=En&n=BA0D657B-1.

'Great Lakes Futures Roundtable, Building a Vision for the Great Lakes and St. Lawrence Region', *Pollution Probe* October 2007.

Hartig, J., M.A. Zarull, T.M. Heidtke, and H. Shah. 'Implementing Ecosystem-based Management: Lessons from the Great Lakes', *Journal of Environmental Planning and Management* 41, 1 (1998): 45–75.

Hartig, P.D., J.H. Hartig, D.R. Lesh, D.G. Lowrie, and G.H. Wever. 'Practical Application of Sustainable Development in Decision-making Processes in the Great Lakes Basin', *International Journal of Sustainable Development and World Ecology* 3 (1996): 31–46.

International Joint Commission. *The IJC and the 21st Century*. Ottawa: IJC, 1997.

———. *Water Use Reference*. Material on IJC Reports and Public Hearings. Available at http://www. ijc.org.

———. *Thirteenth Biennial Report on Great Lakes Water Quality*. Ottawa: IJC, 2006.

———. *Priorities and Progress under the Great Lakes Water Quality Agreement 2005–2007*. Ottawa: Great Lakes Science Advisory Board, 2008.

Ivey, J.L. 'Community Capacity for Adaptation to Climate-induced Water Shortages: Linking Institutional Complexity and Local Actors', *Environmental Management* 33, 1 (2004): 36–47.

Kreutzwiser, R.D., and R. de Loe. 'Water Security: From Exports to Contamination of Local Water Supplies', in B. Mitchell, ed., *Resource and Environmental Management in Canada: Addressing Conflict and Uncertainty*. Don Mills, Ont.: Oxford University Press, 2004.

Internet Sources

Environment Canada, Great Lakes
http://www.cciw.ca/glimr/intro-e.html
Focus, Bulletin of the International Joint Commission
http://www.ijc.org
International Joint Commission
http://www.ijc.org
Great Lakes Commission
http://www.glc.org
Great Lakes Fishery Commission
http://www.glfc.org
Great Lakes Research Consortium
http://www.esf.edu/glrc/
Great Lakes United
http://www.glu.org

Index